MASSACHUSETTS STATE FORESTS AND PARKS

100 YEARS
1898-1998

Presented by the
Conservation Trust
of the
Department of Environmental Management
to commemorate the 100th Anniversary of the
Massachusetts State Forests and Parks System
1898-1998

printed on recycled paper

Stepping Back to Look Forward

Stepping Back to Look Forward

A History of the Massachusetts Forest

Charles H. W. Foster (Editor)

Robert S. Bond
Charles H. W. Foster
David R. Foster
Stephen Fox
Nancy M. Gordon
William A. King
Robert L. McCullough
John F. O'Keefe
William H. Rivers

Distributed by Harvard University for
HARVARD FOREST
Petersham, Massachusetts

Frontispiece: Illustration for *Walden,* by Henry David Thoreau. (New York: The Heritage Press, 1939). Boston Public Library, Print Department, by permission of the estate of Thomas Nason.

Frontis, *Pines* and woodcuts *Pine Cone, Stump,* and *Sumach,* were illustrations for *Walden,* by Henry David Thoreau, (New York: The Heritage Press, 1939). Photographs from the Boston Public Library, Print Department, by permission of the estate of Thomas Nason.

This book is printed on acid-free paper, and its binding materials have been chosen for strength and durability.

Library of Congress Cataloging-in-Publication Data is available.

ISBN 0-674-838-30-0

Printed in the United States of America

Table of Contents

Preface

*T*O A SCIENTIST, a tree is a woody perennial plant, typically large, with a single, well-defined stem and a more-or-less definite crown. Viewed functionally, a tree is an upside-down watershed, defying gravity by taking water and minerals from the ground and transporting them to the top and branch ends, where they are broken down in the presence of sunlight to form carbohydrates. Occurring worldwide, trees hold four-fifths of all the plant tissue on earth and are among the most important producers of organic matter on the planet. The cellulose they produce accumulates in what is called wood — an inert substance with at least 10,000 known uses, the most prominent of which are fuel and raw materials for products of utility to humankind.

Where trees grow in association with one another they are called forests. Although forests are dominated by trees and other woody vegetation, they are actually complex biological communities characterized by plants, animals, and life processes called ecosystems— groups of living things, including humans, that are inseparable from the physical environment with which they interact. Forestry is the art, science, and practice of managing, for largely human benefit, the trees and other associated natural resources that occur on and in association with forestlands.

But there are other important dimensions associated with trees and forests. Writing in *Time* magazine (February 12, 1990), Lance Morrow observed," "At one time, trees were sacred: Gods inhabited them and took their forms. Trees were druidic. They rose out of the earth, gesticulating, tossing their hair. They were the tenderest life-form: cooling, sheltering, calming, enigmatic. Or else they might harbor terrors: beasts and devils in the dark forest. They were, in either case, magic. Still are, of course."

The particular magic of the Massachusetts forest inspired a group of specialists to come together and write individual chapters that together form a collective account of the history of forests and forestry in Massachusetts. But what really triggered this project in the fall of 1995 was the decision by Senator Robert D. Wetmore, a Massachusetts legislator for more than forty years and an active forest land owner, to create the Special Commission on Forest Management Practices (the Wetmore Commission), whose purpose is to assess the potential of the state's 3 million acres of forestland. In the judgment of many forestry observers, this timely examination of present and future policies could be informed appreciably by a thoughtful review of the Common-wealth's forest history.

And so the Massachusetts forest history project began in October of 1995 under the titular auspices of the joint policy program of Harvard University's John F. Kennedy School of Government and the Harvard Forest. With the advice of Dr. Harold K. Steen, then executive director of the Forest History Society, an outline of topics was drawn up, chapter authors recruited, and initial drafts commissioned. Given the objective of preparing a forest history for largely popular consumption within fifteen months' time, the authors were forced to limit their research to mostly secondary materials. Midway through the project, another potential use of the forest history emerged: it would be a document that could mark the celebration of the centennial, in 1998, of Massachusetts' forest and park system. A statewide forestry conference was held at the University of Massachusetts, Amherst, on October 25, 1996, to review the preliminary history findings and recommendations.

The project proceeded literally on faith until the spring of 1996, when the William P. Wharton Trust and the Massachusetts Foundation for the Humanities offered modest core grants to help meet expenses. These philanthropies have since been joined by other contributors: the Arnold Arboretum and the Wetmore Commission. The New England Forestry Foundation has thoughtfully served as the project's primary fiscal agent throughout. Altogether, less than $15,000 has been spent on this unusual project, and it remains to this very date a largely voluntary endeavor.

Even more remarkable has been the mix of intellectual contributors the project has attracted. As you can see from the biographical summaries at the end of the book, the group is eclectic, multidisciplinary, and multi-institutional. Despite substantial differences in age, experience, and attitude, collaboration has never been a problem. Indeed, the group discussions about the lessons of history have at times been inspiring.

And so we offer nine independent views of Massachusetts forest history, each written in an individual style following the author's vision of the subject matter rather than a common chronology. We are deeply indebted to our manuscript editor, Dr. Alice E. Ingerson, a fine anthropologist in her own right, for providing a measure of cohesion without losing the flavor of individuality.

Our collaboration uncovered several common themes. One is the critical importance of the cultural context for the Massachusetts forest over time. Its uses and veritable presence have been largely human-determined. It is, quite literally, of, for, and by the people. The second is the story of constant resilience and change on the part of the forest. Massachusetts grows trees often and well. Third, the diversity of the forest has led to a similar diversity of interests and uses, which adds complexity to future policy decisions but also furnishes its citizens with a substantial range of choices if they can begin thinking less of trees and more of whole forests, less in business cycles and more in real forest time.

Finally, we are convinced that the need for close relationships between forests and communities, so important in the early days of the colonies, may have come full circle. In all parts of America today, men and women of goodwill are joining together in the face of uncertainty to pledge their best collective efforts to conserve and sustain productive forest environments. The Massachusetts experience, dating back as it does to the hardy band of Pilgrims who expressed their common intentions so eloquently in the famous Mayflower Compact of November 1620, seems to have the potential to enlighten literally an entire nation. If so, this Massachusetts forest history will have served an even larger purpose.

Charles H. W. Foster
Cambridge, Mass.
November 1997

Stepping Back to Look Forward

*T*he Indian boy slid off his rush sleeping mat and out from under the warmth of its fur blankets. He lifted the deerskin door flap, being careful not to disturb the ten other family members asleep in the bark-covered longhouse known as Neesquottow, "the house with two fires." Dawn was breaking, and newly returned Canada geese were talking to each other in Plymouth's Town Brook marshes. Sensing the boy's presence, a deer lifted its head at the edge of the woods. The forest of tall pines, oaks, and chestnuts, freed of lower limbs and underbrush by the Indians' constant search for deadwood for their cooking fires, still cast long shadows into the clearing. Early in the spring, when the dogwood leaves were the size of squirrels' ears, his mother and sisters would prepare and plant the little field with corn.

The boy had woken early, his mind still filled with the wonder of his grandfather's account by firelight of how Earthmaker was cast out by the Sky Dwellers, her fall broken by the wings of birds, how the first solid ground was created on the back of a turtle, and the first corn delivered to the earth by a crow. Uninterrupted by his audience, his grandfather had gone on at great length to describe the early world as consisting largely of ice and water, interspersed with scattered strands of dwarf willow, birch, alder, and spruce, and populated by huge animals — mammoths and mastodons — the boy could scarcely imagine.

As the forest grew, his grandfather recounted, the spirit powers encouraged hunting, fishing, and gathering in conformity with the seasons and, later, the cultivation of what the Iroquois called the three sisters: corn, beans, and squash. The souls of the animals taken became spirit helpers, aiding individual human beings to attain true stature and distinction. The son of the pniese (tribal counselor) Hobbamock, the boy had seen with his own eyes the black wolf pelt and rattlesnake belt worn by his sachem (chief), Massasoit. The forest spirits would remain kindly, his grandfather warned, only if the people of plenty did not become a people of waste.

The Massachusetts Forest:
An Historical Overview

CHARLES H. W. FOSTER

T HE EXTENT to which the Massachusetts forest governed Indian life is hard to imagine today. It contributed food directly — fruit, seeds, and acorns and other nuts — and also indirectly, by furnishing habitat for wildlife, headwaters for fish and shellfish, and nutrients for crops grown in forest clearings. Medicines were derived from the forest, as well as housing, which consisted of frameworks of saplings covered by sheets of bark held together by tree-root lashings. Strips of the inner bark of cedar or basswood were used for mats and baskets. Canoes were built from trees felled with stone axes; hollowed out with fire; finished with stone, bone and shell scrapers; and propelled with ash and maple paddles.

Fire was an indispensable tool of the Indian culture. The friction of wooden drills and spindles sparked "touchwood" (often the *Polyporus* fungus found on tree roots). Cooking fires were fueled with windfalls and deadwood gleaned from the forest. Wildfire was the principal instrument used to maintain clearings for crops, obtain ash for fertilizer, and create conditions favorable for wildlife. The forest also yielded the primary instruments for taking game: deadfalls were used for making snares; ash, for longbows; elder, for arrows; and tree bark, for quivers. Not all of the forest was congenial, however, for it was in the wooded swamps ("the abode of owls") that the *pauwaus* (native conjurers) would assemble to seek divine intervention.

Under such circumstances, the natural rhythms of plants, animals, celestial bodies, and weather became the chief determinants of where the Indians lived, what they did, and indeed whether they survived. At best, perhaps 100,000 Indians occupied New England prior to the arrival of the European settlers. They followed what William Cronon has termed the "wheel of the seasons." Despite romantic assertions to the contrary, the Indians' coexistence with nature was more of a practical necessity than a conscious ecological decision. Yet their attitudes toward nature may provide important clues even for modern Massachusetts.

For example, land was valued for its resources, which were held both in private ownerships (such as the plots allocated to a kin group for the growing of crops) and collectively (the hunting and fishing territories of an entire village). Rights were for use of the resources on the land, not for the land itself. These rights could be inherited or even bargained away for consideration. They would be reallocated if not used. Patterns of ownership tended to follow natural features (virtual ecosystem lines). But rivers and streams, rather than providing fixed boundaries as they do today, were reserved as general travel routes through territories. The collection of kin groups, governed lightly by individual sachems with the advice of a council of elders, have been described as virtual neighborhoods, a form of social structure that facilitated collective and highly democratic decisions about resources.

The impact of these cultural influences on the pre-Colonial forest was quite distinctive. The descriptions recorded by the early settlers are somewhat distorted and suspect, conditioned as they were upon putting a good face on New England to the merchant financiers back home. But the forest was probably a mosaic of individual tree stands varying widely in composition — a now-sought-after quality called "patchiness." The dry ridgetops and old burns supported white pine; the moister locations were marked by hardwoods. Although individual tree sizes could be substantial, there is consistent reference in the seventeenth century journals to trees being "not thick." In many locations the forest was "open and without underwood," the result of spring and fall burning by the Indians to improve conditions for game, all in contradiction to William Bradford's journal assertion of a "hidious and desolate wilderness, full of wild beasts and wild men" and traveler John Josselyn's later description of a land "clothed with infinite thick woods."

To the hardy band of Pilgrims who dropped anchor in Provincetown harbor in November 1620, accustomed as they were to an England barely 10 percent forested for centuries, the apparent abundance of natural resources must have been staggering. The forest in particular appeared limitless. It was viewed in two ways: as a storehouse of commodities to sustain the colony and its prospective economic relationship with Europe, and as "an adversary, a barrier, and a fearsome threat to peace and security." The Pilgrims' livelihood would have to be "literally wrenched from nature." To those accustomed to the order of the English countryside, wild New England was evidence of a land simply awaiting settlement under God's providence. Its occupants, the Indians, could claim few rights under concepts of English law because "they did not treat the land as if they owned it."

Upon their arrival on November 11, 1620, the Pilgrims wasted little time in beginning to make use of the Massachusetts forest environment. As Edward Winslow's journal reports, they came ashore to fetch wood, marveling as they did at the profusion of "oaks, pines, juniper, sassafras and other sweet wood" encountered at Wood End in Provincetown, the "deep valleys and excellent black earth" at High Head in Truro, and the "fowl and deer haunted there." Products of the forest made other significant first impressions, yielding materials for the repair of the Pilgrims' shallop and a shower of arrows from their Indian welcomers, which the Pilgrims, in their meticulous fashion, duly noted as tipped with "hart's horn and eagles' claws." Approaching their ultimate settlement site at Plymouth on December 15, 1620, they viewed in the prospect "nothing but woods." The cleared high ground chosen for the plantation, more than likely a former Indian village site, seemed ideal except in one respect. "Our greatest labor will be fetching of our wood, which is half a quarter of an English mile; but there is enough so far off," Winslow noted.

The picture of the Pilgrim-era forest, constructed through the travel diaries of that period, must be regarded as somewhat conjectural. More modern thinking, supported by an examination of sediment cores from Martha's Vineyard and ponds in the Myles Standish State Forest in Plymouth County, suggests a species composition not unlike that of today. Periodic wildfire and a largely dryland environment favored a forest of sprout hardwoods interlaced with pitch and white pine, with such occasional species as chestnut, beech, hickory, and even hemlock occurring throughout. Larger trees were present, as evidenced by the chronicles of such early explorers as Bartholomew Gosnold and John Brererton, and the documented construction of early buildings entirely from native materials.

For 12-year-old *Resolved White, in the house of his step-father, Edward Winslow, it was the grunting and squealing of hungry swine in the Pilgrim village's "beast House" that caused him to stir. Moving carefully so as not to disturb young John and his parents, still asleep in the big four-poster bed, and his brothers Peregrine and Ned alongside him on the floor, Resolved moved past the still-smoldering cooking fire at the end of the clapboard cottage, pushed open the heavy wooden door, and slipped outside. Tree shadows still striped the heavily palisaded village, reminding the boy of his mother's fear of the surrounding forest, the wild beasts and savages that surely lurked there, and her stories of the well-tended fields and intensively managed woodlands she had left behind in her native England.*

But the real excitement for Resolved was his parents' whispered conversation the night before, when they believed the children were asleep, about Edward Winslow's forthcoming diplomatic mission to the Wampanoag's sachem, Massasoit, to explore the "champaign" (open plain) and forested shores of Narragansett Bay, in order to express the Plimoth colony's continuing commitment to peace and friendship. Winslow would be accompanied by Stephen Hopkins and the Indian pniese, *Hobbamock, Massasoit's liaison with the colonists. Much respected as a fine Christian, statesman, scholar, and man of affairs, and as a keen and sympathetic recorder of the New England landscape and its native culture, Winslow was the obvious choice of Governor William Bradford to serve as the Pilgrims' emissary.*

For young Resolved, his stepfather's absence would mean that the boy would have to take over clearing the stones from the family's small allotment of land, fertilizing it with fish from the spring herring run; gathering "underwood," (underbrush) for fuel and the "gads" (long sticks, from saplings) used to make the woven barriers called "hurdles" that kept animals out of the unfenced fields; and fetching water for his mother. The boy did not know it, but in the hands of the colonists, wild New England was on its way to becoming a world of fields and fences.

The Plymouth settlers, accustomed to the unwooded English countryside, were largely unacquainted with a forest environment. Yet as prospective farmers, the Pilgrims were already preconditioned to trades and tools, including in their shipboard complement a full supply of axes and saws; two members of their company were carpenters. The assault on the surrounding forest began promptly, and a group of one-room posthole cottages and a surrounding wood palisade were soon built to provide housing and a measure of security.

The next move was to begin creating the English open-field setting with which they were most comfortable. Lacking wheeled vehicles and draft animals until 1621, and without a sawmill until the Scituate settlement was founded in 1633, the Pilgrims had to undertake the clearing by hand; the resulting felled wood and other cleared materials were dragged to the village, floated down nearby Town Brook, or simply left in place to be reduced by fire. Unlike the Indians, the colonists were capable of harvesting the larger trees — and did. Furthermore, the English tradition of "joining," (piecing together wood fragments) also made it possible for smaller-dimension material to be used. So successful was the forest exploitation that by 1631 the Massachusetts General Court had to begin enacting timber control ordinances for forest burning and the felling of trees and to start rationing fuelwood sources in the interest of conserving supplies and reducing waste.

Another incentive for removing the forest lay in the economics of the plantation. The merchant backers of the settlement expected financial returns for their investment, and the reported abundance of the forest made that a promising prospect. Two hundred pounds of wood samples were sent back to England on the *Anne* in 1623, and forest products became a regular item of trade from 1640 on. Because of the distances involved, New England never became a major exporter of timber to England except for its special role as a supplier of masts for the Royal Navy, but forest products did become a lucrative part of the flourishing trade between the colonies and the West Indies later in the seventeenth century.

The settlers' ambitions of personal wealth also accelerated the clearing of the native forest. The first allocations of land were modest in size and were associated pragmatically with use and need. Larger tracts of forestland were often reserved as undistributed commons for grazing and as sources of fuelwood. In later years, the Massachusetts General Court of the colony came to offer forestland to groups of proprietors willing to found new townships. The proprietors would then divide the land among the settlers in accord with status and need. Further distributions were made by the General Court as rewards for service (for example, bounties to Revolutionary War veterans) or simply as ways to raise revenues.

Toward the end of the Colonial period, the Indian concept of the forest as a resource had been supplanted by its status as a source of commodities. Deforestation was considered not a trait to be decried, but the natural result of the process of cultivation. After all, New England was known to be a region of boundless resources and seemingly inexhaustible wealth, a pristine and empty land simply waiting to be occupied. Loss of woodland was no cause for concern, because, as New England traveler and Yale president Timothy Dwight would later assert, "Forests are furnished by the author of nature with means of perpetual self restoration." As waves of colonists arrived, the fever of settlement began to spread to outlying regions.

For example, in May 1670, in Dedham, Massachusetts, townspeople gathered in the parlor of Lieutenant Joseph Fisher to finalize plans for establishing a new settlement in the Connecticut Valley. The occasion was the disposition of a special award of 8,000 acres from the General Court to compensate Dedham for the loss of 2,000 acres granted to the Natick Indians for the Puritan missionary John Eliot's colony of "praying Indians." Explorers from Dedham had set out in 1663 to find a tract "in any convenient place . . . where it shall be found free from former grants." A one-and-a-half-square-mile plateau of rich soil and abundant meadows, at the foot of a ridge called Pocumtuck by the Indians, appeared to be the perfect site. The area had been vacant since the Mohawks to the north had descended upon the Pocumtucks and destroyed their village. Accordingly, a plan for the division of the land was drawn up in Dedham that included both homesteads and commons. The lots were made narrow both to facilitate ploughing a long furrow and to provide each owner with the needed amounts of cropland, meadow, and forestland. The 43 original proprietors were governed at a distance from Dedham, 80 miles to the east, until an act of the General Court in 1674 permitted the "inhabitanc of pocomtick" to establish their own town of Deerfield.

*T*en-year-old Thankful Sheldon, sound asleep in a pile of comforters in the east bedroom of her father Ebenezer's home in Deerfield, now known locally as the Old Indian House, stirred awake as the early morning sun rose over the Pocumtuck Hills and dappled the walls with light and shadow. Clutching the flannel nightshirt around her neck against the winter chill, Thankful jumped out of bed and ran to the window. Although it was February 1730, not the fateful early-morning hours of February 29, 1704, Thankful could visualize the loud cries and pounding of hatchets on the oaken front door on that day as a surprise assault force of French and Indian warriors came across the ice-bound confluence of the Deerfield and Green rivers, traversed the north meadows, easily scaled the snow-piled stockade, massacred more than 40 settlers, and marched another 100 settlers to captivity in Canada. She recalled her grandfather John Sheldon's vivid account of how her grandmother, Hannah, was shot through the neck by a stray bullet while sitting in bed in this very room.

Much had occurred since those tumultuous days. By 1707, most of the settlers had returned to rebuild the village. There was now talk in her father's tavern of a coming accord between the British and the French and their respective Indian allies. As evidence of increasing peace and prosperity, Thankful could see through her window the rich farmland of the Pocumtuck Plateau, extending as far as the eye could see under its winter blanket of snow. The plateau's fields were already promising surpluses of grain and cattle to be delivered to market down the Connecticut River and east to Boston. And as she watched, the first of the morning's teams sleighed into town bringing a load of wood down from the shrinking Pocumtuck Hills forests to fuel village fireplaces and provide materials for its skilled housebuilders and joiners.

At the time of settlement, the Connecticut River valley appears to have been a land of forested ridges interspersed with fertile plateaus and floodplains, the legacy of glacial Lake Hitchcock, which once extended 150 miles north from Middletown, Connecticut, to Lyme, New Hampshire. The colonists began clearing the land with vigor, harvesting the forest for fuel and deriving from it a variety of products. The wood used in the construction of the eighteenth-century houses provides clues as to the species present at that time. Architectural historians at Historic Deerfield, Inc., have encountered roof shingles made of cedar, external clapboards and internal floor boards of white pine, ceiling beams of pitch pine and hemlock, and frameworks of chestnut and white oak. The size of the individual trees can be deduced by the width of the beams and boards; one interior sheathing fragment measured 32 inches wide.

But by far the biggest drain on the forest was the demand for firewood. Wood was the sole fuel for cooking and heating, and each family of settlers required some 35 cords (61 tons) of wood annually. Although the first sawmill in the Massachusetts portion of the Connecticut Valley was established in nearby Hadley in 1665, the cutting, hauling, and processing of timber used mostly local equipment and labor. Much of this work was carried on in the dark shadow of unremitting Indian hostility and against a backdrop of the coming Revolutionary War with England.

By the early nineteenth century, Connecticut Valley leaders had begun taking a special interest in the flora of the region, including its forest. Descendants of the early Deerfield settlers were in the vanguard. For example, the area physicians Dennis Cooley and Stephen West Williams assembled extensive personal herbaria. The Deerfield native Edward Hitchcock, the first professor of natural history at Amherst College and later its president, maintained a lifelong interest in the geology and natural history of the Connecticut Valley, serving as the appointed head of the 1830 state survey of geology, mineralogy, botany, and zoology in Massachusetts. Hitchcock's extensive correspondence with Professor Benjamin Silliman of Yale University helped fortify Silliman's own concerns about conditions in the valley during the nineteenth century. The president of Yale University Timothy Dwight, traveling throughout New England and New York in 1821 and 1822, contributed his own thoughts about the landscape and resources of the

Connecticut River, describing the "un-common and universal beauty of its banks, here a smooth and winding beach, there covered with rich verdure, now fringed with bushes, now covered with lofty trees, and now formed by the intruding hill, the rude bluff and the shaggy mountain."

Farther to the west, on a 36-square-mile land grant from the Mohhekunnuck and Housatunnock Indians, the Massachusetts General Court was encouraging settlement of "New Framingham" (Lanesborough) and what was later to become Berkshire County. A heavily forested region whose forests were composed largely of deciduous species (beech, birch, and maple), but interspersed with conifers at higher elevations, the northern portion of the county was dominated by Herman Melville's "Most Excellent Majesty," Mount Greylock, at 3,491 feet Massachusetts' highest peak. The slopes of Greylock served as the headwaters of the Hoosic River, a Hudson tributary, the Deerfield River flowing east to the Connecticut, and the Housatonic River, flowing south to Long Island Sound.

In time, farms would be hewn out of the forest within a thousand feet of the summit. Sheep would graze on the western slopes. Lime, iron ore, charcoal, and paper industries would rise and fall in the mountain's shadow. And a vigorous debate would ensue, still unresolved to this very day, over appropriate recreational use and development of the mountain. Virtually stripped of timber not once but twice, the Berkshire forest rebounded to form the basis of some 100,000 acres of secured public land in Berkshire County, including the summit of Greylock itself, which now lies within a state reservation of some 12,000 acres.

But as early as the 1790s, concern had begun to be expressed about the rapid depletion of the Massachusetts forest in western Massachusetts and elsewhere. In an essay foreshadowing the later national forest movement, an unknown author writing in the May 16, 1798, issue of the *Philadelphia Weekly Magazine of Original Essays, Fugitive Pieces, and Interesting Intelligence,* entitled his article "On the Importance of Preserving Forests in the United States." There were other observers from outside the state, for example, the Swedish naturalist Peter Kalm, who wrote of the deplorable condition of the cedar swamps in the Northeast, and the Revolutionary War general Benjamin Lincoln, who suggested a program to promote the planting of acorns because "our timber trees are greatly reduced and quite gone in many parts."

In Sturbridge, Massachusetts, 15-year-old Augusta Freeman looked up from her sewing as her cat, Comfort, named for her grandfather, jumped into her lap and started purring. Distractions like this did not occur often in the Pliny Freeman household, especially since her mother, Delia, had taken ill and left the bulk of the household chores to Augusta. It was now the girl's lot to draw water, fetch wood, milk the cows, and tend the quarter-acre garden that would yield enough vegetables for both summer and winter. Inside, there were seemingly endless meals to prepare and serve. And ever since Delia had read Lydia Maria Child's The American Frugal Housewife, *she demanded that the house be tidied up and swept daily with one of the new Connecticut Valley brooms.*

Glancing out the window, Augusta could see her younger brother Dwight leading the team of oxen as her father, Pliny Freeman, guided the plow and hilled the Indian corn and potatoes. When this was done, it would be time to scythe the first hay in the meadows and harvest the winter crop of oats and rye. When the snows came, Pliny Freeman would take the oxen into his 59 acres of unimproved land and fell logs from the dwindling forest. He would sled them out to the sawmill on Leadmine Brook that he partly owned and trade the roughcut boards for needed supplies and services. Later, in his workshop, he would craft wooden furniture, utensils, implements — especially the ox yokes that were in such demand by the area's farmers. Pliny Freeman, Augusta knew, was a highly respected member of the Sturbridge community, having served as highway surveyor, town assessor, selectman, and currently school committee member.

Of the 40 scholars enrolled in District School 7, Augusta was considered to be one of the best. Thinking of school, she caught a glimpse of herself in the looking glass on the otherwise bare wall, coloring at the thought that young Master Perrin might find her attractive.

Meanwhile, the New Englander Timothy Dwight observed that the labor-saving practice of girdling trees and leaving them to rot in place presented "an uncouth and disgusting appearance." Dwight also observed that the Connecticut River was "now often fuller than it probably ever was before the country above was cleared of its forests." In the opinion of the environmental historian William Cronon, the removal of the forest had become "one of the most sweeping transformations wrought by European settlement in New England."

By the early 1800s, it would seem, virtually everyone in Massachusetts owned a farm. As New England society expanded across available space in response to rapid population growth, clearing forest became part of the farm-making process. But the term "farm" was something of a euphemism, because the proportion of farmers in the workforce actually began to decline as early as 1800. More accurately, a high percentage of Massachusetts households, by the turn of the nineteenth century, simply owned some land.

To be sure, although most farms (like the Pliny Freeman farm in Sturbridge) were not independent, self-sufficient entities in an economic sense, they did contribute a comfortable existence, serve as the focus for families, and provide a base for other entrepreneurial pursuits, many built around the settlers' cultural proclivity for the trades. The 1850 census of occupations listed nearly 200,000 carpenters and joiners in nineteenth- century America, skills that were in great demand as a generation of "country carpenters" began converting the forest into tools, products, and materials for dwellings. The resulting impact on the landscape was quite profound. Through the eyes of gentleman-farmer journalists like Rodolphus Dickinson of Greenfield, Massachusetts, we learn that by 1813 the Massachusetts forest had retreated largely to swamps and hilltops. "This state exhibits, comparatively, no very extensive forests; the cultivated parts of the farms being, in general, accompanied only with proportionate woodlands." Yet, where they do exist, Dickinson wrote, "the forests present a thick and handsome foliage and are uniformly pervaded by a great proportion of shrubbery."

Indeed, in places like Sturbridge, settled in 1729 by proprietors from Medfield, the forest proved stubbornly resilient. As Timothy Dwight observed, "When a field of woods is, in the language of our farmers, cut clean i.e. when every tree is cut down so far as any progress is made, vigorous shoots sprout from every stump." The state census of 1845, near the peak of the period of conversion to farmland, still reported an annual cut of 26 million board feet from Massachusetts forests. The Sturbridge-Southbridge timber supply is known to have sustained area sawmills until the late nineteenth century. By 1850, with 61 percent of Sturbridge recorded as improved land, the early Massachusetts dynamic of subsistence had been replaced by the accumulation of personal wealth and capital. As William Cronon has observed, capitalism and environmental degradation, which had begun in the eighteenth century, were beginning to march across the New England region hand in hand.

The transportation improvements brought about by the opening of the Erie Canal in 1825, the growth of endemic canal systems on the Blackstone, Merrimack, and Connecticut rivers, and the presence of more than 1,000 miles of national railroads by 1835 heralded a dramatic change in the demands on the Massachusetts forest. By 1846, Massachusetts railroads were already consuming more than 50,000 cords of wood annually for fuel, and each mile of track required over 2,500 wooden ties, which had to be replaced every five to seven years. The new manufacturing facilities were imposing unprecedented demands for wood, and the mid-century ironworks, fueled by charcoal, were in the process of devastating the forests around them.

Early in the nineteenth century, concern began to grow about the deteriorating state of the Massachusetts forest. In 1813, the progressive farmers' movement polled its members as to the condition of local timber supplies. The response from West Springfield spoke of "much destruction of wood while growing in our forests by fires purposely or carelessly set." The ideal solution, it was said, would be a condition where growth and consumption became equal.

Cognizant of the declining forest growing stock, the private Massachusetts Agricultural Society offered in 1795 annual premiums for individual efforts to culture forest trees, but so confident were the farmers of the unlimited nature of the natural forest that only one application was received in thirty years. "Let us then abandon the hope of extensive plantations," the society concluded when it terminated the award program in 1825. John Lowell, in his 1818 *Remarks on the Gradual Diminution of the Forests of Massachusetts and the Importance of an Early Attention to Some Effectual Remedy,* commented that "no man dreamt that the day would arrive in which his descendants might regret the improvident profusion of their ancestors." The issue of selective versus clear-cutting was debated in print as early as 1804. The theme was picked up by George Barrell Emerson, in his 1846 report to the General Court on trees and shrubs growing naturally in Massachusetts; he, observed that "the effects of the wasteful destruction of the forest trees are already visible."

In Concord, Massachusetts, where town woodlands had shrunk to barely 10 percent of the town's land area, Henry David Thoreau would declare that "of the primitive wood, woodland which was woodland when the town was settled . . . I know none." As he went on to write in 1860, "The history of a woodlot is often, if not commonly, here, a history of cross-purposes — of steady and consistent endeavor on the part of nature, or interference and blundering with a glimmer of intelligence at the eleventh hour on the part of the proprietor."

Charles Sprague Sargent, in a special report to the Massachusetts Board of Agriculture in 1875, wrote that "the most valuable trees have always been cut, often before they reach maturity, and as no steps have been taken to replace them, it is not astonishing that the poverty of our woodlands has reached a point which compels the inhabitants of the state to draw nearly their whole supply of lumber from portions of the country most recently settled." In light of the difficulties of transporting logs any distance from the forest, nineteenth-century Massachusetts had no option other than a network of small, local, water-powered sawmills built around an ever-dwindling forestland base.

By the late nineteenth century, the residue of wasted and fire-scarred land throughout the state was so extensive as to inspire a group of private citizens, in 1898, to form the Massachusetts Forestry Association. Private pressure subsequently prevailed upon the legislature to establish the office of state forester in 1904, and to enact a remarkable forestland relief measure in 1908, which authorized the state to accept donations of private land for reforestation purposes. These so-called reforestation lots, as well as later strategic acquisitions by the state at costs not to exceed $5 per acre, are the backbone of what Massachusetts citizens now enjoy today as their state forest and park system.

Even as the remnants of the original forest continued to be decimated, Massachusetts' new forest had become re-established on the abandoned agricultural land. Several factors hastened this transformation: westward migration, the movement of people from the farms to the cities, and the competitive advantages of importing food and materials via the new transportation network. By the turn of the twentieth century, the forest was ready to be harvested again — spurring another two decades of exploitation.

In 1907, the production of lumber in New England reached its peak in this century, a cut of nearly 3 billion board feet. Portable sawmills appeared throughout the state, and an entire industry was founded on the harvest of white pine to make boxes. Once again, exploitation was indiscriminate and rampant. Loggers even stripped the timber off the east face of Mount Greylock.

Massachusetts forests were hard hit again during World War I. The principal demand was again for fuel. Since coal was a requisition priority for military use, the state forester organized "Cut A Cord Clubs" and wood exchanges throughout the Commonwealth to supply wood fuel for mills, public facilities, and households. Massachusetts sawmills and experienced woodsmen were sent to England to help the British war effort produce its own lumber.

In 1929, "Black Friday" hit the New York Stock Exchange, and U.S. securities lost $26 billion in value virtually overnight. The resultant Depression was to leave a permanent mark on Massachusetts forests, just recovering as they were from the exploitative period of the early 1900s. On April 5, 1933, President Franklin Roosevelt signed into law an act establishing a Civilian Conservation Corps (CCC), a program that would ultimately engage 2.5 million unemployed Americans in the conservation and development of the nation's natural resources. Massachusetts forests were a direct beneficiary of this program. During the period 1933–42, 63 CCC camps were established on state forest and park lands. Almost 100,000 men were enrolled. CCC crews engaged in reforestation, timber stand improvement, fire suppression, insect and disease control, and the construction of roads, bridges, lookouts, and recreational cabins, facilities that are still enjoyed by the public today.

Just as the CCC camps began to close, the 1938 hurricane struck southern New England, leveling more than half a billion feet of standing timber. Fresh from the experience of the CCC, state foresters with federal assistance established a dozen hurricane clearance camps and salvaged about 150 million feet in Massachusetts alone. Owners of fallen timber delivered logs to designated collection points, where they were stockpiled for later marketing. The constant threat of wildfire did achieve one enduring forest benefit, stimulating the development of our modern cooperative forest-fire prevention and control system. In addition to the work accomplished, the CCC and other forestry camps left an indelible mark on the national ethos. At a time of uncertain economic conditions, CCC enrollees received gainful employment, learned valuable trades, and even earned high school diplomas. In their own words, they became men. More important, CCC veterans gained a lifelong respect for the natural environment. Their sense of the future is expressed eloquently on the bronze memorial installed on the lawn as the visitor drives into the Mohawk Trail State Forest headquarters in Charlemont. Flanked by decorative flags, the plaque reads:

> To those of the veterans Civilian Conservation Corps
> who working here have opened to you and the generation
> that will follow a rare intimacy with the peace and
> refreshment of God's hills.

The finer detail of this broad sweep of Massachusetts forest history is contained in the chapters to follow. John F. O'Keefe and David R. Foster, forest ecologists at the Harvard Forest, start by describing the ecological and land-use history of the Massachusetts forest. The economic historian Nancy M. Gordon then traces the patterns of use and development of its material resources. William A. King of the New England Forestry Foundation shows how human dimensions transformed themselves into private actions and institutions. The state's management forester William Rivers provides an insider's account of the early history of state programs, especially their interrelationship with the private sector. How education contributed to state and private programs, and how the forestry profession developed are explained by Robert S. Bond, a longtime University of Massachusetts faculty member and the former director of Pennsylvania State University's School of Forest Resources. The national conservation context for all of these events is furnished by the environmental historian and writer Stephen Fox. His perspective is followed by the architectural historian Robert L.

McCullough's account of the unique town forest movement in New England and Massachusetts. The concluding chapter, "The Massachusetts Forest Today," by former Massachusetts natural resources commissioner and environmental secretary Charles H. W. Foster, indicates how the lessons of history can be applied usefully to shape future programs and policies.

An Ecological History of Massachusetts Forests

JOHN F. O'KEEFE AND DAVID R. FOSTER

THE FORESTS of Massachusetts present a history of almost con-
tinual change. However, the scale, rates, and causes of these
changes have varied dramatically through time. The relative importance of human disturbance compared to natural disturbance has
steadily increased — gradually at first, as aboriginal activity expanded
and included agriculture, and then dramatically since European settlement. Moreover, the variety, frequency, and extent of human disturbance have generally increased through time and can be expected to
continue increasing and changing into the future.

Any effective forest-management policy to protect the health,
values, and resources of Massachusetts forests must develop from an
understanding and consideration of this history. It is critical that conservation, forestry, wildlife management — in fact, all environmental
decision-making — begin with knowledge and appreciation of the history and dynamic nature of our landscape. Without these, any plan will
almost certainly produce surprises, if not failure. The forests have
reclaimed abandoned farmland and now cover nearly two-thirds of
Massachusetts. As our population expands onto this land, suburban
forest owners, largely unaware of the past changes in our forests and
only slightly more informed of the current ones, must consider the
history and dynamics of these forests in their backyards. We are blessed
with a landscape and climate that are ideally suited for growing trees
and forests, but without an understanding of the past we may unwit-
tingly lose many of the values these forests can provide.

SHOULD OUR HISTORY begin with the arrival of European settlers?
Probably not. The forests they found had long been influenced by
aboriginal activities. For millennia our forests had been evolving into

the landscape that greeted the settlers. One reasonable start for our forests' history is the end of the last glacial period, more than 13,000 years ago.

This chapter is composed of five sections. The first describes the dramatic changes following the melting of the glaciers as our present forests were developing. The second provides a view of the natural factors that help determine the distribution of different types of forest. The third examines the types of disturbance, both natural and human, that shaped the forests prior to European settlement. The fourth describes the amazing changes that our forests have undergone since European settlement as they were cleared for agriculture and have subsequently regrown on abandoned farmland. The final section reviews the current state of Massachusetts forests and the pressures and stresses they are under, and suggests some lessons from their past that might help direct their future management. Table 1 provides a chronology of some major events in our forests' history over the last 15,000 years.

The authors of this chapter are both ecologists on the staff of the Harvard Forest, a research and educational department of Harvard University located in Petersham, Massachusetts. David Foster is director of the Harvard Forest and John O'Keefe is coordinator of the Fisher

Table 1. Approximate chronology for important events in the development of Massachusetts forests.

Approximate Years Before Present (B.P.)	Landscape Condition/Event
> 13,000	Glacial ice
13,000	Tundra
11,500	Spruce woodland and forest
10,000	Human arrival
9,500	Pine forest
8,000	Mixed deciduous forest
5,000	Hemlock decline
3,000	Arrival of chestnut trees
1,000	Native American agriculture
250–350	European settlement
150	Peak of agricultural clearing
85	Chestnut blight
60	1938 hurricane

Museum, a small museum devoted to understanding the land-use history, ecology, and management of New England's forests. Scientists at Harvard Forest have intensively studied the forests of central Massachusetts since the turn of the century and amassed an unparalleled database from these studies. The authors have drawn heavily on this database for information and illustrations, which is the reason for the numerous references to Petersham and north-central Massachusetts in their work and examples. However, they have noted when other areas may not fit these examples and present the story of all Massachusetts forests.

I. POSTGLACIAL FOREST DYNAMICS

At the peak of the last glaciation, over 15,000 years ago, most of present-day Massachusetts was covered by ice up to a mile thick. Cape Cod and the offshore islands, Nantucket, Martha's Vineyard, and the Elizabeth Islands consist largely of what geologists call moraines, piles of debris accumulated at the front of the advancing ice sheet and left behind when the glaciers finally melted. The advancing glaciers not only smoothed and shaped the landscape by scraping and plucking the bedrock as they advanced, they also left behind a layer of ground-up rock, or *till*, which has developed into our present soil. As the glaciers melted, the tremendous volume of water produced seasonal streams that carried and sorted much of this material and deposited sands and gravels wherever they slowed (Strahler 1966). The soils of Massachusetts are a product of this massive natural engineering, with the subsequent addition of organic material from the vegetation that covered the landscape. Along major rivers fine silt was deposited when the rivers overflowed their banks in spring; in some depressions a surplus of moisture allowed thick layers of peat or muck to develop. The resulting pattern of soil types has strongly influenced the types of trees and forests growing in different locations.

Of course, as the glaciers melted, there were no forests in Massachusetts. The climate change that allowed the glaciers to develop limited the modern tree species of New England to favorable locations, or *refugia,* south of the glacial zone, presumably scattered across the southern Appalachians and the eastern coastal plain. The huge quantities of water trapped on land as glacial ice had once been seawater;

consequently, sea level was several hundred feet lower than at present. This exposed vast areas of continental shelf off the present-day East Coast for refugia as well. The forests in these various refugia contained species mixtures unlike any we are familiar with today. As the climate warmed and the glaciers melted the trees began their migration north. The rate of migration of each species was determined by its seed dispersal and its climatic tolerance.

We are fortunate to have a record of the vegetation change following the glacial period in the form of pollen preserved in sediments at the bottom of lakes and ponds and below many wetlands. Each year pollen from plants growing in an area is carried on the wind. When it lands on the water of a pond or lake, it sinks to the bottom and along with other wind-borne material is incorporated into the sediments. These sediments form a layered time sequence, with the oldest at the bottom, which scientists can core into and recover as a thin cylinder or core of mud. The different layers in the core can be dated using radioisotopes. Pollen is extremely resistant to decay and because the pollen of different plants can be identified (generally to genus and in some cases to species), the presence and relative abundance of different species enables paleo-ecologists to reconstruct the major vegetation changes at a site.

The Harvard Forest Black Gum Swamp pollen diagram (Figure 1) shows vegetation changes through time that are typical of those from sites across Massachusetts. As the glaciers melted and the climate warmed, a period of tundra was followed by boreal (northern conifer) forest, then pine forest with rapidly increasing amounts of several deciduous species (oak, birch, beech) by 8,000 years ago. Although mixed deciduous forests have been dominant for about the last 8,000 years, they have changed continually through time, and these changes can tell us much. Different species have behaved quite independently, presumably migrating to Massachusetts from different locations at different rates, each species responding in its unique fashion to combinations of climatic, soil, biotic, and historical factors. The resulting forest communities constantly changed through time. The major influences on these changes are long-term climate change, migration rates of individual species, and natural disturbance processes.

Population dynamics of selected species can help us understand these processes. Hemlock increased rapidly in importance after its arrival about 9,000 years ago. A little less than 5,000 years ago, it

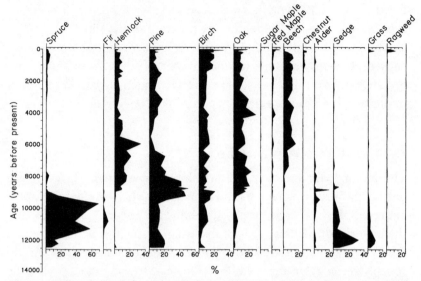

Figure 1. Pollen diagram from the Black Gum Swamp at Harvard Forest in central Massachusetts depicting the major changes in the vegetation over the past 12,500 years. Tundra communities (sedge, grass) were replaced by boreal forest dominated by spruce until approximately 9200 B.P. (before present), when pine and then hardwood tree species became important. Changes in the relative abundance of species resulted from climate change, species migrations, disease (hemlock decline at about 5000 B.P.) and fire until 250–300 years B.P., when European settlement resulted in major deforestation and the increase in agricultural weeds (ragweed), grass, and early successional species. Modified from Foster and Zebryk (1993).

decreased dramatically in a very short time, then slowly recovered. This sudden decline in hemlock is seen in pollen records throughout the Northeast and is attributed to a severe pathogen (insect or disease) outbreak, which dramatically decreased hemlock populations for nearly 1,000 years.

Regional pollen analyses indicate that the period from 8,000 to 5,000 years ago was most likely somewhat milder than the last 4,000 years have been (Davis 1958). During the warm period many common tree species migrated into Massachusetts and some species expanded their ranges well north of their current limits. Fire frequency, shown by charcoal in sediment cores, was also greater at a number of sites (Patterson and Backman 1988). A more recent cooling probably produced the increase in spruce pollen over the last 2,000 to 3,000 years. Yet these changes and forest community dynamics were complex: while spruce, a northern species, increased — evidently in response to gradual cooling — chestnut, a southern species, was also migrating north across Massachusetts. In fact, chestnut is the most recent arrival in the pollen record, not appearing until about 3,000 years ago, much later than the other important deciduous species that occur in the region today.

II. NATURAL ENVIRONMENT

The development and distribution of forest types across Massachusetts during the presettlement period were controlled by the geographic pattern of the landscape, or physiography, the underlying geology, and the patterns of various types of disturbances such as windstorm and fire, which are all interrelated. Massachusetts, excluding Cape Cod, is roughly rectangular, 125 miles (200 km) east to west and 50 miles (80 km) north to south. Today we receive approximately 40 inches (100 cm) of precipitation annually, distributed fairly evenly throughout the year. With a mean annual temperature near 50°F, ranging from a mean of several degrees below freezing in January to a mean of about 70°F in July, our climate today is very well suited for trees and apparently has been for the last 10,000 years.

Within this relatively small compact area, Massachusetts contains six broad physiographic regions: the coastal lowlands, the central uplands, the Connecticut River valley, the Berkshire Mountains, the Berkshire valley, and the Taconic Mountains (Figure 2). The geologic substrate varies across the state. Except for parts of the Connecticut valley, the Taconic Mountains, and the Berkshire valley the soil is generally acidic and fairly nutrient-poor. The soils are generally shallow with patches of exposed bedrock. Elevation generally increases from east to west, reaching a maximum at Mount Greylock (3,487 feet [1,060 m]) in the Berkshires.

As mentioned, these physiographic and geological conditions interact with climate to produce vegetation zones sometimes referred to as ecoregions. Figure 3 shows the Massachusetts portion of a natural vegetation zone map of New England (Westveld 1956). Within Massachusetts these zones are largely determined by climate, which is principally controlled by elevation except in areas with close proximity to the moderating influence of the ocean. Southeastern Massachusetts, all of

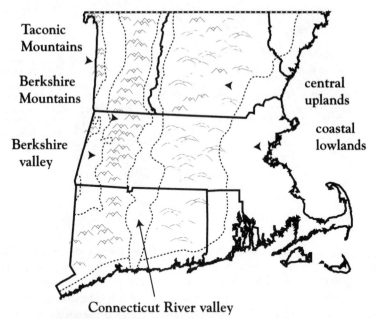

Figure 2. Map of southern New England depicting the major physiographic regions. From east to west they are coastal lowlands, central uplands, Connecticut River valley, Berkshire Mountains, Berkshire valley, and Taconic Mountains. Modified from Wright (1933) and Jorgensen (1977).

Cape Cod, and the offshore islands fall within the pitch pine-oak zone. This vegetation type, occurring on sandy and gravelly soils laid down as glacial moraines or outwash deposits, is characterized by drought-tolerant and fire-adapted species including pitch pine, scrub oak, and huckleberry. This type also occurs on scattered outwash deposits in inland Massachusetts. The remainder of the coastal lowlands, southern Worcester county, and the southern Connecticut River valley fall within the central hardwood-hemlock-white pine zone. This vegetation type represents the northern extension of the oak-hickory dominated forests of the central Appalachians and the Middle Atlantic states.

Generally north and west of the central hardwood zone we find the transition hardwood zone. This zone also extends up the major river valleys in the western part of the state. The transition hardwood zone is characterized by increasing amounts of more northern species such as yellow birch, black birch, sugar maple, and beech; less oak (especially white oak); and the general occurrence of paper birch on heavily disturbed sites. The higher elevations in the Berkshire and Taconic

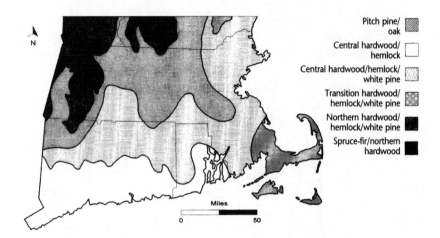

Figure 3. The major forest vegetation zones in southern New England. Glacial sandy deposits forming the area of Cape Cod and extreme southeastern Massachusetts support a dry forest of pitch pine and scrub oak species. Central hardwood forest, a northern extension of the oak-hickory forest type, covers most of the coastal lowland. Transition hardwood forest dominates the central uplands and much of the Connecticut River and Berkshire valleys with northern hardwood forest on the higher elevations in the Berkshires and Taconics and spruce-fir forest on the highest elevations. Modified from Westveld (1956).

mountains and in extreme northern Worcester County fall within the northern hardwood and spruce-fir zones. The spruce-fir zone is restricted to the highest elevations, generally above 2,000 feet, and has red spruce as the dominant conifer, while the northern hardwood zone occurs just below the spruce-fir zone and has hemlock and white pine as its dominant conifers. Both zones have hardwood mixtures dominated by sugar maple, yellow birch, beech, and red maple.

III. NATURAL AND PRESETTLEMENT DISTURBANCE

Natural Disturbance

These natural vegetation zones represent idealized conditions as they have developed over the last two millennia or so, as forests responded to existing physiographic, geologic, climatic, and soil conditions. What major disturbance processes have been active during this time frame? The major natural disturbances affecting Massachusetts forests include windstorm, pathogens (insect and diseases), and fire. Although direct soil evidence of the uprooting of trees may persist nearly 1,000 years (Stephens 1955; Lyford and MacClean 1966), over millennia storm frequency and pattern have undoubtedly varied with changing climatic conditions. Nevertheless, trends can be estimated from observations over the past few hundred years. Two different types of windstorms cause significant damage to Massachusetts forests: tropical storms or hurricanes, and downbursts or microbursts — sudden, straight-line winds — often from the northwest, associated with severe thunderstorms and occasionally accompanied by tornadoes. Downburst winds are probably the dominant wind disturbance in the Berkshires and western Massachusetts. They continue east across central Massachusetts and become somewhat less important in the more stable areas under maritime winds near the coast. While commonly rather local, the potential destructiveness of these events was demonstrated in July 1995, when hundreds of thousands of acres of forest from the Adirondacks of New York into western Massachusetts were severely damaged by an extremely large and long-lived downburst front (Jenkins 1995).

Tropical storms represent the most important wind disturbance in central and eastern Massachusetts. Historical evidence indicates that hurricanes may affect central and eastern areas approximately every 100 years, with the Cape and islands affected somewhat more often (Figure 4). These large, counterclockwise-rotating storms have the strongest winds on their easterly side. Catastrophic hurricanes may be generally restricted to those with tracks paralleling the 1938 and 1815 storms, which produced the greatest damage in areas receiving winds from the south and east, probably typical for severe hurricanes in Massachusetts (Foster and Boose 1992). Hillsides facing south and east would receive repeated hurricane damage, while steep north and west slopes would tend to be protected and may have developed a different vegetation. Western exposures and ridges would be prone to selective damage from the more patchily distributed microburst winds associated with severe thunderstorms.

The only strong evidence for a pathogenic disturbance in the paleoecological record is the widespread hemlock decline nearly 5,000 years ago, mentioned previously (Figure 1). The rapidity and extent of this decline, not associated with declines in other species or identifiable climatic change, points to a species-specific pathogen as the cause. Hemlock remained at low population levels for nearly 1,000 years. It

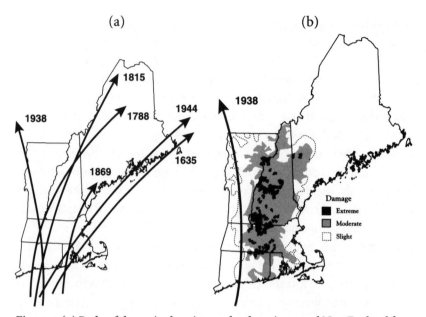

Figure 4. (a) Paths of the major hurricanes that have impacted New England from 1600 to present and (b) the damage (indicated in three categories) inflicted on forests in the region by the 1938 hurricane. Approximately 3 billion board feet of timber were windthrown by the storm, more than 600 lives were lost, and damage costs exceeded $100 million. Modified from Smith (1946) and Foster (1988).

gradually approached its predisturbance abundance at many sites between 1,000 and 1,500 years later (Allison et al. 1986). Forest response to this event differed across the region. Hemlock never fully regained its former importance at some sites, presumably because of competition with recently immigrating species or slight climatic changes over the interim. Of course, this event offers many comparisons with the human-transported pathogens (gypsy moth, chestnut blight, hemlock woolly adelgid) to be discussed later, with which our forests are coping today.

Like windstorms, fire probably differed significantly in its impact across Massachusetts as a result of differences in climate, fuel abundance (vegetation type), and ignition sources (lightning and aboriginal populations). When we look at the impacts of fire, we encounter the first strong evidence of human influence on Massachusetts forests. Charcoal evidence from sediment cores indicates that fires were less frequent and significantly smaller in the Berkshires than in southeastern Massachusetts and on Cape Cod (Patterson and Sassaman 1988). The droughty, sandy soils of the southeastern area supported a much more fire-adapted vegetation largely dominated by pitch pine, scrub oak, and other oaks and huckleberry. Pitch pine, like all conifers, contains resins in its needles that make it much more flammable than our broadleaf, deciduous trees. Huckleberry, although a broadleaf, deciduous species, also contains resins in its leaves and therefore provides a very flammable understory. All the oaks, especially scrub oak, are prolific sprouters following injury. Pitch pine is unique among Massachusetts' native conifers in possessing dormant buds beneath the bark and near the base of its trunk that enable the tree to sprout and survive if the main stem is severely damaged by fire. Moreover, the cones of pitch pine tend to be *serotinous,* which means they may remain closed with seed inside until the heat from a fire triggers an opening mechanism to release the seeds onto the recently burned landscape. Although pitch pines in Massachusetts rarely exhibit this behavior today, it is commonly observed in pitch pines in the frequently burned New Jersey pinelands.

The northern hardwood species — sugar maple, beech, and yellow birch — while capable of sprouting, tend to have thinner bark that provides less protection from understory fires. Hemlock, a major associate in the northern hardwood forest, is also thin-barked as well as slow-growing, long-lived, and incapable of sprouting. Therefore, where these species were dominant, we can conclude that fires could not have been frequent or severe. Moreover, during the growing season, broadleaf foliage normally contains enough water to be nonflammable. This moisture tends to limit the fire season in our broadleaf forests to spring and fall, when the fallen dry leaves will burn in surface or brush fires. In fact, the combination of these factors led some to nickname the northern hardwood forest "asbestos forests."

Aboriginal Impacts

There is considerable debate regarding the extent of aboriginal impact across the broad-scale forest landscape. American Indian populations migrated into Massachusetts shortly after the trees, some 10,000 years ago, but their populations remained quite low until 4,000 or 5,000 years ago. Some researchers speculate that the hemlock decline about this time, and subsequent increase in mast species (*mast* means hard food such as nuts that accumulate on the forest floor) such as oak and hickory, which produce abundant large nuts edible by both wildlife and humans, may have contributed to the increase in aboriginal populations (Mulholland, personal communication).

Archaeological evidence indicates that aboriginal populations — like the incidence of fires — were more numerous in the eastern than in the western part of the state, with settlements also along the major river basins, as shown in Figure 5 (Patterson and Sassaman 1988). There is little evidence that these populations cleared extensive areas for agriculture. Rather, they most likely created a patchwork of cleared areas, abandoned fields, and village sites in a matrix of intact forest. Population density and presumably human impact on the forest gradually decreased moving away from the coast (Whitney 1994), from a high of up to 50 people per square mile on Nantucket to 4 to 10 per square mile in inland eastern and southeastern Massachusetts and the Con-

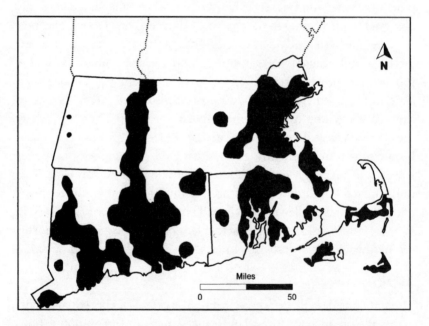

Figure 5. Areas of concentrated aboriginal populations (black) in southern New England during the Late Woodland period (A.D. 1000–1600) preceding European settlement. Populations were concentrated along major river valleys, the coast, and the larger islands of Nantucket and Martha's Vineyard and were low across broad upland areas. Modified from Patterson and Sassaman (1988).

necticut River valley, with probably no permanent settlements in the upland Berkshires.

It is interesting to note that the pattern of high population density (Figure 5) tends to follow the distribution of the central hardwood and pitch pine–scrub oak forest zones on Westveld's map (Figure 3). These would be the forest types most suitable to burning. Although there is still extensive debate over the frequency, extent, and broad-scale impacts of aboriginal burning (Cronon 1983; Whitney 1994), there is general agreement that these populations did burn to create fields and remove and rejuvenate understory browse for deer and other animals they hunted. This burning was probably largely restricted to dry areas with vegetation adapted to fire, but undoubtedly it served to maintain these conditions by eliminating regeneration of fire-sensitive species. In dry periods, human-set fires may even have altered the distribution of fire-sensitive species. Early reports of aboriginal burning indicate that most fires were set in the spring or fall and burned primarily the new litter and other small material that had recently collected on the forest floor. Undoubtedly feedback mechanisms between forest types and aboriginal practices reinforced the distribution of both. Such tight links were most important near the coast and inland up to the "tension zone," where the central hardwood forest met the transition hardwood forest.

We have traced how the postglacial landscape interacted with migrating species and different disturbance patterns to create the pre-European forests of Massachusetts. Several important lessons emerge from this review:

- Both the environment and the forest communities have a dynamic history without long-term equilibrium.

- When forests are seriously disturbed, restructuring can take a long time.

- Most pre-European disturbances were infrequent and distributed unevenly across the landscape.

- The forest communities that the Europeans encountered had been in place a relatively short time, evolving under dynamic conditions (Foster 1995).

What has been the fate of our forests since the arrival of Europeans?

IV. POST-EUROPEAN DYNAMICS

The Colonial Period

European settlement in Massachusetts spread inland from the coast at uneven rates. Essex, Suffolk, Norfolk, Plymouth, and Bristol counties were largely settled by 1675, as was the Connecticut River valley, with settlers moving northward from settlements in the Springfield area that dated from the 1630s. Concentrated in the coastal lowlands and major river valleys, this early settlement pattern closely overlapped the areas where aboriginal practices had most affected the forests. Settlement then spread to much of Middlesex and Worcester counties in the late seventeenth and early eighteenth centuries and expanded into the foothills of the Connecticut River valley during the same period. In 1725 Massachusetts began using land grants to pay off debts, especially for military service (Clark 1983), which encouraged the settlement of the central upland areas. The last areas to be settled, from the second half of the eighteenth century into the beginning of the nineteenth century (Figure 6), were the northern portions of Worcester County and the uplands of the Berkshires.

Initially, clearing occurred quite slowly for several reasons, including lack of markets for excess production and a town organization based on the European model of a centralized settlement and common field system (Whitney 1994, Foster 1995). More than 100 years after its settlement in 1635, Concord was still more than 50 percent forested. This rate of about 0.4 percent deforestation per year was typical of towns in the seventeenth century (Whitney 1994). A shift to a town pattern of dispersed settlement and individual ownership of private land, with all land in the township distributed, led to much more rapid deforestation toward the middle of the eighteenth century. Rates of 0.8 percent to 1.0 percent per year were common in both older towns like Concord and new ones like Petersham in the second half of the eighteenth century (Figure 7). This clearing coincided with a shift toward a market economy, partly driven by a developing beef trade with the West Indies. Animals were a suitable crop on remote hilltown farms during this period because they could be walked to market on the rudimentary roads that precluded the long-distance transport of most products. The difficulty of transport also partly explains the methods most commonly used to clear the forest, girdling

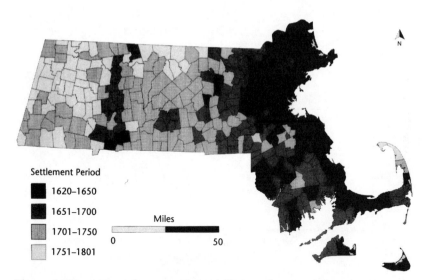

Figure 6. European settlement patterns of Massachusetts showing early settle-ments along the coast and in the southern Connecticut River valley, slowly expanding west and north respectively through the seventeenth century and then more quickly filling the central area during the first half of the eighteenth century. The last areas to be settled were the Berkshires and the north central tier of towns. In a few cases, "late" settlement may reflect town subdivision dates.

and leaving the dead trees in place to fall apart slowly, or cutting the trees and burning them (Whitney 1994). Except where water transport was available, trees were valuable only locally as lumber or firewood. Potash, a relatively more compact and transportable product, was probably the major marketable product from the trees of these early farms.

Pasture suited the landscape of most of Massachusetts quite well. The rockiness of most soils made clearing land for tillage a long and backbreaking chore. It has been said that it took two generations to clear upland farms for plowing, the first to remove the trees and the second to remove the stones. The massive stone walls surrounding abandoned fields across the state attest to the effort required by the second endeavor. And yet the great number of rocks scattered through-out the remaining pastures and second growth woods suggest that the majority of the landscape was never tilled, but rather grazed or at most mowed. The principal exceptions of course were the major river valleys where postglacial alluvial deposits provided excellent tillage after the

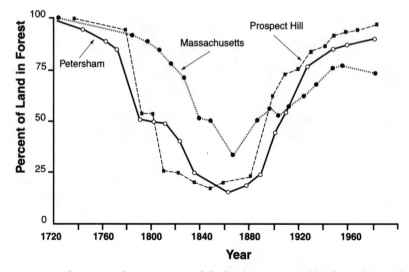

Figure 7. Changes in the percentage of the land area covered by forest during the historical period in the state of Massachusetts, the town of Petersham, and the Prospect Hill tract of the Harvard Forest. Information is derived from the following sources: Dickson and McAfee (1988), MacConnell (1975), Rane (1908), and Baldwin (1942) for Massachusetts; Raup and Carlson (1941), MacConnell and Niedzwiedz (1974), Cook (1917), and Rane (1908) for Petersham; and from Foster (1992) and Spurr (1950) for Prospect Hill.

mere removal of the trees. These areas are most notable for their lack of stone walls.

In upland areas, hilltops were often selected for village centers and initial clearing because they appeared to offer the best agricultural soils, with good drainage and relatively fewer stones. Except for the broad river valleys, inland lowlands often offered poor drainage and a shorter growing season. Land quality and therefore potential use was commonly evaluated on the basis of topography and forest vegetation; see Figure 8 (Whitney 1994, Foster 1995). Initially farmers might clear six to eight acres over the course of several years. When tilled this initial clearing could support a typical family of five to seven (Whitney 1994). During this period low-intensity agriculture combined with artisanship was the dominant employment and economic base of rural Massachusetts. Few individuals provided for all their own needs through their own labor, but through cooperation and exchange townships could be largely self-sufficient. Each town supported a range of artisans, shops, mills, and tanneries. Roads provided internal circulation but relatively poor access to external markets. At the same time, coastal communities were developing extensive fishing and shipping industries utilizing local forests for shipbuilding materials and export products. By the mid-1700s Salem was the most prosperous port in the country and a center of worldwide trade.

Agricultural Period

The late 1700s through the first half of the nineteenth century saw a major transformation of the Massachusetts economy, social structure, and land-scape (Pabst 1941; Merchant 1989; Baker and Izard 1987). The rural economy shifted from home production and local consumption to market-oriented intensive agriculture. Transportation was greatly improved through construction and development of roads, canals, and railroads. Farmers responded to the expanding markets by clearing more forested land and draining wetlands, both often on marginal agricultural sites. Pasture remained the primary land use, as beef and wool were dominant products until canal and rail connections with the west and relaxation of wool tariffs in the 1830s–40s reduced their profitability (Pabst 1941). Most farm families also engaged in home production of some sort (shoes, hats, clothes), and many also earned some income from mills or tanneries. Local industry thrived, and most hill towns reached their agricultural and commercial, as well as population, peaks during this period (Foster 1995). However, this period also represented the start of regional industrial concentration, a factor that together with the developing national transportation network and westward expansion signaled the eventual decline of New England agriculture.

Many towns literally moved downhill, from being ridgetop agricultural villages to being riverside industrial towns. Hill towns without significant water-power resources began a gradual decline. Factories, which began small, employing local residents, often grew tremendously, attracted many immigrants, and produced quantities of textiles, wooden products and tools (Botts 1934). The developing railroad network, which followed the same watercourses that the factories used for power, transported raw materials and finished products to and from the factories. The new roads and railroads allowed many nonperishable

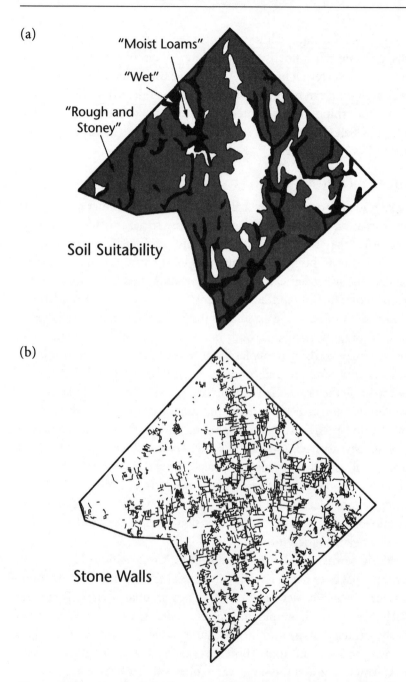

Figure 8. The township of Petersham, Massachusetts. (a) Soil suitability, (b) stonewalls and (c) forest cover from the periods 1830 and 1985 are depicted.

(c)

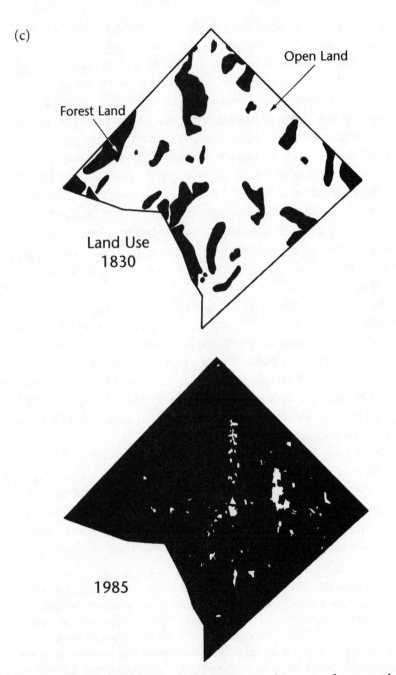

Stone walls and agricultural land are concentrated in areas of more productive soil. Maps are compiled from the atlas of Worcester County (1830, unpublished) and analysis of aerial photographs for 1985.

farm products to be shipped from the Midwest more cheaply than they could be produced in Massachusetts.

Many factors contributed to the decline of Massachusetts agriculture, but depletion of the fertility of the land was not a major one. In fact, there is evidence that the quality of tilled land in hill towns improved through the eighteenth and nineteenth centuries (Jones 1991). The disadvantages of Massachusetts farmland included stony soil and small fields divided by numerous stone walls, which were incompatible with mechanization. Industrial production and improved transportation reduced the need for local production and artisanship, and removed opportunities for supplemental income. Social factors contributing to the decline of Massachusetts hill-town agriculture included attraction to the amenities and income of city life, a declining interest in the agricultural life, and shrinking economic opportunities in small towns.

The pattern of decline was strongly influenced by regional geography. Towns adjacent to such developing industrial centers as Worcester and Fitchburg produced fuelwood, market crops, and milk, while those more distant produced butter, cheese, and hay. The farthest-distant towns declined most rapidly (Pabst 1941; Baker and Patterson 1986). Figure 9 depicts the demographic changes as Massachusetts evolved from a dispersed agricultural state in 1810 through urbanization in 1900 toward suburbanization in 1975.

How did our forests fare during the agricultural period? The gradual clearing of the first half of the eighteenth century became a rapid deforestation by the late eighteenth century that continued until the mid-nineteenth century. This clearing was concentrated on the uplands, while the wetter swamps and steep bouldery slopes were generally left as woodlots. The Berkshires were the last areas to be cleared

Figure 9. Population distribution in Massachusetts. In the agricultural period (1810) density was low (412 000 inhabitants) and remarkably evenly distributed (79 percent in rural areas), with the exception of Boston, Salem, and a few other coastal communities. With industrialization and into the twentieth century there has occurred a tremendous increase and concentration of population in urban and suburban centers. In 1975, 85 percent of the population of 5.8 million individuals was located in urban areas. Many of the rural communities have actually undergone a great decline in population during the past 100 years. Data from the U.S. Census with maps modified from Wilkie and Tager (1991).

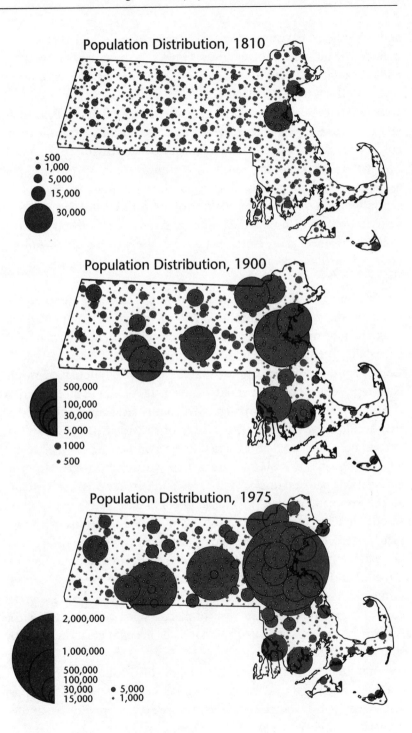

and never were developed for agriculture to the extent that the remainder of the state was. Figure 7 shows the trends of deforestation and reforestation. The statewide peak deforestation was reached about 1860, by which time nearly 70 percent of the land was cleared. Many areas east of the Berkshires show the pattern exemplified by Petersham and the Prospect Hill tract of Harvard Forest, with maximum clearance in the 1840s, when less than 20 percent of the forest remained. The pattern of remaining forest was strongly influenced by regional as well as local geography (Figure 10). For example, in the north-central portion of Massachusetts from the Connecticut River valley to eastern Worcester County, the hills east of the valley, with many rocky ridges, remained more forested, as did the north-south-trending, poorly drained valleys farther east. Most of the rest of the region was cleared.

Of course, even the uncleared areas were harvested intensively for wood by the nineteenth century. The increasing rural populations, peaking in the mid-1800s, required large amounts of cordwood for fuel. Petersham, for example, had a population of nearly 1,800 people in 1840. Assuming an average household size of six, this population would have represented 300 households to heat. If each household used 15 cords per year (a conservative figure when fireplaces are used), together they would have required 4,500 cords of fuelwood per year. The 20 percent of Petersham that remained forested in 1840 represented about 6,000 acres. Because Massachusetts forests can be expected to grow between one half and one cord of hardwood per acre per year, virtually all the woodland growth in Petersham could have been used for fuelwood. These hardwoods were probably managed by means of a "coppice" system, in which trees would be harvested very young (every 20 to 40 years), left to resprout, and then harvested again as soon as the new growth was big enough to burn. Across upland Massachusetts most farms could maintain woodlots to satisfy their fuel needs, but along the coast, where settlement had been in place longer, and near cities, the fuelwood was soon exhausted and had to be brought great distances by ship at considerable expense.

Although fuelwood represented by far the greatest use of the remaining forests in the early 1800s, the forests also faced other demands. Trees (especially hemlock and chestnut) were cut to provide tanbark for tanneries. Lumber was needed for constructing houses, barns, out-

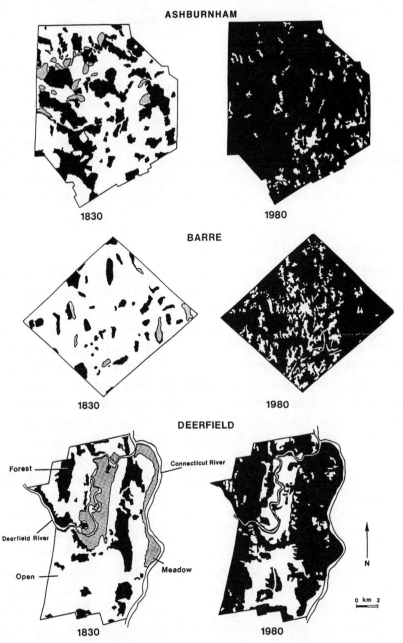

ASHBURNHAM

1830   1980

BARRE

1830   1980

DEERFIELD

Forest

Connecticut River

Deerfield River

Open

Meadow

N

0 km 2

1830   1980

Figure 10. Maps of three townships characteristic of different physiographic regions in central Massachusetts depicting distinctive amounts and patterns of forest, open land, and meadow in 1830 and 1980. Ashburnham, on rocky hills near the New Hampshire border, was least extensively cleared and today is the most forested. Barre, on rolling terrain in the central uplands, was extensively cleared for agriculture but has largely reverted to forest. Deerfield, in the Connecticut valley, was extensively cleared except for a few north-south bedrock ridges and the fertile valley bottom remains in agriculture today.

buildings, and public buildings. Wood was needed for charcoal production, and fences had to be built. The scarcity of wood by the early 1800s
probably accounts for many of the stone walls built along boundaries
and in pastures, where the stones would not have had to be removed for
plowing or mowing. By then stones were much more readily available
than wood. Although stone walls took much more effort to build, they
lasted much longer than wood fences, as is attested by the miles of stone
walls winding through second-growth forests throughout the state
today.

Postagricultural and Modern Periods

The decline of agriculture in the second half of the nineteenth century
was accompanied by a corresponding regrowth of forest (Figure 8).
Our present forest can be divided into secondary forest on land formerly cleared and used for agriculture (plowed or grazed), and primary
forest on land never actually cleared but harvested throughout the
agricultural period (terminology based on Peterken 1996). As we have
seen, the great majority of upland farmland was used for pasture, and
even tilled land may have reverted to mowing or pasture before final
abandonment. The resulting sod surface was not hospitable to many
"pioneer" tree species such as birch and aspen, whose small windblown
seeds would often dry out and die after germinating because the sprouting seeds were trapped in the grass unable to reach mineral soil. The sod
did, however, provide a suitable seedbed for the windblown but larger
seeds of white pine, which colonized vast areas of abandoned farmland.
Pines were much less likely to be cut for fuelwood. Several large pines
left as shade trees in a pasture or along a fencerow could colonize many
acres with dense stands of young pine. Moreover, animals still grazing
these pastures would avoid pine seedlings while devouring most broadleaf species.

These new forests grew quickly, and by the late 1800s supported
renewed harvesting for lumber and especially shipping containers. The
old road system and the new portable steam sawmill, in common use by
the turn of the century, permitted logging throughout the backwoods
areas. Tremendous amounts of "old-field" white pine were harvested,
the volume peaking in 1910–11. During this timber boom, extensive
harvesting of all species across the state resulted in the creation of large
tracts of even-aged, young, low-value stands. Many of these cut-over

stands, considered nearly worthless at the time, were acquired by the state for overdue taxes and formed the basis of our state forest system. The excesses of the timber industry throughout the East at this time gave rise to the conservation movement, which was strongly represented in Massachusetts.

When the old-field pines were harvested they were unable to sprout from the remaining stumps and roots (except for pitch pine, our only native conifer with this ability) and so had to reestablish themselves on the site from seed. However, as the old-field pines grew, various broadleaf species, including oaks, red maple, cherry, and others, usually were established beneath them as their seeds were either carried in by animals or blown in by the wind. All these hardwoods have the ability to sprout from cut or damaged stems. Therefore, even if they were cut back when the pines were harvested, the hardwoods had a tremendous advantage in succeeding the old-field pines, as they could grow much more quickly from their established root systems than could the tiny pine seedlings. This succession from a first generation of old-field white pine to a second generation of mixed hardwoods has been typical across most of Massachusetts. These changes are beautifully depicted in a series of three-dimensional models, or dioramas, in the Fisher Museum at Harvard Forest in Petersham (Figures 11–15; photographs by John Green).

The proliferation of old-field pine across Massachusetts led to problems as well as economic benefit. The vast expanses of young pines fed an epidemic of a native insect, the white pine weevil. The larvae of this insect eat the terminal buds of young pines, thus killing the leader and releasing the branches in the topmost whorl to replace the leader. The resulting trees have a crook in their growth at best. At worst they divide into multiple, spindly stems. In either case the economic value of the trees is greatly reduced. White pine blister rust, a fungal disease lethal to white pine, also spread rapidly through the tracts of old-field pine. This disease requires an alternate host of the genus *Ribes* (currants and gooseberries) for part of its life cycle. During the 1930s the state and federal governments conducted a massive eradication program for *Ribes* in which men literally marched through the woods tens of feet apart looking for and pulling up wild *Ribes* plants. The prevalence of white pine weevil and blister rust also led to the planting of red pine across the state in the 1920s and 1930s, on many sites where white pine might normally have grown or been

Figure 11. 1740 — Initial clearing and subsistence farming.

Figure 12. 1830 — Height of intensive farming.

Figure 13. 1850 — Agricultural abandonment and establishment of old-field white pine.

Figure 14. 1910 — First crop of old-field white pine harvested.

Figure 15. 1930 — The old-field white pine is followed by hardwood.

planted, because red pine is not affected by either pathogen. Although red pine is at the very southeastern edge of its range in western Massachusetts, these plantations have generally done well. Many are now maturing and being harvested.

The extensive old-field white pine stands also played a major role in the most dramatic natural disturbance to affect our forests in the twentieth century, the hurricane of September 21, 1938 (Figure 4). Historically, hurricanes have been a major force in shaping most Massachusetts forests. The 1938 storm followed a track similar to that of other historically significant storms (1788, 1815), but several factors conspired to make it the most destructive storm in our recorded history. The week prior to the hurricane's arrival had been very wet, saturating the soils and predisposing trees to windthrow. The added rain from the storm produced massive property damage from flooding along rivers, compounding wind damage. Large areas of central Massachusetts still supported stands of old-field pine on land abandoned in the late nineteenth century. Even pine stands as young as 30 years of age suffered severe damage if their sites were not protected topographically from the southeast winds. Hardwood stands on similar sites were not as susceptible to damage until they were twice that age (Foster 1988). The expanses of old-field pines set the stage for the unprecedented impact of the storm on our forests, nearly three billion board feet of timber blown down. We had unintentionally created about as vulnerable a landscape as possible. There is evidence that the 1815 storm may have been similar in intensity and path (Figure 4), but it encountered a landscape largely cleared of forest and its impact was quite different.

The vast tracts of blown-down pine presented another problem beyond economic loss and landscape damage, the threat of fire. Fires often follow other disturbances, especially in conifer stands where the resinous foliage and lack of new green sprouts contribute to flammability. With this in mind, and in an attempt to recover some of the value of the blown-down timber, a massive salvage operation was undertaken that recovered much of the windthrown timber. Logging crews were brought in from all over the Northeast, temporary camps were set up, and logs were salvaged and brought to the mills. Because the volume of logs far exceeded the capacity of all the available mills, logs were stored in every available pond in the area. As long as the logs remained underwater, away from oxygen in the air, they were preserved. Many ponds in central Massachusetts were dammed and raised to their present levels in order to accommodate as much salvaged timber as possible. The tremendous volume of lumber produced by the hurricane salvage also drastically lowered lumber values. To stabilize the price, the federal government bought up the vast supply, stamping the end of each log with "U.S." Mobilization for the Second World War finally made use of this vast lumber supply.

Humans have been unwitting accomplices in several other recent forest disturbances as well. With increasing mobility and transport of products, numerous forest pests and pathogens have been introduced from abroad. In many instances these organisms pose special problems because native plants possess little resistance to the exotic pests. Several such "immigrants" have severely affected our forests, and Massachusetts has the dubious distinction of being the introduction site of one major national forest pest. Gypsy moths were introduced into the United States in 1869, when Leopold Trouvelot imported them to Medford with the intention of using them as silkworms to develop a local silk industry. The moths quickly proved unsuited to this use and escaped into the local forests, where they found the native deciduous species, especially oaks and aspen, an ideal food source. Since then gypsy moths have gradually expanded their range, and there have been periodic regional outbreaks during which virtually every green leaf in the forest is consumed, leaving the forest in mid-July looking nearly as barren as in midwinter. Defoliation for two successive years is especially harmful. The outbreak of 1980–81 across the Northeast was particularly severe, causing extensive oak mortality. Today the gypsy moth has spread throughout the Northeast and into the Middle Atlantic and midwestern states and is one of the most destructive forest pests throughout the region.

Probably the most dramatic introduced pathogen to affect our forests has been the chestnut blight fungus. Although the details of the introduction of this fungus are not certain, it was first noticed in New York in 1904, and rapidly spread throughout the range of the American chestnut, passing through Massachusetts in 1913–14. An especially virulent pathogen, chestnut blight is the only disease that has effectively eliminated mature individuals of its host, greatly altering our forests in the process. Chestnut was certainly one of the most useful trees in the nineteenth-century forests, providing abundant crops of edible nuts annually, bark for tanning, and excellent wood that was beautiful, decay-resistant, and as strong as oak but lighter. It also sprouted vigorously and grew very quickly and therefore increased in areas that were repeatedly harvested (Figure 16). By the early 1920s the large chestnuts had been killed throughout the state, but because the fungus gains access to the trees through cracks in the bark and kills them by preventing transport of water and nutrients past the point of infection, effectively girdling them, the roots and base are not affected and can send out new sprouts. Today these chestnut sprouts are common in our woods. Individual stems are usually killed by the time they become several inches in diameter and the bark naturally develops cracks, only to be replaced by new sprouts. Most of the large chestnuts were salvaged for their valuable wood; their decay resistance, especially within the sapwood, means that many stumps still remain in testimony to the former importance of this species. Chestnut's place in the forest has

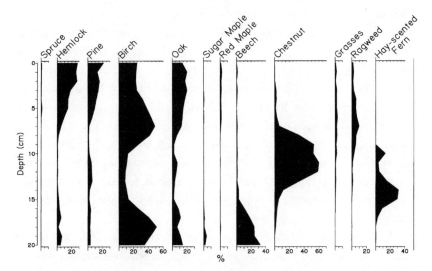

Figure 16. Pollen diagram from the humus soil in a hemlock forest at the Harvard Forest, Petersham, Massachusetts representing the last several hundred years. The site is a primary forest that was never cleared for agriculture but was clear-cut early in the settlement period (at about 18 cm depth in the diagram) and then cut repeatedly for firewood. Tree species respond quite individualistically to the series of human impacts. Chestnut benefited greatly from the cutting activity until it was decimated by blight in 1913. Beech and sugar maple never recovered to presettlement levels of abundance, whereas hemlock, pine, and red maple have gradually increased to the present. From Foster et al. (1992).

been taken by a mixture of species, especially oaks, but its wood and nuts cannot be replaced.

Several other native tree species have also been significantly affected by human-introduced agents, although none so completely as the chestnut. Dutch elm disease, a wilt fungus transported by a bark beetle, dramatically changed the look of almost every town in the state in the 1950s and 1960s as it killed the stately shade trees that lined most of our main streets. The disease is passed from tree to tree by insects above-ground and through root grafts below ground, where the trees are growing adjacent to each other, as in street plantings. This disease was somewhat less traumatic in our forests because elm occurred in mixed stands, primarily near wetlands, and exhibited a greater range of natu-ral resistance than did chestnut. The devastation of the elms in our urban tree stands again demonstrates the susceptibility of human-induced monocultures to various pathogens. More recently, many of our beech trees have been disfigured and killed by beech-bark disease. This disease, caused by the coincident impact of a fungus and a scale insect working together, is spreading steadily south after being intro-duced into the Canadian Maritimes. Most recently, hemlock woolly adelgid is beginning to cause mortality in the southern Connecticut River valley area and has been reported from many other areas of the state as it slowly advances north. This aphidlike insect, introduced on nursery stock from Japan to the West Coast and then to Maryland, poses an extreme threat to hemlock forests because hemlocks have shown little resistance and are incapable of sprouting. Moreover, be-cause of the steep habitats many hemlock stands occupy and the unique microenvironments they create, loss of hemlock would cause extreme changes in many of our forests.

Logging and land conversion to suburban use are the two direct human changes that have most affected our forests over the past several decades. Regrowth after the old-field pine stands and other forests were cut early in this century, and after the 1938 hurricane, has provided an abundant middle-aged and maturing forest, much of which has been and is being harvested with varying intensities. Environmental disputes resulting in limitations on harvesting on federal lands in other regions of the country and a strong export market have put added harvesting pressure on Massachusetts forests. However, despite these pressures the average size of trees in our forests has been steadily increasing (Figure

17). In some instances we have even managed to reduce the impact of suburban development on the forest. Significant numbers of people are now building homes on large forested lots, clearing only immediately around the buildings, and some developments cluster buildings together, reserving the majority of land as forest or open space. While both of these patterns of development alter the forest, they are much less destructive of it than traditional tract development.

Wildlife species have very much been influenced by human-induced changes in the landscape as well as by hunting (Figure 18). Although much of this information is indirect and difficult to gather, most of the large, broad-ranging species were probably largely eliminated during the initial period of forest clearance. This group would include elk, wolf, mountain lion, and moose. Deer were nearly eliminated by the mid-1800s. However, being an edge species, utilizing both open areas for browsing and forests for cover and tolerating human activities, deer have responded so favorably to the return of the forest that they have reached densities detrimental to the vegetation in areas where they are not controlled by hunting (Kyker-Snowman 1989).

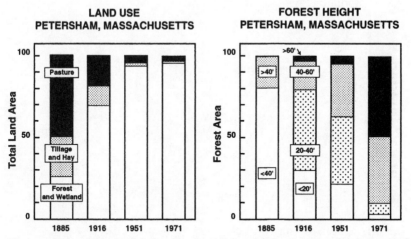

Figure 17. Historical trends in land-use activity and forest structure for the town of Petersham, Massachusetts, during the period of farm abandonment and reforestation. Note that the 1885 data for height structure depicts 40-foot height classes, whereas the later years depict 20-foot height classes. As the township became increasingly covered with forest, there occurred a progressive aging and height increase in the extant forest. Sources include Cook (1917), Rane (1908), and MacConnell and Niedzwiedz (1974).

Beavers were extirpated by the 1700s owing to the value of their pelts. They were successfully reintroduced in 1928 in West Stockbridge and have subsequently expanded to overutilize existing habitat. More recently, wild turkeys have been reintroduced very successfully, and moose have returned on their own as their northern populations have continually increased and migrated south. These three species are all responding to the expansion of our woodland area, as have black bear and fisher which have significantly expanded their ranges and numbers within the past 75 years. Other species, most notably open-land birds such as the bobwhite and meadowlark, have decreased as the forest has regrown and matured.

V. PRESENT CONDITIONS AND FUTURE PROSPECTS

How are the forests produced by the series of human changes since European settlement, in some cases interacting with natural disturbance processes, different from the forests the colonists found? The process of deforestation and reforestation produced different landscape patterns in different places, depending on the distribution of natural

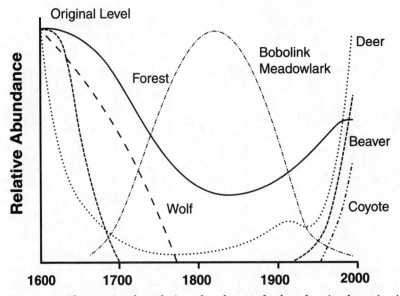

Figure 18. Changes in the relative abundance of selected animal species in Massachusetts over the past 400 years. Whereas the wolf has been eliminated, beaver have been reintroduced and the coyote represents a new species in the landscape. Modified from Bickford and Dymon (1990).

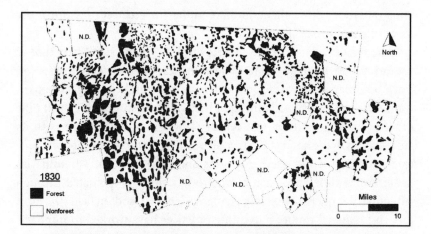

Figure 19. Forest cover (black) for north-central Massachusetts in 1830 at the approx-imate peak of agricultural clearance, and in 1985. Major physiographic regions from west to east include the Connecticut Valley, the rough Pelham Hills, and the undu-lating central upland regions. ND = no data. From Foster et al. (1998).

and subsequent cultural features, including river valleys, wetlands, steep slopes, rock ledges, town centers, and highways (Figures 8, 10, 19).

Today, open, agricultural land is primarily restricted to broad river valleys and the crests of broad ridges. Urban areas first developed along the coast and along major rivers, then along the railroads, which tended to follow the rivers. More recently, suburban development has occurred along and especially near the junctions of major highways. Today, forests predominate outside these zones, and in protected reserves and some wetlands within them, and are under the greatest pressure at the edges of these zones (Figure 20).

The major changes in the geographic pattern and stand structure of our forests have strongly favored a new landscape of even-aged forests and sharp boundaries between forest types. Agricultural clearing and abandonment, heavy fuelwood cutting, intensive harvesting of old-field pine and other species early in this century, and the 1938 hurricane with its subsequent salvage harvesting have all pushed our forests toward an even-aged condition. Land-use regulations and land ownership boundaries create visible differences that tend strongly to be perpetuated through time and subsequent ownership changes. General trends in field size, farm size, and regional timber harvesting practices have worked to impose a repetitive patchwork of forest classes on top of the natural vegetation patterns described early in this chapter. The even-aged structure and imposed pattern present across much of our forest today increase the potential for future disturbances to be more damaging than they might be in a more diverse forest. Moreover, the relative lack of very young forests presents problems for species dependent on such habitat.

Surburbanization and Land Use Change 1950-1980

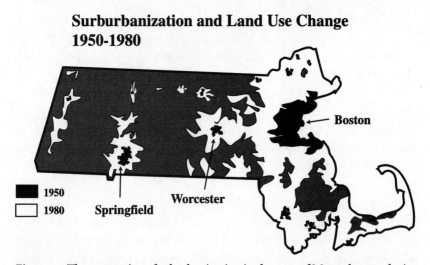

Figure 20. The progression of suburbanization in the state of Massachusetts during the last half of the twentieth century. A growing population and an improved road transportation system have resulted in a conversion of former agricultural and industrial towns to residential communities around the major cities of Boston, Worcester, and Springfield. Modified from Wilkie and Tager (1991).

Ever since the heavy fuelwood cutting in the early 1800s, there have been repeated public concerns about the condition of our forests. As Figure 17 shows, over the past 100-plus years the forests in Petersham have continually increased in area and size, and this trend has been general throughout the state. How has the composition of our forests been affected? Agricultural clearing and subsequent abandonment led to the dramatic increase in white pine discussed previously. Prior to European settlement white pine was probably found principally on sandy outwash soils, on sites heavily burned by Indians or following a natural disturbance, and as scattered, emergent individuals in old stands. Following agricultural abandonment, especially of pastures, white pine proliferated throughout most of the state on sites it would never have occupied in the absence of clearing and grazing. Despite intensive harvesting and the 1938 hurricane, white pine remains much more widely distributed and dominant today than it was before. The repeated fuelwood cutting and agricultural burning practiced in the nineteenth century would have favored an increase in invasive, pioneer species intolerant of shade such as gray and paper birch, aspen, pin cherry, and black cherry, as well as species that sprout prolifically such as chestnut, oak, red maple, birch, and hickory. Chestnut is probably the species that responded most favorably to nineteenth-century disturbances because it sprouts prolifically from dormant basal buds and is capable of phenomenal rates of height and diameter growth when reproducing vegetatively (Zon 1904; Paillet and Rutter 1989).

Figure 16 traces the changes in tree species abundance from the agricultural period to the present, as recorded in the pollen collected in the humus soil in a hemlock woodlot in Petersham. The most striking feature is the tremendous increase in chestnut followed by its virtual elimination following the blight. The other major changes are the decreases in several long-lived, shade-tolerant species, including hemlock, sugar maple, and beech, during the agricultural period. Both hemlock and beech are very sensitive to fire and could be largely eliminated from upland areas by repeated fires, a rather common agricultural practice. The site represented in Figure 16 is a moist lowland, and hemlock has become dominant there following the loss of chestnut to the blight. Oak, pine, and red maple have also increased, replacing beech and sugar maple.

As our forests have grown back and matured following the tremendous cutting at the turn of the century, the loss of chestnut in the teens, and the 1938 hurricane salvage, in conjunction with our more recent suppression of fires, there has been an increase in long-lived, shade-tolerant species, including hemlock, sugar maple, and to a lesser extent beech. However, these species, especially beech, remain well below their presettlement distributions based on early survey and pollen records. Oak, which requires at least moderate disturbance for successful regeneration, may be generally more common than before settlement.

The recent maturation of considerable areas of Massachusetts forest has led to significant new harvesting. At the same time, the developing environmental consciousness from the 1960s to the present has increased awareness of what is happening on our woodland and has led to the regulation of forest cutting practices (Massachusetts General Laws, chapter 132, sections 40–46), which, in turn, has increased the quality and extent of professional forest management across the state. Moreover, the requirement to file a cutting plan that includes a map for all harvests greater than 25,000 board feet has enabled the compilation of maps of current harvesting patterns (Figure 21) at much finer detail than has been possible in the past. The growing understanding that forest stands or ownerships do not function in isolation but must be considered within a regional or ecosystem context (for example, with respect to disease spread or wildlife habitat) points up the importance of such regionally mapped information.

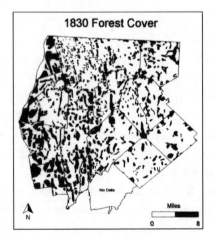

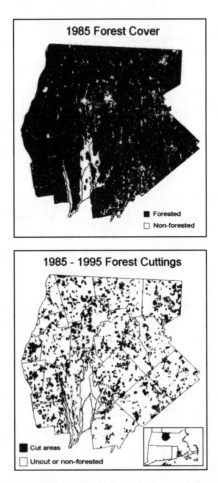

Figure 21. Maps of the north Quabbin region of Massachusetts showing forest cover at the height of agricultural clearing (1830) and in 1985 and the areas on which some type of forest cutting was conducted during the period from 1985 to 1995.

The growing environmental interest has led to the discovery of remnant patches of old-growth forest, once assumed to have been entirely eliminated through the extensive clearing and harvesting in the nineteenth and early twentieth centuries (Figure 22). Although exact definitions of these remnants of the presettlement forests vary considerably, these areas typically contain dominant trees well over 200 years old and show minimal evidence of human disturbance. At present between 500 and 1,000 acres (depending on exact definition and extent of disturbance allowed) of old-growth forest are recognized in Massa-

Figure 22. General location of currently recognized old-growth sites (at least 10 acres) in Massachusetts. The majority of these sites are on steep, rocky slopes along the headwaters of streams in western Massachusetts that were unsuitable for agriculture and inaccessible to harvesting. Adapted from Dunwiddie and Leverett (1996).

chusetts (Dunwiddie and Leverett 1996), and this amount continues to increase as more areas are investigated by scientists with increasingly better understanding of what they are looking for — which is not necessarily huge old trees. Many of these remnants are small patches of barely 10 acres — which according to one current, working definition is the minimum size necessary to prevent significant edge impacts — but some are considerably larger. Most are located on steep, rocky slopes, often on headwater streams, where they were inaccessible for harvesting from either the stream valley or the broad ridges and were somewhat protected from natural disturbances.

Not even these sites offer protection from some recent human disturbances, which are subtle but pervasive. These include atmospheric pollution and rising carbon dioxide (CO_2) levels, with implications for future global warming. While neither of these forces has had serious, measurable impacts on our forests as yet, both have the potential to significantly alter them in the future.

Inputs of atmospheric nitrogen (NO_x), an important component of atmospheric pollution, increase as one moves farther west and to greater elevations in Massachusetts (McNulty et al. 1990). Nitrogen is the major limiting nutrient for plant growth in our soils. Initially nitrogen works as a fertilizer, but at higher concentrations it may saturate the soils and become damaging, even leading to nutrient loss through leaching (Aber et al. 1989). Low-level ozone is another pollutant with potential serious forest impacts. Pollutant impacts are extremely complex, and the effects of long-term chronic exposure to and accumulation of these compounds is still largely unknown.

Elevated carbon (CO_2) levels affect plant growth, competitive interactions, leaf chemistry and thus organic-matter quality, as well as potentially changing the global climate. We do not yet understand how forest communities and ecosystem processes might ultimately be changed by elevated CO_2 levels, nor do we know the local effects of global warming. Massachusetts forests do have some impact on the global CO_2 level. Because they are still relatively young and growing, and our landscape is still recovering from agricultural clearing, our forests take up and store significant amounts of CO_2, slightly offsetting the increases from fossil fuel burning and deforestation. CO_2 levels and pollution are both international issues that will require unprecedented levels of cooperation if they are to be managed.

CONCLUSIONS

We have traced changes in Massachusetts forests from a time when there were no forests through natural forest development and change, aboriginal impacts, European settlement and forest clearance, reforestation and regrowth, and down to the present, when the state is nearly two-thirds forested again. What comparisons can be made between change under natural processes and the more recent changes from human disturbances? Although our forests have been very dynamic throughout geologic and historical time, human-induced changes over the past 300 years have been much more frequent, varied and extensive than most changes in previous forest evolution (Table 2). These changes were superimposed upon natural disturbance processes, and where they interacted, as in the 1938 hurricane, the impacts were substantial. On the whole, human disturbances have been more frequent and more systematic in both time and space than their natural counterparts. Human activities have tended to mask natural forest patterns by overlaying imposed patterns on them and homogenizing them.

Table 2. Forest disturbances through time with their impacts scaled as low, moderate, or high on four measures: frequency, area, community (species) changes, and geographical specificity. There is a general trend toward increasing frequency, area, and community change and decreasing geographical specificity in the post-European settlement disturbance period.

Disturbance	Frequency			Area			Community			Geographical Specificity		
	L	M	H	L	M	H	L	M	H	L	M	H
Migration	▬	▬				■	▬	▬			■	
Pathogens	■					■	▬	▬			■	
Fire (natural)	▬	▬			■		■					■
Windstorm–Hurricane	▬	▬			■		▬	▬			▬	▬
Windstorm–Downburst	■				■		▬	▬			■	
Fire (aboriginal)	▬	▬		▬	▬			■			▬	▬
Agriculture	■				■				■		■	
Logging	■				▬	▬		▬	▬		▬	▬
Introduced pathogens	■				■			▬	▬	■		
Pollution	■				■			?		■		

L = low; M = medium; H = high

The forests across the state today are quite different from those the colonists and Indians saw — quite different from those 60 years ago. Undoubtedly they will continue to change, but will likely continue the recent trends of increasing in volume and storing carbon. Changing ownership patterns will increasingly affect forest development. Over the past 50 years the average size and term of forest ownership have both consistently shrunk, as more people have found their place in the woods and as our population has become even less agrarian and much more mobile. These trends, along with expanding low-density development on wooded lots as suburbs encroach on rural areas, will certainly influence our forests and their management into the next century. At the same time, demands for forest conservation, preservation, and recreation will all probably increase, especially on public lands, as the amenity, recreation, and watershed-protection values of our forests increase even more rapidly than their resource or development values. Humans — directly, indirectly, and in conjunction with natural processes — will continue to be the dominant force acting on our forests, which are certain to change. The forests covering nearly two-thirds of Massachusetts today are testimony to the resilience of our landscape in

the face of centuries of unplanned human activity and natural disturbance. However, as we continue to increase the stresses on our forests,
we will need to use our increasing understanding of forest ecology and
history to plan for a future in which the forests will continue to meet
our demands for both amenities and products.

As long as they have lived in Massachusetts people have influenced
the forest, and the forests have influenced the people. Hugh Raup,
former director of the Harvard Forest, once suggested that "the principal role of the land and the forests has been that of stage and
scenery: the significant figures have always been the people, and the
ideas they have had about what they might do at specific points in
time with the stage properties at hand. At each such point in time an
actor could play his role only by the rules he knew — in terms of his
own conception of his relation to the play of which he was part"
(Raup 1966). A closer examination of some of these roles occurs in the
chapters that follow.

🍃 LITERATURE CITED

Aber, J. D., K. J. Nadelhoffer, P. Steudler, and J. M. Melillo. 1989. "Nitrogen
Saturation in Northern Forest Ecosystems." *BioScience* 39: 378–86.

Allison, T. D., R. E. Moeller, and M. B. Davis. 1986. "Pollen in Laminated
Sediments Provides Evidence For a Mid-Holocene Forest Pathogen Outbreak." *Ecology* 67: 1101–1105.

Baker, A. H., and H. V. Izard. 1987. *Production Changes and Marketing Strategies
of Worcester County Farmers, 1780–1865: A Case Study of the Wards of
Shrewsbury.* Society for History of Early American Republic, Izard, Dublin.

Baker, A. H., and H. I. Patterson. 1986. "Farmers' Adaptations to Markets in
Early Nineteenth-Century Massachusetts." In: pp. 95–108, *Proceedings of
the Dublin Seminar.* Antiquities Society, London.

Baldwin, H. I. 1942. *Forestry in New England.* National Resources Planning
Board Publication 70, Boston, Mass.

Baldwin, H. I. 1949. *Wooden Dollars: A Report on the Forest Rresources of New
England.* Federal Reserve Bank of Boston, Mass.

Bickford, W. E., and U. J. Dymon. 1990. *An Atlas of Massachusetts River
Systems: Environmental Designs for the Future.* University of Massachusetts
Press, Amherst.

Botts, A. K. 1934. "Northbridge, Massachusetts, a Town That Moved Down
Hill." *Journal of Geography* 33: 249–260.

Clark, C. 1983. *The Eastern Frontier: The Settlement of Northern New England 1610–1763.* Knopf, New York.

Cook, H. O. 1917. *The Forests of Worcester County. The Results of a Forest Survey of the Fifty-Nine Towns in the County and a Study of Their Lumber Industry.* State Printing Office, Boston, Mass.

Cronon, William. 1983. *Changes in the Land: Indians, Colonists and the Ecology of New England.* Hill and Wang, New York.

Davis, M. B. 1958. "Three Pollen Diagrams from Central Massachusetts." *American Journal of Science* 256: 540–570.

Dickson, D. R., and C. L. McAfee. 1988. *Forest Statistics for Massachusetts, 1972 and 1985.* Resource Bulletin NE-106, U.S.D.A. Forest Service.

Dunwiddie, P. W., and R. T. Leverett. 1996. "Survey of Old-Growth Forest in Massachusetts." *Rhodora* 98: 419–444.

Foster, D. R. 1988. "Species and Stand Response to Catastrophic Wind in Central New England, USA." *Journal of Ecology* 76: 135–151.

Foster, D. R. 1992. "Land-Use History (1730–1990) and Vegetation Dynamics in Central New England, U.S.A." *Journal of Ecology* 80: 753–772.

Foster, D. R. 1995. "Land-Use History and Four Hundred Years of Vegetation Change in New England." In: pp. 253–321, B. L. Turner, A. G. Sal, F. G. Bernaldez, and F. DiCastri (eds.), *Global Land Use Change: A Perspective from the Columbian Encounter.* SCOPE Publication. Consejo Superior de Investigaciones Científicas, Madrid.

Foster, D. R. and E. R. Boose. 1992. "Patterns of Forest Damage Resulting from Catastrophic Wind in Central New England, USA." *Journal of Ecology* 80: 79–98.

Foster, D. R., and T. M. Zebryk. 1993. "Long-Term Vegetation Dynamics and Disturbance History of a *Tsuga*-Dominated Forest in Central New England." *Ecology* 74: 982–998.

Foster, D. R., G. Motzkin, and B. Slater. 1998. "Land-Use History as Long-Term Broad-Scale Disturbance: Regional Forest Dynamics in Central New England." *Ecosystems* 1:96–119.

Foster, D. R., T. M. Zebryk, P. K. Schoonmaker, and A. Lezberg. 1992. "Land-Use History and Vegetation Dynamics of a Hemlock (*Tsuga*) Woodlot in Central New England." *Journal of Ecology 80*: 773–786.

Jenkins, J. 1995. "Notes on the Adirondack Blowdown of July 15, 1995: Scientific Background, Observation, Responses and Policy Issues." Wildlife Conservation Society Draft Report, December 1995.

Jones, N. 1991. "An Ecological History of Agricultural Land-use in Two Massachusetts Towns." Senior thesis. Hampshire College, Amherst, Mass.

Jorgensen, N. 1977. *A Guide to New England's Landscape*. Globe Pequot Press, Chester, Conn.

Kyker-Snowman, T. 1989. "1989 Quabbin Forest Regeneration Study." Metropolitan District Commission (MDC) Publication.

Lyford, W. H., and D. W. MacLean. 1966. "Mound and Pit Relief in Relation to Soil Disturbance and Tree Distribution in New Brunswick, Canada." Harvard Forest Paper 15.

MacConnell, W. P. 1975. "Remote Sensing 20 Years of Change in Massachusetts." Massachusetts Agricultural Experiment Station Bulletin No. 630.

MacConnell, W. P. and Niedzwiedz, W. 1974. "Remote Sensing 20 Years of Change in Worcester County, Massachusetts, 1951–1971." Massachusetts Agricultural Experiment Station, University of Massachusetts, Amherst, Mass.

McNulty, S. G., J. D. Aber, T. M. McLellan and S. M. Katt. 1990. "Nitrogen Cycling in High Elevation Forests of the Northeastern U.S. in Relation to Nitrogen Deposition." *Ambio* 19: 38–40.

Merchant, C. 1989. *Ecological Revolutions. Nature, Gender and Science in New England*. University of North Carolina Press Chapel Hill.

Mulholland, M. Personal communication.

Pabst, M. R. 1941. "Agricultural Trends in the Connecticut Valley Region of Massachusetts, 1800–1900." *Smith College Studies in History* 26: 1–135.

Paillet, F. L., and P. A. Rutter. 1989. "Replacement of Native Oak and Hickory Tree Species by the Introduced American Chestnut (*Castanea dentata*) in Southwestern Wisconsin." *Canadian Journal of Botany* 67: 3457–3469.

Patterson, W. A., and A. E. Backman. 1988. "Fire and Disease History of Forests." In: pp. 603–632, B. Huntley and T. Webb (eds.), *Vegetation History*. Kluwer, Dordrecht.

Patterson, W. A., and K. E. Sassaman. 1988. "Indian Fires in the Prehistory of New England." In: pp. 107–135, G. P. Nicholas (ed.), *Holocene Human Ecology in Northeastern North America*. Plenum Publishing, New York.

Peterken, G. F. 1996. *Natural Woodland: Ecology and Conservation in Northern Temperate Regions*. Cambridge University Press, Cambridge.

Rane, F. W. 1908. *Fourth Annual Report of the State Forester of Massachusetts for the Year 1907*. Wright and Potter, Boston, Mass.

Raup, H. M. 1966. "The View from John Sanderson's Farm." *Forest History* 10: 2–11.

Raup, H. M., and R. E. Carlson. 1941. "The History of Land-Use in the Harvard Forest." *Harvard Forest Bulletin* 20: 1–64.

Smith, D. M. 1946. "Storm Damage in New England Forests." M.S. thesis. Yale University, New Haven, Conn.

Spurr, S. H. 1950. "Stand Composition in the Harvard Forest as Influenced by Site and Forest Management." Ph.D. thesis. Yale University, New Haven, Connecticut.

Stephens, E. P. 1955. "The Historical-Developmental Method of Determining Forest Trends." Ph.D. thesis. Harvard University, Cambridge, Mass.

Strahler, A. N. 1966. *A Geologist's View of Cape Cod.* Natural History Press, Garden City, N.Y.

Westveld, M. V. 1956. "Natural Forest Vegetation Zones of New England." *Journal of Forestry* 54: 332–338

Whitney, G. C. 1994. *From Coastal Wilderness to Fruited Plain: A History of Environmental Change in Temperate North America from 1500 to the Present.* Cambridge University Press, Cambridge.

Wilkie, R. W., and J. Tager. 1991. *Historical Atlas of Massachusetts.* University of Massachusetts Press, Amherst.

Wright, J. K. 1933. "Regions and Landscapes of New England." In: pp. 14–49, *New England's Prospect: 1933.* American Geographical Society, New York.

Zon, R. 1904. "Chestnut in Southern Maryland." U.S.D.A. Bureau of Forestry Bulletin 53.

The Economic Uses of
Massachusetts Forests

NANCY M. GORDON

Since time immemorial, man has used the forest in a variety of
ways to support his existence. When Europeans realized that there
was a whole new world, on the other side of the Atlantic, for them to
explore and exploit, they had reached a point where their own forests
had become a scarce resource. But the forest in the new world seemed
limitless, and those who moved to the new world to live set about
immediately to utilize the forest and its products to improve their living
standard.

At first, the forest was seen primarily as a source of furs, the next
best thing to the gold and silver the Spaniards had staked out for
themselves far to the south. But once Europeans, especially Englishmen, determined to move permanently to the new world, they found
that the forests there supplied a wide variety of needs. These needs
changed over time, but to this day the forest supplies products without
which modern man could not live.

THE SEVENTEENTH CENTURY: CREATING A MARKET

When the Pilgrims first set foot on Massachusetts soil, in November of
1620, a bleak scene met their eyes. There was very little vegetation on the
sandy shore, and where trees grew, inland, they were often interspersed
with dense thickets. Even though the Pilgrims chanced on some abandoned Indian larders and corn fields, the next few years would be hard
ones for the seekers of a religious haven.[1]

Not so the Puritans who followed and, under the leadership of John
Winthrop, staked out a place on Massachusetts Bay. To be sure, the
immediate coast, with its salt marshes and sand flats, was almost as
bleak as that around Plymouth. But not far inland the forest began, and

the settlers of Massachusetts Bay, driven as much by a desire for new economic opportunities as for religious security, made haste to take advantage of the adjacent forest.[2]

The flood of settlers that poured into Massachusetts Bay in the decade between 1630 and 1640, often called the Great Migration, were convinced believers in Calvinist theology but were also, most of them, men of some means as well; nowadays we would call them middle class. They had owned property, some personal, some real estate in England; and they had sold off their possessions before they left to provide themselves with the funds they would need to create a new existence in the new world.

The first need was houses for protection against the harsh New England winter. House building went on apace in the new settlements on Massachusetts Bay, the settlers adapting the styles that had been familiar to them in old England to the resources available in New England. They built timber frame houses, felling the numerous oaks in the woods adjacent to the new settlements, hauling them by ox teams to the chosen site, and erecting modest dwellings. They filled in the spaces between the beams with mud and straw, but they sheathed the outside, and later the inside, with clapboards. These were not made by sawmills or even by pit-saws, the conventional method of sawing boards in the England of their day, but were, as the settlers would have said, "riven." Bolts of wood were chopped from a log and then split into thin layers with a frow, a wedge-shaped tool that was hit with a hammer. If the wood was straight-grained, a relatively smooth piece was the product, but those who were meticulous could make it smoother with a draw knife. In place of the masonry-clad houses the immigrants had known in England, these wooden, clapboard-sheathed houses became the norm in New England. This was without doubt the first use of the forest by the new immigrants to New England.[3]

The first houses were generally roofed with thatch — the marshes along the coast could provide ready material for thatched roofs — but before long the settlers adopted a practice of the Dutch traders in New Netherlands to the south, the shingle. These too could be riven, and where cedar was available a good, sound roof could be made. Shingles were also made from pine. Moreover, shingles were slightly less liable to catch fire than the thatched roofs they replaced, which was an important consideration, since the new residents of New England built huge fires in their houses to keep themselves warm during the long winter. The forests, that then seemed unlimited, provided fuel in abundance. After the deprivation in England, where fuelwood had become scarce and expensive, the New Englanders could afford to indulge in generous fires on the hearth.[4]

Although the settlers in Massachusetts Bay proved adept at making use of the wood they found available to them, many of the goods they needed could not be hand made in the new environment. These goods, notably glass and metal products, had to be imported from England. During the first decade, the resources (English currency and letters of credit) most immigrants brought with them from England paid for these necessities, and as long as new immigrants kept pouring in, the money to buy such goods came with them. But in 1640, for reasons both political and economic, immigration almost ceased, and with that cessation came the end of the financial resources of the new immigrants. What happened then has often been described as a depression, which lasted for most of the next two decades. But there was still a need for British products. How to pay for them was the burning question of the day.[5]

This need for foreign exchange led to a pressing search for products that could be traded elsewhere, either in exchange for other products that could be sold for English currency or credit, or that could be shipped directly in Europe and sold there. Some of the earliest settlers had had visions of great wealth gained from the fur trade; but except for the new settlement created by John Pynchon on the Connecticut River at the present site of Springfield, the settlers had little opportunity to interact with Indians who, in turn, could bring in the number of furs that would generate good European credit. And even the Pynchons found that, after a decade or so, the fur trade was petering out. The Dutch, located on the upper Hudson River, had built better ties with the Indians who had access to the vast trapping grounds in the interior of the continent.

But the new settlers were determined men, and they were driven by necessity. Necessity soon produced an answer: the many white oaks in the forests adjoining the Massachusetts Bay settlements could be cut up to make barrel staves. In the seventeenth century barrel staves, especially white oak barrel staves that could be made into water-tight (or, more accurately, wine-tight) barrels were in rapidly rising demand.

Figure 1. *Woodcutters at work in a nineteenth-century woodlot. Illustration for* Walden, *by Henry David Thoreau, (New York: The Heritage Press, 1939). Boston Public Library, Print Department, by permission of the estate of Thomas Nason.*

White oak barrel staves, crudely manufactured by hand with frow and draw-knife, began to earn that vital foreign exchange that Massachusetts so desperately needed. The market was not in England, but in Spain, and, especially, in the so-called "wine islands," the Azores, the Canaries and Madeira, where recent Spanish immigrants had created a thriving industry in the mild climate raising grapes that were quickly turned into wine. Wine was in high demand in England especially among the upper and growing middle classes. So staves went to the islands, wine went from there to England, and the New England shippers were paid off in commercial credit in England.[6]

At the same time that Massachusetts was being settled by Puritans, the British West Indies islands, especially Barbados, were being settled by other Englishmen. These men soon discovered a market niche that supports the Caribbean islands to this day: sugar cane, made into sugar and molasses. So great was the profit that the West Indies soon became devoted almost entirely to the raising and processing of sugar. The local forest was soon exhausted, and the continued need for wood fuel and building materials created a market that the New Englanders were eager to fill. New England sent livestock, timber and fish to the islands, where they were exchanged for sugar and molasses, some of which were brought back to Massachusetts Bay, but most of which went to England. There they were sold and earned for the New Englanders the desperately needed credit with which to buy manufactured products.[7]

But before the New Englanders could reap the rewards of this triangular trade, they had to get the barrel staves, the fish and livestock to the wine islands and to the Caribbean. That meant ships. Once the settlers in Massachusetts Bay had satisfied their need for housing, they began building ships. A large portion of the ships' frame was hewn from local white oak, which had many of the same qualities as the English oak. New England's white oak, however, proved most useful when built into a ship in Massachusetts. Attempts were made to sell white oak logs in England, where the shortage of oak was acute, but were not very successful, because the oak was shipped immediately after being felled, rather than being allowed first to dry. (Time was money then as it is today.) The holds of the ships of that time tended to be dank (few ships were totally water-tight) and filled with decay organisms. These infected the wood cargo, so that logs shipped to British shipyards had already begun to decay before they could be used. For constructing ships in Massachusetts, however, they were highly satisfactory; and in shipbuilding the settlers of Massachusetts Bay and their descendants found a niche in world trade that lasted two centuries.[8]

The first ship built in Massachusetts Bay colony was the *Blessing of the Bay,* launched in 1631 in Malden. It was followed in 1633 by the *Rebecca,* built in Medford. Both were relatively small ships, intended for the coastal trade. But by 1636 the ocean-going vessel *Desire* slid down the ways in Marblehead. The *Desire* was followed by many others, for building ships in New England, despite the shortage of skilled shipwrights, was far cheaper than in England, because wood was so readily available. By 1660 shipbuilding was a major industry in the Bay Colony; all the places with access to the rivers that flowed into Massachusetts Bay became busy shipyards, though Boston supplied the financing. Throughout the colonial period New England continued to enjoy a great advantage in the shipbuilding industry, for its costs were below European costs.[9]

One major advantage of the New England shipyards, besides the availability of oak ship timbers, was access to pine masts. For several centuries British shipyards had had to rely on Baltic sources for masts, produced from Scotch pine. But as ships grew steadily larger, and carried more sail, larger and taller masts were needed. But large masts made of Scotch pine had to be pieced together. However in New England's old growth forests were many white pines, a yard and more in diameter. A single tree could furnish the mainmast of a British man-of-war. The rule of thumb was that a mast tree would have the same height in yards as it had in inches of diameter, so that a 36-inch-diameter tree would yield a 36-yard mast — over 100 feet tall. Many of these trees were significantly larger. White pine masts such as these were available no place else in the world, and the men of Massachusetts Bay, skilled traders, soon learned to capitalize on this fact.[10]

The first mast was shipped from New England to England as early as 1634. But it was contemporary European politics that opened up real opportunity. The Dutch and the English were lively trading competitors in the seventeenth century, and in the 1650s the Dutch acquired control of the sea lanes to the Baltic. This victory effectively shut off England from her traditional mast supply. At that point the New England masts came into their own. By 1670 Portsmouth, in what is now New Hampshire but was then part of Massachusetts Bay colony, was regularly sending ten mast ships a year to England.[11]

The late seventeenth century saw a substantial restructuring of the political landscape in northern New England, where most of the great pines were located. In 1680 New Hampshire was struck off from Massachusetts Bay Colony, and made a separate royal colony. By contrast, Maine, which had hitherto been the preserve of private royal grantees such as Sir Ferdinando Gorges, in 1677 became part of Massachusetts. The Bay Colony bought out the rights of the Gorges heirs for the sum of 1,250 British pounds, and Maine became the District of Maine within Massachusetts. The reconstruction of the Bay Colony's government as a royal colony in 1691 included both Maine and Plymouth within its boundaries. Plymouth and the islands remained permanently part of Massachusetts, but in 1820 Maine became a separate state.

Harvesting the pine masts, located mostly in New Hampshire and southern Maine, became a separate industry. To fell the great trees without splintering them when they hit the earth required great skill. Generally, a "bed" of smaller trees was dropped first, to create a cushion for the mast tree when it came down. Then it had to be limbed and skidded to a navigable river, mostly the Merrimac, which drains much of New Hampshire but flows into the Atlantic at Newburyport, in Massachusetts, and the Piscataqua, which drains southern Maine and flows into the ocean at Portsmouth. At one of these two ports the felled tree was loaded into specially designed ships that carried only masts. These ships had a loading port in the rear, and they were of exceptional size — at least 500 tons, some as much as 1000 tons. They could carry anywhere from 40 to 100 large masts, with some smaller masts and spars as well; such a cargo of masts would be worth many thousands of pounds.[12]

By the end of the seventeenth century, as Britain was about to embark on a series of wars for control of the sea lanes that proved to be the foundation stone of the British Empire, the British Navy came to require a steady supply of pine masts from New England. This need led the British Government to attempt to reserve all large pine trees — in time this came to mean all more than two feet in diameter — for the use of the navy. Timber inspectors were appointed whose task it was to roam the woods of New Hampshire and Maine to stamp the famous symbol, the "King's Broad Arrow," on the trunks of trees that were to be kept for the British Navy. The colonists resented deeply this attempt to restrict what they believed was their right to fell any tree for which they had a market, either as a single piece or cut up into boards. The conflict festered throughout the eighteenth century until resolved by the American Revolution. Meanwhile the mast business became a highly organized affair, involving American firms generally headquartered in Boston doing the felling and the shipping, and British merchants securing the contracts with the navy.[13]

When the Pilgrims set forth for New England, there were no sawmills in Old England. Boards were hand hewn or else were laboriously produced by two men pushing and pulling a large saw through a log located over a pit. The man in the pit was known as the pitman, and when machinery took over his role, the connecting rods to the lower end of the saw became known as pitmans. But labor, though abundant in old England, was in very short supply in New England, and the old method was quickly abandoned in favor of water-powered sawmills. Moving a single blade up and down through a log does not require a vast amount of power, and many of the streams that crisscross the New England countryside generally afforded enough power for a sawmill. Because of the great need of the colonists for lumber to build houses, sawmills were one of the first enterprises, often linked to a grist mill, to be established in the colonies. The early history of New England sawmills is obscure, but by the 1630s a number of them are known to have existed in Massachusetts. As the settlers spread out over eastern Massachusetts, just about every new town commissioned one of its new inhabitants to erect a sawmill, and in return provided certain advantages, among them water privileges, a stream-side lot on which to erect the mill, and early tax exemption. Still, it took capital to set up a sawmill: estimates are between 400 and 750 British pounds. Such costs often meant that sawmills were started by several men. Visitors can view examples of early sawmills at Sturbridge Village, or at Henry Ford's Greenfield Village outside Detroit, Michigan. That mill came from Georgetown, Massachusetts. It was bought by Ford, dismantled and re-assembled in Michigan.[14]

Most of the lumber produced by these early mills was used locally, but commercial operations were not long in coming. Numerous mills on the Merrimac and the Piscataqua sawed out lumber for sale abroad, especially in the West Indies. In the seventeenth century, very little was

Wood Products as Percent of All Massachusetts Products, 1837–1995

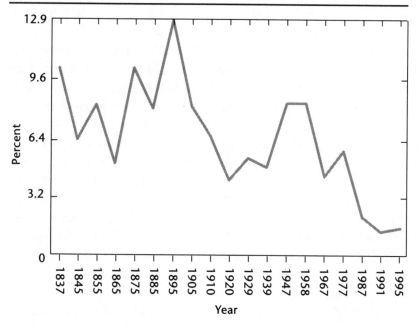

exported to England, because the cost of transportation prevented it from being competitive with Baltic lumber. Only in years of war, when foreign navies were able to control access to the Baltic, did significant amounts of American lumber go directly to England.

As the seventeenth century wore on, some minor products of the Massachusetts forest came to market. Aware that the need for iron and iron products was a heavy drain on the foreign exchange earned by Massachusetts traders, the General Court encouraged the development of local iron manufacture. The necessary ingredients were at hand on the North Shore in the vicinity of Lynn. An attempt was made to set up an early iron works in Saugus, making use of the readily available bog ore, the gabbro rock containing lime for flux to be found on Cape Ann, and the vast supply of wood for fuel. The wood, of course, first had to be turned into charcoal, and the proprietors of the Saugus Iron Works were granted timber rights, along with water rights and tax exemptions, by the General Court in 1645. Though the Saugus Iron Works was not commercially successful, it did lay the basis for a charcoal iron industry in Massachusetts that lasted until the twentieth century.[15]

Early settlements in Massachusetts were along the coast and in the

Connecticut River valley, for the obvious reason that water transport was the only economical way to travel. Roads were virtually nonexistent. For this reason, central Massachusetts, especially Worcester County, remained a wilderness until the eighteenth century. But even in the seventeenth century, new settlements had to be hacked out of the forest, for the supply of Indian clearings for agriculture was quickly exhausted. It was time consuming and expensive to clear land for agriculture, but the colonists were rewarded for their effort in the production of potash, and its more refined cousin, pearlash. When the trees for a new farm had been cut down and burned, the ash was collected and boiled down to make potash, needed in the manufacture of glass (at first all imported from England), soap and gunpowder. In the seventeenth century, most of the potash produced in the colonies was used locally, but by the eighteenth century, when Worcester County began to be settled by the sons and daughters of the large families in eastern Massachusetts, potash became a commercial product. It was relatively light in weight in relation to its value, so it was worth transporting, even overland. It was to become a major earner of foreign exchange in the eighteenth century.[16]

Once the colonial towns had become well settled and their inhabitants well established on the farms that supported most of them, there was a need for better communication. The rivers were immensely useful for transport, but sometimes there was a need to travel overland to reach areas not accessible by navigable rivers. Crossing rivers became a real headache, so many towns moved as quickly as they could from ferries to bridges; thus was born the timber bridge. The first such bridges were built in the Boston area, notably the Cradock bridge over the Mystic River at Medford. Another early bridge crossed the Charles River between Cambridge and Boston. To build these bridges, stone-filled cribs were established at intervals in the river, and wood stringers connected them. The deck was planked. The Cambridge-Boston bridge that was built in 1662 lasted till the end of the eighteenth century.[17]

THE EIGHTEENTH CENTURY:
EXPLOITING THE ATLANTIC MARKET

During the English Civil War (1642–48) immigration into New England virtually ceased, but with the restoration of the Stuart monarchy in 1660, immigration resumed, though at a slower pace. The religious fervor that had driven the Great Migration was replaced by a quest for greater economic opportunities. Combined with the large natural increase of families long settled in New England, the new migrants put acute pressure on the land supply in the older settlements. This land shortage had two consequences: it drove younger sons to create new settlements in the parts of Massachusetts not already settled, those parts not close to a navigable river, and it increased the proportion of the population deriving its living from efforts other than farming.

The most important alternative to farming was trade. The trade with the West Indies, initiated and developed in the seventeenth century, blossomed in the eighteenth. Although precise figures exist only for a four-year period between 1768 and 1772, many inferences can be drawn from those data. Staves and completed barrels continued to occupy a central position, though many more completed barrels were exported than in the prior century. Approximately half of all timber-related exports from Boston were staves and barrels.[18]

Although the British government attempted through legislation to organize the trade of the empire according to self-sufficiency principles popular at that time — the concept called mercantilism — American traders were practitioners of freedom of the seas. The Navigation Acts, passed in the mid-seventeenth century to counteract the Dutch success in global trade and restrict intercolonial traffic to British ships, were now enforced with greater vigor. But canny Yankee shipowners either found ways to get around the rules or they simply ignored them, trading with only a minimum of precautions not just with the British West Indies but with the Caribbean islands of other European nations as well. Not just staves but boards as well were in high demand in the West Indies, and the New Englanders, with Boston the focus of the financing if not the management of the trade itself, took full advantage of the continuous Caribbean market for wood products. Some five-sixths of the boards and half the staves exported from New England ports went to the West Indies.[19]

British mercantilist doctrine was employed not just to direct trade into channels that benefited the Empire, but also to protect the markets of British manufacturers against upstart colonial enterprises. But despite all attempts to ban the production of iron ore, colonial entrepreneurs managed to evade the efforts of the British to control their activities. As a result, manufacture of pig iron and cast iron products grew in the colonies, and these products actually became an important item of trade between the colonies and Britain itself. Such manufacture required ample supplies of charcoal that had to be supplied by the local, that is, the Massachusetts forest.

Among the permitted items of trade between the colonies and Great Britain was lumber. The shortage of native-grown timber in England was acute, and although a steady import of Baltic timber helped alleviate the shortage, New England pine found a niche market of some significance in Britain. Oak and pine from New England were evidently used for house construction in Britain, especially in the latter part of the century when the population began to increase as industrial growth created new livelihoods. Even though English houses continued to be substantially of masonry construction, they needed oak timbers for their frames, and they needed pine to finish the interiors. By the 1770s American lumber imported into Britain exceeded that brought from the Baltic.[20]

The most valuable of American wood products continued to be ships. Here New England, and especially Boston, reigned supreme. Forty percent of the tonnage built in the American colonies was built in or around Boston in 1769. That percentage had dropped to 35 in 1770, and to 32 percent in 1771, but Boston still outran other shipbuilding colonies by a wide margin. New Hampshire was second, Rhode Island third. The value of the wood used in constructing the hull of a ship, combined with the cost of the labor in assembling it, equaled half the cost of the entire ship. Next to Boston in shipbuilding activity in Massachusetts were Charlestown, Salem and Scituate. Shipbuilding, like many enterprises in the eighteenth century, was often a family business. Notable among the shipbuilding families were the Barstows and the Briggs, building ships on the North River near Salem for more than a century. Other important shipbuilding families were the Beckets in Salem, and the Hoods and Hallowells in Boston.[21]

White oak continued to be the preferred material for construction of the hulls, and these oak trees continued to be the foundation of Massachusetts' shipbuilding dominance. Some shipbuilders, however, became adventuresome: in 1719 a shipbuilder in Duxbury built a ship of "wild cherry wood."[22]

New England shipbuilders' main advantage, however, was their access to large white pine masts. With Maine part of Massachusetts since 1677, the producers of masts from the "virgin" forests of Maine along the Piscataqua, Kennebec and Penobscot rivers that made the interior of the state accessible were formally as well as financially Massachusetts businesses. They were run largely from the financial center of the colony, Boston.[23]

The new Massachusetts charter of 1691 incorporated a provision that reserved for the use of the British Navy all pine trees above a specified size that were not growing on land already granted to an individual — essentially, that is, the public lands as they later came to be known. Legislation soon followed to confirm this reservation. In 1711 the British Parliament passed the first of a series of acts, called "An Act for the Preservation of White and other Pine trees growing in Her Majesty's Colonies . . . for the Masting of Her Majesty's Navy." This Act applied the reservation contained in the Massachusetts charter of 1691 to all pine trees growing between Maine and New Jersey. In 1721 the reservation was enlarged to include all pine trees of any size not growing in an established township, and requiring a license if anyone wished to cut a pine. The removal of the earlier size limit (a minimum of two feet in diameter) was intended to ensure future supply.[24]

Concern about future supply also underlay a system of bounties or special premiums on American masts and "naval stores" instituted in 1704 and paid by the British government to the naval contractor. Except for a brief lapse, between 1725 and 1729, this system of bounties or premiums continued until the Revolution. During this time the navy paid out almost 1.5 million British pounds in bounties to the contractors who supplied these items to the navy, though a significant part was for "naval stores." (After a brief attempt in the late seventeenth century to develop the production of "naval stores" — tar and pitch essential for making ships watertight — in Massachusetts, the business shifted to the southern colonies, where it remained.)[25]

Perhaps partly because the felling and processing of mast trees was largely controlled by capitalists, either in Boston or in London, the average settler deeply resented the "king's broad arrow" policy. Most settlers felt that on land not clearly owned by an individual, the logs belonged to whomever took the trouble to fell the trees. Moreover, as the number of sawmills grew and the market for lumber expanded, there was an alternative use for the large pines.

In the late seventeenth century the office of Surveyor-General of the Forest had been created for the colonies to enforce the mast reservation, but until the mid-eighteenth century the whole process was riddled with corruption. One Surveyor-General accused the Massachusetts General Court of creating paper townships so that the pine trees within such townships would not be subject to reservation for the navy. Besides, most of the large pines still standing were well up the rivers, and policing the timber cutters was simply not possible with the minimal staff the Surveyor-General had. His staff was paid, anyway, out of his own salary, so the incentive for him was to employ as few as possible. The resentment against British restrictions on American enterprise that began in the early years of the century escalated in the 1770s until it played a part in triggering the explosion called the American Revolution.[26]

Notwithstanding all the difficulties, some 4,500 American masts actually made it to the British Navy in the eighteenth century, though one authority estimates that these constituted less than one percent of the trees that would have been eligible had the policy been strictly enforced. Those trees that did not make it intact to the navy generally found their way to the numerous sawmills dotting nearly every stream in Massachusetts and heavily concentrated along the major rivers. Even when the Surveyor-General or his minions succeeded in confiscating a group of logs that they thought should be reserved for masts, the logs often found no buyer when auctioned in the colonies. Or sometimes they mysteriously disappeared and were lost to the authorities because they were promptly sawn into boards. No successful condemnation sales were recorded.[27]

THE WATERSHED YEARS, 1775–1825:
TRANSITION TO A NATIONAL MARKET

The years between 1775 and 1825 were years of profound change in American society, in its economic underpinnings, and in the role government played in shaping those underpinnings. Prior to the Revolution, the 13 colonies had been an integral part of the old British colonial system, based on the notion that the colonies should supply raw materials to the mother country, which then made them into usable products. The New England colonies never fitted well into that system, yet New Englanders had managed to adapt reasonably well to it. Their efforts were devoted to economic activities that supplied niches in the mercantilist system: staves for the variety of packaging materials needed before many raw materials could be transported, notably sugar, molasses and alcoholic beverages; ships to move the staves to where the raw materials were; ships to move the packaged raw materials to market in England. Even potash and pearlash, products of new settlement, temporarily filled a niche in the British market. In the four years of the colonial period for which records have survived, 1768–1772, Massachusetts exported more potash and pearlash than any other colony.[28]

But the Revolution changed all that. The mainstay of the New England economy was the trade with the West Indies, and the Revolution virtually wiped that out. American vessels were refused permission to bring goods directly to the West Indies. Under the Navigation Acts this trade was reserved for British vessels. Moreover, during the War the British navy had captured so many American merchantmen, many operating as privateers, that few American merchantmen were available to pick up trade after the signing of the peace agreement in 1783. Though subsequent negotiation between the U.S. and Great Britain reopened part of the trade between New England and the British West Indies to American vessels, the trade never recovered the dominance of American foreign trade it had had before the Revolution.

The cessation of hostilities ushered in a severe depression in New England, especially devastating in such overwhelmingly agricultural areas as western Massachusetts. Repayment on debts owed Boston financiers, postponed during the Revolution, now fell due. Deferred taxes also had to be paid. The resulting foreclosures led directly to Shay's Rebellion; its failure served to convince many that, as soon as the western lands opened up, they should move there. That is why the population of such western Massachusetts hilltowns as Shutesbury fell from 1,000 in 1800 to 250 in 1900. Western Massachusetts recovered only slowly in the early decades of the nineteenth century. Indeed, until 1840 and the advent of railroads it was largely (though not wholly) a self-sufficient world that existed on its own agricultural output and on barter exchanges among the inhabitants.[29]

The eastern part of the state recovered much faster. In this recovery it was helped by the beginnings of industrialization, first in Rhode Island under Samuel Slater, then in the environs of Boston. To be sure, the industrialization took place first in the manufacture of textiles but since the early textile machines were largely made of wood this new industry created a great opportunity for the craftsmen who worked in wood.

Industrialization made other demands on the state's wood supply. Early industry was still water-powered, and continued to be so at least till 1850. The small dams that created the mill ponds that assured a steady flow of water over the water wheel were primarily made of large timbers. The water wheels themselves were made of wood. Earlier, the water-driven mills had operated intermittently, usually in the spring and summer when the flow of water was greatest. Now, however, there was an incentive to keep them going all year round. This in turn meant greater wear on the parts of the water wheel, requiring more frequent replacement.

Heating the barnlike structures that housed the new industry made ever greater demands on the fuelwood supplied by the Massachusetts forest. The concentration of population in industrial centers meant that supplying fuelwood was no longer just a household effort, but rather a business. Massive quantities of fuelwood were burned in Massachusetts' early industrial centers; no one knows exactly how much, but one estimate is that every winter from one to four and a half cords per capita were burned in the northern states. The quantity probably exceeded that cut for sawing into lumber by a wide margin, and this at a time when most Massachusetts land had already been cleared for farmland.[30]

Massachusetts' premier industry of the eighteenth century, shipbuilding, recovered between 1790 and 1810. Before the Revolution, Massachusetts customarily launched about 125 vessels each year; in 1784 only 45 were built. But that situation quickly improved, and until 1812 Massachusetts led the nation in tonnage built. Wood was still available in coastal areas, but its price was rising, causing some shipbuilders to move their operations upriver. Between 1790 and 1810 the total tonnage of vessels whose home port was in Massachusetts doubled. This was the heyday of Salem as a port, and the vessels that called Salem home were built either in Salem itself or on the nearby North River or the Merrimac. The lower Merrimac between Haverhill and Newburyport bristled with shipyards; in 1810 alone, some 12,000 tons of shipping were built and launched on the Merrimac.[31]

The new American government in many respects simply adopted for itself the economic thinking that had earlier guided the British government. For example, Massachusetts passed a law in 1783, reserving for itself all pines over two feet in diameter. The legislation required permits to cut such trees; the fine for cutting without a permit was a hefty 30 pounds, and even lesser white pine trees cut without a permit could bring a fine of three pounds. Other regulations were added. Every town in the Commonwealth had to have a surveyor of wood and shingles, whose responsibility it was to inspect and attest to the quality of the product. Any vessel shipping wood products, especially staves, out of Massachusetts had to have a certificate showing that the product had been inspected in the town in which it had been produced. A penalty of 12 shillings per thousand board feet was imposed on anyone attempting to ship wood products that had not been inspected. The same legislation also set quality standards, specifying, for example, the width and length of clapboards and shingles.[32]

On the national scene, too, some leaders believed that the future of the United States could only be guaranteed if the country developed its own industry through active intervention by government in the market. Initially, these leaders had little influence over policy, as long as southerners with their tobacco and cotton to export and their desire for cheap imports dominated the government. But as the nineteenth century wore on, the notion of national self-sufficiency gained ground. This was to be the dominating outlook in the years that followed.

THE NINETEENTH CENTURY:
THE FLOWERING OF THE NATIONAL MARKET

The nineteenth century was a time of profound change for the forests and people of Massachusetts. A Rip Van Winkle who went to sleep in 1700 and woke again in 1800 would have been, no doubt, surprised at the density of the population, but not at the way they lived and worked. By contrast, one starting a long sleep in 1800 and awakening in 1900 would have been totally confounded. The difference was largely due to technological change. In 1800 activities were hand- or animal-powered, at best water-powered, whereas in 1900 the steam engine had taken over. Candles and oil lamps were being rapidly replaced, first by gas lights, then by electric lights. Goods that had moved by ships powered by wind in the sails now were moved by ships powered by steam engines or by railroads using the same source of power. Men who were overwhelmingly farmers in 1800 were overwhelmingly industrial workers in 1900, and most lived in towns and cities, not down on the farm. Where, in 1800, many exchanges were still barter exchanges, by 1900 there were only cash or credit transactions.

These changes profoundly altered the use of Massachusetts forests. Earlier, wood products had been made primarily of local wood, because the cost of transporting the wood any appreciable distance was so high. Now wood from around the world was available. Moreover, Massachusetts residents had increasingly come to be workers in manufacturing, because the supply of productive (and profitable) farmland had long been exhausted. So wood products from Massachusetts came increasingly to be secondary wood products — made from boards already sawn. The high value-added product came to dominate Massachusetts' trade in wood prducts.

The businesses that handled wood products changed, too, in the nineteenth century. Before, wood that was sold either in raw form or partially worked up was nearly always the work of a single individual or of one with a partner and perhaps half a dozen laborers. But gradually wood products, secondary wood products, came to be produced by industrial processes that required substantial investment in machinery and a significant labor force. This shift, in turn, required capital to be invested in the plants and the machinery; in the latter part of the century this capital was usually assembled by corporate organizations.

These changes are visible in the many ways in which wood, still one of nature's cheapest and most available raw materials, was put to use in nineteenth-century Massachusetts. Since the arrival of the Pilgrims, one of the most important uses of Massachusetts wood had been for the construction of houses. This remained true even in the nineteenth century, for the rapidly growing industrial towns needed dwellings for the hordes of industrial workers that flocked there for employment. These houses continued to be built overwhelmingly of wood, but the technique was profoundly altered by the development of the balloon-frame house in Chicago in the 1830s. Henceforth, house framing was no longer of post and beam, hewn from native oak, but of 2-by-4-inch sticks sawn, as often as not, from trees growing in parts of the United States far distant from Massachusetts. Though dwellings remain a high value-added product, much of the wood in them is no longer from the Massachusetts forest. One exception to that generalization remains true, at least for the nineteenth and the early twentieth centuries: the trim moldings with which the Victorians embellished their houses often began as a Massachusetts pine.[33]

The profound technological shift of the nineteenth century also had a major influence on how these houses were heated. Throughout the nineteenth century and well into the twentieth, farmhouses continued to be heated by fuelwood cut on the farm. In towns and cities, however, by the end of the century the houses were overwhelmingly heated by coal. Cheap railroad transportation made the switch from wood to coal possible, as did the availability of furnaces able to provide central heating in place of the stoves and fireplaces that had formerly done the job.[34]

Though changes in the standard of living are often hard to document, some of these can be detected in the type of household devices used. Early in the century woodenware — bowls, buckets and basins — was extremely common; by the end of the century these items had largely been replaced by sheet metal products. The coal scuttle had to be made of metal; the bathtub came to replace the wooden tub in the kitchen where the weekly bath took place.[35]

But if metal replaced some items of everyday use, others remained made of wood. Even in the eighteenth century, local cabinet-makers had supplied increasingly well-off householders with furniture that served both to show that they had "arrived," as well as to provide greater comfort. The nineteenth century built on this base, but added immense improvement in the system of manufacturing, copying the concept of "interchangeable parts" devised at the Springfield Armory. Furniture parts no longer need be cut out by hand — they could be machined on power lathes and even cut to exactly duplicated dimensions on power saws controlled by jigs.

Two centers for furniture making developed, one in Boston, the other in Gardner, in Worcester County. Gardner, which came to be known as the "Chair City," produced chairs and tables particularly, and not just for the well-off, but for the average family at prices the average family could afford. In time, Gardner had some twelve companies making chairs, with a total annual output of some two million a year. The effects of large numbers of tables, chairs, chests of drawers, bedsteads, vanities and the like at modest prices can be seen in pictures of Victorian houses stuffed with furniture.[36]

Boston developed another secondary wood specialty, musical instruments. Without television to entertain, families had to create their own entertainment, and they did so with the piano and the parlor organ. Grand pianos were still made in the Boston area in the twentieth century, utilizing sugar maple veneer glued into the traditional shape of the grand piano body. The sounding board probably came from somewhere else — spruce is the preferred species for sounding boards, especially spruce with tight annual rings — but at least some of the maple veneer probably came from Massachusetts forests.

Down on the farm, too, manufactured wood was still the norm. Hay had become the principal crop of Massachusetts farms since the West had taken over the cultivation of grain. First the Erie Canal, then the railroad could bring in grain at prices with which Massachusetts farmers could not compete, but hay to feed local horses was still overwhelmingly grown locally. By the middle of the century hay began to be harvested and processed with implements made largely or wholly of wood. Horse-drawn rakes, for example, were generally of local design and manufacture. The first reaper, that invented by Obed Hussey of Nantucket in 1833, used numerous wooden parts. Most agricultural

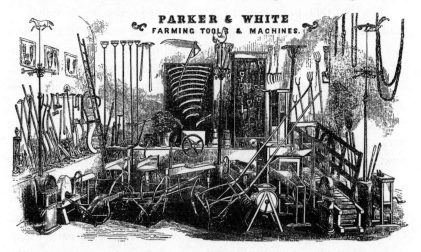

Figure 2. Hand tools made from wood, displayed at a fair held in Boston in 1853. FROM Gleason's Pictorial Drawing Room Companion, *volume 5 (1853). Courtesy of Widener Library, Harvard University.*

equipment of the nineteenth century combined both wood and steel. Scythes, still widely used for mowing, had a steel blade but a wooden handle. Shovels and hoes had metal at the business end, but wooden handles. One of the most notable manufacturers of hand tools used in agriculture was the Ames firm of North Easton. By 1857, Ames was making 2,400 shovels and spades every day, one-third of all the shovels and spades made in the United States.[37]

Though the shift from wood to other materials was slow, it did impact the way in which wood was used by industry. The mill dams of the turn of the century had all been made of wood. But by mid-century, they were tending to become either hybrids, using both wood and masonry, or wholly of masonry construction. The dam across the Connecticut River built at Holyoke in 1848, for example, was first made of wood, but no sooner was it tested than it failed — it went, as the famous telegram to its Boston financiers reported, "to hell by way of Willimansett." But it was immediately rebuilt, and this time it was anchored to bed rock with metal bolts; the dam itself was a mixture of timber and rubble. It was replaced in 1900 with a masonry dam. However, at Lawrence the initial dam built in the 1840's was of masonry, and from mid-century onward, dams created to hold back water, at least on major rivers, were almost invariably masonry. Water wheels gave way to turbines, made after mid-century of metal. Later in the century water power itself itself, with its uncertainties, was replaced by steam power.[38]

Although wooden-hulled ships were now powered by steam as well as by sail, the shift to steam power heralded another, more fundamental change that decimated the Massachusetts shipbuilding industry: the shift to metal hulls. The growth of the American iron and steel industry in distant Pittsburgh made this change possible. By the end of the century the era of sailing ships, except for recreation, was definitely over.[39]

Notwithstanding, Massachusetts continued to have a small iron industry of its own, smelting with charcoal. Not until the twentieth century did the iron and steel industry learn how to control the chemical composition of its product. Until then, charcoal-smelted iron had advantages, particularly when used to produce wrought iron, then worked into horseshoes. As long as local transportation was powered by the horse, which remained true until after World War I, there was a

Distribution of Wood Products Dollar, 1995

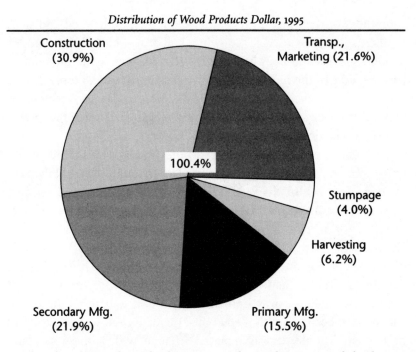

Construction (30.9%)

Transp., Marketing (21.6%)

100.4%

Stumpage (4.0%)

Harvesting (6.2%)

Secondary Mfg. (21.9%)

Primary Mfg. (15.5%)

market for charcoal-smelted iron. But the replacement of the horse-drawn carriage by the internal combustion engine killed the small Massachusetts iron industry.

Despite these changes new uses for wood helped to sustain the wood market. From early in the nineteenth century Massachusetts had had a large shoe industry, supplying much of the nation. Initially the industry had used local hides, but later it began importing them from the West Coast and from South America. In the early years, these hides required tanning after arrival, for which first the bark of oaks and later of hemlocks proved of great value. Only the development of synthetic chemicals late in the nineteenth century freed the tanners from dependence on the bark of trees.[40]

The transportation revolution made possible by the development of the railroads provided a vast new use for the products of Massachusetts forests. One of the earliest railroads in the United States was the Beacon Hill Railroad, built early in the nineteenth century to haul earth dug off Beacon Hill to the harbor to fill in the marshy areas along the shore. The impetus for this enterprise was the drastic shortage of house lots in Boston at the turn of the century. The loaded cars going downhill were attached by pulleys to the empty cars, and pulled the latter uphill. For everything except power source, however, this road served as a prototype, clearly revealing the advantages of rail for the movement of heavy, low-value materials.[41]

The first true railroad in the Commonwealth was the Boston and Worcester, which opened for traffic in 1835. Linking Worcester with Boston and subsequently directly with the harbor opened up vast new commercial opportunities for central Massachusetts. Seven years later, the construction of the Western Railroad forged rail ties between Boston and Albany, where for the first time western agricultural products barged in on the Eric Canal could be loaded onto cars heading for Boston. When rail lines were completed across the nation, such agricultural products were moved entirely by rail. This connection spelled the death of tillage farming in Massachusetts, except in a few specially favored localities such as the alluvial plains of the Connecticut River valley.

The Boston and Worcester and the Western Railroad became the Boston and Albany in 1867. The road was financed by canny Boston investors, was well run, and throughout the nineteenth century was prosperous and profitable. The construction of a series of very local lines in central and western Massachusetts opened up those parts of the Commonwealth to the national economy, enabling producers of goods in that region to sell their products nationwide.[42]

Each mile of new railroad required 2,640 railroad ties. The most desired material for the ties was white oak, the same white oak that had earlier supplied ships' timbers and barrel staves. Even after the railroad was built, ties continued to be needed: the normal life span of a white oak tie was seven to eight years. Generally, some 350 ties per mile were renewed each year. In 1882, the cost of white oak ties in Massachusetts was 50 cents each, but by the end of the century the price had begun to rise, even though the development of creosoting had, by that time, lengthened the life of ties. The first creosoting facility in Massachusetts was built by the Old Colony Railroad in 1865 in Somerset. Creosoting proved to prolong the life not just of ties, but of bridge timbers as well, an important consideration, since all early railroad trestles were built of wood.[43]

Wood provided a major part of the materials used in the construction of early railroads, not just for the ties. Initially, the rails were also made of wood, with iron straps laid on the top surface to retard wear.

Only the rapid development of the iron industry in Pittsburgh and vicinity made possible the substitution of iron rails for wooden ones, soon themselves to be replaced by steel rails with the introduction of the Bessemer converter in the last quarter of the century. Besides the rails, the cars of the early railroads were largely made of wood well into the twentieth century. Last but by no means least, all the early railroad engines generated their steam power with wood fires. All the early railroads had piles of firewood at strategic points along the route, as did the early steamships. Wood-fired engines used a vast amount of firewood until they were replaced by coal burners late in the century.

Perhaps the most important technological innovation of the nineteenth century, especially when viewed from the perspective of the late twentieth century, was the adaptation of wood to the making of paper pulp. From the early years of the nineteenth century there had been a paper industry in Berkshire County, using first rags collected from individuals, later scraps from the rapidly growing textile industry. The first paper mill in the county was established in 1801. Wood was important in the manufacture of rag-based paper because the tubs and the beaters used to reduce the rags to fiber were made of wood. Their heavy use required frequent replacement. The leader in Berkshire papermaking was Zenas Crane, who moved from eastern Massachusetts to Berkshire County in the early years of the nineteenth century. He had learned the trade in his brother's paper mill in Newton Lower Falls.[44]

Crane saw the advantages of Berkshire County for paper-making: access to a new supply of rags, the presence of several turning mills that could produce wood elements for the early machinery, and an ample supply of firewood to heat the buildings and the vats that cooked up some of the ingredients, notably size. Made from animal wastes; size gave the paper its smoothness and stiffness. The beating machines, known as Hollanders, were largely made of wood and had to be frequently replaced.[45]

People began thinking about substituting wood for rags as the basic raw material for paper early in the nineteenth century. That thinking intensified as a world-wide shortage of rags developed by the middle of the century. The key invention that made possible the use of wood pulp was the Keller-Voelter machine devised in 1847 in Germany. This machine duplicated the work of the Hollander but with wood, reducing it to fiber. In the 1860s a group of Americans led by Frederick Steinway, the piano manufacturer, organized a company to import Keller-Voelter machines, and shortly thereafter began manufacturing the machines themselves. Their firm was located in Curtisville, in the Berkshires, and in 1867 they sold one of their machines to the Smith Paper Company of Lee. That year Smith Paper produced the first wood-based paper pulp in America.[46]

The new technology spread rapidly in the 1870s. The wood, from spruce or fir trees, was drawn from the forests of the Berkshires, and by 1885 the Smith Paper Company alone was using 30–40 cords a week. A number of textile mills in the Berkshires were converted to paper mills, and some new mills were built to take advantage of this new technology. By 1890, however, the Berkshire County forests were denuded of usable wood for pulp, and one of the Smith mills was shut down in 1891 for lack of raw material. Meanwhile, mills had sprung up in Holyoke, using pulpwood floated down the Connecticut River, not just from Massachusetts but from Vermont and New Hampshire as well. Paper production became such a central activity in Holyoke in the last two decades of the nineteenth century that the city earned the title, "the paper city."[47]

Meanwhile, as American industry turned out more and more products that had to be shipped to reach their ultimate market, the packaging industry, once based almost exclusively on barrels of various sizes made from staves and hoops, now shifted to wooden boxes. The barrel was fine for bulk products and even served satisfactorily for the thousands of apples shipped from Massachusetts to the West Indies in the nineteenth century. By late in the century, however, shippers needed smaller containers that were better adapted for shipping fragile manufactured products, as well as batches of items already packaged in small containers such as metal cans that were then sold directly to the consumer. Meanwhile, too, the abandoned Massachusetts farms had produced a fine crop of pasture pines, that could be used to make boxboard that could, in turn, be assembled into small crates. This industry lasted through the rest of the nineteenth century and well into the twentieth, with firms in the business persisting until after World War II.

THE TWENTIETH CENTURY:
JOINING THE GLOBAL MARKET

The trends initiated in the latter half of the nineteenth century continued in the twentieth, largely driven by technology. Wood products
became ever more concentrated in secondary manufacture, their
higher value reflecting both the capital investment in the processing
machinery and the high cost of skilled labor. Both these factors had
played an important role in Massachusetts' economic development
from an early period, and continued to do so.

Ships offer an outstanding example of these trends. The wooden
vessels that had played such a part in the success of Massachusetts, first
as a trading colony, then as a major participant in world-wide trade,
were replaced in bulk shipping by iron, then steel vessels. But Massachusetts continued to build ships of wood. Some of these were for the
fishing fleet whose market expanded with the growth of population,
but others were luxury vessels for recreational use.[48]

Massachusetts forests not only contributed the material for the
construction of small boats for recreation, but they themselves offered
recreation directly. Massachusetts state forests saw a steadily rising
number of visitors until about the eighth decade. Although the amount
of income generated by "gate receipts" for daily visits, seasonal passes,
and the use of campsites remained relatively small compared to the very
large value of all the products turned out by Massachusetts manufacturers, the state forests provided recreational opportunities for those
who could not afford to own their own private recreational land.
Growing numbers of residents of the state (and of other states) chose to
"own their own," as the increasing fragmentation of ownerships in
Massachusetts reveals. People who first acquired a taste for forest
recreation from public forests wanted their own private forest, and
went out and bought one. Though no figures are available on the dollar
value of the recreation pursued on privately owned woodland, it surely
constitutes a very important use of the Massachusetts forest.[49]

Secondary processing of wood continued to be the place where
money was to be made. By the last decade of the twentieth century over
half the returns from wood processing were concentrated in the manufacture of mirrors and picture frames (6.1 percent in 1992), wooden
boxes and crates (36.6 percent), millwork — windows, doors and inte-

Figure 3. Pine plantation thinnings being received at the yard of a local sawmill (location unknown), typical of the scale of the Massachusetts wood-processing industry during the first quarter of the twentieth century. Lantern slide collection, Massachusetts Department of Environmental Management.

rior trim (16.7 percent) and wooden kitchen cabinets (15.6 percent). Although there are anecdotal reports of large quantities of Massachusetts logs being exported, in value they account for only .4 percent of all Massachusetts wood products. Rough sawn hardwood lumber comes in at 2.1 percent, rough sawn softwood lumber at .3 percent, measured by value, the only way in which these very different products can be compared.[50]

Technology had a profound effect on the market for railroad ties, important in the previous century. The advantages of using creosote preservatives — the greater longevity of ties in place and the reduced need for replacements — had been fully demonstrated by the beginning of the twentieth century. But the railroads themselves suffered a deep decline with the vast expansion of the national highway system after World War II, when a lot of freight and an overwhelming proportion of passengers switched to trucks and cars. Now, railroad ties are only a niche market, and the nationwide system of rail lines can find the ties where they are least costly. The Massachusetts white oak ties that commanded premium prices in the late nineteenth century are effectively priced out of the market.[51]

Late in the century a new market opened in Massachusetts for forest products: the use of wood chips as a fuel to generate electricity. Political events played a role when the OPEC oil crises of the 1970s with their tremendous price spikes led to a search for alternatives to oil-fired generators. The simultaneous price inflation of oil and the various disasters that overtook the nuclear power industry led industry leaders to look around for a low-cost way of firing up steam generators. While burning wood chips for fuel has its own technological drawbacks, it has become a use for the low quality wood that abounds in all New England forests. Massachusetts currently has one wood chip power generator located in Westminster.[52]

The paper industry, in the late nineteenth century a major user of wood from the Massachusetts forests, has undergone a total transformation. Present-day paper manufacture enjoys genuine economies of scale. By the late twentieth century, only paper mills that could produce on a vast scale could be profitable in what had become a global industry. As the cost of a new basic paper plant approaches $1 billion, new plants are generally sited near a large resource base. That is why Maine is still a major producer of bulk paper, while in Massachusetts the "paper city," Holyoke, has become essentially a paper-converter city. Its plants buy bulk paper produced elsewhere and turn it into products for the ultimate consumer. The only true paper plant still in Holyoke produces only rag-based paper.[53]

Perhaps the most important new use of the products of the Massachusetts forest is one that its residents once took for granted: water, water that is pure because it is filtered through forested watersheds. Massachusetts is one of the most densely populated states in the United States, and civilized society requires a substantial quantity of water to maintain health standards, and that water needs to be pure. The more technologically advanced industries also consume water for their manufacturing processes: about 35 percent of the water produced by the

Metropolitan District Commission (which supplies water to a large part of eastern Massachusetts) is process water — water used in manufacturing processes. Once water became a public utility and no longer came from backyard wells, it was first priced by the municipal authorities who delivered it to each household at the cost of distribution. Cost of distribution is still an important factor in the pricing of water, but now scarcity is also part of the equation. The wholesale price of MDC water went from $120 per million gallons (the price established by the legislature) in 1962 to $200 per million gallons in 1974 and $240 in 1975. Since then its price has risen dramatically, to $875.95 per million gallons in 1995, reflecting the limits on supply. It is projected to rise even more rapidly in the years ahead, to between $2212 and $2506 per million gallons by the year 2002. Considering that MDC water supplies all or most of the water needs of about 40 percent of the population of the state, the water produced by Massachusetts forests is worth about $200 million annually. Even though this is less than one percent of the gross state product, it is a product no one in the state can do without.[54]

CONCLUSION

Urban Americans of the late twentieth and early twenty-first centuries take the forest products that surround them for granted. They shouldn't. Wood saved the early settlers from freezing in the harsh New England winter, because it supplied the material to make the wooden houses that are still the hallmark of New England. Wood heated those houses. Wood supplied the packaging material that enabled the products of the new world-wide economy to be traded globally. Without barrels of New England white and red oak it would have been difficult, if not impossible, to send Caribbean sugar and molasses to European consumers. Equally indispensable to this trade were the wooden ships that slid down the ways of Massachusetts shipyards in increasing numbers from the first days of settlement.

Wood contributed fundamentally to the manufacture of other products as well. Wood ashes boiled down by new settlers clearing a forest for farming supplied the potash needed to manufacture glass, soap and gunpowder. Wood converted to charcoal made possible the processing of the bog iron ore of Massachusetts into bar iron that in turn was converted into usable iron products: plows and guns and horseshoes.

After America gained national independence and began to build a national economy, wood, nature's most abundant raw material, provided the parts for the machines that made industrial production possible. The dams and the millponds that made water power a usable resource, the textile and paper-making machines that supplied an ever-enlarging consumer market as the population of the United States grew, all contributed essential items to the economic advance of the country.

As the engine of technology moved ahead, uses of the Massachusetts forest changed. The wood that heated houses, factories and stores was replaced by coal, made available by railroads that depended heavily on wood for their initial construction and that still rely on the wooden tie. While the railroads brought wood from other places to Massachusetts for the construction of houses, the millwork of modern houses comes in part from the trees of Massachusetts. Massachusetts wood was used, not directly as lumber (though the state still produces some $50 million worth of lumber annually) but rather as the raw material to be turned into furniture, musical instruments, and kitchen cabinets. Though the cardboard carton has replaced many boxes as the shipping container of choice, wooden boxes are still preferred for some products, and Massachusetts still produces a lot of boxes — over $200 million worth in 1992.

Civilization has come to depend on two products of Massachusetts forests that figure largely in the life styles of Massachusetts residents at the end of the twentieth century: recreation and water. As the machine has released men and women from the drudgery necessary to survival in earlier centuries, the residents of Massachusetts have come to need the outdoor experience to refresh their lives. Forests are the setting for a significant part of the recreational activities of the state's residents — and of residents of other states who come to Massachusetts because of the quality of her forests. Both residents and tourists rely on the water that flows out of that forest in pure form to maintain a standard of cleanliness that was once unheard of but is now the basis of civilized living. Without the human-forest interaction of more than three centuries, Massachusetts would still be that "hideous and desolate wilderness" William Bradford first observed as the Pilgrims landed on Cape Cod in November of 1620. The Massachusetts forest has played an indispensable part in the long passage from then to now.

NOTES

1. William Bradford, *Of Plymouth Plantation, 1620–1647*, ed. S. E. Morison (New York: Alfred A. Knopf, 1952), 62; S. E. Morison, *The Maritime History of Massachusetts, 1783–1860.* (Boston: Houghton-Mifflin, 1961) 4; James E. Defebaugh, *History of the Lumber Industry in America* (Chicago: (American Lumberman, 1907) 2: 178–79.

2. Robert C. Winthrop, *Life and Letters of John Winthrop* (New York: Da Capo Press, 1971) 2: 44; Alexander Young, ed., *Chronicles of the First Planters of the Colony of Massachusetts Bay from 1623 to 1636* (New York: Da Capo Press Reprint Edition, 1970) 339.

3. Cark W. Condit, *American Building*, 2nd ed. (Chicago: University of Chicago Press, 1982), 6, 20; Michael Williams, *Americans and Their Forests: An Historical Geography.* (Cambridge: Cambridge University Press, 1989), 73–74; Charles F. Carroll, "The Forest Society of New England," in: Brooke Hindle, ed., *America's Wooden Age: Aspects of its Early Technology* (Tarrytown, NY: Sleepy Hollow Press, 1975) 28–29; Defebaugh, *Lumber Industry,* 2: 186–88; R. G. Albion, *Forests and Sea Power: the Timber Problem and the Royal Navy,* (Cambridge, Mass.: Harvard University Press, 1926), 102–03; Charles E. Peterson, "Early Lumbering: A Pictorial Essay," in Hindle, *America's Wooden Age,* 78.

4. Condit, *American Building,* 6–7; Williams, *Americans and Their Forests,* 102–03.

5. Stephen Innes, *Creating the Commonwealth* (New York: Norton, 1995), 286, 288, 295; Morison, *Maritime History,* 11–12; Joseph J. Malone, *Pine Trees and Politics* (Seattle: University of Washington Press, 1964), 2.

6. Charles F. Carroll, *The Timber Economy of Puritan New England* (Providence: Brown University Press, 1973), 78; Carroll, "Forest Society," in Hindle, *America's Wooden Age,* 25; Bernard Bailyn, *The New England Merchants in the Seventeenth Century.* (Cambridge, Mass.: Harvard University Press, 1955), 44.

7. Carroll, "Forest Society," in Hindle, *America's Wooden Age,* 25, 28; Bailyn, *New England Merchants,* 83, 86; Carroll, *Timber Economy,* 84, 124; Innes, *Commonwealth,* 296; Morison, *Maritime History,* 288; Malone, *Pine Trees,* 2.

8. Albion, *Forests and Sea Power,* 23; Morison, *Maritime History,* 14–15; Malone, *Pine Trees,* 2.

9. Innes, *Commonwealth,* 287, 289, 293; Joseph A. Goldenberg, "With Saw and Axe and Augur: Three Centuries of American Shipbuilding," in:

Brooke Hindle, ed., *Material Culture of the Wooden Age.* (Tarrytown, NY: Sleepy Hollow Press, 1981), 98–99, 104; Morison, *Maritime History,* 17.

10. Albion, *Forests and Sea Power,* 31; Bailyn, *New England Merchants,* 132; Carroll, *Timber Economy,* 87–88.

11. Albion, *Forests and Sea Power,* 166–67, 234–238; Malone, *Pine Trees,* 2; Carroll, *Timber Economy,* 105; Defebaugh, *Lumber Industry,* 2: 182; Bailyn, *New England Merchants,* 103, 124, 132–33.

12. Ibid., 133; Albion, *Forests and Sea Power,* 236–238.

13. Ibid., 232, 243; Defebaugh, *Lumber Industry,* 2: 181, 200–01.

14. Innes, *Commonwealth,* 303; Peterson, "Early Lumbering," in Hindle, *America's Wooden Age,* 70; Howell, Charles. "Colonial Watermills in the Wooden Age," in Hindle, *America's Wooden Age, 120;* Malone, *Pine Trees, 2;* Williams, *Americans and Their Forests,* 95, 96, 100; Defebaugh, *Lumber Industry,* 2: 185, 198–99.

15. Richard H. Schallenberg, "Charcoal Iron: The Coal Mines of the Forest," in Hindle, *Material Culture,* 278, 291–92; Bailyn, *New England Merchants,* 66; Williams, *Americans and Their Forests,* 106; Innes, *Commonwealth,* 243, 244, 246, 256.

16. Williams, *Americans and Their Forests,* 101.

17. Condit, *American Building,* 24; Christopher Clark, *The Roots of Rural Capitalism: Western Massachusetts,* 1780–1860 (Ithaca, NY: Cornell University Press, 1990) 69.

18. Malone, *Pine Trees,* 7–8, 82; Albion, *Forests and Sea Power,* 275–76.

19. Ibid., 275.

20. Ibid., 250–52, 275; Malone, *Pine Trees,* 131.

21. Goldenberg, "With Saw and Axe," in Hindle, *Material Culture,* 109, 116; Williams, *Americans and Their Forests,* 93.

22. Morison, *Maritime History,* 19.

23. Carroll, *Timber Economy,* 115, 119; Malone, *Pine Trees,* 5, 10.

24. Ibid., 5, 10, 26–27, 40, 54, 70–71, 75–80, 98; Albion, *Forests and Sea Power,* 253–54, 258.

25. Defebaugh, *Lumber Industry,* 2: 205; Malone, *Pine Trees,* 35, 37.

26. Ibid., 20, 58–59, 106, 123, 136, 138–39, 141; Albion, *Forests and Sea Power,* 251.

27. Malone, *Pine Trees, 53–54,* 132; Albion, *Forests and Sea Power,* 251.

28. Williams, *Americans and Their Forests,* 75.

29. Morison, *Maritime History,* 32, 38; Clark, *Roots of Rural Capitalism,* 66.

30. James H. Eves, "Shrunk to a Comparative Rivulet: Deforestation, Stream Flow and Rural Milling in 19th Century Maine," *Technology and Culture* 33 (January 1992), 38–65; Williams, *Americans and Their Forests,* 78, 80–81.

31. Morison, *Maritime History*, 34, 96, 97, 101, 152; Goldenberg, "With Saw and Axe," in Hindle, *Material Culture*, 121.

32. Defebaugh, *Lumber Industry*, 2: 206–08.

33. Ibid., 2: 223; Herbert Gottfried, "The Machine and the Cottage: Building Technology and the Single-Family House, 1870–1910," *IA, The Journal of the Society for Industrial Technology*, 21 (1995), 47–68.

34. Clark, *Roots of Rural Capitalism*, 197, 263.

35. Ibid., 83, 101, 183, 233–34; Morison, *Maritime History*, 131.

36. Ibid., 85, 367; Defebaugh, *Lumber Industry*, 2: 131; Clark, *Roots of Rural Capitalism*, 99.

37. Howard S. Russell, *A Long, Deep Furrow: Three Centuries of Farming in New England* abridged by Mark Lapping (Hanover, NH: University Press of New England, 1982), 239.

38. Morison, *Maritime History*, 102, 290. Tom Juravich, William F. Hartford and James R. Green, *Commonwealth of Toil: Chapters in the History of Massachusetts Workers and Their Unions* (Amherst, Mass.: University of Massachusetts Press, 1996), 61, 67; Terry S. Reynolds, *Stronger Than a Hundred Men: A History of the Vertical Water Wheel* (Baltimore: Johns Hopkins University Press, 1983), 276–77.

39. Morison, *Maritime History*, 349; Goldenberg, "With Saw and Axe," in Hindle, *Material Culture*. 122–23.

40. Morison, *Maritime History*, 266–67.

41. Frederock L. Gamst, "The Context and Significance of America's First Railroad, on Boston's Beacon Hill," *Technology and Culture* 33 (January, 1992), 66–100.

42. George P. Baker, *The Formation of the New England Railroad System*. (New York: Greenwood Press, 1968), 3, 7–9, 23; Sherry H. Olson, *The Depletion Myth: A History of Railroad Use of Timber* (Cambridge, Mass.: Harvard University Press, 1971), 12–15, 17.

43. Ibid., 63.

44. Judith A. McGaw, *Most Wonderful Machine: Mechanization and Social Change in Berkshire Paper Making, 1801–1885* (Princeton: Princeton University Press, 1987), 15, 20.

45. Ibid., 41, 178, 206.

46. Ibid., 201–03.

47. Ibid., 162, 204–05.

48. Morison, *Maritime History*, 318.

49. Muriel More, *Massachusetts Forest Resources: A Working Guide to Action* (Amherst Mass.: Department of Environmental Management, 1985), 40–41.

50. United States Department of Commerce, 1992 Census of Manufactures: Forest Products (Washington, DC: Government Printing Office, 1995), passim.

51. Olson, *Depletion Myth*, 63.

52. Senator Robert D. Wetmore, personal communication.

53. Nancy M. Gordon, "Parsons Paper: High Quality Is Their Specialty," Holyoke *Transcript-Telegram*, March 18, 1975, 24; Nancy M. Gordon, "Parsons: First in Paper City," Holyoke *Transcript-Telegram*, January 20, 1979, 40. This may change as recycled paper gains wider use. There is still a business, in Massachusetts, of gathering up used newspapers and selling them to facilities that reconvert them to pulp that, in turn, can be reprocessed into paper. As more de-inking plants come into being, more of this may occur in Massachusetts, which does have a large resource base in used paper.

54. Metropolitan District Commission, "A History of the Development of the Metropolitan District Commission Water Supply System," pamphlet ([Boston]: Wallace, Floyd Associates, 1984); Massachusetts Water Resources Authority, "MWRA Wholesale Water Charges." pamphlet ([Boston]: MWRA Rates and Budget Department, 1996).

The Private Forestry Movement in Massachusetts

WILLIAM A. KING

We turn to the natural world about us when the creations of men fail, and we don't have to pay an admission or even a green fee to draw fresh strength and inspiration from the fields and the woods and their inhabitants. To conserve these sources of refreshment for the future seems to me a particularly worth while objective.
— *William Pickman Wharton*

I N THIS CHAPTER I will examine the evolution of the private forestry movement in Massachusetts from the perspective of the associations and organizations that, sometimes to great effect and sometimes faltering along the way, have given the movement momentum and vitality. That movement has contributed many remarkable personalities to historic developments in national conservation, state government, and education. Like the forests themselves, the private forestry movement is dynamic, vital, and ever changing. Its history invites us to question causes and effects and ask why these people and their enterprises behaved as they did and what we can learn from them that may help to guide the footsteps of those who will assume future leadership of private forestry in Massachusetts and beyond her borders.

Although the private forestry movement in Massachusetts first took concrete form in the late nineteenth century, Massachusetts had long offered fertile ground for such enterprises. Shortly after the Revolution, General Benjamin Lincoln, having vanquished (with the help of others) the British, cast his martial eyes upon a landscape where "timber trees were greatly reduced and quite gone in many parts."[1] The worthy general thereupon set out to promote the planting of acorns. By the mid-1800s, private nurseries, capitalizing on reforestation projects, also provided shade trees for village streets and parks. An example, described by Robert McCullough in *The Landscape of Community*,[2] was Jacob Manning's nursery in Reading, Massachusetts, which is said to have served "wealthy patrons." In 1876 and 1878, the Massachusetts Society for the Promotion of Agriculture offered prizes for improved arboriculture, which spawned reforestation experiments.[3] Charles W. Eliot, son of the former president of Harvard University and a landscape architect of international reputation, was the driving force that led to the creation by the Massachusetts legislature, in 1892, of the Trustees of Reservations, a quasi-public although privately supported organization that to this day preserves and manages areas of extraordinary natural beauty for the benefit of the people. As the nineteenth century drew to a close, the stage was set for the formation of New England's first private forestry associations.

THE BIRTH PANGS OF THE PRIVATE FORESTRY MOVEMENT

Shortly after the midpoint of the nineteenth century, Alexis de Tocqueville, an acute observer of the democratic process in America, wrote:

> If men living in democratic countries had no right and no inclination to associate for political purposes, their independence would be in great jeopardy, but they might long preserve their wealth and their cultivation; whereas if they never acquired the habit of forming associations in ordinary life, civilization itself would be endangered. . . . An association may be formed for the purpose of discussion, but everybody's mind is preoccupied with the thought of impending action. An association is an army; talk is needed to count numbers and build up courage, but after that they march against the enemy. Its members regard legal measures as possible means, but they are never the only possible means of success.[4]

As the advent of the twentieth century approached, thoughtless exploitation, uncontrolled fires, and expanding urbanization had put much of America's forestland seemingly on the brink of ruin. Such a condition was ripe for attack by the democratic process of association.

Responding to the broad perception that a crisis in the management of the nation's forests was at hand, democratic processes of association went to work in Massachusetts and far beyond. The early Massachusetts forestry organizations emerged in the context of a larger drama being played out on a national scale. In 1875, Dr. John A. Warder, a physician and horticulturist from Cincinnati, had summoned concerned men and women from across the United States to a meeting in Chicago, where the American Forestry Association was chartered. The subsequent emergence of the American Forestry Association as a political force of considerable consequence lends credence to de Tocqueville's thesis of the processes of democracy being carried out through the formation of voluntary associations. Under the leadership of Dr. Bernhard E. Fernow as its general secretary, the association "became a potent agency, not only in education but in politics. . . . Dr. Fernow was an able, strong-willed German forester, who organized his campaigns with the thoroughness and determination of a Bismarck. The ground swell of conservation began to show practical results."[5] (For a more detailed profile of Dr. Fernow, see Robert S. Bond's "Professional Forestry, Forestry Education, and Research" in this volume.) Among the initiatives spawned by the association was the formation by the National Academy of Sciences of a National Forest Commission to report on the future of the great forest reserves being created in the American West, the forerunners of the national parks and forests. As waves of settlers staked out claims to the western lands of the United States, the creation of these preserves was becoming imperiled by mounting political opposition to what many settlers perceived as locking up the nation's natural resources. The National Forest Commission was chaired by Harvard's eminent dendrologist and the founder of the famed Arnold Arboretum, Dr. Charles Sprague Sargent. Its secretary was Gifford Pinchot.

In "Massachusetts' Contributions to National Forest Conservation" (in this volume), the historian Stephen Fox recounts Sargent's sense of hurt and betrayal as Pinchot, as he ascended to positions of power, became a leading apostle of a more utilitarian forestry than that espoused by Sargent and others. Pinchot and President Theodore Roosevelt were joining forces to forge an unparalleled partnership in conservation. While Pinchot had his detractors in the man Fox calls the "growling and irascible" Sargent and in John Muir, among others, he was virtually deified by a cache of adoring young foresters who became his disciples. Colonel Greeley, the author of *Forests and Men* (1951), was one of these, writing euphorically of Pinchot's appointment as secretary to the National Forest Commission:

> At this point the young "Lion of Judah" enters the story of America's forests. He brought into it a fervor of religious intensity and a magnetic personal leadership that have rarely been equaled in the American drama. For the next fourteen years the astonishing vigor in the planning and execution of successive moves for national conservation largely expressed the zeal and energy of Gifford Pinchot.

Greeley continues:

> Ancient astrologers foretold world-shaking events from the proximity of heavenly bodies. But who could predict the consequences of the simultaneous presence in Washington of two very dynamic and forest-minded men — Theodore Roosevelt in the White House and Gifford Pinchot in the Bureau of Forestry?
>
> Both were men of great idealism and men of action. . . . They made a great team as crusaders of conservation, and they put over one of the most effective selling jobs in our history.
>
> My first glimpse of "T.R." was at the meeting of the American Forestry Association in Washington, in 1905. This meeting sounded the bugles for legislation which transformed the reserves into national forests and transferred them from the Department of the Interior to the Department of Agriculture. As a young recruit in the Bureau of Forestry, I was thrilled when the President threw down his manuscript and strode across the stage. With shaking fists and flashing teeth he thundered "I am against the man who skins the land."[6]

While Roosevelt, Pinchot, and their colleagues were leading the great American crusade for forest conservation, their direct influence on the private forestry movement in Massachusetts is, at best, a matter of speculation. Dr. Char Miller, Professor of History at Trinity University in San Antonio, Texas, and a leading authority on the life of Gifford

Pinchot, has found among the Pinchot Papers in the National Archives the text of an address Pinchot gave on November 30, 1895 at a meeting in Boston of a remarkable association called the Saturday Club, whose membership was drawn from the leading luminaries of that time in letters, law, philosophy, and progressive intellectual thought, including Charles W. Eliot, Oliver Wendell Holmes, William James, Frederick Law Olmsted, and Charles Eliot Norton. Pinchot's talk was curiously prophetic of the philosophy of forest management so vigorously advocated fifty years later by Harris Reynolds and his colleagues as discussed later in this chapter. After describing at length his enthusiasm for the practices that he had observed in the management of the ancient Sihlwald Forest in Zurich, Switzerland (which later became the inspiration for Reynolds), and extolling the virtues of wise utilization of the American forest's timber resource, Pinchot offered his prescription for "the Metropolitan Reservations which have recently been added to the park area of Boston — the Blue Hills, Middlesex Fells, Stony Brook, and Beaver Brook — with a total of something over 6,000 acres," concluding with this proclamation:

> . . . for the value of the forest as a public pleasure ground, for the well being of the trees upon the reservation, and for the enormous value of an example of true forestry in New England, I believe the application of forest management to the Boston Reservations would be wholly feasible, widely useful, and altogether appropriate.

Unfortunately, only nine of the thirty-six illustrious members of the Saturday Club are recorded as having been in attendance at Pinchot's talk and, of these, only Charles Eliot would seem likely to have had any profound interest in the subject of forest management. One searches in vain for evidence that Pinchot's admonitions found any fertile ground in the forestry practices that were evolving in Massachusetts with the dawning of the twentieth century.

Ironically, at the turn of the century, notwithstanding the far-reaching changes in national forest policy led by the titanic figures described above, scarcely an acre of forestland — federal, state, or private — was under systematic management. A notable exception was George W. Vanderbilt's famed Biltmore estate in North Carolina. Dr. Carl Alwin Schenck, a German born and educated forester, came to

America in 1895 to take over the estate's management from Gifford Pinchot and started the Biltmore Forest School. The Biltmore School was the first forestry school in the United States. Although it was subsequently eclipsed by the forestry schools at Cornell, the University of Minnesota, and Yale, among others, it was notable for its "hands-on" innovative methods of instruction. To the citizens of New England, however, the vast carpets of green that once characterized the New England forests had been stripped of their best timber, their rivers were polluted, and they appeared to be nearly devoid of wildlife. Stephen Fox relates the exasperation voiced by Henry David Thoreau when viewing his beloved Concord stripped of its pine forests by the "heedless practices of local farmers."

True to De Tocqueville's observations concerning the natural proclivity of Americans to form voluntary associations, it was in response to this bleak scene that the first private-citizen forestry organizations in New England, serving the interests of both private landowners and the town forests, were organized. In order of founding, they were:

Connecticut Forestry Association	1895
Massachusetts Forestry Association	1898
Society for the Protection of New Hampshire Forests	1901
Forestry Association of Vermont	1904

THE WOODS LOOKED MORE RAGGED

The Massachusetts Forestry Association fulfilled the vision of its nine founders, led by Joseph S. Nowell and Allen Chamberlain, both of Winchester. While commuting home from their offices in Boston on a dreary December afternoon in 1897, Nowell and Chamberlain observed from their train window that "the woods they saw along the right of way looked more ragged than they had only a few years before . . . and the street shade trees seemed no better."[7] The nine "men of good will" (James H. Bowditch, Myron S. Dudley, D. Blakely Hoar, Warren H. Manning, Jacob U. Pierce, Walter C. Wright, and the renowned landscape architect Frederick Law Olmsted) framed a charter for a new association "to introduce judicious methods in dealing with forest and woodlands; to arouse and educate a public interest in this subject; to promote the afforestation of unproductive lands; to encourage the planting and care of shade trees."[8]

THE RETURN OF THE PRODIGAL

Figure 1. The "woods looked more ragged" because they were growing on spent timberlands and abandoned farmland. A driving force behind the new private forestry movement was the need to place these lands under professional management. Cartoon from the Twenty-sixth Annual Report of the Massachusetts Forestry Association, Bulletin 138, *issued in 1923.*

The Massachusetts Forestry Association was renamed the Massachusetts Forest and Park Association in 1933 and is referred to throughout this chapter simply as the MFPA. To make the organizational nomenclature more confusing, the Massachusetts Land League, organized in 1970 and discussed later in this chapter, was renamed the Massachusetts Forestry Association in 1985. Finally, not content with one name change, the MFPA became the Environmental Lobby of Massachusetts and then the Environmental League of Massachusetts (ELM). Here is a genealogical chronology to guide us through this labyrinth. In this chart, time marches from top to bottom, and approximately simultaneous events appear on about the same line.

1890		
1900	1898 Massachusetts	
1910	Forestry Association	
1920		
1930	1933	
1940	Massachusetts Forest and Park	
1950	Association (MFPA)	1944 New England Forestry
1960		Foundation (NEFF)
1970		1970
1980	1981 Environmental Lobby of	Massachusetts Land League
1900	Massachusetts (ELM)	1985 Massachusetts
2000	1993 Environmental League of Massachusetts (ELM)	Forestry Association (MFA)

The circumstances of the MFPA's founding and its early history offer up some intriguing questions. In the roster of names of the MFPA's nine founding fathers, we look in vain for the redoubtable Charles Sprague Sargent and ponder the question: Why was Dr. Sargent not among them? We can surmise that while Sargent's passion for the planting and cultivation of all sorts of trees and his love of forest and wilderness aesthetics would have been compatible with the founders' purposes, he was, first and foremost, a scientist, deeply committed to science for its own sake and thus not drawn to the MFPA's embrace of scenic and cultural values to the exclusion of science. Further, Sargent's energies were largely devoted to the national arena until, embittered by the consequences of the arguments with Pinchot and his camp over their advocacy of using science to further the aims of industry and utilitarian forestry, he withdrew into the seclusion offered by his beloved Arnold Arboretum.

Why did science seem to play only a minor role in the MFPA's affairs? The birth and early flowering of the MFPA coincided with the emergence of professional forestry as an academic discipline. Professor Bond describes the early recognition of forestry education at Harvard University through the work, initially, of Sargent and Alexander Agassiz and subsequently Richard T. Fisher, J. G. Jack, and Austin Cary. None of these learned gentlemen appears among the MFPA's early leadership, and the concerns of the MFPA seem to have had little or nothing to do with formal forestry education. Allen Chamberlain, for example, was a journalist and writer who contributed numerous articles to the publications of New England conservation organizations.[9] It seems a reasonable inference that the private forestry movement in Massachusetts had its roots in the literary and cultural activities that were blossoming at the time, fueled by an ethic among the educated and wealthy elite to dedicate themselves to public service.

However this may be, the leaders of the MFPA certainly were not above the political fray, as we will see when we look at their achievements and those of their successors.

THE EARLY DAYS OF THE MFPA

Led by Nowell as its first president and Chamberlain as its first secretary, the embryonic MFPA embarked on an extraordinary number of initiatives, chronicled in Richard Applegate's *Massachusetts Forest and Park Association: A History, 1898–1973*. In its first year, believing that legislation could prove to be an invaluable tool for managing environmental issues, the MFPA "went to Beacon Hill to fight commercialization of Mt. Greylock, the state's highest mountain."[10] It seems ironic that, nearly a century later, this battle still goes on as evidenced by a recently publicized plan, trumpeted by the state and blessed by former Governor William Weld, to create an extensive development at the foot of the mountain.

A curious catalyst for one of the MFPA's early efforts was one Leopold Touvelot, a Medford naturalist of French extraction, who conceived the notion that the cocoons of French gypsy moths could be used to produce a substitute for silk; to this end he imported in 1869 a handful of gypsy moth caterpillars, creatures that, Touvelot observed, voraciously consumed every shred of the large helpings of greenery that he fed to his captive charges. To Touvelot's horror, fearing that if gypsy moths were allowed to multiply in the wild, they would cause massive destruction, the caterpillars escaped. The naturalist's entreaties to the Department of Agriculture, alerting it of the peril, fell on deaf ears, and the moths promptly became, and to this day remain, a scourge of increasingly epidemic proportions. In an effort to attack the destruction wrought by these creatures, the office of moth warden was created. Partially in response to the need for finding further ways to control the gypsy moth infestation, the MFPA in 1902 began the lobbying that resulted in legislation establishing the office of the state forester and a state forest nursery.[11] In 1906, encouraged by the success of its earlier lobbying efforts, the MFPA established a Committee on Legislation to advance the association's interests in the Massachusetts legislature and the governor's office.

In addition to its forays into political activism, the MFPA planted shade trees, mostly European lindens, on Beacon Street. These have withstood the ravages of wind, disease, and time to stand as a monument to the enduring beauty of what today is becoming known as the "urban forest."

THE ADVENT OF HARRIS REYNOLDS

In 1911, Harris Reynolds succeeded Allen Chamberlain as executive secretary of the MFPA. After graduating from West Virginia University in 1909 with the degree of bachelor of science in civil engineering, Reynolds attended Harvard University, where in 1911 he earned a degree in landscape architecture. Harris barely had time to practice either of the professions for which he trained when he assumed the leadership of the MFPA, a position that he would hold with great distinction until his sudden death in 1953.

During his long tenure as its executive secretary, Harris Reynolds' name became virtually synonymous with the MFPA. An exemplary apostle of de Tocqueville's assertion that the work of democracy is most effectively carried out through voluntary associations, Reynolds held to his conviction that a private, citizen-driven organization is the most powerful mechanism, and, when necessary, weapon, that can be brought to bear on forest-related conservation issues. Testimony to the wisdom of this belief is borne out by the MFPA's achievements under Reynolds' guidance and direction:

- The MFPA played an important role in convincing Congress to pass the Weeks Act in 1917, which, among other things, established the White Mountain and Green Mountain National Forests, containing nearly 900,000 acres of forested lands.

- In 1914 the MFPA secured from the Massachusetts General Court $90,000 for the acquisition of state forests.

- In 1920, Reynolds caused the MFPA to bring before the General Court an initiative petition, the first ever, for the purchase of 250,000 acres for the Massachusetts state forest system. It had 31,000 signatures, and 100,000 acres were purchased.

- Reynolds became known as the father of town forests; there were 127 in Massachusetts by 1953.[12]

- Under Reynolds, the MFPA promoted the establishment of the state forest fire warden system.

- The MFPA sponsored and secured passage of a law requiring each town to elect a tree warden.

- Reynolds led the MFPA's battles against the destructive effects of insects and disease.

- The MFPA continued to develop and implement the organization's recommendations for town conservation land-use plans, commencing with MFPA-prepared plans for Wayland and Groton (1951 and 1952, respectively), with the assistance of a planner and a forester.

These plans called for identifying and inventorying natural resources within each town and suggested public actions for their protection.

- The MFPA organized a conference of experts to consider ways to obtain and use scientific information about natural resources, resulting in the creation of the Massachusetts Conference on Land Economic Survey and a new topographic survey of the state.

- The MFPA facilitated passage of legislation intended to prevent the discharge of industrial effluents into the state's streams and rivers.

- The MFPA published *Forest and Park News* and, in cooperation with the Harvard Forest, numerous forestry bulletins.

- Reynolds reorganized the Massachusetts Conservation Council, Massachusetts' citizen clearinghouse.

- Reynolds served on various state committees and headed three major national committees.

Throughout Harris Reynolds' long tenure as secretary of the MFPA, the association engaged in a host of environmental initiatives both within the state and beyond its borders. In 1920, the MFPA joined a battle to prevent the flooding of 8,000 acres of Yellowstone National Park. The following year the asociation worked to create a Roosevelt Sequoia National Park, secure additional land purchases for national parks, oppose transfer of the national forests from the Department of Agriculture to the Department of the Interior, and encourage federal appropriations for the control of blister rust. Closer to home, the association proposed a forestry center for New England. Over the ensuing decades, Reynolds led the MFPA in such diverse efforts as forest-fire prevention, highway beautification, a plan, defeated in Congress, to establish an Everglades National Park, legislative approval of a topographic resurvey of Massachusetts, additions to the state forests, and, sadly, unsuccessful battles against Dutch elm disease.

The MFPA's roll of achievements under Harris Reynolds' leadership is eloquent testimony to his belief that the power of government can work to great effect when properly harnessed so as to make possible goals identified and advocated by associations of enlightened citizens. However, to this conviction there was one very notable exception: Reynolds, particularly in his later years, harbored an abiding skepticism about the ability of government, federal or state, to effect positive change in the hands-on management of privately owned forested lands and the promotion of New England's private forest economy.

Reynolds was a prolific correspondent. Shortly before his death in 1953, he wrote the following clear statement of his convictions on this subject:

> For more than half a century in this country, we have followed the theory that forest management was a function of government. This has meant government subsidies to [these] small owners and the virtual socialization of the forestry profession. . . . Ten years ago the Massachusetts Forest and Park Association reached the conclusion that all of its efforts through public subsidies since its organization in 1898 had failed to bring the woodlot under management. The countryside was still pock marked with clear-cut forest lands, constituting a fire menace and an eyesore in the landscape.

Reynolds' solution to the failure of government agencies to bring the smaller woodlots under management was the formation of the New England Forestry Foundation, discussed later in this chapter.

Harris Reynolds is affectionately remembered by his son Clinton Reynolds, currently a member of the foundation's corporation, as a colorful and forceful personality. Reynolds' attachment to his pipe was a trademark. Much to his wife's annoyance, the pipe was always "in his mouth," even while he was swimming. Clint Reynolds recalls that in 1929 and 1930 his father was engaged in building houses along Pinehurst Road in Belmont. The family had just assembled for lunch when one of the boys observed smoke rising from a nearby house lot where their father had been at work. By the time the Belmont Fire Department arrived at the scene, Harris Reynolds and his sons had extinguished the blaze, the cause of which would remain forever a mystery, since Reynolds assured the firemen that he could not have been at fault as he had "banged out" his pipe. Reynolds' vision of the mass destruction that might have ensued from this incident inspired him to demonstrate yet another of his talents, that for poetry, in an epic entitled "The Careless Smoker":

A fool there was and his pipe he lit
   (Even as you and I)
On a forest trail where the leaves were fit
To become ablaze from the smallest bit
Of spark — and the fool he furnished it.
   The day was windy and dry.

The forest was burned to its very roots,
   Even beneath the ground.
With the flowers, the birds and the poor dumb brutes,
Old Hoary oaks, and the tender shoots
Which might have made logs but for such galoots
   Allowed to wander around.

The lumber jack has now passed on
   His pay-day comes no more
And the screech-owls haunt the camp at dawn
Where the cook's tin pan woke the men of brawn
But the mill is silent, the trees are gone,
   The soil and the forest floor.

A deadly sight are those hills of rocks
   Which once were beds of green
No hope for the human, no food for the flocks
The floods must be held by expensive locks
And the harbor is silted to the docks,
   The ships no more are seen.

But the fool smokes on in the forest still
   Leaves camp-fires burning too
While the patient public pays the bill
And the nation's wealth is destroyed for nil.
If the law doesn't get him, Old Satan will
   When his smoking days are through.

Richard Applegate's history of the MFPA and other written accounts of its earlier activities resonate with the dramatic successes of Harris Reynolds. Less has been written about Reynolds' quiet but remarkably influential sometime comrade-in-arms, William Pickman Wharton of Groton, who was elected to the MFPA's executive committee in 1911. Remembered today by some Groton old-timers as Billy Wharton and by others as Mr. Wharton, this self-effacing gentleman, a modest man of both great wealth and great influence, often could be seen walking Groton's fields and woods dressed in the simple attire of a local farmer. Wharton served as president of the MFPA from 1936 to 1960 and was an original incorporator in 1944 of the New England Forestry Foundation. A listing of Wharton's memberships and offices found in the fiftieth-year account of the Harvard class of 1903 provides eloquent testimony of his eclectic interests. Here is an excerpt:

> *Memberships:* National, Massachusetts, and New Hampshire Audubon Societies; American and Massachusetts Forestry Associations; Society of American Foresters; National Parks Association; Wilderness Society; American Ornithologists Union; Friends of the Land; Northeastern Bird Banding Association; Society for Protection of New Hampshire Forests.

> *Offices Held:* Selectman of Groton, 1921–1924; currently, chairman, Town Forest Committee, and member, Planning Board; secretary and vice-president, National Audubon Society, 1912–1941; secretary, American Bison Society, 1910–1914; president, National Parks Association, since 1938; Massachusetts Forest & Park Association, since 1936; chairman, Massachusetts Conservation Council, 1942–1949, Massachusetts State Forestry Committee, since 1943.

A contemporary and friend of President Franklin D. Roosevelt at Groton and Harvard, Wharton was an adviser to Mr. Roosevelt on a range of matters, including forestry policies and the establishment of national parks. Stephen Fox's chapter in this book provides a thoughtful insight into this remarkable figure in American conservation.

THE NEW ENGLAND FORESTRY FOUNDATION

By the early 1900s, many of the farm fields and pastures that had dominated the Massachusetts landscape had been abandoned. Land, in many cases acquired by municipalities through tax foreclosures, could be bought for as little as a dollar per acre. The landowners who began to replace the farmers were diverse. Some were essentially absentee city dwellers who lived and worked far from the properties they purchased, while others were local individuals who often acquired property through inheritance or picked it up as "tax land." Bolt mills, charcoal kilns and other utilizers of wood created local markets for logs and provided an incentive for timber speculators to own large tracts of woodland, hoping to make fast profits from the demand generated by the local markets. For the most part, these people knew nothing of forestry practice or forest stewardship.

The abandoned farms were yielding to stands of pine, much of which was becoming marketable. Portable sawmills sprang up, resulting in extensive clearcuts. Because of a widespread lack of enlightened professional management, the woods that grew on this land generally contained very poor quality timber. Woodland owners needed expert advice and management assistance if they were to enhance and retain the quality of their forests. Once again, it was Harris Reynolds who brought his enormous talent and energy to attacking this problem: he identified a critical need for an enterprise that would offer to the owners of private forestlands a complete range of services, from timber cruising (inspecting land for possible lumber yield) to marking timber to be cut for both thinning and harvesting to overseeing cutting to securing the best markets for the harvest. Reynolds envisioned that this new enterprise would educate landowners by demonstrating that, with proper management, the timber resources of their forestlands could be renewed and sustained virtually in perpetuity. In today's parlance, this concept would be called sustainable forestry.

The inspiration for Reynolds' vision for wise management of the Massachusetts forests dated back to August 1913 when he honeymooned in Europe with his new bride, Alice Hecker, who was of German descent. Combining romance with scholarly investigation, Reynolds managed to conduct a study of European community forests, concentrating on some of the most famous German and Swiss city forests and the Black Forest. The honeymooning party was actually a threesome: the resourceful William Wharton went along to help with the study and to indulge his passion for observing birds and their habitats. The establishment of the town forest movement in this country is believed to have been the direct result of their forest studies on this trip. Reynolds' detailed notes on one of the forests they visited, the Sihlwald (extolled, as previously noted, by Pinchot in his 1895 Boston lecture), describe the organizational structure for the management of what in 1913 was a 1,000-year-old forest situated within the city of Zurich:

Forest warden
Assistant
3 clerks
8 forest maids
120 workmen the year round. Double in the winter.
1 mill foreman

Regarding the responsibilities of the eight forest maids, Massachusetts Extension Forester David Kittredge tells us that "women were, and to a large extent still are, used for planting purposes in European forests. They are considered superior planters."

Drawing on the experience gained in his travels abroad and the application of his learning to the management of community forests, Harris was ready to take the next step. M. Richard Applegate recounts in *New England Forestry Foundation: A History:*

> On July 12, 1944, while war still raged over much of the world, the New England Forestry Foundation was incorporated in Boston to start and carry on a new kind of war — the battle to enhance and make better use of the forests of New England. The problem was to reach and to help the many, many individual owners. It was to educate them by doing what they couldn't do for themselves. It was to prove that forestry makes economic sense, and that an owner is willing to pay for a complete forestry service that can handle all of the details, from recommendation, to financial arrangement, to formal supervision of logging. This the government cannot and should not do.[13]

If Harris Reynolds' initiative is characterized as a war, the New England Forestry Foundation was his weapon of choice. Characteristically, Reynolds sought recruits to extol the virtues of his proposal. Many of the initial responses were far from encouraging.

In the light of Reynolds' disdain for the role of government in private forest management, one can only imagine his reaction to the following response from Perry H. Merrill, Vermont's state forester and one of New England's most influential forestry leaders.

> December 31, 1943
> My reaction to your foundation proposal is adverse at the present. Perhaps with more information, I might be convinced of its value.

Your proposition is nothing more than the establishment of another land holding organization, which is quasi-public instead of public. Why not let the towns, county or state own or manage the lands? I see no greater inducement to the individual to give their lands to the foundation than to a public corporation. The tendency would be to donate cut-over or burned over land for which little can be done regardless of who holds it.

I doubt if you would get enough acreage to help the forestry situation. Suppose you got 50,000 acres; that would be only a drop in the bucket.

(Quite contrary to Merrill's comment, Harris Reynolds, as noted above, was not seeking to create "another land owning organization"; he was a passionate advocate for sound forestry management practice.)

From C. Edward Behre, assistant to the chief, United States Department of Agriculture Forest Service, he received the following:

February 7, 1944

I have your letter of January 20 and have discussed your proposal for a Forestry Foundation with several people here. It is my feeling that the scheme is quite impractical and is unlikely to affect more than a small segment of the private forest land problem. Because there would be no incentive for income, the tendency would be for management to be inefficient, both from the standpoint of forest practice and business administration. . . . There would be a tendency to sell stumpage too cheaply, thus undermining ordinary private owners or giving an undue advantage to the processors. This holds untold possibilities for playing favorites and diverting the income to the pockets of some self-seeking clique.

It seems to me that if the land cannot be held privately, it would be better for it to be in public ownership rather than in a foundation which might be dominated by a small group of generous contributors.

I also have difficulty in understanding why technical aid provided to small owners by the foundation foresters is any less obnoxious than "subsidies from the public till."

From Harold O. Cook, Director of Forestry, the Commonwealth of Massachusetts Department of Conservation, came the following:

March 24, 1944

I have been thinking over the plan of your Forestry Foundation, and have come to the conclusion that the most valuable part of your program is liable to be overshadowed by the forest land acquisition and management portion of the project.

However, the Massachusetts commissioner of conservation, Raymond J. Kenney, in an encouraging letter dated April 21, 1944, appeared to share Harris Reynolds' vision. Addressing the challenge posed by the creation of the foundation, Mr. Kenney, with extraordinary foresight, wrote:

I read with interest in the *Forest and Park News* of April of the progress being made in the formation of the New England Forestry Foundation. I believe that this organization can be made an important factor in the development of forestry in Massachusetts and New England to supplement the present activities of the State and Federal agencies.

As you know, one of our important problems with respect to forestry in this State is the matter of non-resident ownership, and I believe that an agency which can take over the management of forest lands owned by non-residents will be an important factor in meeting our problems.

No doubt there are many people, residents and non-residents alike, who would hesitate to relinquish title to their property but who would be glad to enter into an arrangement whereby their forest lands would be put under sound management practices. I have in mind an arrangement similar to that which is in common practice with respect to the management of business real estate today or even in the management of personal property in the nature of stocks, bonds and similar securities.

I feel that once the Foundation gets under way, it will be found that many owners will want not only competent forestry advice but the actual management of their property, involving the harvesting of mature timber, stand improvement work or replanting where necessary, and that they will be ready and willing to pay a reasonable fee for such a service. I feel that such an arrangement would make it possible to extend over a wider area the services and resources of the Foundation than would be possible if it became largely a land-holding corporation.

Realizing that good forestry and good wildlife management work hand in hand, I should hope that the Foundation would also employ a competent wildlife consultant, and undoubtedly many owners would desire that management plans for their lands involve wildlife management wherever possible as well as forest management.

In short, I believe that there is a great possibility for the future of a well-organized forestry foundation in this and adjoining states, and compliment the Massachusetts Forest and Park Association for initiating the project.

Certainly Harris Reynolds must have smiled at these remarks from James J. (Jack) Storrow in a letter dated September 25, 1947:

As I probably told you before, when you first started the Foundation I thought it was a rather crazy and entirely impractical idea, and just barely worth a trial. Since then I have been perfectly amazed at its splendid success, and I think you have something that ought to be developed throughout the country, because this success shows that not only have you managed it well, but that it fills a great and widespread need.

Mr. Storrow, the scion of a distinguished Boston family, soon became a staunch friend of the foundation, serving as its vice president from 1951 to 1970. A lover of the sea and the forest, Jack Storrow devoted his life to the causes of conservation and to helping others less fortunate than himself.

And so it came about that Harris Reynolds, together with his colleagues in the MFPA, founded the New England Forestry Foundation, which, as its name implies, embraces all New England. Central to Reynolds' vision for his beloved foundation was his belief that its high calling would be to educate New England's private woodlot owners through applied forestry management and that, accordingly, it would enjoy to the full the status of a charitable enterprise. The NEFF indeed was created as a charitable, nonprofit corporation under Massachusetts law.

THE NEFF FORESTERS

The plan, devised and put into operation by the MFPA and the NEFF, called for the creation of forest management centers (described below), each under the direction of a trained consulting forester. J. Milton (Milt) Attridge, a graduate of the University of Maine, became the foundation's first truly successful full-time forester, joining the foundation in 1946 and serving as its chief forester from 1954 to 1967. In 1967 he became a member of the foundation's corporation. Attridge, who is now a vigorous man of 85, recalled his early years for Applegate:

> Many young growing stands were liquidated that way [clearcut-ting immature trees] to give the owner hardly enough profit to make it worthwhile at all. There were no provisions for leaving growing stock or seed trees then. Over the years we've managed to change that a good deal.

Under Attridge's leadership, the NEFF built up a cadre of professional consulting foresters, at one time numbering 22, who demonstrated through their work for landowners the enlightened forestry practices that the NEFF's founders envisioned. Each NEFF forester was (and is) responsible for a geographically defined area called a "center," the size of the center being largely determined by the distance involved in adequately serving the needs of the landowner/clients under the partic-ular forester's care. For example, a center was established to provide consulting foresty to landowners in New Hampshire's lakes region, another covers the Merrimack valley from southern New Hampshire into eastern Massachusetts, and so on. Today there are 11 centers and 1 subcenter, under the direction of 14 full-time consulting foresters, located in Maine, New Hampshire, Vermont, and Massachusetts. The foundation also has a small but growing client base in Connecticut. Through these centers, nearly 1,500 landowners, accounting for ap-proximately 350,000 acres, are served by these foresters.

"ISLANDS OF PEACE"

Since its incorporation in 1944, the NEFF has accepted gifts of over 100 properties, many of them designated by the donors as memorial forests — currently more than 18,000 acres of woodlands. In addition, the foundation currently holds conservation easements on approximately 3,000 additional acres. M. Richard Applegate, in his twenty-fifth anniversary history of the NEFF (1944–69), waxed eloquent on the subject of the memorial forests. A forest is

> ... a memorial that keeps on growing, a delight to the eye, a haven for birds and small animals, a place of peace for the wandering lover of nature, an escape from exhaust fumes, blaring horns, neon signs, and rock-and-roll transistor radios. It is a memorial which ... keeps on giving ... which looks eternally young ... and which our own young or their young might never see if these islands of peace are not put aside by thoughtful donors.[14]

It should be added that while rock-and-roll is seldom encountered in the foundation's forests, these same "islands of peace" resonate to the sounds of the ax, the saw, and the skidder, as virtually all of them have been and continue to be actively managed for timber production.

The foundation's first donation of a memorial forest in Massachusetts was received in 1952 as a bequest from Dennis E. Hartnett. Known as the Hartnett-Manhan Memorial Forest, this property, 148 acres along the Manhan River in western Massachusetts, is of "considerable historical interest, since it contains an abandoned lead mine which may have provided bullets for the Revolutionary War, and where Patriot Ethan Allen apparently was once occupied as a lead miner."[15]

Of the total number of forested properties owned today by the foundation, 41, comprising more than 5,400 acres, are situated in Massachusetts. John T. Hemenway, the foundation's secretary-treasurer following the death of Harris Reynolds in 1953 and currently the foundation's honorary director, deserves much of the credit for NEFF's success, largely through his tireless dedication to attracting donations of forests to the foundation. The management of all these properties has been, and continues to be, a major responsibility of the foresters who formerly were employed by and now are affiliated with the foundation.

THE HIKING CLUBS

As Robert McCullough notes in *The Landscape of Community,* New England's hiking community has played an important role in forest

Recreation and Nature Study Are Assets of the Forests

Figure 2. The concept of forests as sites for recreation, education, and nature appreciation ("islands of peace") led to a reconstituted Massachusetts Forest and Park Association and to the system of memorial forests currently maintained by the New England Forestry Foundation. Vignette from Harris Reynolds's 1925 monograph Town Forests: Their Recreational and Economic Value and How to Establish and Maintain Them.

protection by expanding the base of political support for responsible long-range forest policy and by forging close associations with forestry groups. Among the earliest hiking clubs in Massachusetts were the following:

Cyrus Tracy's Exploring Circle in Lynn	circa 1850
The Alpine Club in Williamstown	1863
The White Mountain Club of Portland, Maine	1873
The Appalachian Mountain Club	1876[16]

The Appalachian Mountain Club (AMC) survived and prospered, and currently boasts over 75,000 members throughout the Northeast. Throughout its 122 years, the AMC has been based in Boston; for much of that time it has occupied its present headquarters at 5 Joy Street on Beacon Hill where, in addition to offices and meeting rooms, there is an extensive library that contains a wealth of material relating to the mountains and forests of New England. The club also has established a splendid visitors' center at Pinkham Notch in Gorham, New Hampshire, which serves as the headquarters for the club's famed chain of huts in the White Mountains, and where numerous workshops and field trips on conservation, forestry, and ecology are conducted.

Over the years the AMC has acquired substantial wooded properties, including its 1,800-acre Cardigan Reservation in Alexandria, New Hampshire, but so far the club has not engaged in active forest management, preferring to focus its resources upon public forest protection, research, outdoor recreation, and education.

The AMC's leaders, however, often have played important roles in Massachusetts forestry. For many, participation in the AMC has been a catalyst for increased awareness of and appreciation for the private forestry movement in Massachusetts and elsewhere in New England. Allen Chamberlain, cofounder of the MFPA, joined the AMC in 1897, became its president in 1906, and contributed numerous articles to *Appalachia,* the club's historic journal of mountaineering and care for the land. Thomas D. Cabot, an ardent white-water canoist and AMC president in the 1930s, served for many years as a member of the corporation of the NEFF and during his long lifetime acquired hundreds of acres of land that have been a model of exemplary forestry practices, portions of which have been donated by Mr. Cabot to the NEFF. In the early 1960s, John Hitchcock of Princeton, Massachusetts, served as president of the AMC, subsequently as president of the MFPA, and as a director and generous contributor of land to the Massachusetts Audubon Society. C. Francis Belcher, the AMC's executive director from 1956 to 1975, in his *Logging Railroads of the White Mountains,* wrote a fascinating account of how, at the turn of the century, wood-burning locomotives were utilized to haul millions of board feet of timber from New Hampshire's forests to feed the mills downstream on the Pemigewasset and Merrimack rivers. This practice resulted in disastrous forest fires ignited by sparks from the engines' smokestacks, which helped precipitate the passage of the Weeks Act in 1917, establishing New Hampshire's White Mountain National Forest. I myself served on the AMC's board of directors (its "council") from 1962 to 1975 and as its president in 1973 and 1974; in 1997 I was elected to a seventh one-year term as president of the NEFF.

THE WOODTICKS — A "NOTORIOUS AGGREGATION"

Much has been written by and about Benton MacKaye. MacKaye, from Shirley Center, Massachusetts, was a man of strong intellect and personality. Long associated with the initial concepts of the Appalachian Trail and the Wilderness Society, MacKaye, "ever the theorist . . . fused forestry, conservation, wilderness advocacy, and planning into a lifelong quest for habitable communities."[17] MacKaye loved loosely organized assemblages, which he termed "notorious aggregations." One such notorious aggregation, the Woodticks, which traditionally convened on Mount Monadnock (from 1937 to the early 1950s), brought together among other notables MacKaye, Allen Chamberlain, Harris Reynolds, William Wharton, and one Elmer D. Fletcher (Flooche), whose work with the U.S. Forest Service had been instrumental in the establishment of the White Mountain National Forest. Massachusetts State Forester Harold O. Cook frequently joined the Woodticks, as did a number of New Hampshire foresters. In this manner MacKaye assembled many of New England's most prominent figures for the purpose of brainstorming and formulating forest policies. (One ponders what de Tocqueville would have thought of such an informal democratic association. No doubt he would have made an exemplary Woodtick.) It has been said of MacKaye that he was more a dreamer than a doer. Be that as it may, some of his dreams are with us today in very tangible form.

MACKAYE'S TWO CATEGORIES OF OPEN SPACE: INDUSTRIAL AND CULTURAL

In describing the creation by Massachusetts Governor Alvan T. Fuller in 1928 of the Committee on Needs and Uses of Open Spaces, McCullough notes that Benton MacKaye, retained as a consultant to the committee, began his report on his work by "distinguishing two categories of open spaces: industrial and cultural. Forests grown for timber or for protecting watersheds embodied the former; lands utilized primarily for recreation, the latter." State and town forests, MacKaye observed, exemplified both types. From there, he moved to the crux of his proposal: a system of cultural areas shaped as belts or open ways designed to mitigate the expansion of urban environments and offer escape from civilization."[18]

It is interesting to note that MacKaye used the term "cultural" to refer to the human reshaping and stewardship of the landscape, as in "horti*culture*," rather than in either of word's two more common contexts: cultural differences (as in Polish versus Russian culture) or in reference to the fine arts (painting, sculpture, classical music). Prior to the advent of the 1960s, the term "cultural" as used by MacKaye could be said to define many of the initiatives undertaken by the MFPA and the singular men who led these efforts: namely, the establishment of national and state parks and forests; the beautification of parks and roadsides; the protection of choice landscapes; field ornithology; floodplain zoning; the regulation of inland and tidal waters; controlling pests and diseases; and, by no means of least importance, the acquisition and preservation of forestlands.

MacKaye's use of the term "cultural" in this context has not gained general acceptance, but most of the activities, apart from those relating to forestry or forest management, in which Chamberlain, Reynolds, Wharton, and their colleagues engaged now are encompassed by the term "conservation." William Wharton is reported to have said in 1970, "I've never found anything more interesting in my ninety years than my work in conservation." In the winter 1995–96 issue of *The Woodland Steward*, Bob Ricard wrote of the era prior to the 1960s as "The First Generation: The Early Conservation Movement."[19]

By contrast, forestry, or forest management, as practiced by the NEFF, appears often to have been viewed in the rather narrow context of what MacKaye would have termed industrial timber production. For example, a report dated January 1956 for a prospective client of the foundation describes the goal of the NEFF as follows:

> The sole purpose of the Foundation is to grow more and better timber in New England and to bring all of our forest lands into full production. There is no business opportunity in New England today that equals the possibilities in forest management. Every forest acre has the power to produce a certain amount of wood and the art of the forester is to capture that power in the form of commercial timber. For the first time, the forester has been given the authority to determine WHAT, WHEN AND HOW trees shall be harvested. Forest management is beginning to be accepted as an integral part of the forest economy.

It thus appears that, as the first half of the twentieth century drew to a close, forestry and conservation were proceeding along somewhat parallel but increasingly separate and divergent paths, a course that eventually would prove potentially perilous to the NEFF's ability to fully honor Harris Reynolds' high ideals for the foundation's overriding charitable purpose as educator of the private woodlot owner.

COMING OF AGE

The passing of Chamberlain, Reynolds, Wharton, MacKaye, and their contemporaries raised the question of whether the private forestry movement and the organizations that fueled its achievements would survive without their leadership. In the 1960s, changes were in the wind that would profoundly affect the fate of the MFPA and the NEFF and lead to the formation in 1970 of the Massachusetts Land League. The publication of Rachel Carson's *Silent Spring* in 1962 aroused environmentally concerned citizens in Massachusetts, New England, and across America. The commitment of Houghton Mifflin to publishing *Silent Spring,* at a time when Carson's assault upon the use of pesticides had brought down upon her a firestorm of criticism from powerful forces in industry and government, can be credited to the steadfast support of the publisher's distinguished editor and renowned conservationist, Paul Brooks of Lincoln, Massachusetts. Outrage over the massive defoliation of Vietnam and Cambodia by United States military incursions; the publication of Carson's book; the advent of Earth Day in 1970; the sprawl of urban and suburban development; concern that revaluation of land and rising tax burdens, driven in part by state-mandated 100 percent valuation, would lead to the liquidation of family land holdings; and the abandonment of family farms — all these factors contributed in the 1960s and '70s to "a second wave of strong citizen participation in environmental matters and spawned a variety of new forest conservation organizations in the region."[20] The environmental movement was in full sway; the venerable bulwarks of the private forestry movement in Massachusetts, the MFPA and the NEFF, could not but be affected by this new wave of environmental activism.

THE RESPONSE OF THE MFPA TO
THE ENVIRONMENTAL MOVEMENT

The MFPA's Annual Report for 1962 noted that only a small part of the Association's budget was devoted to lobbying; nevertheless it characterized the MFPA as a "legislative watchdog" on matters relating to conservation. "By 1960 it was becoming obvious that the interests of the Association were gradually turning toward [acting as]a basic lever of conservation legislation for protection of the natural resources of the Commonwealth."[21] The position of executive director of the MFPA, created in 1963, was initially filled by John Hemenway, who continued as the secretary-treasurer of the NEFF. But Hemenway found it difficult to do justice to both positions, and within a year he recommended Benjamin W. Nason for the MFPA job.

Nason, a former NEFF forester in New Hampshire, had just received his law degree from Suffolk University in Boston. Richard Applegate's history of the MFPA notes, "Armed with a lawyer as well as a man fully acquainted with forestry problems, the Association finally went all the way toward becoming the Legislative Arm of Conservation in Massachusetts."[22] By the time Nason assumed the office of executive director, the MFPA had become essentially a lobbying organization, a conversion brought about, at least in part, because the MFPA was the only citizen conservation group that legally could devote a substantial portion of its resources to lobbying. Reflecting this change in its focus, the name of the MFPA was changed in 1981 to the Environmental Lobby

Figure 3. A gathering of the informal association called the "wood ticks" at Wapack Lodge on Mount Monadnock, New Hampshire, May 25 and 26, 1946, included many New England and Massachusetts forestry leaders. Left to right (front row): White Mountain National Forest activist Elmer (Flooche) Fletcher, regional planner Benton MacKaye, New Hampshire state forester John Foster, MFA secretary Harris Reynolds, the University of New Hampshire's Karl Woodward; (back row): Connecticut state forester Austin Hawes, New Hampshire extension forester Kenneth Barraclough, MFA executive committee member William Wharton, and forester Lawrence Rathbun of the Society for the Protection of New Hampshire Forests. Courtesy of Dartmouth College Archives.

of Massachusetts and subsequently, in 1993, to the Environmental League of Massachusetts (ELM). In order to become a lobbying organization, ELM had abandoned its 501(c)(3) public charitable corporation status. The transition from the MFPA to ELM is captured in a recently recorded interview with Alexandra Dawson, now retired as professor and supervisor of the interns at Antioch College in Keene, New Hampshire, as follows:

My first experience with them was in the late sixties and then I started working for Conservation Law Foundation in the early seventies so I saw more of them. They were part of the environmental group that all hung out at 3 Joy Street. There was a group feel. It was very evident that most of these groups didn't have the staff or the tax status to do lobbying and I think that's what finally drew them to ELM. The people who ran around it were very interested in legislative work and it was there in Boston.

Ms. Dawson's reference to her "group feel" experience at the Conservation Law Foundation is explained by the fact that, in 1975 and 1976, the Appalachian Mountain Club, headquartered at 5 Joy Street in Boston as noted above, completed the purchase of the adjoining properties at 3 and 4 Joy Street. The space thus acquired by the AMC was leased to the Conservation Law Foundation (CLF) for its headquarters at 3 Joy Street and, next door, to the New England regional chapter of the Sierra Club, thereby creating a consolidated environmental command post. This project was brought to fruition through the leadership of then AMC president Ruby Horwood, the first (and until now only) woman to serve as president of that venerable organization and my immediate successor in that office. Being right in the midst of this command post, the CLF, at 3 Joy Street, became an ideal place to "hang out."

Under the direction of Nason and his successor, Michael Ventresca, the ELM was active in a broad spectrum of legislative efforts, including the following:

> Abolition of the Mount Greylock Tramway Authority and the Mount Greylock Reservation Commission and transfer of responsibility for the 8,800-acre Mount Greylock reservation to the Department of Natural Resources
>
> Funding for water pollution control
> Appropriations for land acquisition and recreational development
> Establishment of the Cape Cod National Seashore
> Enactment of the Massachusetts Wilderness Act
> Protection of inland wetlands
> Protection of the Appalachian Trail in Massachusetts
> Regulation of billboards
> Adoption of an Environmental Bill of Rights
> Enaction of a Farmland Assessment Act
> Enaction of a Massachusetts Clean Waters Act
> Provision for reviewing power-plant siting

It is evident from a tally of ELM's legislative efforts that, swept up in the many currents of the environmental movements of the 1960s and 1970s, the organization had become diverted from its historic focus on behalf of private forests and forestry. As a consequence, the organization's prominence in private forestry in Massachusetts was greatly diminished. Dr. Robert Bond, currently president of the MFA, writing in *The Woodland Steward,* quotes former longtime Massachusetts Chief Forester Harold O. Cook's opinion that "the Massachusetts Forestry Association, established at the turn of the century, became the Massachusetts Forest and Park Association (MFPA) in 1932. . . . The original MFA provided the leadership for forest conservation in the Commonwealth early in this century. When ELM was created, a void was left for advocacy exclusively for forest stewardship in the state."[23]

THE ELM IN THE 1980S:
ATTEMPTS AT COALITION BUILDING

In the late 1970s, ELM was experiencing frequent changeovers in staffing, erosion of its membership, and difficulty in using its limited financial resources to best advantage. To remedy these difficulties ELM recruited Kelly McClintock as its director. McClintock, who had been managing the affairs of the Conservation Law Foundation, set about stabilizing ELM, increasing professional salaries and achieving greater staff continuity.

On picking up the reins of ELM, Kelly McClintock soon formed the opinion that, in the era of environmental activism that characterized the 1980s, the Massachusetts legislature was besieged by the lobbying efforts of too many organizations, each promoting its own single-issue agenda, with disappointing results as a consequence. McClintock observed that many such organizations, each known for having a broad, well-defined and well-focused agenda, were scatter-shooting a succession of narrowly-focused environmental lobbying efforts at the legislature with, at best, a confusing result. McClintock's response to the problem harkens back to the observations of de Tocqueville with respect to the power of voluntary association; he organized coalitions to present fewer and more broadly defined agendas for legislative approval. This approach, in McClintock's view, worked well as long as each participating coalition maintained its identity of purpose and worked from a broad based agenda, a strategy that in time broke down as coalition members appeared to lose their former focus. In a recent interview, McClintock mused on the initial success of these efforts and the problems that later ensued:

> Agenda building was a focus of ELM. The eighties were as active environmentally as an era could be. The problem was there were, perhaps, too many agendas. Legislatures don't have to pay attention to any of them as single issues and ELM wanted to boil down priorities and present a solid front to the legislature of Massachusetts. To do this, ELM and other members of the coalition had to devise elaborate ways of stepping on the fewest toes. For several years this agenda building worked, but for it to work all the organizations had to have broad agendas. Groups such as the Defenders of Wildlife had to address land protection, for example. The problems arose when organizations began to lose their initial focus and funding sources that were interested in specific issues were more hesitant to donate money. Subsequently organizations began to retrench and refocus on specifics and the coalition became smaller and smaller.

Although Kelly McClintock's work at the ELM during the 1980s appears to have done little to fill the void in forest advocacy referred to by Harold Cook and Professor Bond, his experience with both the successes and failures of coalition building raises questions about how funding and other supportive resources may be affected by the "partnering" approach to forestry-related activities currently coming into vogue and discussed later in this chapter.

THE INITIAL RESPONSE OF THE NEFF TO THE ENVIRONMENTAL MOVEMENT

As the old MFPA was converting itself into ELM, the lobbying arm of the Massachusetts environmental movement, it and the NEFF began to drift apart. The NEFF went on doing pretty much what it always had done: managing the woodlands of its clients and its own memorial forests in Massachusetts and elsewhere in New England and adding to its inventory of memorial and other forest properties. The NEFF continued to pride itself on the accomplishments of its cadre of consulting foresters and principally identified itself with them.

Although the NEFF attracted a band of enthusiastic and devoted supporters, not all accounts of the foundation's doings are particularly flattering, partly owing to current perception of some of the techniques that were employed at that time in the practice of forestry. In light of today's concerns for the environment and for health in the workplace, the following rather graphic description by a parent of the activities of two boys employed in the 1970s by the foundation to do summer work, utilizing a substance that at the time was approved by the state, provides a startling contrast to the methods now being employed in the woods by the foundation's foresters.

> When two of my offspring were in high school, they worked for a summer for [the foundation]. I have never forgiven myself for letting them do that. [Their supervisor] had them outdoors in minimal clothing spraying, what's called frilling the trees that you don't like. You chop around the bark and spray them with this stuff, it was clearly toxic material and I'm sure there were things all over the cans about wearing protective clothing but it was ninety degrees and they were out there practically naked. My son said it dried all over you and looked like blood, it was reddish. He was going around and here came this lady through the woods, she was horrified, and he spoke to her, saying "Lady, lady, it's all right," but she turned and raced off in the other direction.
>
> So that was very bad, I don't know whether it's going to end up taking their lives at a relatively early age, but I have ever since then felt that the problem at that time was a profuse attitude of "Oh I use that all the time and I'm not sick." The idea that toxicity is measured by your keeling over on the spot was about the level of sophistication that was employed by the forestry community at that time and I think that remains quite unforgivable.

Throughout the 1960s, '70s and '80s, the NEFF was primarily known for its professional foresters and their hands-on work in the field. It maintained a low profile and as a 501(c)(3) public charity [nonprofit entity], attracted relatively little attention. In 1984, Hugh Putnam, a NEFF forester from Vermont, was given the title of executive director and succeeded John Hemenway as the foundation's chief of staff. For the next decade, in the public eye, the NEFF, apart from its highly respected cadre of professional consulting foresters, was rarely identified with forestry-related environmental initiatives.

INTO THE VOID

It has been said that nature abhors a vacuum. The same is true of human institutions. With the ELM scattering its legislative shots across a broad spectrum of environmental causes, the NEFF lingering in relative obscurity as an environmental organization, and no other then-existing private forestry organization assuming a position of leadership in Massachusetts, others were moving aggressively in the arena of activities relating to forests and forestry in Massachusetts and beyond.

To our north, the venerable Society for the Protection of New Hampshire Forests (SPNHF), a powerful and respected presence with a reputation extending far beyond New Hampshire's borders, was aggressively pursuing forestland protection, public education, and the role of a private organization in affecting forestry and conservation policies at the state and local levels. In no small measure the SPNHF's success has been attributable to its historically close working relationship with state forestry and New Hampshire's political leaders, including, for many years, its governors. On Massachusetts' southern border, the Connecticut Forest and Park Association successfully retained its identity with forests and parks while serving as the principal lobbying arm for the Connecticut environmental community.

Here in Massachusetts, according to Keith Ross, longtime forester and conservationist and currently vice president and director of land protection for the NEFF, with the influence of the private organizations waning, the state forester assumed greater importance. Gilbert Bliss, the Massachusetts director of forests and parks in the Department of Environmental Management, with his colleagues Jack Lambert, Tom Quink and Ken Beaujean, among others, were achieving remarkable success in working with the Massachusetts legislature in the 1980s. Gil Bliss takes particular satisfaction in two legislative achievements: updating the Forest Classification Act (Chapter 61) and the Forest Cutting Practices Act, both in 1981. Bliss recalls, with respect to the latter, that the environmental movement was spawning a plethora of initiatives for wetland restrictions. Individual towns were adopting their own wetlands bylaws, potentially creating a crazy-quilt of inconsistent and conflicting wetlands regulations. This led to state legislation bringing wetlands protection under the jurisdiction of what is now the Department of Environmental Protection. Bliss and his colleagues, with the full cooperation of then House Chairman Dick Moore, were able to make the Cutting Practices Act dovetail effectively with the wetlands protection restrictions, preserving the ability to engage in timber harvesting in a manner compatible with the wetlands ordinances. Other legislative initiatives addressed the treatment of wood-using businesses as mature industries, provision for registration of foresters to avoid victimizing consumers of forestry services, and a variety of activities in urban forestry. Bliss recalls the decades of the 1960s and 1970s as periods of exceptional rapport with state legislators, including Senator Robert Wetmore, then chairman of the state Senate Committee on Labor and Industries. Bliss's prescription for success in the legislative arena was bringing factions together in "big forum discussions" and conducting MFPA-based studies as a basis for formulating public policies.

The Commonwealth's prominence in forestry and forest conservation was reinforced when Governor Francis Sargent, as part of a reorganization of state agencies under state cabinet members, in 1971 appointed Charles H. W. Foster of Needham as the Commonwealth's first secretary of environmental affairs. Holder of a Ph.D. in geography and environmental engineering from Johns Hopkins University, Dr. Foster had previously served as Massachusetts commissioner of natural resources, president of The Nature Conservancy in Washington, D.C., and president of the New England Natural Resources Center in Boston. Charles Foster later became dean of the Yale School of Forestry (now the Yale School of Forestry and Environmental Studies), and currently is an adjunct professor at Harvard's Kennedy School of Government.

On the private forestry front, a new venture was coming to the forefront, helping to fill the void in regard to forests and forestry activities. In 1970, Bob Russell, a retired urban planner who owned a tree farm in Princeton, Massachusetts, and his wife, Betty, recognized the need for an educational organization to advocate the care and stewardship of land in Massachusetts and became the founder of the Massachusetts Land League. This organization's name was changed to the Massachusetts Forestry Association in 1970, so once again there was an MFA in Massachusetts. Greg Cox, executive director of the MFA, wrote in "MFA: 25 Years and Still Growing" in *The Woodland Steward:*

> With the help of Worcester County Regional Extension Specialist Fred Giebel, Russell put together a workshop for landowners on ways to productively manage their property. From that meeting came the Massachusetts Land League.
>
> The Land League was organized to provide information and services to help landowners manage and keep their land as privately-owned open space. . . . Although the League promoted a variety of productive land uses, encouraging better woodland management was a primary goal from the outset. Bob's ownership of woodlands made him aware of the possibilities that many landowners overlooked. With woodlands covering more than 60% of Massachusetts, if the League wanted to keep as much land undeveloped and productive as possible, it had to reach woodland owners.[24]

In a recent interview conducted by Robert Bond, Russell offered the following reflections:

> The Audubon societies and like-minded organizations prefer to sit on the land as is. My intent has been to promote growing trees as a crop. In this way you can produce a financially rewarding harvest and create an environment that gets people into the woods and fields. MFA, while focusing on trees, is a very broad kind of thing, looks at land as a total entity. The MFA was designed for an audience that needed a home.

Greg Cox, in *The Woodland Steward,* profiles the MFA from 1986 to 1995 as follows:

> Although slow to be realized, the 1985 plan for MFA to expand its membership and its influence has been a success. From just 191 members in 1985, membership rose to more than 800 by 1990, and over 1,000 members now. During the same time, MFA has become an important part of forestry in Massachusetts, helping sponsor and revitalize the Tree Farm Program and the educational program, Project Learning Tree.
>
> MFA has also been involved in all the major issues facing

woodland owners here during the last ten years: acid rain, Chapter 61, Quabbin deer management, the Generic Environmental Impact Report, global warming, endangered species, private property rights, revisions to the Forest Cutting Practices Act, forester licensing, ecosystem management, and so on. Because MFA represents a sizable group of private woodland owners, and their lands represent the bulk of the state's forest, MFA's concerns are increasingly important to policy discussions.

Just as the Land League first began with a workshop for landowners, every year MFA sponsors workshops on topics of interest. Recent workshops have covered everything from having a careful timber harvest to estate planning and protecting vernal pools. For those who want to see good woodland management in action, MFA holds Woods Walks around the state each year, showing off how different woodlands are cared for. With MFA's help, in 1995 the Tree Farm Program revived its annual Field Day, a very successful event it hopes to repeat each year around the state.

As MFA has grown, it has also expanded the land conservation role which Bob Russell envisioned for the Land League at the very beginning. MFA has helped landowners make arrangements which will allow them to protect their land from future development while continuing responsible forest management. This has resulted in nearly 1,000 acres being conserved as forests, including a 90-acre section of old growth forest in the Berkshires.[25]

When asked to distinguish their perceptions of the distinction between the MFA and the NEFF, both Russell and Bond responded that the NEFF generally has been thought to be a New England regional, rather than a Massachusetts, organization focused primarily on forest management; in addition the NEFF, until recently, has not been perceived as engaged to any significant extent in the work of conservation, education, or public policy.

RECENT CHANGES IN THE NEFF

In 1992, the New England Forestry Foundation organized a group comprising people from both within and outside its ranks, dubbed the "By '98 Committee," for the purpose of reexamining every aspect of the organization's mission, structure, and programs. The new mission statement contained in the By '98 Committee's final report reads:

MISSION STATEMENT

The New England Forestry Foundation's mission is to counter the deterioration of New England's unique forest resources due to fragmentation and the lack of management by promoting forest land stewardship, responsible forestry practices and multigenerational forest land planning.

This mission embraces:

• Demonstration of the multiple benefits — ecological, aesthetic, recreational and economic — of forestland stewardship

• Practicing and teaching new forestry concepts

• Provision of a balanced and credible perspective on public policy issues affecting forest land conservation

• Delivery of a full range of forestland stewardship services

• Preservation, through sustainable yield forestry, of a working landscape that supports New England's economic welfare and quality of life

The By '98 Committee's final report was presented to the NEFF Board of Directors in December 1992. In retracing the history of the foundation and determining the course of action for the NEFF's future, the directors considered the early history and origins of the foundation.

When Harris Reynolds launched the foundation as a charitable enterprise in 1944, the foundation's consulting foresters were seen as pioneers, teacher-educators who fulfilled the charitable mission of the foundation by enlightening and educating the landowner through their hands-on work. These foresters were more "cultural" than "industrial," by Benton MacKaye's criteria. Over time, the number of consulting foresters multiplied in Massachusetts and elsewhere in New England, and the profession of consulting forestry in general and the work of the NEFF foresters in particular were increasingly perceived as less unique, less charitable in nature, and more akin to a profession, practiced primarily for profit, with education subordinated to a primarily commercial purpose. Were Benton MacKaye with us today, one can surmise that he would classify the NEFF as "industrial." Although the NEFF foresters continued to promote the notion that they were "educating by doing what others only preach," by the early 1990s the foundation was encountering, in Massachusetts and elsewhere, confusion on the part of donors, grant makers, and the public over the foundation's 501(c)(3) charitable purpose, and a perception that the foundation was not "aboard" in the environmental movement that had been sweeping Massachusetts and New England. Also, the NEFF foresters were confronted with a dilemma: they were expected through their work as consulting foresters to generate the revenues necessary to keep the foundation going and at the same time to fulfill its stated educational purposes.

As a consequence of these deliberations, the foundation board, in 1993, approved and implemented a major reorganization of the enterprise. A for-profit business corporation was organized with the name "New England Forestry Consultants, Inc. (NEFCo); the foundation holds a portion of NEFCo's outstanding capital stock but itself remains a 501(c)(3) charitable corporation. Following completion of this reorganization, the former foundation foresters have become employees of NEFCo and the proceeds derived from their services are income to NEFCo. After paying all its expenses and setting aside a prudent amount for reserves, NEFCo's remaining net earnings are available for bonuses and other compensation adjustments for the foresters; none of these monies are distributed to the foundation. For its part, the foundation, which derives its income from dues, donations, grants, proceeds from timber harvests on its own properties, and the earnings from a modest endowment, makes grants to the NEFCo centers to support the work of the foresters in the area of education and forest policy. The foundation has undertaken to clarify and redefine its work, focusing its resources on land protection, education, and regional public policy in Massachusetts and across New England, and thereby has begun to move into the mainstream of the environmental movement, sharing in principle many of the announced objectives of the MFA described above.

GROWTH OF ENVIRONMENTAL ACTIVISM

While the MFA under Bob and Betty Russell's stewardship had been staking out its claim as an advocate for the land in general and the forest in particular, and the NEFF had continued in its traditional ways, the environmental movement in Massachusetts and across New England was bringing a multitude of new faces to front and center. Two of the country's most powerful and well-funded activist organizations, the Sierra Club and the Wilderness Society, had established beachheads here and, in the 1960s and 1970s, were staking out positions of prominence in the environmental movement. At the same time the Massachusetts Audubon Society had expanded its efforts into a broad spectrum of environmental initiatives and was experiencing dramatic growth in membership and endowment. The highly respected Trustees of Reservations was aggressively adding to its impressive treasure trove of magnificent properties throughout Massachusetts. New fledgling organizations began to spring up in Massachusetts and elsewhere, among them the avowedly radical RESTORE: The North Woods based in Concord, Massachusetts. As the NEFF, following its reorganization, has undertaken to raise its profile and "come to the table" with the host of stakeholders in the environmental community, this venerable and now re-energizing organization necessarily has encountered some harsh and divisive voices. Powerful advocates for wilderness preservation both nationally and regionally are locked in verbal — and in some places physical — combat with loggers, the timber products and paper industries, property rights advocates, government officials, and a host of other interest groups. The traditional civility that historically has characterized dialogue among disputants here in New England is beginning to yield to a strident rhetoric among polarized factions.

The MFA and the NEFF — organizations committed to both the preservation of the New England forests and the active management of these forests for timber production and other uses — have sought to stake out a middle ground. Many of the NEFF (now NEFCo) foresters, rightfully proud of their traditional standards of caring for all aspects of the woods wherein they work, are concerned that the forces of protectionism, driven by activist organizations that are thought to be the standard-bearers for locking up the forests as wilderness, will inevitably undermine their profession and their way of life. New terms such as "ecosystem-based management" and "ecoregionalism" are being advanced as necessary corollaries to the traditional forestry profession. There is concern on the part of many of these traditional allies from the forestry profession, the mills, and the timber products industries that the MFA and the NEFF will yield the middle ground to the entreaties of what are perceived as the environmental extremists. From the other direction, as centrist organizations, we are buffeted by criticisms that we are vulnerable to being co-opted by the sinister forces of the industry and property rights people.

These concerns recently came to the front and center when the NEFF, in October, 1995, applied for and was admitted to membership in the Northern Forest Alliance, a coalition of more than thirty environmental organizations concerned with the future of the 26,000,000 acres of forest, extending across New York, Vermont, New Hampshire, and Maine, know as the "northern forest," or the "great north woods." Currently, two officers of the NEFF, myself being one, serve on the Steering Committee (the policy making arm) of the Alliance. Demands that the NEFF withdraw from the Alliance have come from representatives of the timber products industry, the logging industry, and the timberland owners associations of two states; from the NEFCo foresters; and from some mill owners, among others, all asserting that the NEFF has allied itself with those who seek to lock up the northern forest as wilderness and therefore has abandoned its historic commitment to active forest management. Notwithstanding these criticisms, the NEFF has continued its membership in the Alliance, arguing that a centrist organization having expertise in sustainable forest management is essential to the deliberations of the Alliance in formulating its agenda for the future of this extraordinary forest resource.

What will be the future challenges for the private forestry movement and the enterprises that support it? What opportunities will there be for those organizations that seek to provide forums for rational debate and enlightened discussion of issues? Charles Thompson (recently appointed the NEFF's Managing Director), in "The Next 50 Years — Anything's Possible" (*The Woodland Steward*), speaks to these issues and raises some provocative questions about the future:

> What about the period from 1970 to 1995? In the course of his article on the growth of MFA, Greg Cox mentions a number of important forest issues, including taxation, regulation of cutting practices, and global environmental problems. But perhaps the most significant forestry occurrence since 1970 has been the perceived separation of forestry from "environmentalism." Although

forest conservationists were the pioneer environmental activists in the U.S., traditional, centrist groups such as MFA came to be viewed with increasing suspicion by an environmental movement that favored forest preservation over forest conservation. The good news is that recently the quality of dialogue within our region — among those with varying priorities — has begun to improve. At the national level, polarization seems to be at least as severe as it has ever been.

Who in 1945 would have predicted these events and trends? Not many. What's in store for the next 50 years? If you have confidence in your predictions, you're delusional or a genius. I can do no more than ask a few questions: will the climate change, the oceans rise and the forests change in response? How will the tug of war over property rights and public rights sort itself out? Will the chestnut be successfully restored? What dread pathogens will whisk away which species? How will the need to protect water quality play out in the woods? Will forest taxes be so high that only the very wealthy are able to own land? Will 10 acres be a big woodlot? Will the metric system really take hold, so that a 10 acre woodlot is really a 4.5 hectare woodlot? Will there be space colonies? Will paper be made from trees? Will lumber be a curious oddity? Will other renewable resources, especially fisheries, rebound? Will we be able to afford the luxury of individual transportation? If so, with what fuel? And so on.

What do YOU think? Send us your predictions and we'll bury a time capsule.[26]

Let us place a copy of this book in Charlie Thompson's time capsule. When the time capsule is opened 50 years from now, all the answers will be known.

SOME LINGERING QUESTIONS ABOUT LEADERSHIP AND PARTNERSHIP

In the course of writing this narrative of the private forestry movement in Massachusetts, some tantalizing questions have arisen, the possible answers to which provide fertile ground for study and speculation.

The story of the private forestry movement in Massachusetts re
veals that an impressive, even overwhelming, array of initiatives burst
upon the scene at the turn of the century and, in myriad ways, have
continued to the present time. A small number of enormously energetic, talented, dedicated men, with acute powers of observation and
the ability to change the course of events, emerged and led the way.

When asked why all this had not occurred earlier in the nation's
history, one of the authors of this book suggested that earlier people
simply had to work so hard to make ends meet that there was no luxury
of time for such endeavors. This theory presupposes the emergence at
the end of the nineteenth century of a "leisure class" of well-educated,
thoughtful individuals for whom the requisite devotion of time and
energy had become possible. If this theory is valid, it might be supposed
that a similar burgeoning of creativity was taking place in the arts and
sciences, recreation, and other activities. This offers a topic for further
investigation and discussion.

Men such as Chamberlain, Reynolds, Wharton, and MacKaye often
are referred to as "giants" in the private forestry movement in Massachusetts. In the early days, they seem to have been coming or going
through every door that we pass through. Some today lament that we
no longer find such "giants" in our midst. During authors' workshops
for this book, this concern provoked the following observations.

> These individuals were not "giants" at all. Referring to them as such is a
> distortion, creating "bigger-than-life" images of a relatively small
> number of ordinary individuals who happened to be on the scene
> when events called upon them to become actively involved.

> The work of the environmental movement and the role of private
> forests and forestry in relation to it have become usurped by large,
> complex, well-financed organizations characterized more by bu-
> reaucratic layers of management than by individual genius. The
> identity of the individual becomes subordinated to that of the
> enterprise that he or she serves, and the modern form of leader-
> ship is exercised collectively rather than individually.

> If collective leadership is the order of the day in the world of
> forests and forestry, is there a place for ordinary mortals from

diverse places and backgrounds? The affirmative evidence is heartening. In a world previously dominated by men (whether of the "giant" variety or otherwise), the Society for the Protection of New Hampshire Forests has chosen Jane Difley, formerly executive director of the Vermont Natural Resources Council and past president of the Society of American Foresters, to succeed Paul Bofinger as president/forester. The Appalachian Mountain Club recently has elected the second woman president in its 120-year history. Youth groups from the inner city are learning the rudiments of forestry through Boston's innovative Eagle Eye Institute. Men and women from business and the professions, many of whom have spent their working lives in urban surroundings, volunteer countless hours and give generously of their resources in support of the NEFF, the SPNHF, the MFA, and a host of other organizations that work or are concerned with forests and forestry. One can envision that when Charlie Thompson's time capsule is opened, the private forestry movement will have wholeheartedly embraced the strengths that can come from such diversity.

Historically, it has not been unusual for those working as staff or volunteers with each environmental or natural resource organization to boast of its unique qualities and capabilities while failing to give adequate recognition to the merits of some of its peer enterprises. But this is changing. Recent experience appears to demonstrate that, to an increasing degree, the preservation of significant amounts of privately owned wooded acreages and application of the methodology of ecosystem-based management both require the combined efforts and resources of multiple organizations and interested individuals as well.

Recently, a major forestland protection project, covering over 250 acres, was successfully completed in New Boston, New Hampshire. In this project, the SPNHF, the NEFF, New Hampshire Audubon, the local watershed association and several adjoining property owners collaborated to achieve the desired result. The days seem to be passing when the better "pitch master" makes the deal. It is becoming more difficult, if not impossible, for a single organization to go it alone. The people who staff the private forestry organizations such as the SPNHF, MFA, and NEFF bring different backgrounds, training, talents, and skills to their work, all of which contribute to a successful result. It also has been suggested that this willingness to work together can be attributed to increasing numbers of women in positions of responsibility in the environmental community. Bearing in mind Kelly McClintock's experience with the erosion of financial support for organizations joined in coalitions, the question arises of whether "partnering" poses such a risk for the future of these enterprises as they outgrow a measure of historic parochialism and acknowledge the values each brings to the table.

Perhaps these observations, and others found in this chapter, can help illuminate the way for future thoughtful dialogue and direction in the ever-evolving drama of the private forestry movement.

📖 NOTES

1. Bob Ricard, "Paving the Way, Sustaining the Future: New England's Forest Conservation Organizations," *The Woodland Steward* 25, no. 6 (Winter 1995–96): 4.
2. Robert McCullough, *The Landscape of Community* Hanover, N.H.: University Press of New England, 1995), p. 118.
3. Ibid., p. 117.
4. Alexis de Tocqueville, *Democracy in America,* edited by J. P. Mayer and Max Lerner and translated by George Lawrence (New York: Harper & Row, 1966), p. 178.
5. William B. Greeley, *Forests and Men* (New York: Doubleday, 1951), p. 57.
6. Ibid., p. 64.
7. M. Richard Applegate, *Massachusetts Forest and Park Association: A History* 1898-1973 (Massachusetts Forest and Park Association, 1974), p. 3.
8. Applegate, *Massachusetts Forest and Park Association: A History,* p. 3.
9. McCullough, *Landscape of Community,* p. 119.
10. Applegate, *Massachusetts Forest and Park Association: A History,* p. 3.
11. Ibid., p. 4.
12. A detailed account of Reynolds's contributions to the town forest movement is found in McCullough, *Landscape of Community* (see note 2).
13. M. Richard Applegate, *New England Forestry Foundation: A History* (New NEngland Forestry Foundation, Inc., 1969, 1975, 1982), p. 12.
14. M. Richard Applegate, *New England Forestry Foundation 1944-1969 25th Anniversary* (New England Forestry Foundation, 19TK), p. 19.
15. Applegate, *New England Forestry Foundation: A History,* pp. 23, 24.
16. McCullough, *Landscape of Community,* p. 238.

17. Ibid., p. 277.
18. Ibid., p. 289.
19. Ricard, "Paving the Way," p. 4.
20. Ibid., p. 5.
21. M. Richard Applegate, *Massachusetts Forest and Park Association: A History*, p. 50.
22. Ibid., p. 53.
23. Robert Bond (MFA president), quoting former Chief Forester Harold O. Cook in "Presidentís Notes," *The Woodland Steward* 25, no. 6 (Winter 1995–96): 3.
24. Greg Cox (MFA executive director), "MFA: 25 Years and Still Growing," *The Woodland Steward* 25, no. 6 (Winter 1995–96): 18, 19.
25. Ibid., 20, 23.
26. Charles Thompson, "The Next 50 Years: Anythingís Possible," *The Woodland Steward* 25, no. 6 (Winter 1995–96): 21.

Massachusetts State Forestry Programs

WILLIAM H. RIVERS

✤

ODAY, THE MASSACHUSETTS Department of Environmental Management, the Commonwealth's leading forestry agency, manages 280,000 acres of state forests and parks, administers programs that both regulate and promote forest management on 2.9 million acres of private forestland, and protects these same forests from fire, insects, and disease. The state's official involvement in managing the environment had its beginnings at the turn of this century. The DEM itself is relatively recent; its immediate predecessors include a number of organizations and state administrative units that ultimately became the Department of Environmental Management in 1975. All were involved with developing policy for Massachusetts' public and private forests. These entities include the Trustees of Reservations, the Massachusetts Forestry Association, the Office of the State Forester, the State Forest Commission, the Department of Conservation, the Department of Natural Resources, and others you will read about in this account.

The first major step taken by the Massachusetts legislature to become more directly involved in forestry matters was in 1892. In the 1890s there was no state-owned forest or park land in Massachusetts, with the exception of several thousand acres of desolate sand dunes and contorted pitch pine on the outer reaches of Cape Cod, known as the Province Lands. This once-productive forest had been common land since the early days of the Massachusetts Bay Colony. For almost 300 years it had been cut repeatedly to provide both lumber and fuelwood for nearby Provincetown. The organic matter and the nutrients in the sandy soil became so depleted that they could barely support tree growth. It was a classic example of a land that had been taken beyond the limits of sustainability — the Massachusetts Bay Colony's "Dust Bowl."

But the Province Lands were not representative of Massachusetts forests. At the turn of the century, much of the land in the rural areas of the state that was not under the plow or pastured was in transition from abandoned farmland to forest and consisted primarily of what was known as "old-field" white pine. While the biological process of succession was under way on hundreds of thousands of acres across the state, an ever-increasing demand for the products that could be manufactured from this second forest was being created in an economy that transcended Massachusetts and reached to foreign shores. A great deal of unregulated timber harvesting, fueled by both greed and ignorance, was undertaken to fill that demand. Estimates of the amount of timber harvested ranged from five to ten times the amount of that harvested today — from a forest about half the area of today's. The slash (tops and branches of trees that have been harvested for lumber) left in the wake of this cutting made Massachusetts' woodlands a virtual tinderbox. This circumstance and the fact that there were no organized rural fire-suppression agencies led to uncontrolled wildfires that often burned for days and scorched tens of thousands of acres of woodland each year.

Figure 1. Early-twentieth-century state fire truck used to assist town forest wardens in the suppression of forest fires. Edgar S. Burton lantern slide collection, Massachusetts Department of Environmental Management.

Figure 2. Standard forest fire fighting hand tools used before the development of the Fitzhenry-Guptill pump and the modern, mechanized brush-breaker. John H. Thurston lantern slide collection, Massachusetts Department of Environmental Management.

A public outcry against these conditions prompted the Massachusetts legislature to establish the Trustees of Reservations in 1892, which was authorized "to purchase, preserve and administer areas of unusual scenic, historic or natural interest for the benefit of the public." Its first accomplishments were to carry out a study regarding the advisability of establishing a park system in the metropolitan Boston area. Over the next eight years, one of the most revered park systems in the world was created at a cost of over $6 million as nearly 10,000 acres were acquired and connected by 17 miles of parkway. Included in this system were the Blue Hills and the Middlesex Fells Reservations.

In the latter part of the same decade, a private organization presented to the state its first state forest reserve. In 1897, a number of conservation-minded citizens united to form the Massachusetts Forestry Association (MFA). At that time, Mount Greylock in northern Berkshire County, the Commonwealth's highest peak, was under assault by loggers. The highly visible east face of the mountain had been clear-cut and plans were being made to harvest the timber on its north slope. There was a great deal of local concern about this and it was brought to the attention of the MFA. The association lobbied for and received $25,000 from the state legislature and secured $16,000 in donations from private sources to acquire the Greylock summit as the first state reservation in 1898. This was the beginning of a movement to acquire public forest land in Massachusetts; six years later the Commonwealth would have a state forester; and eventually the means would be created to put a system of forest reserves in place.

🍂 The Place of Foresters and Forest Policy in State Government

THE STATE FORESTER'S OFFICE

In 1904 the Commonwealth of Massachusetts, by an act of the legislature, created the Office of the State Forester and appropriated the sum of $5,000 to support the office. On August 12 of that year Alfred Akerman, who had been the state forester of Connecticut, became the first man appointed to the post of state forester. The responsibilities of the position were clearly stated in Chapter 409, Acts of 1904: the state forester was to promote the "perpetuation, extension, and proper management of forest lands within the Commonwealth, both public and private."

One of the state forester's many duties was to conduct a course of instruction at the Massachusetts Agricultural College (which ultimately became the University of Massachusetts, Amherst) on the art and science of forestry. Akerman's perspective on the course was as follows:

> This course is designed to prepare prospective farmers for the management of their woodlots. It is not designed to fit men for the practice of the profession, which usually takes two or three years of close application after the undergraduate courses have been finished. The course at the Agricultural College would no more fit a man for the practice of forest engineering than a short course on home sanitation would fit a man to practise medicine.

The first course was held in February and March of 1905. It consisted of 12 lectures and 2 field exercises and had an enrollment of 29 men.

Further, "The state forester may, upon suitable request, give to any person owning or controlling forest lands aid or advice in the management thereof," and charge the landowner or organizations he lectured to for traveling and subsistence expenses. The act also gave the state forester the authority to establish a forest nursery on the grounds of the Massachusetts Agricultural College at Amherst.

In his first year in office, Akerman began two projects that would last for several years: a study of the growth and yield of eastern white pine, in cooperation with the U.S. Forest Service and Harvard University, and the development of a forest map of the Commonwealth, in cooperation with the state Bureau of Statistics of Labor. A forestry library of 141 books and pamphlets was also assembled, both as reference material for the staff, and for the benefit of "all who may wish to use it."

In the previous eight years the legislature had appropriated $6 million for the acquisition of metropolitan parks and additional amounts to acquire a number of state reservations, but Akerman felt that "the Commonwealth ought to extend its policy of park reservation to include genuine State Forests." He also suggested that portions of the existing state reservations could produce timber "without any reduction in their value as parks. . . . But the lands mentioned are small in area, and the State might well follow the precedent established by several other states, and acquire lands for the purpose of growing timber on them." By then the state of New York had acquired a 1.4 million-acre forest reserve, and Pennsylvania, 572,000 acres of public forestland. Citing a recent 900-acre land purchase by the state of Connecticut, Akerman declared that "large areas of overgrown, stony, abandoned pastures, cutover lands that have been burned repeatedly, scrub oak lands and the like, that are in such condition that an individual owner cannot afford to improve them" could form the basis for a state forest system in Massachusetts. Such lands could be acquired for less than $5 an acre — a statement that those who followed him would wish hadn't been made. Not until 1955 would this ceiling be eliminated. Akerman went on to describe further uses of such reservations. They would:

> . . . furnish recreation grounds for the people. This use for recreative purposes under reasonable restrictions is not inconsistent with the production of timber. . . . The educational effect of well-managed State forests is one of their chief advantages. They should, as far as is consistent with their economical management,

be widely distributed over the State, in order that they may serve as object lessons in practical forestry.

Akerman's third annual report, submitted on September 15, 1906, ended with an announcement of his resignation. He had been elected chairman of the Forest Engineering Department at the University of Georgia, his alma mater. In a note to the governor he stated:

> I do not leave the service of the Commonwealth because of dissatisfaction with my work; on the contrary, I have enjoyed my service here as only one man who loves to fight for a good cause. Nor does the place in Georgia carry a larger salary; but I believe that it offers a better opportunity to forward the cause for which we foresters are working, and I feel it my duty to go.

After 25 months of service Akerman could look back on successfully laying the foundations for many of the programs that are still with us almost a century later.

Frank William Rane assumed the position of state forester immediately following Akerman's departure in 1906. Rane had spent the previous eleven years at New Hampshire College (now the University of New Hampshire), where he taught agricultural economics and forestry. Initially he saw his charge as being "to carry forward the work already in hand and get thoroughly in touch with the purpose of the office." In a letter addressed "To All Interested in the Forestry Problems of Massachusetts," he extended an invitation "to consult my office at any and all times on forestry matters, and let it be generally known that the office is established by the state to accomplish great good for the whole state in general and each individual in so far as practicable." Three months later, in closing his first annual report, Rane pointed out the need for the enactment of some "practical laws" to do the following:

- Improve forest-fire protection
- Regulate forest taxation
- Develop a state-forest reserve policy
- Develop an educational program to enlighten citizens on the great economic importance of the forest crop

In 1910, Rane increased his general staff to include a total of four assistant foresters charged with moth work, forestry management, nursery work, and one to be a general assistant. Two motorcycles were purchased for the foresters' use. He also had an administrative staff of one secretary and four clerks. The increased staff necessitated a move from the drafty office in Room 247A of the State House to the tenth floor of number 6 Beacon Street.

Basking in the wake of a major budget increase, Rane, speaking to the Third National Conservation Congress in Kansas City in September 1911, stated:

> Speaking of fishing and game, forestry, natural history and Appalachian clubs, I am frank to say that I believe there are no people on earth who are more in love with nature herself, heart and soul, than our Massachusetts people. We have organizations galore, and they are not only organized, but bubbling full of real activity, and are accomplishing things. Were you the State Forester of Massachusetts, I can guarantee that you could spend your whole time simply lecturing on conservation or forestry, as the demands are so great and the work so popular.

Rane had the support not only of the general public, but also of the legislature. In the closing paragraphs of his 1914 annual report, he stated:

> I am pleased to say that with the legislation of the last General Court, the general program outlined by this department for securing the fundamentals of a State forest policy, which has extended over a period of eight years, has been covered. We are, therefore, now in a position to exert our best energies in accomplishing results. Let us all have a part in this splendid work.

By then, the legislature had created a Bureau of Forest Fire Control, had established a process to acquire a system of state forest reserves, had established a demonstration reforestation program and several forest-tree nurseries, and had put in place a more equitable approach for taxing forestland.

Following this period of great gains, Rane faced difficult times during the First World War, when his program was depleted by decreased appropriations and the resignations of a number of his staff to serve in the military. The greatest demands placed on his program during this period centered around developing supplies of fuelwood to alleviate shortages of coal brought about by increased wartime demands. Nearing the end of his tenure, a tired Rane, looking back over the previous year, stated in his 1919 annual report:

> When an organization is running well and its policies are clearly defined and understood, there is little trouble meeting all ordinary emergencies. When, however, such calamities as war conditions break in upon a department like this and fairly strip it of labor, both skilled and ordinary, and materials of all kinds advance in price while appropriations remain the same, or are made less, it inevitably follows that a department is powerless to do aught else than to adapt itself to the new conditions.

CREATION OF THE DEPARTMENT OF CONSERVATION

In 1918, a state constitutional convention was held whose end result was a complete reorganization and reduction in the number of agencies, boards, and commissions in the state government into just 20 departments. The Office of the State Forester, the State Forest Commission, the Commission of Fisheries and Game, and the Department of Animal Industry were combined into a newly formed Department of Conservation which included a Division of Forestry, a Division of Fisheries and Game, and a Divison of Animal Industry. A. L. Bazeley of Uxbridge was appointed commissioner of the Department of Conservation and also the director of the Division of Forestry.

This reorganization also created the position of Chief Forester. Harold O. Cook, a 1907 graduate of the Harvard Forestry School, who went to work for the State Forester's office that same year was appointed to that position. He served in that capacity until his death in May of 1962. Of particular note were his efforts in overseeing the implementation of the CCC program in 1933. In eulogizing Cook in his 1962 annual report, Director Raymond J. Kenney stated: "Perhaps no monument of marble or bronze will be erected to his memory but wherever forests grow on hill or in dale — there will be his lasting memorial unmarred by winter snow or summer sun." Interestingly, a granite memorial bearing his name was placed in a meadow in the Colrain State Forest in 1967 and that forest renamed in his honor.

Cook was followed in the Chief Forester's position by John H. (Jack) Lambert, Jr. who served in that capacity until his retirement in 1976. While a student, Lambert began his career with the agency in the 1920s as a member of a forest inventory crew involved with preparing a county by county inventory of the state. State forester Robert Parmenter was his supervisor. After his graduation from the University of Maine and later the Yale Forestry School he served a brief stint (ended by the Depression) with the Hollingsford and Whitney (now Scott) Paper Company in Waterville, Maine. He came to work for the Department of Conservation in 1932 and served in several short-lived temporary positions. He eventually became the supervisor of the Beartown State Forest in Monterey in December of that year. He was promoted to forester during the CCC era where he was placed in charge of the planning and overseeing the forestry activities of the CCC camps in the southern Berkshires. Following that he worked as a district fire warden and district forester and was the district forester in the northeastern part of the state prior to assuming the office of Chief Forester in 1962. The indefatigable Lambert's name was often associated with "special projects" that were in addition to his normal duties. The most notable of these was his assignment as an assistant to the State Forestry Committee in the 1940s in the development and early administration of the Forest Cutting Practices Act.

During Bazeley's tenure with the department (1920–1933), a significant amount of state forestland was acquired and great progress made in many other aspects of the department's work, particularly the accommodation of recreational use of state forestland. In 1931, no doubt prompted by increased demands for recreation in the state forests resulting from widespread automobile ownership and the free time created by the Great Depression, the legislature created a Division of Parks within the Department of Conservation.

In 1933, Samuel York of Cummington was appointed to succeed A. L. Bazeley as Commissioner of Conservation. That year the Department of Conservation was reorganized. Now the conservation commissioner acted as state forester and had three divisions under him: the Division of Forestry, the Division of Parks, and the Division of Fisheries and Game.

In 1935, Ernest J. Dean of Chilmark was appointed by Governor

James Curley to succeed York as Commissioner of Conservation. Both York and Dean served in the tumultuous Depression years; their tenures were indelibly marked by the activities of the Civilian Conservation Corps (CCC), which had a a tremendous impact on the state forests and on the establishment of a system of state recreation facilities.

The late thirties saw the Department of Conservation roiled by political controversies. The cleanup work following the 1938 hurricane prompted a number of allegations about fraudulent contracts. During the same period, there was a general dissatisfaction about the conduct of the department. This was related primarily to the practice of relying on political patronage to fill management positions rather than utilizing technically trained career employees. In 1939, no less than eight different proposals for the reorganization of the department were considered by the legislature.

The end result of all of this turmoil was the passage of Chapter 491 of the Acts of 1939, which created five divisions within a newly reorganized Department of Conservation: the Divisions of Forestry, Parks and Recreation, Wildlife Research and Management, Fisheries and Game, and Marine Fisheries. Raymond J. Kenney, who had joined what was then the Fish and Game Commission in a clerical position in 1918 was appointed Commissioner of the Department in 1940. Prior to that Kenney had served as the Director of the Division of Fisheries and Game from 1931 until 1936 and, following that, to various positions within the Division of Forestry. Kenney served as commissioner until 1944 when he returned to the Division of Forestry and was replaced by Archibald Sloper. Kenney would serve the Commonwealth in various positions (his last appointment was as the Director of the Division of Forests and Parks, from June of 1945 until his death in 1963). Kenney was followed by former District Fire Warden Francis B. Mahoney who served until 1966 when he retired and was succeeded by Bruce Gullion, a former Service Forester from Berkshire County. Gullion served into the period of the Department of Environmental Management which began in 1975. Commissioner of Conservation Archibald Sloper served until January of 1948 when he was succeeded by Arthur Lyman who had been the Commissioner of the Massachusetts Department of Corrections. Lyman served as Commissioner through the last years of the Department of Conservation and briefly into the era of the Department of Natural Resources in 1953.

THE DEPARTMENT OF NATURAL RESOURCES AND THE DEPARTMENT OF ENVIRONMENTAL MANAGEMENT

In 1953 the legislature again reorganized the agency: it created a Department of Natural Resources, governed by a board, made up of five individuals appointed to staggered terms by the governor. Arthur Lyman remained on as commissioner of the agency for a brief time until Francis W. Sargent, who would later become governor, was appointed the new department's second commissioner by the members of the Board of Natural Resources. He served from 1953 until 1959.

The Division of Forestry and the Division of Parks and Recreation were combined into a single Division of Forests and Parks, which was comprised of the Bureaus of Forest Development, Fire Control, Insect Pest Control, and Recreation.

The third commissioner was Charles H. W. Foster, who was appointed to fill the vacancy left by Sargent when he left to head the national Outdoor Recreation Resources Review Commission, which was in existence from 1959 until 1962. In 1971, with the creation of the Executive Office of Environmental Affairs, Dr. Foster became the Commonwealth's first secretary of environmental affairs. The Division of Forests and Parks remained basically unchanged, but as of 1975 it was under the Department of Environmental Management, as the Department of Natural Resources was renamed in that year. Its commissioner, Arthur W. Brownell, reported directly to the secretary of environmental affairs. Basically, this administrative structure remains in place today.

🍃 Forest Protection

WILDFIRES

Though forest fires blackened the landscape early in this century, there was no means by which the damage could be quantified. Informal estimates by Akerman and Rane placed the acreage burned each year in the tens of thousands — often up to 100,000 acres. The first attempt at creating an organized fire-suppression system in Massachusetts was in 1907, when the legislature passed a law empowering the selectmen in each of the Commonwealth's towns to appoint a forest warden, their salaries to be the responsibility of the individual towns. The state forester could, from time to time, require the fire wardens to supply information to him relating to forest acreage, reforestation work, insects and disease conditions, and forest fires. For their time spent on these activities for the state they were to be compensated by the state forester at the rate of 35 cents an hour. In his 1907 annual report, State Forester Frank Rane stated:

> Through this law we now have a thoroughly systematized plan of usefulness, a natural channel through which it is believed much good to our forest interest must result. When we once get a corps of competent forest wardens, one in each of our three hundred and twenty (eligible) towns, who can intelligently handle forest fires and other forestry matters of vital concern, we shall have made great progress, both from the economic and aesthetic standpoints.

Within one year, 343 wardens had been appointed by the towns and cities having forest land within their borders. To give his cadre of wardens their "proper credentials," Rane distributed numbered badges. His vision for the forest wardens went far beyond fire control work:

> As I stated last year, the State Forester hopes to so educate his wardens that they will become, in a sense, town foresters, who shall keep the importance of forestry and how to perpetuate and manage the same practically directly before the people. With such an organization, when gypsy moths, pine blight, fires, etc. are troublesome, or, on the other hand, when people desire to reforest lands or thin and give proper care to their woodlots, in either case here is a man to whom they may look for advice.

In 1910 there were 1,531 forest and grass fires in the state, affecting a total of 42,808 acres. State Forester Rane would declare that "the fire demon each year lays its insidious claws on a valuable portion of our natural heritage." The principal causes of these fires were "railroad locomotives" (34 percent), "unknown" (25 percent), "burning brush" (8 percent), "smokers" (6 percent), and "boys" (6 percent). Some of the other, lesser causes listed for that year include: berry pickers, carelessness, children playing (as opposed to "boys"), fire balloons, fireworks and fire crackers, mayflower parties, steam sawmills, and steam rollers.

In 1911 significantly more fires were reported (2,536) and more acreage was burned (99,693 acres) than in the previous two years. Most of the fires occurred during a droughty spring — over 90,000 acres burned by June. That year proved to be a banner year not only for forest fires in the Commonwealth but for the state forester's fire control budget as well. The passage of the Weeks Law that same year, which provided federal financial assistance to states that had established fire control organizations, was no doubt influential as well. That year the Massachusetts legislature appropriated $10,000 to create a forest fire control agency; the same amount was allocated for the general forestry and the reforestation accounts.

This generous budget allowed Rane to appoint Maxwell C. Hutchins as the Commonwealth's first state fire warden and allowed him to begin the process of assembling what has evolved into today's Bureau of Forest Fire Control. Hutchins was recruited from New York, where he had been employed by the New York Forest Service in the Adirondack region for seven years. He set about his work that fall by organizing the Commonwealth into five districts and appointing a district fire warden in each one. He and his wardens were mandated by statute to "aid and advise" the municipal forest wardens, unlike the case in some states, where the state fire control organization has complete jurisdiction over fire suppression activities. Public support for fire control as well as other forestry programs continued. Along with the legislation that created the Bureau, there was a provision allowing the state to reimburse smaller rural towns for 50 percent of the cost, up to $250, of fire-suppression equipment that they might purchase. With this encouragement many towns began to assemble efficient fire fighting forces with equipment they might not have been able to afford otherwise. Hutchins's budget for the bureau continued to grow, and for 1915 it was $28,000, almost three times his first budget.

In closing his 1924 annual report Hutchins stated:

> I do not feel that this report would be complete without saying a word here about the splendid spirit shown by my assistants, the district fire wardens. They are in constant attendance at the fires in their districts, often being absent from home day and night, sometimes obliged to snatch such rest as they can get by sleeping

out on the ground. . . . There is no reward for such service as this, the men simply doing it as a matter of duty. But at least the public should know that such service is being given.

The Bureau of Forest Fire Control continued to grow. In 1929 there were 9 districts; in 1950 a twelfth district was added, and today there are 13 fire districts. Interestingly, district thirteen is not shown on any map, nor is it listed on any roster. However, there is a district fourteen! Legislation providing for a state patrol system was enacted in 1929. Initially, only Barnstable County took advantage of the law by putting two fire patrolmen in place. Eventually, all fire districts would have at least one patrolman.

Another early goal of Hutchins's was to erect across the state a total of 15 "observation stations," as they were then called, along with the necessary telephone lines and a staff of observers. Massachusetts only had one fire tower at that time, in Plymouth, which had been built by the town. The first of these new observation stations, put into operation on August 14, 1911, was the observatory on the top of the Summit House on Mount Wachusett in Princeton. A similar arrangement was made in the Mount Tom Summit House in Holyoke. In that first year, towers and their communications systems were put in place at 17 locations; two more than Hutchins's goal. Some were constructed of wood or were former windmill towers. Some of these did not even have cabs to protect the observer from the elements.

The following winter, Hutchins' staff prepared maps and developed a triangulation system that would be used

> . . . in extreme cases where the observer is not sure as to the exact location of a fire. This system is not in general use, as far as known, in any other section of the country, Massachusetts being the first to adopt it for forest fire purposes. By this method fires can be located more quickly and much more accurately than would otherwise be possible.

The system proved to be quite effective. In 1914 observers in the 24 stations in operation spotted 3,013 fires out of a total of 3,181 that were reported that year.

Public interest in the program was great: in 1930 the fire-tower sites attracted 100,000 visitors "from every state in the Union and nearly all the foreign countries." Eventually, picnic tables and fireplaces were installed at a number of towers and were well received by the recreating public. The towers suffered with each major hurricane, but they were always replaced quickly. At the peak of the program, in the 1950s and 1960s, approximately 50 towers were in operation. Today those that are still in operation, are supplemented by aerial surveillance from fixed-wing aircraft during severe fire weather.

Two major forest fire laws enacted early in the century had a profound effect on both the occurrence and the severity of forest fires. The first of these was the "Permit Law" (Chapter 209, Acts of 1908) that required any person having an open air fire to receive a permit from the town forest warden. Presumably the forest warden would only issue permits when burning could be done safely, although this did not always prove to be the case. The second of these laws was the "Slash Law" (Chapter 101, Acts of 1914), which required landowners and timber harvesters to treat the slash left from logging by lopping it and removing it from the areas adjacent to property lines. Both of these laws have been amended a number of times since their passage, but they remain in effect today.

Beginning in the 1940s, through the efforts of U.S. Forest Service publicists, Smokey the Bear, an orphaned black bear cub from the Lincoln National Forest in New Mexico, became the symbol of the nation's forest fire prevention program. The Forest Service made available all manner of promotional material, ranging from bumper stickers to comic books, for distribution by the Bureau of Forest Fire Control. Several Smokey suits were acquired and were employed at schools, fairs, parades and other public gatherings to get the prevention message across to schoolchildren as well as adults. The Smokey character is one of the most universally recognized symbols today in American advertising.

As the science of forest fire control became more sophisticated, meteorology was increasingly recognized as a basis for planning fire suppression activities. Beginning in 1919, forecasts from the Blue Hills Meteorological Bureau were used as a basis for planning daily activities. In 1927 a cooperative venture between the U.S. Weather Bureau, the U.S. Forest Service, and the Department of Conservation established four weather stations across the state. By 1931 both WBZ and WEEI radio were broadcasting daily forest fire weather reports during the fire season. Hutchins assessed the service as follows:

> We find it a distinct advantage, especially during a drought, to be able at a moment's notice to get weather forecasts which we can transmit to our observers, as so much depends not only on upon when rain is expected, but also upon wind direction and velocity, all of which play an important part in extinguishing forest fires.

This much-appreciated service continued through the 1930s, but was halted in the interest of national defense in 1942 for fear that it would provide enemy aircraft with useful information.

On April 12, 1927, the relative humidity dropped to 10 percent, the lowest reading ever recorded in the state until that time. During the 13-day period following that date, 1,251 fires were reported by the observation towers. Although the total number of fires during that period was not especially high, the difficulty of controlling them was reflected by the fact that the average acreage burned per fire was approximately 50 percent greater than in the two previous years. Nineteen thirty also proved to be an especially difficult year for fire control forces in Massachusetts with periods of drought occurring in both the spring and fall. That year a total of 72,998 acres were burned by 1,922 fires, the worst year since 1911. The high rate of unemployment resulting from the Depression may have exacerbated the situation. Hutchins stated that not only the extreme weather was to blame for the great number of fires that year, but also many of the unemployed, some of whom were

> . . . engaged in extinguishing fires and were continually increasing them that they might lengthen their time of employment. We also had an increasingly large number of boys and young men who were constantly starting new fires not for the purpose of employment but who were possessed with a mania for starting fires.

Cape Cod and Plymouth County, owing to the extremely flammable nature of their pitch pine and scrub oak vegetation, have been the scene of many large wildland fires. According to Hutchins:

> Each year great waste and destruction from forest fires seem to visit some section of the Cape country. This condition has continued so long and become so common that not only are many thousands of acres reduced to acorn brush deserts, but from their being burned over every few years as they accumulate enough vegetation to feed the flames, there is little likelihood of conditions

improving until something is done. It is generally acknowledged that these fires originate from mayflower gatherers and berry pickers.

These fires often burned several thousand acres at a time and, on at least two occasions, cost firefighters their lives. Two Plymouth firefighters were killed in 1937 and three firefighters were killed in a fire on the Shawme State Forest in Sandwich in 1938.

Myles Standish State Forest was the scene of perhaps the most serious Massachusetts forest fire in this century. At three in the afternoon on May 7, 1957, three incendiary fires were set in the southwest corner of the forest. Winds were from the southwest at 20 to 25 miles per hour and the forest was tinder-dry. Two of the fires were controlled quickly. The third one gained momentum while the other two were being extinguished. By the time firefighters reached the third fire, it was too late. By the end of the day, the fire had traveled 12 miles and burned 12,500 acres, 3,000 on the forest itself, much of it white pine plantations that had been established in the 1920s and 1930s. On its way to the ocean, where it finally stopped, the fire jumped Route 3 and several backfires that had been set to stop it.

On May 23-25, 1964, another serious fire burned on the Myles Standish State Forest. On the first day it consumed 1,000 acres. On the third day, several outbreaks merged to form one fire that burned 4,500 acres in 2 hours and 15 minutes.

As stated previously, the railroads were the single greatest cause of forest fires in the Commonwealth at the turn of this century, causing as much as 42 percent of all fires. At that time it was estimated that there were over 2,000 locomotives operating on 2,500 miles of right-of-way in Massachusetts. The first legislation directed at the problem was to require spark arresters on all locomotives and establish a number of state inspectors within the state's Railroad Commission to enforce the law. While this was somewhat effective in dealing with local traffic, a number of tramp locomotives from out-of-state lacking the spark arresters continued to cause fires. In 1909 legislation was enacted that required the railroads not only to pay for damages from fires caused by their trains, but to reimburse the cities and towns for the cost of extinguishing the fires they caused. Eventually, it became more cost-effective for the railroads to undertake hazard-reduction work along their rights-of-way. In 1929 Hutchins stated: "It is only within very recent years that the railroad officials have realized that it was to their advantage to expend money for prevention (spark arresters and fuel reduction along their tracks) rather than to pay fire payrolls for fighting fires." That year railroad fires, once the leading cause of fires, accounted for less than 20 percent of the Commonwealth's forest fires.

The state forester's staff assembled two fully equipped fire wagons in 1910 as demonstrations of how the town fire wardens might assemble their own equipment:

> The larger wagon is intended for two horses, and costs, all equipped, about $450. The equipment consists of fourteen chemical extinguishers; fourteen galvanized cans, each holding two extra charges of water and chemicals; shovels; rakes; mattocks; and spare chemical charges. The equipment is carried in racks and cases, not only so that it will ride safely, but also so that it can be conveniently carried into the woods. Eight men can find accommodation on this wagon. The smaller wagon, drawn by one horse, has all the equipment of the larger, but less in amount. It will carry four men, and costs, all equipped, about $300.

Prompted by a number of large fires in 1913 that could not be brought under control by several inefficient town forest-fire organizations, Hutchins reported that there had been

> ...6 serious fires that were allowed to burn several days without extinguishment.... A careful investigation of these 6 fires has revealed in each case the presence of one or more common causes, namely, inefficiency in the town forest fire organization, lack of proper forest firefighting equipment and indifference on the part of the general public until such time as the fire assumed sufficient proportions to threaten their villages and homes.

As a consequence, Hutchins proposed that the Department of Conservation acquire "at least two motor trucks equipped with modern fire apparatus and capable of carrying from 10 to 15 men trained in forest fire work." He suggested that one of these trucks be stationed on Cape Cod and another in central Massachusetts so that any serious fire in the eastern part of the state could be reached in two or three hours.

In 1916 the State Forester's Office purchased the first fire truck to be used as a demonstration to the towns of an ideal fire truck. It carried "three double forester pumps, six extinguishers, five one-man pumps, ten 5-gallon Marshfield cans for water, six shovels, six wire brooms, two axes and two grub hoes." The unit went on tour that summer and fall and was exhibited at a number of fairs.

"We have had an opportunity this year of giving the power gasoline pump a thorough tryout and it certainly has proved its usefulness" was Hutchins' comment following the 1924 season's trials of portable pumps manufactured by the Fitzhenry-Guptill Company of Cambridge. That year, four pumps went into use, in Carver, Westborough, Winchendon, and Westfield, and the following year, 10 more units were purchased. There were plans to acquire more pumps and trucks for conveying them when funding would permit. By 1928 the department had 22 of these units in service.

The Fitzhenry-Guptill pump was quite heavy compared to its contemporaries, weighing close to 300 pounds, but its durability and efficiency overshadowed the weight limitations. It was also unaffected by sand and other debris, and it could use from 4,000 to 5,000 feet of high-pressure one-inch hose.

As more of the pumps came into use, efforts were made to construct "water holes" throughout the state forest system. These water holes might be "an abandoned well, a hole dug in a swamp, or a natural pool in a running brook. . . . They serve the same purpose as a fire hydrant on a city street." The system of water holes would be expanded substantially by the CCC (Civilian Conservation Corps) and later by state forest crews. In addition to their value as water sources for firefighting, water holes also benefited wildlife and were attractive landscape elements.

Hutchins' 1934 report concerned itself with the matter of communications:

> The importance of the radio in forest fire prevention has been demonstrated in a small way at our Hanson and Harvard towers. Two-way sets were tried out and results obtained were very satisfactory. There is no question but radio will play a very important part in the future in our forest fire work. It is simply a matter of funds to equip our observation towers and district cars with two-way sets so that the men in the field can get in direct touch with

the fire situation. I believe that within a very short time radio equipment will be within reach of not only our department but also the various town wardens.

An experiment in the use of two-way radios was undertaken at Myles Standish State Forest in 1935. One radio was installed in the fire tower and another in the superintendent's car. Although these were only amateur sets, they had an effective range of 10 miles. Following this impressive demonstration, the county forest wardens association lobbied for an appropriation of $2,000 to equip five towers and three patrol cars with radios. In 1936 additional monies were sought for radios for five towers and three patrol cars in southeastern Massachusetts, and in 1937 monies were appropriated for radios in Worcester County. In time, the entire agency would be dependent on radios, not only for firefighting but for day-to-day communications.

In 1935 the department replaced four older trucks with custom-built new fire trucks that Hutchins felt were more suitable for forest-fire fighting than anything on the market. The larger of these trucks had a front-mounted 100-gallon-per-minute pump, a 500-gallon tank, and a portable pump with 4,000 feet of hose. These units were stationed at the Myles Standish and Shawme state forests. Two smaller units in the central part of the state had smaller tanks, but otherwise carried the same pumps and hoses.

The largest single addition to the department's stock of firefighting equipment came in 1939 in the wake of the 1938 hurricane. Fourteen cab-over-engine, short-wheelbase trucks, each equipped with a 100-gallon power takeoff pump, a portable Fitzhenry-Guptill pump, 2,500 feet of one-inch hose, and 500 feet of one-and-one-half inch hose were purchased. These trucks, added to the department's existing 24 units, brought the state's total number of fire trucks to 38.

Of perhaps even greater significance that year was the introduction of what was claimed to be the first "brush-breaker," a truck invented by Charles Cherry, superintendent of the Myles Standish State Forest. The unit was equipped with a 1,000-gallon tank with rear-mounted pumps and was capable of being driven through brush and small trees. Today, these vehicles have evolved into high-clearance, four-wheel-drive vehicles surrounded by a rugged pipe frame for pushing over small trees.

Skid plates protect their undercarriages, and they are equipped with a water- or foam-delivery system.

Maxwell C. Hutchins retired on December 26, 1943, after 31 years of service to the Bureau of Fire Control. Through his pioneering efforts he had built one of the most effective wildland-fire fighting organizations in the Northeast.

INSECTS AND PESTS

In 1868 a visiting instructor in astronomy at Harvard University, Dr. Leopold Trouvelot, was engaged in trying to breed a variety of silkworm that could survive in New England's harsh climate. His plan was to cross-breed the Asian silk moth with the hardy European gypsy moth. When the cages were damaged, a number of the caterpillars escaped into his suburban Medford neighborhood. Trouvelot warned of their potential danger in several entomological papers and stated that efforts should be made to eradicate them. His warnings went unheeded for several years while the insect established a viable population. Ten years later, in 1889, the gypsy moth population had reached alarming proportions and in 1890 the legislature appropriated a sum of $25,000 for its control. Initially this task was delegated to the Massachusetts Board of Agriculture.

To complicate matters, another insect of European origin, the brown-tail moth, was discovered in Somerville in the early 1890s. At first its origins were unknown, but eventually circumstantial evidence pointed toward shipments of dormant rose bushes from France and Holland made to a florist's greenhouse near the Somerville depot of the Fitchburg Railroad. By 1897, a serious infestation, two miles in diameter and centered around the greenhouse, was under way. The infestation "made up in severity what it lacked in extent":

> In the central district the devastation was almost complete. The pear and apple trees, on which the majority of the winter webs had been spun, were first stripped. Such remarkably large numbers of these insects were harbored by these trees that their leaf supply was soon consumed, and the half-grown caterpillars were forced to migrate in search of food. In this migration shade trees suffered

as severely as fruit trees from the attacks of the insects. Willows, elms, maples and lindens often were completely defoliated. In their mad search for food the insects swarmed along fences and sidewalks, making the latter slippery with their crushed bodies, and even entered houses. Rose bushes, grape vines, garden crops and even grasses were consumed by the hungry insects. By the middle of June the trees in the central infested district appeared as if swept by fire (Fernald and Kirkland, 1903)

Not only was the defoliation of fruit and shade trees problematic but, in addition, the bodies of the older caterpillars and, to some extent, the moths contained microscopic hairs that caused severe rashes when they came in contact with one's skin. One did not necessarily have to come in direct contact with the caterpillars to be affected. The skins cast by the larvae in molting and pupal cases contained these same hairs. The slightest breeze in a heavily infested area was enough to expose individuals to this discomfort. People could not work outside of their homes in their yards or gardens without being "poisoned" by these hairs. Fernald and Kirkland (1903) cite this description of the affliction by Dr. O. A. Givson of Somerville:

The trouble began with an intense irritation; then an eruption appeared, resembling exzema [sic], with a sort of watery blister on the top. There was intense irritation all over the body, on the head, arms and limbs. I saw numbers and numbers of cases of this poisoning; I should say nearly a hundred cases in all came under my observation. The irritation seemed to remain, and was much worse than that caused by poison oak or poison ivy, and was not so easily gotten rid of. . . . Some cases were decidedly obstinate, but no case was serious enough to menace the life of the patient.

Vaseline, numerous coal-tar disinfectants and alcohol were applied topically to reduce the inflammations. "So prevalent is the dermatitis from the caterpillar in the metropolitan district in the summer months that druggists put out special lotions for the brown-tail moth itch, many of which are meritorious" (Fernald and Kirkland, 1903).

The localized infestation of 1897 spread rapidly in a northeasterly direction following gale winds on July 12-14 of that year. These winds coincided with the peak of pupal emergence and scattered moths all the way to Seabrook, New Hampshire, 40 miles away. Eventually the pest made its way into Kittery, Maine, on a shipment of household goods, and to St. Johns, New Brunswick, presumably on a vessel that had sailed from Boston.

In 1898 the Massachusetts Board of Agriculture was directed "to take charge of the work of exterminating the brown tail moth" in addition to its previously assigned duties relating to gypsy moth control. Control efforts for both the gypsy moth and brown-tail moth consisted of spraying with various arsenical compounds; wrapping tree trunks with burlap, under which the larvae would hide in the daytime, after which they could be killed by crushing; painting egg masses with creosote; and applying a sticky compound first made up of printers ink, coal tar, or other sticky substances and, later, a commercial compound known as "Tanglefoot" in bands around tree trunks. Another method used for the control of the brown-tail was to remove the nests in which the larvae overwintered and destroy them by burning or other means. While this was effective on small numbers of trees whose nests could be reached from the ground, it was obviously not efficient on tall trees where climbing was necessary.

After 10 years, the gypsy moth control program, which began in 1890, appeared to be so effective that the Massachusetts state legislature appointed a committee to study the need for continuing the control program. In part, the committee's report stated:

> It appears that the fears of the farmers throughout the state have been unnecessarily and unwarrantably aroused, evidently for the purpose of securing the effect of those fears upon the matter of the annual appropriations. . . . We do not share these exaggerated fears, and the prophecies of devastation and ruin are unwarranted and in the most charitable view are but the fancies of honest enthusiasts.

During the next five years, unencumbered by any control program, the gypsy moth increased in both numbers and range, expanding northerly in a band along the seacoast through southern New Hampshire and into southern Maine, and southerly through Plymouth County and over the western half of Cape Cod. In addition, two new, large infestations were discovered in Providence, Rhode Island, and

Stonington, Connecticut. The infested area now included 124 cities and towns and 2,224 square miles in Massachusetts alone. This prompted the Massachusetts legislature to act again and create the Office of Chief Moth Suppressor in 1905 under the Board of Agriculture, with a sizable staff to be headed by Archie Kirkland, who had been involved in the earlier suppression efforts. That same year the Board of Agriculture and the federal Bureau of Entomology established a laboratory, first in North Saugus and later in Melrose, and began importing and studying parasites of the gypsy moth from Europe and Asia for release. One of the most prominent of these (not a true parasite, however, as it does not attach itself to its host) was the European calasoma beetle — a large (1 to 1.5 inches), voracious, iridescent beetle. Unlike the two native species of calasoma beetles, both the larvae and the adults prey upon lepidopterous insects in their larval and pupal forms.

Kirkland's generous budget prompted allegations of waste and inefficiencies. It was even suggested that his men spread the pest to ensure that their jobs would be secure. Because of the controversy, the legislature moved the responsibility for controlling the gypsy moth to the supervision of the state forester. As Chief Forester Harold O. Cook would later observe, placing the chief moth suppressor under the state forester in 1909 was "truly a case of the tail wagging the dog" — at the time the chief moth suppressor's budget was eight times that of the state forester's. From that point on the State Forester oversaw all moth suppression activities until 1921. At that time, following the creation of the Department of Conservation, George A. Smith, who had worked in the suppression program for many years, was placed in the newly-created position of Superintendent of Moth Work. Smith served in that capacity until his death in 1936.

The battle against the gypsy moth and the brown-tail moth continued. In the next 10 years the gypsy moth spread well into Worcester County. In 1912 the Bureau of Entomology took over the entire program of experimentation with parasites, as the rapid spread of the pest was rightfully perceived as an interstate problem. The chief moth suppressor and the municipalities were responsible for control efforts in the "infested area," and the federal Bureau of Entomology was responsible for quarantine, control and scouting activities in the "barrier zone" along the western edge of the infested area — where, it was hoped, the moths' spread could be stopped. By 1922 the barrier zone had become the Berkshire County line. The brown-tail moth never extended its range, nor was it as destructive in later years as the gypsy moth, although occasional, localized infestations occur to this day in eastern Massachusetts. In 1963, Charles S. Hood, Chief of the Bureau of Insect Pest Control, stated: "Natural enemies and disease have, in recent years, reduced the brown-tails almost exclusively to pests of beach plum in certain coastal areas." One can only wonder if the parasite introductions made early in this century are responsible for this.

In time, it became apparent that "Tanglefoot" and burlapping were not economical methods of gypsy moth control. The development of horse-drawn, kerosene-powered sprayers and the introduction of sprayers mounted on motor trucks in 1911 made spraying with lead arsenate and creosoting egg masses the control methods of choice. As the official reports asserted, spraying "has become one of the most efficient methods used in suppressing injurious insects, it being beneficial to the crop and detrimental to the insects." For a brief period it was felt that "improvement thinnings" in forested stands that reduced or eliminated favored food species was a viable control method. However, the high cost of this method ($32.88/acre as opposed to $9.44/acre for spraying, as of 1910) and perhaps its impracticability in most situations as a result of inappropriate stand composition and the potential for seriously understocking the residual stand led to its falling from favor in 1920. Other control efforts consisted of destroying neglected orchards, which were held to constitute a menace because of their attractiveness to gypsy moths, and treating stonewalls, which were ideal places for the moths to lay their eggs, with spray and creosite.

Concerns about the safety of spraying were voiced by some, but public sentiment supported the program. Questions were raised about lead arsenate's effects on songbirds, and whether it might be a causal factor in the spread of infantile paralysis, but the public's concern over the damage caused by the pests was so great that little attention was paid to these suggestions.

In addition to suppression efforts, the state moth superintendent administered a warehouse program whereby the state purchased equipment and materials in large quantities and passed the savings along to the towns. Each year one of the largest purchases of materials was lead arsenate. In 1916, one million pounds were purchased. The shipment filled 29 railroad cars and was valued at $81,000.

TREE DISEASES

While the battle was being waged against the insects, two tree diseases made their way into the United States. One of these was white pine blister rust, which was discovered in Massachusetts in 1910. It is believed to have been brought here on a shipment of nursery stock from Germany. Unfortunately, it was not discovered until several years after its introduction. Although an embargo was placed on foreign seedlings in 1912, infected seedlings had already been planted across the state.

At first it was thought that the disease would only affect nursery and young plantations and not large trees, but that proved not to be the case, prompting a great deal of debate within the forestry community as to whether or not it was still practical to establish plantings of eastern white pine. In commenting on this issue in 1916, State Forester Frank Rane spoke about the efforts by some "to discourage and thwart all our laudable reforestation endeavors." Two years later, in 1918, a committee representing 12 northeastern states and Canada passed a resolution stating that white pine blister rust was not menacing enough to stop the planting of white pine.

The disease continued to spread rapidly throughout the state and by 1927 had infected trees in 236 towns. Initially, control of the blister rust was the responsibility of the state Department of Agriculture; eventually it became a joint effort with the U.S. Department of Agriculture. The only involvement of the state forester was on state-owned forest land.

Control of the blister rust was undertaken by eliminating its alternate host, plants of the *Ribes* genus (gooseberries, currants, etc.), by pulling the plants from the ground. In 1922 the program was administered through eight federal agents and 21 temporary state employees. That year 200 landowners cooperated in the program. In practice, the state paid for the foreman of the crew and the landowner for the laborers. A great deal of this work was accomplished by the CCC. In later years, most of the state was on "maintenance," that is, the *Ribes* had been eliminated from most areas and the work now consisted of scouting with occasional removal. This practice continued for many years under state auspices utilizing federal funds.

Chestnut blight was first noted in the vicinity of New York City in 1904. Within a few years, this disease would virtually eliminate one of the most important tree species in the eastern United States, the American chestnut, and change the composition of the eastern hardwood forest from the southern Appalachians to New England. In 1912 it was estimated that American chestnut stands were concentrated in the central part of the state and constituted the equivalent of one-sixth of the total forest area of the state. The species was said to be either "scanty or wanting" in the extreme northeastern and southeastern portions of the state and the higher elevations in the Berkshires.

At first there was a great deal of debate over whether chestnut blight constituted a menace and whether or not it was truly a disease or merely a condition caused by climatic extremes. That year State Forester Rane concluded, "It is believed to be unnecessary for us to worry at present over the Chestnut Bark Disease in Massachusetts." Nothing could have been further from the truth. In 1909, Robert Edson, the forest warden in Wilbraham, noted the first occurrence of the disease in the state. By 1911 it was reported in 72 towns . . . in 1913, in 200 towns . . . and in 1914 it was said to be found "nearly everywhere chestnut grows."

At first the state forester's office published two bulletins that dealt with identifying the disease and offered suggestions for controlling it or at least slowing its spread. In 1912 the disease's severity was recognized, and perhaps not coincidentally, the book *Chestnut — Its Market in Massachusetts* was published. It was clear that the only thing left to do was to salvage the dead and dying trees.

In 1908 Massachusetts industries used approximately 4 million board feet of chestnut lumber, one half of which was utilized by the furniture industry and much of which was used locally for bridges: "Perhaps the most important [use] for the native article [American chestnut] is in bridge construction. It is especially adapted to this, owing to its durability when exposed to moisture. . . . It is difficult to form any estimate of the amount of lumber employed in bridge and building construction, since these uses are largely local" (*Chestnut — Its Market in Massachusetts*).

Chestnut's resistance to decay also made it valuable for railroad ties, which had an average service life of eight years, and for telephone poles. The elimination of this species as a forest tree was a loss not only from an economic standpoint but also from an ecological one: many species of wildlife — for example, many species of birds, squirrels and white-tail deer — depended on the fall crop of nuts to build up their body fat and ready themselves for winter. The nuts were also gathered by rural residents and sold, or dried and stored for later use. Today the American chestnut continues to survive as rootstocks throughout its former range. Unfortunately, as soon as the sprouts achieve any size they are killed back to the roots by the disease.

AERIAL SPRAYING

Although the chestnut blight had everyone's attention for a time, the battle against the gypsy moth still continued, but the financial burden of the program was gradually shifted to the municipalities. By 1926 the state only employed seven division (district) superintendents. The actual work of spraying and other control work was done by the towns. During the late 1920s and through the 1930s, the WPA (Works Progress Administration) and CCC federal jobs programs devoted a great portion of their energies to gypsy moth, brown-tail moth, and blister rust control. Harry B. Ramsey was appointed chief moth suppressor in 1937, following the death of George A. Smith, and was succeeded by his son Harry L. Ramsey in April 1942.

Attempts to confine the gypsy moth to the barrier zone were unsuccessful. By 1943, scattered infestations were reported in the Albany and Schenectady areas of New York and in Pennsylvania. During the 1940s two control methods were instituted that would change the methods of gypsy and brown-tail moth control. In 1942, 1,200 acres were sprayed with lead arsenate from the Department of Conservation's autogiro. It was felt that it would not be long before conventional aircraft could be employed using substances that were much less toxic to warm-blooded animals than lead arsenate. This substance proved to be DDT, which had proved itself to be a very effective insecticide in wartime use. Eventually DDT was employed in low-volume, mist-blower applications and in low-volume aerial applications from fixed-wing aircraft.

The first large-scale application of this material from the air was in 1948, when 7,000 acres on lower Cape Cod were sprayed. It was later reported, "The results have shown the value of air spraying, especially where we can secure complete kill, lower costs, and an immense saving in time and labor, with no injury to humans or warm-blooded animals." The following year 250,000 acres were sprayed on Cape Cod by airplane, helicopter, and ground equipment. It was said that wildlife and birds were more abundant than ever and that collateral benefits included a lack of weeviling in white pine and an 85 percent reduction of the tick population.

In 1949, 500,000 acres were sprayed on the Cape and in Plymouth County with an ultimate goal "to eradicate the gypsy moth to all intents and purposes from the confines of Massachusetts and at the same time to effect the saving in governmental cost of a minimum of $800,000 a year." A mixing plant was established at the Plymouth Airport in 1950, where kerosene, solvents, and concentrated, technical-grade DDT, purchased in bulk, were mixed at a savings of over $100,000 per year as opposed to purchasing the spray material in dilute form. Several years later it would be mixed at the Department of Conservation's service building in Stow.

Various aircraft were employed in this work, including Bell helicopters that carried a 50-gallon payload, Stearman biplanes that carried 100 gallon payloads, and former B-17 bombers that carried 2,700 gallons. Precautions were taken to maintain a minimum altitude of 500 feet over mink farms lest the hyperactive animals kill their young when exposed to the loud noise of the aircraft. All told, 27 mink ranches were sprayed and only two reported any kit mortality. It was also a matter of policy to not spray either fish hatcheries or stocked trout ponds. The program was extremely effective. In 1952, an optimistic Conservation Commissioner Arthur Lyman stated that the gypsy moth could be eradicated in the next five years.

With the establishment of the Department of Natural Resources in 1954, the chief moth suppressor, Harry L. Ramsey, became the chief of the Bureau of Insect Pest Control. The scope of the bureau's activities was expanded to include three major areas of emphasis: (1) insect pest control, (2) the control of Dutch Elm disease, which had been rampant since 1951, and (3) matters relating to agriculture and public health, including blister rust control, poison ivy, wood ticks, and other nuisances. By 1958, 3 million gallons of DDT solution had been sprayed on the Commonwealth, and it was felt that the gypsy moth had finally been brought under control. That year only 10,000 acres of state-owned land were sprayed. In 1959, following a controversy over the privatization of the DDT mixing plant, Harry Ramsey retired and was replaced by

Charles S. Hood, an entomologist who had worked for the Maine Forest Service. Without the mixing plant, there was no need for the 75,000 pounds of technical DDT that was in stock, and it was traded for 249 50-gallon drums of finished (25 percent emulsion) insecticide supplied by the Nu-Brite Chemical Company.

Although not related to forests per se, Dutch elm disease control consumed a great deal of the bureau's efforts in the 1950s. This introduced disease was spread by the elm bark beetle. The principal control measures were spraying to control the beetle and the removal of infested trees to deprive the beetle of a place to breed. Unfortunately, these control efforts only slowed the demise of the Commonwealth's elm-lined village streets — it did not save the trees.

During the late 1950s and early 1960s, there was mounting criticism of the use of pesticides and on several occasions legislation was introduced to control their use. The Massachusetts Pesticide Board was established in 1962 charged with regulating the use of pesticides and training applicators and issuing them licenses. The publication of Rachel Carson's *Silent Spring* in 1962 further increased public sentiment against the use of pesticides, both in Massachusetts and nationally.

Reforestation and Timber Management

REFORESTATION LOTS

The legislature responded to Akerman's and Rane's pleas for the establishment of a system of forest reserves by passing the Reforestation Act on May 1, 1908, which authorized the acquisition of lands "for the purpose of experiment and illustration in forest management." While it would not create the forest reserve system the state foresters had requested, it was, nevertheless, a move in that direction.

The price of the land acquired under the act could not exceed $5 per acre, and no more than 40 acres could be acquired in any tract in a given year. If they wished, the former owners, or their heirs or assigns, could repurchase the parcel within 10 years for the purchase price plus 4 percent interest and the cost of any improvements made by the state forester. The law also stated that the state forester should "replant or otherwise manage all land acquired . . . to produce the best forest growth both as to practical forestry results and protection of water supplies."

During the first year, close to 1,000 acres were turned over to the state for reforestation purposes, though only 160 acres were actually purchased by the state to remain in state ownership. In most instances, the parcels were acquired with the option for the owners to repurchase them.

In his discussion of the legislation in his 1908 annual report, State Forester Rane stated: "With our depleted, neglected and waste lands reharnessed and made a live factor throughout Massachusetts, one of our natural resources will be headed in the right direction." Rane's plan was to replant as many of the lots as appropriations would allow and to plant one or more lots in each town in the state. Planting costs in the first years of the program ranged from $6 to $10 per acre. While much of the planting stock was acquired from sources in the United States, including the State Forester's nursery in Amherst, 500,000 white pine transplants were imported from Germany in 1909 to satisfy the demand (unfortunately, these were probably the source of the white pine blister rust).

To expedite the work in remote areas where no room and board was available for the planting crew, the State Forester's office built five, 12-by-12-foot shed-roofed, portable steel shacks that could each accommodate a 12-man planting crew. The shacks were constructed of panels of galvanized iron that could easily be transported and erected using bolts and clamps. The only wooden parts were the door and two window sashes. The shacks were part of a kit containing camp equipment, cooking utensils, and planting tools. Each crew member furnished his own bedding.

By 1913 there were 4,489 acres in the program, 1,000 of them owned by the state with no redemption clause. By 1927 the Reforestation Act had passed its experimental stage, and the following year the policy of accepting any new lots was discontinued. This was due primarily to the fact that when the lots were not redeemed the Department of Conservation was forced to take under its control a great number of isolated, small tracts across the state for which efficient administration was impossible.

FOREST TREE NURSERIES

In 1906, under the legislation that created the office of the state forester, the state's first forest-tree nursery was established on the grounds of the Massachusetts Agricultural College. State Forester Akerman's vision for the nursery was that, in addition to supplying trees for reforestation, it would be a part of the course of instruction in forestry he was required to teach at the college. Apparently, the trustees of the college did not share Akerman's enthusiasm for this endeavor, for in his second annual report (1906) a perturbed Akerman stated:

> Through an inexplicable delay on the part of the trustees of the college to act in the matter, work on the nursery did not begin last spring until all the good land available for the nursery had been assigned for other purposes. The only ground left was the worst for a forest nursery that there is on the college grounds. Rather than throw away the seeds that had been collected, the nursery was begun.

The nursery's purpose was to provide seedlings at cost to private woodland owners "operating under a systematic planting plan" and "free of charge to State Reservations." Initially, trees were planted in several separate areas at the college totaling three acres. In the spring of 1907, 4,450 chestnut and 100 red oak seedlings were sold to the public for $3 per thousand.

Akerman's plan called for expanding operations over the next several years until an annual output of 125,000 seedlings was reached. In 1906 the stock on hand was 152,000 trees of varying ages, 90,000 of which were white ash, 45,000 white pine, and the balance a mix of species. It is unknown why white ash was in such favor in those early years. Perhaps it was merely a matter of having a large supply of seed on hand. The writer is unaware of any successful surviving white ash plantations, and the only reference found relating to one is a comment by Harold O. Cook in *Fifty Years a Forester* regarding the 1910 plantings in the Colrain State Forest (now H. O. Cook State Forest), where 110,000 white ash were planted: "The ash trees we planted did not do so well in Colrain State Forest because deer and rabbits browsed on them and trampled them." This was the probable fate of most of the white ash produced at the nursery.

The following year the trustees of the college were more generous and allowed the nursery operations to be relocated to a more favorable site. The following year, R. S. Langdell, a graduate forester and former student of Rane's, was placed in charge of the facility, a tool and packing shed were built, and all operations consolidated at the new site.

In 1907, Rane stated, "As State Forester I am very anxious to get just as many trees set out on our waste and unproductive lands as possible." To stimulate public interest in planting trees, he promoted what might be referred to today as an introductory offer of a quarter-acre planting package consisting of 150 white pine and 150 white ash seedlings for the price of $1. By the end of the year, 120 individuals had responded to his offer. That same year, in a circular letter sent to school superintendents throughout the state, he advertised a packet containing 12 white pine, 24 white ash, 12 red spruce, and 5 beech seedlings. It also contained seeds — 900 white pine, 12 chestnut, and 50 white ash seeds and 25 acorns. The purpose of the packet was to encourage schools to establish a small forest-tree nursery on their grounds. Bulletin no. 4 published by the State Forester's Office, which contained instructions for handling and care of the nursery, was also enclosed. The packet cost $1, and 47 schoolteachers placed orders. In his letter Rane stated:

Our new power sprayer complete. This outfit was planned and built by the State Forester's department. Four-cylinder engine, triplex bronze pump, 300 pounds pressure capacity, weight 3,000 pounds. (Illustration from the Eighth Annual Report of the State Forester, 1911.)

It is hoped that in this small beginning we may foster in the young, our coming generation, not only a fundamental economic recognition of forestry, but return to Massachusetts and New England the natural beauty we all would so much love to see.

In 1908, whether Rane's promotional activities were responsible or not, public orders for planting stock increased and the Amherst nursery could not meet the demand. With the passage of the Reforestation Act in 1908, Rane came to the realization that the Amherst facility alone could not begin to satisfy the demand for planting stock on both the soon-to-be-acquired reforestation lots and on private land. Thus, the sale of stock to private individuals was discontinued. That year, fatefully, the demand for stock for planting on the reforestation lots was met by purchasing 500,000 three-year-old white pine transplants from Germany that were infected with blister rust and an equivalent amount from domestic growers and the Amherst facility; 929 acres of "state plantations" were started that year.

The high cost of privately produced stock ($5 per thousand as opposed to $2.25 per thousand) prompted Rane to propose enlarging the Amherst nursery to fully meet the needs of the Reforestation Act. If the trustees of the college would not allow a doubling in size, "it will necessitate making plans elsewhere." The Amherst nursery was also in need of improvements as it needed a reliable water supply, a better work shed, and fencing to reduce the damage that "has repeatedly resulted from animals getting loose and trampling the beds." Apparently permission was granted to expand, for the nursery remained at the college and the improvements were made.

The results of a successful one-acre planting experiment in Woodstock, Vermont, made in 1876 were responsible for the promotion of Norway spruce as a desirable species to use in reforestation work in Massachusetts. In 1908 Rane wrote: "At age 32 the Vermont plantation yielded 172½ cords per acre valued at $1,120.00. For the first time the State Forester expects to set out quite a large number of Norway spruce in Massachusetts the coming spring." Until the Amherst facility could supply these trees, they were purchased from European sources.

As the acreage of reforestation lots grew, so did the demand for planting stock. Nurseries were established in East Sandwich to grow species "suitable for planting on Cape land." A nursery for transplant stock was established at Hopkinton in 1910. At the end of that year the Amherst facility had on hand over 5 million seedlings and over 300,000 transplants; the Hopkinton facility, 250,000 transplants; and the East Sandwich facility, 482,000 seedlings.

Another expansion of the system took place in 1913 when a nursery was established on the state farm at Bridgewater with a plan for expanding it to 10 acres the following year. Other than the great amount of available space, the main advantage of using this facility was the free labor provided by the inmates in planting 500,000 transplants that first year. Only the foreman's salary was paid by the State Forester.

The following year (1914) a seven-acre tract "having remarkably fertile soil" was leased in the village of Barnstable to replace the East Sandwich facility, which was discontinued because of the lack of a dependable water supply and infertile, sandy soil. At Amherst, the three "shanties," referred to as sheds when they were first built, were torn down in 1915 and replaced by a one-and-a-half-story cottage, quite likely the core building of the present-day regional headquarters.

By 1916 an official state "nursery policy" was in place. The Amherst and Barnstable nurseries were to be regarded as the primary nurseries in the system. Seedlings would be raised there for transplanting to auxiliary nurseries. Transplants would be raised in the primary nurseries only if space allowed. The Hopkinton facility was phased out that year and auxiliary nurseries for raising transplants were established at Myles Standish and Otter River state forests, and at Norfolk State Hospital. In the 1920s, auxiliary nurseries were opened at the Savoy Mountain, October Mountain and the Swann (Monterey) state forests. Small-scale "display" nurseries were also maintained at the Erving, Mohawk Trail, Windsor, and D.A.R. state forests.

There were two primary reasons for creating auxiliary nurseries. One was the great difficulty in transporting trees over inadequate roads to the planting sites during the spring mud season. The other was a matter of economy — 40,000 seedlings could be shipped for the same cost as 3,000 four-year transplants. The display nurseries' role was primarily educational, although stock produced in them was usually planted locally.

The Barnstable nursery was eventually phased out and replaced by one at the Shawme State Forest, which by 1931 became the major source of planting stock for the Cape. Eventually, the roles of the Amherst and

Clinton facilities were clearly defined — the Amherst facility would be used for producing seedlings that would be shipped to Clinton for transplanting and eventual distribution.

The labor shortages during World War I beset nursery operations as well as the other activities of the State Forester's Office. Because of a shortage of men in the planting crews, only a fraction of the acreage of previous years was planted on the reforestation lots. In addition, the discovery of white pine blister rust several years prior to the war caused a great deal of anxiety on the part of the public and reduced the demand for white pine planting stock. Unfortunately, this species made up about two-thirds of the stock on hand in the state nurseries. To move this surplus of older stock, Rane's staff, through "considerable advertising and other methods of salesmanship" sold 600,000 trees for a minimal amount of money, but at least the nursery beds were cleared. Seed was also in short supply during the war years, due not only to a war-time labor shortage that meant reduced seed collection, but also to the fact that much of the seed used by the nurseries, particularly Norway spruce, Scots pine, and Austrian pine, was imported from Europe.

During the life of the nursery program, stock on hand and distributions varied greatly, and it seemed that supply and demand would never be in balance. By 1924, interest in planting picked up and it looked as though the supply would not be able to satisfy the demand. It was hoped that another 70 acres of suitable land could be acquired so that an annual production goal of 4 million to 5 million trees could be met. In 1925, through an arrangement with the Metropolitan Water District (now the MDC), a suitable tract of 25 acres was acquired in Clinton near the Wachusett Reservoir. Over the next several years the Clinton facility was developed with an ultimate distribution goal of 3 million transplants per year.

Beginning in the late 1920s, prompted by the promotion of the practice by Robert Parmenter, the extension forester, there was an increasing interest in planting trees for Christmas trees. The department responded by making more balsam fir and Norway spruce available. In the early thirties the effects of the Depression were felt as the total distribution dropped by 33 to 50 percent of what it had previously been. However, several years later, the availability of CCC labor and an accelerated state forest acquisition program in the mid-1930s caused a brief resurgence, and some 4 million trees were distributed in 1935.

With the exception of several display nurseries, by 1940 only the Amherst (15.7 acres), Bridgewater (14.6 acres), and Clinton (20.5 acres) facilities remained in production.

Another severe labor shortage accompanied the onset of World War II. High school boys, college students, and inmates of state facilities were used as sources of labor. Women students from Massachusetts Agricultural College and Smith College "in particular proved to be excellent workers in the nursery." Again, the seed of some species were in short supply, repair parts could not be had, and many items of mechanical equipment were used beyond their ordinary lifespans. The end of the war did not bring an end to shortages and inflated prices. Postwar seed prices for some species were five times their prewar levels.

Following World War II, distributions dropped below 1 million trees per year. Although demand was up, the stock on hand, which normally would have been 12 million trees, was only 4 million. This shortage led to limits on the number of trees any one landowner could purchase. Even this rationing and a radical rise in the prices of trees, the first one in 25 to 30 years, failed to diminish interest in planting. During the 1950s, annual distributions varied from a half million to 1 million trees. Most trees planted on the state forests were used to reforest areas burned by large fires on the Myles Standish State Forest in 1957 and on the Martha's Vineyard State Forest in 1946. Two tractor-drawn Lowther wildland tree planters were acquired and used to plant the burned areas. After some experience with the machine, it was said that "the machine planting was much superior to the hand planting, not only because it was cheaper but also because it does a better job." No mention was made of the fact that the workers who operated the machine considered this work to be very unpleasant due to the fact that they were tossed about like rag dolls as the bulldozer pulled them through the planting area.

The demand for Christmas-tree stock increased in the 1950s. In his 1958 annual report, H. O. Cook stated: "We are still disturbed by the demand for stock to grow Christmas trees. The fact [is] that many of the landowners do not realize that they not only have to grow the trees but they have to market them."

The Bridgewater nursery was closed in 1955. The soil at that facility had a high clay content, and recent winters with little snow cover had caused a great deal of winter damage from frost heaving. A radical change in policy took place that same year: a switch from transplants to three-year seedlings. It had become common practice in other states to supply three-year seedlings for distribution rather than the larger, more expensive four-year and five-year transplants. This not only shortened the time needed to grow a salable tree with equal survival and comparable vigor, but also reduced by 25 percent the nursery area needed and saved the labor required for transplanting.

A lack of mechanized equipment and a reliance on expensive hand labor (25 people were employed in nursery operations at the Amherst and Clinton nurseries in 1956) began to take their toll on the program. Appropriations did not keep pace with the cost of supplies and equipment. Over the preceding 20 years, prices of supplies had doubled but appropriations had remained almost constant. In 1960 two catastrophes occurred that set the program back. On April Fool's Day two youths from a nearby reform school set fire to the Clinton headquarters building, and it burned to the ground. In addition, a heavy accumulation of snow that winter attracted large numbers of mice to the seedling beds. After the snow melted, it was discovered that over 300,000 trees had been girdled and killed by the hungry rodents. The Clinton facility was rebuilt over the next two years, but production continued to decline. The last large-scale digging there took place in the spring of 1967, leaving Amherst as the sole remaining facility.

The 1960s saw a continued decline in the demand for trees used for reforestation purposes and an increased demand for Christmas trees. In addition, there were now a number of private nurseries offering a greater variety of species at competitive prices without restrictions on ornamental uses or required state inspections and approval of planting sites. Over the years federal monies had been supplied to the state to support reforestation activities, but by 1962 the federal share had been reduced and only paid 12 percent of the program's expenses. The cost of producing seedlings that year was $31 per thousand; they were being sold for $20 to $30 per thousand.

In the mid-1960s bird repellents and fungicides were developed that made direct seeding a practical method of reforestation, until their toxicity caused the practice to be banned. During this period, annual distributions from Amherst continued to drop from approximately 500,000 to 250,000 trees. In 1969, almost half of the 262,000 trees distributed were surplus trees purchased from the New York State Nursery in Saratoga Springs, New York.

The Amherst nursery closed after the spring shipping season in 1970. In the 1970 annual report of the Bureau of Forest Development, Chief Forester John H. Lambert, Jr., stated:

> Due to prohibitive unit costs, nursery operations will be discontinued this year. The U.S. Forest Service estimates that a production of at least six million seedlings annually is needed for a marginal operation.

🍃 Supporting and Regulating Private Forestlands

After his first full year (1906) as state forester, Alfred Akerman was able to state, "The offer of practical assistance which the Commonwealth makes to owners of woodlands has been responded to with alacrity." In those early years, the demand for this service exceeded the agency's ability to provide it. In the first full year of operation, Akerman and Assistant State Forester Ralph C. Hawley traveled 13,533 miles in the course of delivering lectures and other activities. They also made woodlot examinations on 34 properties totaling 6,545 acres.

To make up for a paucity of practical information on forestry, the State Forester's Office produced a great many publications for use by the general public. Akerman's hope was to reduce the many inquiries for advice of a general nature that took up so much of his staff's time. He and his staff began compiling information and publishing bulletins and leaflets. "Forestry in Massachusetts," "Forest Thinning," "Practical Suggestions for the Massachusetts Tree Planter," and "Massachusetts Trees, How You May Know Them" were among those written. Some were of a technical nature, such as *Forest Mensuration of the White Pine in Massachusetts,* first published in 1908. This fact-filled, 51-page, pocket-sized publication was prepared from a great amount of data that had been gathered over a three-year period by Assistant Foresters Hawley and Cook and contained volume tables, financial data and other information of value to forest managers. The publications must have been quite popular — by the end of 1906, 35,000 copies of bulletins and leaflets had been distributed. As time went on and more federal publications became available the demand for these more provincial materials diminished and little effort was put into creating new titles.

Later, Frank Rane's expectations of his newly created corps of town forest wardens — "they may become, in a sense, town foresters" — never really came to pass. Few, if any, had formal forestry training, and, for the most part, they were unpaid volunteers. In addition to advice about tree planting and forest-improvement work, land owners wanted to know how to sell timber. No doubt there was some pressure on the foresters to inflate estimated volumes of timber offered for sale, for in 1917 Rane felt the need to explain, "We want the landowners to understand that in making estimates of woodlots this department must be fair to the possible purchasers as well as the owners, and that we cannot make our valuations high to satisfy the seller at the expense of the purchaser."

Through the years, the department's foresters responded to requests for technical assistance. During the CCC era, there was little time and personnel for this work, but once World War II was under way, the demand for forest products prompted the creation of two federally supported "farm foresters" who spent most of their efforts helping landowners market their timber for use as strategic materials.

Eventually these farm foresters would become service foresters and the program would expand to today's 14 districts. The original emphasis of their work, providing assistance to private landowners, has gradually changed to that of administering federal assistance programs and administering the Forest Cutting Practices Act (chapter 132) and the Forest Tax Law (chapter 61).

In addition to these early one-on-one contacts with the public, the state forester and his staff were in great demand to give lectures about forestry. In 1907, to maximize the use of their time, a minimum audience size of 100 persons was set and the sponsor was charged for the speaker's expenses. Forty-five lectures were given that year.

EXHIBITS

The department also developed a number of elaborate exhibits for sportsmen's shows and agricultural fairs. A most unusual approach was the result of a collaboration between the state forester, the Massachusetts Board of Agriculture, and the Massachusetts Agricultural College. Between March 30 and April 2, 1910, the Boston and Albany Railroad provided "five observation cars fully equipped with exhibits representing every branch of forestry and agriculture." One car was devoted entirely to forestry and contained a number of exhibits ranging from photographs of forest fires, good forestry practices, and spraying apparatus to specimens of living calasoma beetles, gypsy moth and brown-tail moth caterpillars, and other insects. This "Better Farming Special" made 18 stops across the state and "was met by hundreds of farmers who, in many instances, had driven miles to enjoy the privilege of listening to the lectures on the many themes relating to farming. . . . The enterprise from start to finish was declared a pronounced success, and without doubt proved to be a valuable factor in stimulating and advancing the farming and forestry interests of Massachusetts." Because of the success of the Better Farming Special, the New England Investment and Security Company, which controlled about 1,000 miles of trolley line in central and western Massachusetts, offered the use of their facilities in a similar fashion for a three-day excursion several weeks later, which was also very well attended.

It is difficult to imagine the work that went into these exhibits. In 1937, Dennis Galarneau, the district forester in western Massachusetts (1922-40), and his staff put together a forestry exhibit at the Eastern States Exposition in West Springfield. The exhibit occupied the entire north wing of the building and consisted of models of forest stands undergoing various silvicultural treatments, a forest-tree nursery, a forest fire, a watershed, and a state forest recreation area complete with dolls representing people in various recreational activities. It was estimated that about 98,000 people visited the exhibit.

THE EXTENSION FORESTER

In 1924, Congress passed the Clarke-McNary Act, which in addition to replacing the funding of fire-control activities under the Weeks Act (which expired on July 1, 1925) also provided for cooperation between the federal and state governments in several other areas. One of these was in "farm forestry extension." Initially, Massachusetts was to receive $1,500 per year to fund this activity. The money was to be disbursed through the Cooperative Extension Service at Amherst. Through an agreement with the Extension Service, foresters Cook and Parmenter, who already devoted a large part of their time to this type of work, were to be regarded as "extension foresters" and the funds used to pay for a portion of their salaries." By 1929 Parmenter was listed in the roster of the Department of Conservation having an extension function. That year he developed a very ambitious five-year plan that included the establishment of a number of demonstration areas in conspicuous locations and the support of county extension agents. After the program had been in operation for three years, Parmenter stated:

> Woodland owners ... have been satisfied in the past to allow nature to give them whatever crop she desired, but they are now fully awake to the fact that they can improve the quality just the same as they can that of any other product which they are raising. This awakening of the owners of woodland to their prospective value is one of the most promising factors in our forestry work.

Eventually, the indefatigable Parmenter would give radio talks on topics such as "Forest Weeding," "Farm Forest By-Products" and "The Management of Weeviled Stands." He would also develop 4-H forestry clubs and travel throughout the state becoming involved in just about every imaginable forestry activity.

In 1932 Parmenter traveled to the west coast to ascertain, among other things, the potential effect that lumber-producing region might have on the New England lumber industry. After a rather lengthy discussion about denuded hillsides with no reproduction, fire-scarred areas, etc. he went on to say that: "...this section of the timber producing world would not be a menacing factor to the New England lumber market in the years to come." Nothing could have been further from the truth.

In November 1935 Parmenter was transferred to the staff of the Massachusetts State College at the request of President Baker, and the position of extension forester has been administered by the college and then the university ever since. Parmenter served the department in a variety of roles for 19 years prior to his departure in 1958. He was replaced by John H. Noyes, who served as extension forester until his promotion to associate dean in 1965. Despite the transfer of the extension function to the college, the department's foresters have continued to supply "practical advice" to landowners and others engaged in managing forestland through the service forestry program to the present time.

THE CUTTING PRACTICES ACT

The first attempt in this century at what one might remotely call a forest cutting practices act came in 1922, when a fire-prevention law was passed requiring that operators of "portable sawmills and others engaged in lumbering activities" notify the state fire warden of where they were operating and be subject to inspection. In time, most of these mills switched from burning slabs to gasoline or diesel fuel, which were less likely to cause sparks, and they ceased being regarded as the menace they once had been. However, the large accumulations of slash were still a concern. And how was the law accepted by the lumbermen? "There was a general spirit of cooperation that is very gratifying," the state forester reported in 1925.

During the late twenties and thirties, there was little interest in forest cutting practices for several reasons. The Depression had severely limited markets, and consequently there was very little activity in the timber industry. Another factor was that the forests had not fully recovered from the heavy cutting at the turn of the century. However, in 1940, in the shadow of a threat of federal regulation of forest harvesting practices and with a rapidly increasing demand for timber because of conflict overseas, Governor Saltonstall appointed a special advisory committee to study the forestry issues facing the Commonwealth. The result of the study was the recommendation to pass legislation (legislation was passed in 1941) to accomplish the following:

1. To create regional state forestry committees to develop standards leading to the elimination of destructive cutting practices
2. To make a major change in the tax law to tax forestland at a reduced valuation: limit assessments to no more than $5 per acre, create a method of deferring taxes on the timber until harvest, set a flat rate of 6%, and provide an exemption for personal use
3. To provide free demonstrations of forestry practices to owners of woodlands

Four regional state forestry committees were created to ascertain the most appropriate cutting practices for their respective areas. On the basis of the subcommittees' recommendations, legislation was again filed the following year to create a single State Forestry Committee to develop minimum standards for forest cutting. On the committee, appointed in 1943, were William P. Wharton (chairman), the chairman of the Massachusetts Forestry Association; Harold O. Cook, state forester and member ex officio; and three lumbermen, Harry L. Cole from Boxford, Walter C. Jones from Amherst, and Charles J. Kittredge from Dalton. John H. Lambert Jr., the district forester for the northeastern part of the state, was given the temporary assignment to provide technical assistance. The State Forestry Committee met on several occasions in various locations throughout the state and finally presented its proposed regulations to Commissioner Kenney, who approved and promulgated them on May 15, 1944, in the Forest Cutting Practices Act.

The regulations that were promulgated by the Department of Conservation accomplished several things. They defined "desirable species" of trees whose establishment should be promoted and stated that the standard logging practice shall be that of leaving seed trees of these desirable species to restock the land. The regulations went on to specify how many trees of various sizes shall be left as seed trees. In regard to clearcutting the regulations stated that a minimum number (1,000 per acre) of established seedlings of desirable species shall be in place before clearcutting. The regulations went on to state that, "To further protect growing stock care in logging is of great importance where there is considerable immature timber or young growth already established." And finally, "The measures to be used in a given lot necessarily will have to be determined by the State Forester's representative and the operator on the ground."

By the end of 1945, the four district foresters had prepared 275 cutting plans covering the harvest of 59 million board feet of timber on 14,000 acres of forest land. These figures did not include an additional 42 million board feet that was salvaged from the hurricane of September 1944 in southeastern Massachusetts. The State Forestry Committee expressed general satisfaction with the law, but allowed that there was room for improvement, particularly in dealing with a small number of operators who refused to cooperate.

The need for strategic materials during World War II caused a significant increase in timber-harvesting activity. By the end of the war over 400 sawmills were operating in the state. The Department of Conservation's foresters worked closely with the War Production Board to help lumber producers make their operations more productive and to help them fill defense contracts. The Korean conflict prompted similar attention on the part of the agency's foresters in the 1950s.

TAXATION OF FORESTLANDS

In 1913 the Commission on the Taxation of Wild and Forest Lands was created by a legislative resolve to study the forest tax laws of the Commonwealth and of other states and countries (State Forester Alfred Akerman was a member). The impetus for the creation of this committee was that at that time, not only was forest land itself taxed, but the timber thereon as well. As the timber grew and increased in value so did the tax burden. This had the effect of encouraging landowners to harvest their timber before it had reached maturity. This also promoted extremely heavy cutting and, in the long run, reduced potential profits to landowners and, in a general way, put the practice of forestry in an unfavorable public light.

One of the committee's recommendations, made in its report to the legislature, was that the then tax laws be amended to "relieve the growing timber crop of the unfair burden under which it now labors." The forest tax laws evolved over many years until 1981 when the legislature enacted the version in use today.

The aim of the new legislation was that the State Forester's Office should encourage private forest landowners to better manage their land. Under the new law, the owner of at least 10 acres of contiguous forestland not developed for nonforest use, upon its certification as forestland by the state, may now become eligible for an assessment reduced to 5 percent of the property's fair market value for a period of 10 years, during which a forest management plan must be developed and carried out. Declassification as forestland (if, for example, the landowner decides to develop the land in some way) is permitted upon payment of the accumulated taxes plus interest. The municipality has the right of first refusal to purchase the property within 120 days of notice of declassification.

Many Massachusetts forest landowners have taken advantage of these special tax provisions. Nearly 12 percent of the eligible forest land base (private timberland) has already received certification, and new owners are enrolling at a rate of 4 percent a year. Although the

Commonwealth may not be known for its timber production, it is recognized as a leader in many areas of forest resource use and conservation and as a state in which there are high standards for stewardship of its forests. Massachusetts' public and private foresters can take much credit for this reputation.

🍂 State Lands: The Forests and Parks

Today's Department of Environmental Management has approximately 280,000 acres of land under its jurisdiction. These lands occur as State Forests, as State Parks and as State Reservations. There is little distinction between the three categories — except on paper. They are all managed for multiple uses, although, generally speaking, the State Parks and the Reservations are managed with greater emphasis on providing recreational oppportunities. Unlike some other states' and federal park lands the harvesting of timber is not precluded. However, when it is done, it is used as a means of achieving another objective — such as improving wildlife habitat or maintaining diversity — rather than an end in itself.

THE STATE FOREST COMMISSION

As discussed above, under "Reforestation and Timber Management," State Foresters Akerman and Rane had both strongly advocated the establishment of a system of forest reserves. Though the Reforestation Act of May 1, 1908, did authorize the acquisition of lands "for the purpose of experiment and illustration in forest management," land acquired under the act did not serve as the system of state forest reserves envisioned by both Akerman and Rane, whose purpose they foresaw as acquiring large tracts of land that could be managed for timber. In 1913, the legislature's Commission on the Taxation of Wild and Forest Lands had again made recommendations concerning not only the management of small, privately owned woodlots but also the acquisition of large-scale forest reserves. The commission advocated the creation of a State Forest Commission whose purpose would be to transform the state's 1 million acres of "wild, unproductive areas [into] forested areas which would on their maturity have a commercial value." As Rane later explained:

It is obvious that our forest problems differ in some respects from those of other states where virgin forests have been acquired by legislative enactment and are being scientifically managed. In Massachusetts the problem is essentially one of reclamation.

The State Forest Commission, created in 1914, had three members, the state forester and two members appointed by the governor. The first members Frank Rane, the State Forester, Harold Parker, and Harvey N. Shepard who had been affiliated with the Appalachian Mountain Club. It was empowered to acquire, by purchase or otherwise, land suitable for timber cultivation. But support was not universal for this project. Critics of the plan to acquire large tracts of forest as state forest preserves deemed it to be socialistic. In defense of itself and its purpose, the State Forest Commission stated in its first annual report:

No person or corporation will to any large extent assume to do what will have so remote a return, and meantime large portions of the state are unused, — producing nothing, — and like bad associates are continually extending their evil influences. The further and sufficing answer is that by such public methods we are securing a commodity in our midst which otherwise we must import, at least in a very large degree, and at the same time we are setting a practical example for others to follow.

As with the demonstration reforestation lots a ceiling of $5 per acre was placed on these purchases. These lands would be under the care and control of the state forester, who "shall proceed to reforest and develop such lands and shall have power to make reasonable regulations which in his opinion will tend to increase the public enjoyment therefrom and to protect and conserve the water supplies of the commonwealth."

Harold Parker, a civil engineer, former chairman of the Massachusetts Highway Commission, chairman of the commissioners of the Mount Wachusett Reservation, and a former member of the General Court, was elected chairman of the commission. Parker's work with the Highway Commission gave him a knowledge of the state's geography that few had at that time. The commission's first act was to send a circular letter to mayors, selectmen, and forest wardens throughout the state soliciting ideas as to whether any lands in their towns might be suitable for reforestation purposes. The commission's goal, stated in the letter, was to acquire forests distributed throughout the state so that they would be accessible to a large number of people and serve as "object lessons" in forest management. Two restrictions were applied to the lands sought in this first solicitation. One was that, by law, the land could be worth no more than $5 per acre; the other was that the commission hoped to secure these lands in tracts of no less than 1,000 contiguous acres for efficiency of administration. Although no land was purchased in its first year, the commission did enter into negotiations for several tracts.

The commission's second annual report included a section extolling the virtues of eastern white pine:

> The woodland and waste land in Massachusetts of today, it is probable, was originally covered with white pine to a very large extent; it is the characteristic tree of New England. It is suited to all the natural conditions, it is very easily planted and cared for, it has fewer insect enemies than most trees, and reaches maturity in a comparatively short period. It can be used in more ways than any wood known. Investigations made by the experts of the State Forester indicate that a well cared for pine forest will increase 1,000 feet B. M. [board feet] per acre per year. It can readily be calculated what would be the net gain to the State or its citizens if all of the estimated 2,000,000 acres of woodland and waste land within our borders were fully developed and cared for.

The report went on to state "that where the reforesting of the waste lands is to be undertaken it should mainly be by the planting of white pine. And further, every state forest established by the Commission (or proposed) is adapted to the growth of white pine above all other trees."

The Commonwealth's first state forest, the Otter River State Forest, comprising 1,800 acres of light, sandy soil in the towns of Royalston, Templeton, and Winchendon, was established in 1915. The house and barn on the property were repaired for the use of "those in charge of the forest operation." That first year, 75,000 seedlings were planted in the forest.

Although it remained unnamed, the second state forest acquired was to become the Myles Standish State Forest: "south and east of Plymouth town; it extends beyond the limits of Plymouth into Carver." The forest was planned to eventually cover 10,000 acres of what was described as "typical Cape Cod land, every acre of which is capable of growing white, red and Scotch pine. . . . It is uniformly covered with a scant growth of scrub oak and occasional clumps of jack pine [most probably pitch pine] and white pine." Much of this infertile land was tax-delinquent and its ownership could not be determined. These areas were acquired by eminent domain within a predetermined boundary. The third property acquired that year was an 800-acre tract in the towns of North Andover and Reading. This property would become the Harold Parker State Forest, named for the commission chairman after his death on November 29, 1916, following a brief illness.

To the commission, it was apparent that one of the first undertakings on the state forests should be the establishment of

> . . . a fire protective system. Because of the flammability of the State Forests in Barnstable, Plymouth and Dukes counties special measures were taken to cut their area up into 200 acre blocks, each surrounded by a fifty-foot wide fireline with a road in the middle and a ten-foot wide plowed strip at each extreme edge.

In 1916, the commission investigated other large tracts of land in Wendell in "the territory along the Millers River and its tributary waters . . . cut over by lumbermen who had no thought of future needs." Following logging, the area had burned over several times, ". . . so that now thousands of acres present the aspect of a dreary desert." The commission's investigations also included several thousand acres of land in Douglas and East Douglas that had experienced a similar fate. These lands would be acquired as funds became available.

Two legislative resolves were passed in 1916 directing the State Forest Commission to investigate the advisability of acquiring two specific forest reserves: one encompassing Mount Grace, in Warwick, and another encompassing a portion of the Mohawk Trail in Franklin and Berkshire counties. The studies were requested because it was estimated that the cost of acquiring them would exceed the $5 per acre ceiling and because the lands involved were not "unproductive or waste lands" as required by law. Nevertheless both tracts were regarded as desirable acquisitions by some members of the legislature.

In June of 1916, Forest Examiner Frank L. Haynes was dispatched to the Franklin County town of Warwick to gather information about establishing a state park or forestry reserve at Mount Grace. The proposed 1,728-acre reservation, extending three miles north to south and one half to one and a half miles east to west, surrounded the 1,620-foot-high mountain and was located directly north of the village of Warwick. On the basis of Haynes's report, the commission concluded that a state forest could "be administered properly from a commercial standpoint and still afford every opportunity for recreation and pleasure; and that such a forest at the prices named will be profitable to the Commonwealth."

One problem associated with the purchase would be "the removal of the predominating hardwood growth at a profit" so that those areas could be planted with white pine. Some urgency was associated with this recommendation, for the chestnut blight had already killed many trees, and more mortality would surely follow. In light of these circumstances, the commission recommended that if the land were acquired, a $10,000 appropriation should be made to establish a sawmill and harvest the hardwoods and mature pine so that the area could be planted.

After completing his fieldwork on Mount Grace, Haynes traveled to the northwestern part of the state to gather information and prepare a report for the commission on the "practicability and advisability of establishing a state forest along the Mohawk Trail in the counties of Franklin and Berkshire." The Mohawk Trail was fast becoming a major tourist attraction. On at least one day in 1915, 700 cars traversed the Trail. Haynes's methodology was to divide the area along the trail into three distinct sections: Charlemont to Drury, Drury to Whitcomb's Summit, which marks the dividing line between between the Deerfield and Housatonic watersheds, and from Whitcomb's Summit west to the eastern side of the Housatonic valley in North Adams.

Because it was basically undeveloped, the first section was suitable for a state forest as prescribed by law and could be made "nearly self-supporting." But to acquire this land, a special appropriation would be required, because the price would be about $10 per acre — twice the maximum set by law.

The second, central, section of the study area, along the plateau from Drury to Whitcomb's Summit, was felt to be more suitable for acquisition as park land because of the "delightful views over the hills to the east and north." If this land were to be acquired for park purposes, a wide strip would have to be purchased to preserve unobstructed views.

The fact that most of the land was actively farmed raised its value to an estimated $40 per acre. Yet its acquisition was deemed necessary because otherwise its natural beauty "might be defaced by the erection of cheap stands and unsightly camps."

In the westernmost section, there were no long-distance views, with the exception of "the brink of sudden descent" (now known as the Hairpin Turn): "In short, nothing exists here that is different from hundreds of other wild uplands."

The commission's recommendation was to purchase only the first section as a state forest, to have "the beauty of the precipitous valley preserved forever at a cost not unreasonable, both by reason of its location and character."

The total cost of acquiring all three sections was estimated to be $114,300. Some years later, in 1920 and 1921, the legislature appropriated monies to implement the purchase of the Mount Grace and Mohawk Trail State Forests.

In 1927 the Department of Conservation (the State Forest Commission ceased to exist in 1919) was asked to study the feasibility of expanding the Mohawk Trail State Forest to include the area west of the forest from Drury to the Hairpin Turn. It was estimated that what could have been acquired for $75,000 in 1916 would cost nearly $1 million to purchase in 1927. The proposal was ruled impractical and no further action was taken.

A fourth state forest, Savoy Mountain, initially consisting of 1,100 acres, was purchased in 1918. In 1919, Mrs. Susan Ridley Sedgwick Swann donated 1,000 acres in the town of Monterey to the Commonwealth in memory of her husband, Arthur Wharton Swann; this became a portion of what is now the Beartown State Forest.

In 1922, the largest contiguous parcel of land in the state under single ownership, the 10,000-acre Whitney estate in the towns of Washington, Becket, Lenox and Lee, was acquired and renamed the October Mountain State Forest. Because it was valued in excess of $5 per acre, state monies had to be beefed up with donations from the people of Berkshire County to acquire it. That same year, Mrs. Ellen S. Auchmuty of Lenox donated 1,000 acres abutting the westerly boundary of the first tract, and the Department of Conservation purchased the 500-acre Dewey tract, which shared a common boundary with both properties. Prior to these acquisitions, the city of Pittsfield had taken 2,000 acres adjacent to the Whitney tract for the protection of its municipal watershed. This 13,500-acre parcel is now one of the largest tracts of contiguous open space in the state forest and park system.

The State Forest Commission's work continued through 1919, when its functions were absorbed by the newly formed Department of Conservation.

STATE FOREST MANAGEMENT

In addition to the more basic physical improvements, one of the Department of Conservation's highest priorities was to conduct an inventory and forest-type survey of all the state forests. This effort was led by Dennis Galarneau, who was the district forester in western Massachusetts from 1922 until 1940. According to the State Forester's 1926 annual report of the Commissioner of Conservation:

> In order to properly manage and develop the state forests it has been necessary to survey the conditions as they exist within the boundaries of each forest. Through a method of survey the land has been subdivided into types in accordance with the distribution of growth found. The location of the various types has been indicated by lines and symbols on maps of convenient size. In order to make the types more comprehensive these maps have been colored, each type being represented by a separate color. In carrying out these surveys, data also has been secured relative to the composition of the growth by species, size and crown density; areas of cut, burned, brush land, open land and plantations have been located; and the location of streams, lakes or ponds, roads, buildings and other improvements have been noted. This information has likewise been added to the maps.

For the first 20 years of the state forest system, the on-the-ground management of the forests was the responsibility of the district fire wardens. As the system became more extensive, it became apparent that more resources were needed. Accordingly, in 1937, 33 of the state forests were placed under the control of 15 forest supervisors and 8 remained under the district fire wardens. In 1935, Commissioner of Conservation York put forth a proposal to divide the state forests into six districts, with a staff of as many foresters of "unquestionable technical ability," and a resident superintendent in charge of each of 23 state forest areas.

Prior to this the only thing resembling a district was Galarneau's assigned area in western Massachusetts.

Not until 1940, under Raymond J. Kenney, would any form of districting be put in place. His plan called for the creation of three forestry districts across the state. Further, Kenney went on to define their work as having three distinct categories: (1) general forestry, including nurseries, state forest management and technical assistance to private landowners; (2) fire prevention and control; and (3) moth suppression. As a result of the increased forestry activity on both state and private land, Commissioner Kenney in 1942 added another forestry district in central Massachusetts and placed Charles Woodman in charge. The federal government, through the U.S. Forest Service, shared the cost of two farm foresters in Berkshire and Essex Counties. These foresters were initially regarded as an extension effort although they were administered through the Department of Conservation. In 1950, the number of forestry districts was increased from four to six by splitting the western and southeast districts. Each district then consisted of no more than two counties. Worcester, because of its great size, was the exception to this and had one forester assigned to it.

GIFTS OF LAND

Not all the state forests were purchased; a number were gifts by public-spirited Massachusetts' citizens.

In the late 1920s, two women's organizations made gifts of state forests to the Commonwealth. The first of these was the 1,020-acre Daughters of the American Revolution State Forest in Goshen, which was dedicated on April 9, 1929. The second was the Massachusetts Federation of Women's Clubs State Forest in Petersham and New Salem. A first, eight-acre, parcel was presented to Commissioner Bazeley on October 9, 1930, at a ceremony at the forest "in the presence of a large number of club women and conservationists." Over the next several years the federation acquired more land to add to this original tract. In August of 1933 the final transfer of land was accomplished, bringing the total up to 950 acres, and a tablet was put in place at the entrance. The D.A.R. State Forest and a portion of the Federation of Women's Clubs State Forests were acquired as wildlife preserves with no hunting allowed.

In 1937, Mr. Bradley W. Palmer gave the Department of Conservation 1,902 acres in Ipswich and Topsfield, to be known as the Willowdale State Forest. Of this, the 1,235-acre Pine Swamp tract was to be managed as a wildlife sanctuary. In reference to the department's acquisition of a wildlife sanctuary, Commissioner Ernest J. Dean stated: "It is not the intention of the department to add to the acreage of so-called posted land unless a wildlife program is immediately instituted and continued which will warrant closing the areas to the hunters." Following the death of Mr. Palmer the remainder of his estate in Topsfield, Hamilton, and Ipswich — 721 acres — was transferred to the department to be managed as a state park, and an additional 157 acres were added to the Willowdale State Forest. The final transfer took place in October of 1944.

In 1934, two gifts of land were accepted by the department for use as parks. The widow and daughter of Roland C. Nickerson donated a 1,727-acre tract in East Brewster, on Cape Cod, to the Commonwealth to be dedicated in his name. The property contains four ponds having a total acreage of 328 acres, of which the largest, Cliff Pond, is 208 acres. And over a period of several years in the 1930s John C. Robinson donated 1,021 acres abutting the Westfield River in Agawam, West Springfield, and Westfield, which became a state park named in his honor — The John C. Robinson State Park.

In 1940, Joseph Allen Skinner presented to the department 256 acres in Hadley and South Hadley, which became the Joseph Allen Skinner State Park. Earlier, in 1915, the property had been the subject of an investigation by the State Forester's office regarding the feasibility of purchasing it as a State Reservation. Although its acquisition was recommended, the legislature had refused to fund the $40,000 purchase price. The new park was the site of a large hotel — the Summit House, with breathtaking views of the Connecticut River valley — that could accommodate 60 to 75 people; it had been reconstructed in 1851 to replace an earlier one built in 1821. There was also a tramway on the property that carried visitors from the "halfway area" up to the hotel, which, although popular with the public, proved to be a maintenance nightmare. The tramway was eventually dismantled, but the Summit House remained and was restored in the 1970s.

Other gifts included Demarest Lloyd Memorial Park, a 200-acre tract on Buzzards Bay in Dartmouth, donated by Demarest Lloyd's widow in March 1953 in memory of Mr. Lloyd and her son. The 424-acre Lyndon Bates Memorial Park in Hancock was donated by the Bates family to be used solely as a wildlife sanctuary. Wahconah Falls State Park, 47 acres in the towns of Dalton, Hinsdale, and Windsor was a gift from the Crane Company of Dalton in 1942.

HARD TIMES

During the early Depression years, the monies appropriated for acquisition were allocated to forest management and other improvements: "Many purchases contemplated were laid aside in order that we might employ more men on our forests to relieve slightly the employment situation." In 1930, the governor and the legislature supplemented the regular forest appropriation with $25,000 to hire unemployed workers. These extra funds allowed the department to engage an additional 350 men to work for a six-week period on 20 state forests. As the Depression grew worse, the legislature made more monies available for this purpose. In 1931, the sum of $103,000 enabled the Division of Forestry to put 1,440 men to work on 54 state forests. The following year another $110,000 was appropriated and 1,288 persons were employed. Throughout the Depression, several federally funded relief programs, such as the Emergency Relief Administration (ERA) and the Works Progress Administration (WPA), were also used to supply labor for work on the state forests on a project-by-project basis. In 1938, over $200,000 in WPA monies were spent on state-forest improvements.

THE CIVILIAN CONSERVATION CORPS

The Civilian Conservation Corps (CCC) came into being as a result of New Deal legislation passed in 1933; its purpose was to provide work and vocational training for unemployed single young men through conserving and developing the country's natural resources. The creation of the CCC determined the direction of many of the Department of Conservation's activities for the remainder of the 1930s. That year the department applied to the federal government for the maximum number of camps that could be accommodated on existing state land. By July 1933, 31 camps had been established in the state housing 5,600 boys and 600 World War I veterans who were residents of Massachusetts.

The 31 superintendents and 300 foremen were recruited by the Department of Conservation. For the most part the participants were "not only under-nourished and under-developed boys, but boys who in the majority of cases had never known what it was to work. These factors seriously delayed our program until the boys could be conditioned." Their work was broken down into seven categories: "camp establishment, road building, silviculture, fire hazard reduction, pest control, recreation, and fish and game."

Commissioner Samuel York regarded the work of creating forest recreation areas as "the perfect work relief project." The CCC employed two landscape architects, Egbert Hans and Wayne Stiles, to plan these recreational improvements — Hans was assigned to the area west and Stiles to the area east of the Connecticut River. The camps in the forests with the greatest potential for recreational development were administered by the National Park Service, and the remainder by the U.S. Forest Service. The program accomplished so much in its first year that Commissioner York stated in his annual report for 1933:

> It is unfortunate that the present economic work in some of our forests is approaching exhaustion and unless sufficient additional acreage is acquired within the next three months, some of our camps will have to be transferred to other states where Massachusetts boys will do for other states what should be done for this commonwealth.

Responding to his concerns, the legislature funded the acquisition of an additional 40,000 acres of state forest land over the next three years. Due to these increased holdings, the department applied for and received permission to construct 22 more CCC camps, bringing the total number of camps statewide to 53.

By the end of 1934, the program had carried out silvicutural work on 8,856 acres and built "202 miles of road, 288 water holes and ponds, 90 tent sites, 16 bathing beaches, 12 cabins, 298 fireplaces, 66 picnic groves, 50 park areas and 106 miles of foot trails." The actual number and locations of CCC camps in Massachusetts varied considerably from year to year. A total of 165 sites of former camps have been identified. This large number is attributable to the fact that it was not unusual to have satellite camps at major work sites. It should also be noted that a number of camps were not on state forestland: three were municipal camps, three were on MDC land, and four gypsy moth camps were located along the barrier zone in the Connecticut River Valley; they were located on private land in the towns of Belchertown, Greenfield, Millers Falls, and Westfield. It is probably fair to say that in 1933, at the peak of the CCC program, the most working camps on state forest land at any one time was between 40 and 50. From that point on, the camps were gradually phased out. The last two camps, SP-19 at Nickerson State Park and SP-24 at Robinson State Park, were closed in March 1942, when the CCC was abolished by Congress.

STORMY WEATHER

Fortunately, the CCC program was in existence during two of the most severe meteorological events of the century. The flood of March 1936 tested the ability of the department and the CCC workers to deal with natural disasters. The worst damage reported was in western Massachusetts, particularly the watersheds of the Connecticut and Millers rivers; the Merrimack valley also sustained considerable damage. The water at the Hampden County Improvement League building on Memorial Avenue in West Springfield was nine feet deep. Accounts of the relief work accomplished by CCC workers include clearing landslides from the Mohawk Trail; placing 65,000 sandbags on the bulkhead of the Holyoke Dam; removing silt deposited in the main streets of Andover, Haverhill, North Andover, and Lawrence; reconstructing a 120-foot bridge across the Ware River in Thorndike; spending 3,400 man-days cleaning streets and cellars in West Springfield; rescuing people and cattle that had been trapped by floodwaters in Northfield; repairing miles of washed-out roads; removing six to ten inches of silt from the streets and the basements and first floors of 150 homes in Hadley; and burying dead cattle and other animals that were victims of the flood.

The second of these natural catastrophes was the hurricane and flood of September 21, 1938, which has been called

> ... not only the worst catastrophe of the kind to come to the New England section, but, measured in the destruction of life and property values, the worst that ever occurred anywhere in the United States at any time in recorded history.

Over the 10-day period preceding the hurricane winds as much as 15 inches of rain had fallen, not only filling rivers and streams, but softening the ground, allowing trees to be easily tipped over when the hurricane winds started to blow. The greatest flood damage was sustained by the area west of the Connecticut River, where the shallow soils, steep terrain and narrow valleys exacerbated the effects of the heavy rainfall.

Although millions of acres, particularly in the southern New England states, received some degree of damage, the central part of Massachusetts, the so-called "pine area," received the most wind damage: some 600,000 acres were damaged to the point that fire hazard-reduction work was warranted. An estimated 1 billion board feet of merchantable timber was blown down. Of this, 600,000 million board feet was deemed salvageable. Within a month of the storm, the New England Timber Salvage Administration (NETSA) was formed within the U.S. Forest Service and an administrative hierarchy created that included a director in each of the New England states. The Massachusetts legislature also passed emergency legislation in April of 1939 to create the Massachusetts Timber Salvage Administration, whose purpose was to determine the best methods to deal with the aftermath of the storm and to advise landowners as to what their options were. While it was in existence, it was overshadowed by NETSA although it worked very closely with it.

There were three distinct types of tasks that had to be accomplished following the storm: the elimination of the increased fire hazard, the salvage of downed material, and the repair of the tremendous damage that had been wrought by the floodwaters that accompanied the storm. To deal with the fire hazard-reduction work the NETSA created 10 resident DA (Department of Agriculture) camps in central Massachusetts in May of 1939. Eight of these, located in Ashburnham, Harvard, Pepperell, Townsend, Royalston, Warwick, and two in Petersham, were staffed with 50 men each. Two camps with 100 men each were located in Petersham and Winchendon. In addition, an estimated 15,000 WPA workers were involved in the cleanup throughout New England during the winter of 1938-39.

In the state forests an estimated 6 million board feet of damaged timber was on the ground. The Division of Forestry, the CCC workers, and 500 temporary workers set about the work of cleaning up through the 1938–39 winter and spring. They were able to salvage more than half of the damaged timber: 2.75 million board feet were sold to the NETSA and another 1.3 million were processed by an expanded crew at the Mount Grace State Forest on a sawmill manufactured by Chase Turbine in the neighboring town of Orange.

In addition to salvaging timber, repairing the damage to the state forests included repairing roads and bridges that were damaged by the flood, which required heavy construction equipment. Although the CCC had some heavy construction equipment at its disposal, it was insufficient to deal with the aftermath of the storm. No one Massachusetts construction firm was willing to undertake the cleanup work and wait a number of weeks before it would be paid. The Benjamin Foster Company of Philadelphia was the only large firm to come forward and assume the task of repairing the damage on the state forests. Because of the magnitude of the job and the fact that winter was fast approaching, there was little time for detailed planning and preliminary estimates. The Foster Company agreed to do the work on a cost plus basis and began work on October 5, 1938. By the end of the month 2,500 men were at work on 30 of the state forests. The work was finished before the following spring.

Over the next two years, the cleanup efforts were gradually phased down. The last of the 10 U.S. Forest Service DA camps was closed in December 1940. It was estimated that three million board feet of small, scattered, and deteriorating timber that was uneconomical to salvage remained on the ground on the state forests, and another 250,000 acres containing submarginal timber was left untreated in central Massachusetts "largely along the New Hampshire line from Dracut to Northfield and extend[ed] south for 5 to 15 miles." The chief fire warden faulted the NETSA for much of this remaining hazard, because its utilization standards would accept only logs greater than eight inches in diameter at the small end, which left many upper logs and unlopped tops in the woods.

WORLD WAR II

During the thirties the CCC improvements to the Department of Conservation's recreation areas continued to attract more and more visitors, but the outbreak of hostilities in Europe and the Pacific brought this all to a halt. America had little time to play. Shortages of many strategic materials, particularly automotive items such as gas and tires, led to rationing, and bans on pleasure travel caused attendance figures at state forest and park facilities, particularly the more remote ones, to plummet. Furthermore, the work of the forest and park staff near urban areas was made difficult by children unattended by their elders, who were presumably either away at war or at work in the defense industries.

The same shortages that reduced attendance made getting to work difficult for many of the Conservation Department's employees. Some had to resign for that reason, and others left their jobs to take employment in higher-paying defense industries closer to home. In addition, a number of employees either were drafted or enlisted in the armed services. By 1943, 38 staff members were on active duty. Labor shortages prompted the department to hire high school boys to tend the Bridgewater nursery, and young women from Smith and Massachusetts State College worked at the Amherst nursery. German prisoners of war housed at Fort Devens were put to work at the Clinton nursery.

To help alleviate the wartime fuel shortage, the Cut-a-Cord program was resurrected from the days of the 1915 fuel crisis. Through the program, people could buy standing wood that they cut themselves for $1 per cord; in 1943, 200 people took advantage of the program.

In several instances, transfers of land were made from the state to the federal government in the interest of national defense. The largest of these was a tract of approximately 7,000 acres located in the towns of Bourne and Sandwich that became an extension of the Camp Edwards (now Otis Air Force Base) artillery impact area on Cape Cod. This left approximately 1,700 acres of state forestland in a three-mile-long strip one half to one mile wide along Route 6 from the Sagamore Bridge to Route 130.

A one-square-mile block was taken from the center of the Martha's Vineyard (now Manuel F. Correllus) State Forest and transferred to the U.S. Navy for use as the Martha's Vineyard Naval Air Station. It was used as a training facility for pilots of the "Hellcat" night fighter. The area is now the Martha's Vineyard Airport. One of their target ranges was located at what is now South Beach, which is now administered by DEM and the town of Edgartown and the island of No-mans Land off Martha's Vineyard's southwest coast.

During the war, the creation of three 40-to-50-man public service camps for conscientious objectors in Petersham, Royalston, and Ashburnham helped to alleviate the Department of Conservation's personnel shortage, at least locally. These men were used for fire control, water-hole construction, and hazard-reduction work relating to hurricane slash.

Despite the great amount of lumber salvaged after the 1938 hurricane, by the war years there was a shortage: the war effort required immense quantities of lumber and other forest products. A significant amount of timber was harvested from the state forests to help meet the need for strategic materials. By the end of the war, the harvest amounted to 2.5 million board feet from these young forests. For Conservation Department projects, even abandoned CCC camps were dismantled and the lumber was used.

Lumber was not the only material needed from the state forests. Mica was another sought-after material, necessary in the manufacture of radio equipment. In 1943 the forester for western Massachusetts made a considerable effort working with the Chester Granite Company prospecting for mica on the Chester State Forest. As the state forester later reported, "Although federal and state geologists found outcroppings of considerable promise, the prospecting work so far carried out has given discouraging results. Good mica is scarce and much needed in the war effort."

THE POSTWAR ERA

After the war, a number of factors led to a rapid intensification of use of state forest and park facilities. Thousands of veterans returned, started families, and bought now readily available automobiles. The 40-hour work week, which had become the norm, afforded ample leisure time on the weekend with the automobiles easing the rigors of travel. Attendance at state forest and park recreation facilities trebled from what it had been before the war.

Because of minimal staffing at these facilities and increased recreational use, ordinary maintenance activities were often deferred, especially the road system that the pre-Depression crews and the CCCs had rehabilitated or built. There were an estimated 700 to 800 miles of roads in the state forests and parks system, and most of them were in need of serious repair. Help seemed to be on the way in the late 1940s when a special appropriation of $25,000 was made for road-maintenance equipment — but the seven tractors purchased proved to be inadequate. Finally, in 1953, the legislature appropriated funds to the Department of Public Works, and nine major thoroughfares that passed through state forests (10 miles of road) were reconstructed and blacktopped. While utilizing the resources and expertise of the DPW seemed like a reasonable approach, the differing standards between a gravel state forest road and a paved state highway prevented this relationship from working.

The demands on the department's forestry staff increased along with the demand for recreation. In the postwar period, state forest crews spent half of the year on forestry work and the other half — during the high-use season centering around the summer months — on work related to recreation such as keeping recreation areas clean, selling tickets, etc. This arrangement meant that the crews had to carry out forestry work during the most difficult time of the year for outdoor work. The situation was also exacerbated by the fact that in some cases workers were allowed to take their own vacation time only during the off-season. In 1948, State Forester Harold O. Cook suggested that forestry and recreation activities be separated completely.

Through the years, there has never been a lack of special projects to take state forest workers away from their regular duties. One unusual activity in 1949 that took up a significant amount of the forest personnel's time was a survey to locate hazardous abandoned wells on the state forests. This was prompted by the death of a small child in California who had fallen into a well. Two hundred wells were located and were rendered harmless by filling them with rocks and other material.

THE PRISON CAMPS

In May 1952, the Department of Corrections and the Department of Conservation established a forestry camp for 50 prison inmates at the Myles Standish State Forest in Plymouth. This concept had been considered by the Department of Conservation for some time and was brought to fruition under Commissioner Arthur Lyman, a former commissioner of the Department of Corrections. Lyman pointed to successful cooperative programs in New Hampshire, Michigan, Wisconsin, and California as examples of his vision for Massachusetts. However, not everyone shared his enthusiasm for the program. Similar camps proposed for the Douglas, Beartown, and Harold Parker state forests were withdrawn when local citizens voiced their objections. Later, two more camps were established: at the Monroe State Forest, in 1955, and the Warwick State Forest, in 1964. The inmates carried out a number of tasks for the Conservation Department. In addition to constructing new facilities and undertaking road maintenance and forest-improvement work, they manufactured thousands of picnic tables, concrete fireplaces, and signs for recreation areas.

The Monroe camp was closed following a murder in North Adams committed by an inmate on work release. The Warwick camp was phased out in the late 1980s because of inadequate waste-disposal facilities. Most of its staff was absorbed by a new correction facility on the grounds of the former Gardner State Hospital. The camp at Myles Standish State Forest is still in operation.

ACCELERATED FOREST MANAGEMENT

By the late fifties the need was seen to intensify and refocus forest-management acitivities. In 1960 the foundations were laid for an accelerated forest management program whose purpose was to improve the forests of the state forest and park system. The specific areas it targeted were timber stand improvement that was no longer being accomplished by crews whose priorities had changed to recreation; administering forest products sales; and establishing a continuous forest inventory system on the state forests. Initially participating in the program were three foresters, each with one assistant, and three summer crews of six forestry students each.

In 1961, to streamline the operations of the rapidly growing agency, five regions and five regional supervisor positions were created. These staff members were responsible for the coordination of all of the 4 bureaus within the Department of Natural Resources within their respective regions. This administrative structure is still in place today, although some regional boundaries have changed.

𝔊 Recreation and Wildlife

In the early 1900s, it was recognized that the production of timber could coexist and even enhance recreational activities on public land. In reference to existing state reservations, State Forester Akerman stated: "The reservations that have been made so far are distinctly for park purposes; there are, however, considerable areas in these areas that could be used for timber growing." If portions of them were managed for timber, "their park features would be enhanced," because if they were managed in the proper context they would have more diversity and hence, resilience to pests and storms, more diverse wildlife habitats and the practices could have been used to create a more pleasing visual appearance. Consequently, the development of permanent campsites became one of the major activities engaged in on the Myles Standish State Forest in its early years of operation:

> There has been a great demand for camp sites and, therefore, surveys were made of College, Fearings, Widgeon, Clew (sic, Curlew) and Rocky Ponds, and on these ponds, two-hundred and fifty camp sites with 100 feet shore frontage and 200 feet in depth have been laid out. Charge Pond has been reserved for the Boy Scouts and Barretts Pond for the Girl Scouts.

By 1920, 150 sites had been leased. The first public campground was developed at College Pond in 1920 and was continually upgraded throughout that decade. An auto camp was developed at the Mohawk Trail State Forest shortly after its acquisition in 1921. During the 1924 season, the facility "was used overnight by 1,050 auto parties, containing about 3,500 people, representing 28 states and 4 Canadian provinces. Five cars were from California."

While the department did promote recreational use in some areas, it was clear that the priority in those early years of the state forest system was the production of a forest crop. In 1925, the state forester observed: "We are setting apart and growing these forests for the reason that we need the lumber. The fact that such a forest will be a beautiful thing on the landscape must of necessity be a secondary consideration." Prior to the CCC era minimal recreational facilities had been developed at some of the state forests, they were neither elaborate nor particularly inviting:

During the year 1932 we improved the camping places on our State forests. There are now 19 camping grounds on our forests, many supplied with water and all equipped with tables. There are in all 71 tables with benches, 70 fireplaces, and 10 comfort stations or toilets. Nine of these camping grounds are for overnight use and week-end camping, and are among those equipped with fireplaces, tables and comfort stations.

Over 50,000 people enjoyed these various camping grounds during the season. About 100 tables with benches are in process of being made at the present time, and we expect to construct several more fireplaces, as our present equipment does not suffice for the public demand.

By 1932, two hundred permanent camp lots had been leased at Myles Standish State Forest. The new areas developed by the CCC were so well received that Commissioner York was prompted to state: "We have discovered that recreation is the most important by-product of our forest area." To deal with this increasing interest in outdoor recreation, the department developed under Commissioner York what was known as "The Massachusetts Plan of Conservation" in 1934. It called for the eventual creation of 26 state reservations, all of them within 20 miles of a large population center. Commissioner York summed up a rather simplistic, three-point approach to resource allocation on these properties as follows:

> Having set aside recreational areas and a wildlife sanctuary, or game refuge, in one of the forest-parks, all the rest of the area is turned over to the state forester to be developed on a strictly forestry basis; in other words, to be devoted to raising a timber crop. . . . Upwards of 75 percent of any one given area will be devoted to forestry, thus forming perfect surroundings for wilderness recreation and the restoration of the wildlife that is so valuable to the Commonwealth.

Also, to minimize administrative difficulties in the complex management of these areas, Bazeley felt that the minimum size of these areas should be at least 5,000 acres. This acreage would justify a full-time superintendent and would allow enough room for both recreation areas and a wildlife sanctuary. Eventually, a total of 40,000 acres were acquired and 21 of the 26 areas in the "Massachusetts Plan" were established.

The public's response to the recreation facilities built by the CCC was much greater than anyone would have thought, due no doubt to the factors enumerated above, plus the fact that outdoor recreational activities could be engaged in at little or no cost. In 1934 user fees (25 cents for the use of a table and fireplace, $2.50 a week for a tent site) were instituted at five areas on a trial basis. The thought was that the cost of acquisition and development of these recreation areas should be borne by the taxpayers in general, but that the cost of their maintenance should be borne by the users through fees.

Another initiative begun during the CCC era was the development of winter sports areas to accommodate downhill and cross-country skiing and snowshoeing. Facilities were developed at the Mount Grace, Mohawk Trail, Chester, Brimfield, Pittsfield, Beartown, and East Mountain state forests. The most elaborate facility was at the Pittsfield State Forest, where 13 trails and a well-equipped base lodge were developed by the CCC. Snow reports were provided to local newspapers and radio stations, and these areas were very well received by the public. Several of these areas continued to be used heavily throughout the World War II years, with weekend ski trains running from New York City to Pittsfield and Great Barrington.

State reports indicated that in 1937, 2,000 persons used the East Mountain State Forest area in Great Barrington and "a few hundred" used Beartown. During the winter of 1938, "in spite of a poor ski season last winter, there were at least 4,500 skiers" using the East Mountain area and 2,500 using Beartown. In 1939, these facilities "were taxed to capacity whenever the snow conditions were favorable during the winter season." In 1940, it was reported that 6,100 persons had used the Pittsfield facility, and "thousands of persons enjoy Mount Grace's ski trails and slopes in the winter."

In 1944, a report by the Division of Parks and Recreation stated that the Chester and Brimfield ski areas had not been used at all for three or four years, and by 1947 it was becoming apparent that the efforts put into the development of winter recreation facilities despite some early successes were not paying off, though the reason for this remained a bit of a mystery.

In his 1947 annual report of the Division of Parks and Recreation, Director George J. Keville stated:

> With the end of the war, and gasoline rationing, it was anticipated that there would be a great impetus to the areas where there were skiing facilities. The snow conditions were good, if not excellent, for skiing yet the patronage wasn't what was anticipated. The New York, New Haven and Hartford Railroad ran their special Sunday trains from New York to South Lee and Pittsfield. The report of this company was to the effect that travel in these "specials" was light, and they could offer no plausible explanation. . . . This Division is vitally interested in all types of recreation, but it is the opinion of the Director that the cost of clearing away new ski trails, and building ski tows is so prohibitive that no new areas should be opened for skiing purposes.

WILDLIFE

In their early years some state forests were managed as game sanctuaries where game was protected and was often propagated, as the 1918 Report of the State Forest Commission stated:

> We have arranged with the Fish and Game Commission so that bird and animal life is protected in these forests, and there is no reason why they shall not be used for the recreation of the people of the Commonwealth.

In fact, on the Myles Standish State Forest the protected deer herd proved to be a nuisance. It was reported in the 1923 annual report of the Department of Conservation that "deer have become too plentiful and they are injuring the young pines in the nursery and the plantations." By 1924, the problem had become worse:

> Deer continue to cause damage to the plantations and nursery. . . . It has been demonstrated in the Myles Standish State Forest that deer and a State Forest do not always get along well together, and in such an event the deer will either have to be driven off, or else reduced in numbers to a harmless minimum.

In 1926, a fence had to be erected to protect the nursery from the deer, but the deer continued their onslaught. In 1927, the fence of barbed wire put around the nursery to keep out the deer proved inadequate and was replaced with woven wire. Apparently, that fence worked, or some other means of control was employed, as no further mention was made of the problem.

In a discussion about conflicts that might be caused by the management of these lands for both forestry and wildlife, Commissioner Bazeley cited the question of whether to eliminate underbrush which, although of value to wildlife, "may be an intermediate host in the spreading of diseases of our trees." Eventually, the bottom line was that "the development of a forest is a business proposition, and such considerations as can be given to the welfare of the wildlife on the area are of decidedly secondary importance."

The policy of allowing hunting on the former Whitney Game Preserve, now October Mountain State Forest, opened Commissioner Bazeley to public criticism, since the tract had been closed to that activity while it was in the hands of the Whitney family. In defense of the policy, Bazeley stated in his 1922 annual report:

> The foundation of our policy in the management of the forests is that they shall serve the greatest number of people. With the increasing tendency on the part of private landowners to post their lands against hunting and fishing the time is fast coming when the sportsman of small means will have no place to hunt or fish unless he does it on State forests. . . . The Commissioner is desirous of doing the best thing possible for the forests, both public and private, and for the sportsmen, both rich or poor.

In 1925, legislation was passed allowing the commissioner of conservation to declare an open season on deer in the state forests upon the issuance of a written permit. During the early part of the CCC era (1934) a program was developed to establish wildlife sanctuaries on the state forests, undertaken in cooperation with the Division of Fisheries and Game, which was a part of the Department of Conservation. The approach was to designate from 10 to 25 percent of a forest's area and treat it

> . . . from a strictly wildlife standpoint. The object is to provide year-round food for animals or birds which it is desired to in-

crease and protect. Therefore, berry-bearing bushes, apple trees, hawthorns and grains are planted and open spaces and water provided within this area, so that it is possible for wildlife to exist. The inner area is closed to hunting.

Initially, these areas were established on Shawme, Beartown, Savoy, and October Mountain state forests, and a number of others were under consideration. Citing the success of a similar program in Pennsylvania, Bazeley stated: "Where hunting is prohibited in such an inner area, the area surrounding this territory actually becomes a hunter's paradise." When the program was fully implemented, in 1938, there were 18 refuges with a total area of 15,527 acres established within the state forest. In 1937, it was reported in the Department's annual report:

> Approximately 44 miles of graveled fire lanes have been constructed as well as 50 water holes for fire protection. To supply cover, 247,560 coniferous seedlings have been established in scattered groups adjacent to feeding grounds, escape covers have been established, 7.3 miles of food strips cleared, cultivated and planted, and 42.75 acres of food patches established. By the planting, transplanting, grafting and pruning of some 20,000 fruit-bearing shrubs and trees, including 2,839 malus grafts, the winter food situation, as it affects wildlife, has been greatly improved in many areas.

Although Bazeley promoted habitat management on the state forests, he was quite critical of the Division of Fisheries and Game's program of stocking both fish and birds for harvest by sportsmen, stating that their program was "merely carrying water in a sieve" — i.e., the animals stocked seldom became established populations being caught or shot immediately after their introduction through this "put and take" program. The habitat management work went on for several years, and the program was substantially completed by the fall of 1940 (there had been a hiatus after the 1938 hurricane, when cleaning up became the highest priority).

The first annual report (1940) of the new Division of Wildlife Research and Management that was created as part of the reorganization of the Department of Conservation noted a shift in the department's policy regarding the management of the state forests for forest wildlife that was in place during the CCC era. It stated: "In general, good forest management seems to be also good wildlife management, but certain modifications of the forester's proven methods are apparently going to prove desirable for the benefit of wildlife."

WOODLANDS AND WATER RESOURCES

Most of Massachusetts' 359 cities and towns depend for their water on surface water supplies drawn from forested watersheds, so it is not surprising that woodland-water relationships have received priority attention over the years. Forests are now known to protect water quality, moderate runoff to streams and reservoirs, and, in some instances, actually increase water yields. The management of forested watersheds can also improve wildlife habitats, furnish recreation, produce materials and economic returns from the harvesting of timber and other products, and improve landscape diversity and aesthetics as it can on other forested lands. The Commonwealth's approximately 80,000-acre holding of land and water at Quabbin Reservoir in central Massachusetts (some two thirds of the entire watershed) is a case in point. The Metropolitan District Commission/Massachusetts Water Resources Authority (MDC/MWRA) water supply system of which it is a part currently serves 2.4 million water users, about 40 percent of the population of Massachusetts. The land is also managed for timber production, and for wildlife and is of course one of the state's major recreational facilities.

According to the MDC's Natural Resource Specialist, Thom Kyker-Snowman, two forms of change, often powerful and oppositional, have been at work in the Quabbin forest throughout time. Disturbances have ranged from major natural climatic shifts and events to the abandonment and reclamation by forest of formerly cleared agricultural land. In that regard, the Quabbin forest mirrors events described elsewhere in this history. The pre-Colonial forest at Quabbin was likely a patchwork of varying composition due to natural disturbance, though stands of mature, mid-to-late successional species of great size are also in the historic record. This mosaic of forest types occurred again as a result of the history of human use of the area.

Chapter 321 of the Acts of 1927 made possible a general taking of land at Quabbin; farms and commercial properties were acquired and removed; the reservoir site was cleared of trees; four entire townships were officially discontinued; and ultimately, about 500 families were displaced. Shortly after its acquisition, the MDC embarked upon an active program to reforest the 10,000 acres of open upland it had acquired. Most of this work was accomplished in a period of 10 years. During this time, two major floods and a catastrophic hurricane also occurred.

Today, Quabbin is a model of sound watershed management. The MDC's Land Management Plan for 1995-2004 contains the long-term goals of assuring the availability of pure water for present and future generations; effectively managing, protecting, conserving, and enhancing its natural resources; ensuring public health and safety; and preventing adverse environmental impacts from degrading watershed resources. At the same time, Quabbin has been able to host a varied and flourishing population of forest wildlife (including several endangered species), serve as the site for some 700,000 low-intensity recreational visits each year, and return $300,000 annually in revenues from timber sales.

🍃 State Forestry Programs: Summing Up

It might be interesting to ponder how Alfred Akerman or Frank Rane would view the state of forestry in Massachusetts today after nearly a century of evolution. No doubt they would be pleased to note that the forest tax law has been used successfully to "relieve the growing timber crop of the unfair burden" that it once labored under. They would also be pleased that some state foresters are still dispensing "practical advice" to those who seek to improve the management of their land, although the demand for this advice has diminished with the growing corps of private consulting foresters. This advice has not always been well taken. In spite of the fact that there may very well be more standing timber in the Commonwealth today than at any other time since the days of the Massachusetts Bay Colony, the quality of that timber is not as good as it would be if woodlands had been intensively managed. Since they had departed the scene before the debates that raged about the regulation of forest practices at both the state and national level through the 1930s and 1940s, Akerman and Rane would probably puzzle over a forest cutting practices act that, today, deals more with water-quality issues than forest-management practices.

Akerman and Rane would be quite pleased to see that the system of forest reserves they advocated and pushed for has grown to over a quarter of a million acres — not the 1 million-acre goal put forth on several occasions, but still a respectable accomplishment. The fact that these lands have not been nurtured sufficiently would certainly be a disappointment to them. The thousands of acres of planted conifers, both native and introduced, that were not always suited to the site and, consequently, did not flourish could certainly be considered an "object lesson" in forest ecology. Neither forester would be pleased that the relationship between timber production and forest recreation that they both envisioned as blissful coexistence has instead often become contentious; they would be astonished that in a society that consumes vast amounts of wood, often drawing upon supplies from other parts of the world, in some quarters the idea is championed of not managing the forests at all.

How would Akerman and Rane react to today's myriad of special interest groups? Not that they did not exist a century ago — it's just that there are more causes being championed today than in their time. It would be a bitter pill for them to swallow that the once highly visible Office of the State Forester is now buried deep within a bureaucracy of secretariats, departments, divisions, and bureaus, and that its piece of the fiscal pie is smaller than ever before. And, few members of the public would come to listen to Akerman and Rane lecture about forestry — they could not begin to compete with cable or satellite TV.

Nowadays these early state foresters would not encounter the fervor that centered around efforts to reclaim the many acres of "waste and unproductive lands" at the turn of this century, since no one is currently predicting a timber famine. Instead, they would note a public that, more often than not, takes for granted the forests that cover almost two-thirds of the Massachusetts landscape.

Yet, Akerman and Rane could probably be convinced that better days for forestry are in the offing — that as global forest resources continue to shrink, Massachusetts forests will become more cherished than they ever have been. As happened a century ago, public interest in the forest's fate will be renewed. The dialogue about how these forests will be used will result in better management for both commodity and noncommodity values, and state forestry agencies, which are as much an extension of society today as they were a century ago, will play a large part in helping bring about this renewal. In short, both Akerman and Rane would undoubtedly be optimistic about the future.

 SOURCES

1. Various *Annual Reports* of the state forester, the State Forest Commission, the commissioner of the Departments of Conservation and Natural Resources, the Division of Forests and Parks, and the Department of Environmental Management, 1904–1971.
2. *Fifty Years a Forester* by Harold O. Cook, in cooperation with Lewis A. Carter, published by the Massachusetts Forest and Park Association, 1961.
3. *Massachusetts Forest and Park Association: A History,* by Richard Applegate, published by the Massachusetts Forest and Park Association, 1973.
4. *Massachusetts Forest and Park News,* various issues, 1937–1940, Massachusetts Forest and Park Association.
5. *Forests and Forestry in the United States: A Reference Anthology,* compiled by the Association of State Foresters, Ralph R. Widner, editor, 1968.
6. Personal communications with past and present DEM staff, particularly Bernice O'Brien, DEM Regional Headquarters, Pittsfield.

Professional Forestry, Forestry Education, and Research

ROBERT S. BOND

❧

DEVELOPMENT OF professional forestry in the Commonwealth of Massachusetts paralleled that of the United States in the late nineteenth century, although Massachusetts was not one of the nine states that had established a forestry administrative unit prior to 1900.[1] The early beginnings of forestry education came with the passage of the Morrill Act in 1862, which provided federal funds to states to establish and maintain a college in each state to teach agriculture and the mechanical arts. Massachusetts was the third state to agree to the stipulations to acquire such funding, a portion of which went to establish the Massachusetts Agricultural College, at Amherst, which admitted its first class in 1867.[2]

THE MASSACHUSETTS AGRICULTURAL COLLEGE

Although forestry was not initially part of the curriculum of the Massachusetts Agricultural College, it was noted as a subject to be taught as early as a year following the entry of the first class in 1867. Emphasis was primarily on tree planting and arboriculture (the science of the cultivation of trees and shrubs), not on forestry (the scientific management of forests for the continuous production of goods and services). Arboriculture was recognized in the curriculum in 1869, and a year later George B. Emerson, author of *Trees and Shrubs of Massachusetts,* was employed as a lecturer on the subject of arboriculture. The lectures covered "the planting and care of Trees for the production of Fuel, Timber, Fruit or other purposes."[3]

The third president, William S. Clark, was a former professor of chemistry, botany, and zoology at Amherst College, where he had graduated in 1848. He earned a Ph.D. in chemistry and botany from the

University of Goettingen in Germany. His interest in tree growth fostered the teaching of a course on this subject. Forestry was noted in the curriculum periodically during the 1880s, and in the botanical department there was a subsection headed "Forestry" in 1887. Subject matter focused on nursery and tree culture, and a course titled "Forestry and Landscape Gardening" was a six-hour elective until 1893, when it was dropped from the curriculum.[4]

One of the most significant mileposts in the recognition of professional forestry at the Massachusetts Agricultural College was a series of lectures by Dr. Bernhard E. Fernow, given in 1894 (sometimes reported as being in 1887) when he was chief of the Division of Forestry of the U.S. Department of Agriculture. Fernow was a German forester who had been trained in Prussia and had come to the United States in 1875, married an American, and became a citizen in 1883. In his annual report as chief of the Division of Forestry, he notes that the Massachusetts Agricultural College was one of seven colleges offering instruction in forestry. He and another German, Dr. Carl Schenk, and Gifford Pinchot, American but trained in France, were the initiators of professional forestry in the United States. These three men founded the earliest professional educational programs for forestry: Schenk operated the Biltmore School in Asheville, North Carolina, on the Biltmore Estate; Fernow formed the New York State College of Forestry at Cornell in 1898; and Pinchot and his family were the driving force behind the Yale School of Forestry, founded in 1900. Only the Yale program survives today.

Dr. Fernow's lectures obviously made an impact on the student community at the Massachusetts Agricultural College. Over subsequent years, *Aggie Life,* a student publication, carried a series of articles advocating the teaching of forestry. As is common today, students wanted to prevent the destruction of forests and to protect and conserve them from exploitation. The college's administration was slow to react to the students' urging, for little happened for nearly 10 years after the turn of the century.

THE HARVARD FOREST: A UNIQUE FOREST EDUCATION AND RESEARCH PROGRAM

In 1872, the year Arbor Day was founded, James Arnold, a New Bedford merchant, bequeathed to Harvard University $100,000 for the purpose of acquiring 125 acres of the Bussey Farm. Charles Sprague Sargent was appointed the Arnold Professor of Dendrology and Director of the Arboretum. The purpose was to culture, create and, maintain on the Bussey estate in Jamaica Plain, near Boston, a collection of all trees, shrubs, and herbs, both native and exotic, that could be grown out of doors in that climate. The result was the well-known Arnold Arboretum, which has "contributed materially to our knowledge of the taxonomic and silvical characteristics of the trees and shrubs that have been included in it."[5] This initiated Harvard College's interest in trees and forests. It was some 35 years later, in 1907, that the less well known but equally impressive Harvard Forest in Petersham was acquired to serve as a forest demonstration area, a research station, and a teaching and field laboratory for students.

Forestry education received recognition at Harvard University because two members of the university's faculty, Charles S. Sargent and Alexander Agassiz, were interested in forestry issues and served on the Forest Commission of the National Academy of Science, formed in 1896 to consider reserving from settlement lands that were in the public domain. These lands were later to become national forests and public grazing lands. (Today administered by the U.S. Forest Service and Bureau of Land Management.) In addition, Dean N. S. Shaler of Harvard's Lawrence Scientific School and later head of the U.S Geological Survey, was also a proponent of forestry education at Harvard. The importance of his role is indicated by his depiction with Professor Richard T. Fisher, first forestry instructor at the Harvard Forest, in one of the museum dioramas at the Harvard Forest, and the naming of the main building for him. Harvard president Charles W. Eliot, was also nationally involved with conservation and forest issues as exemplified by his service as the first president of the National Conservation Association in 1909, a position from which he resigned a year later in favor of Gifford Pinchot.

Forestry teaching at Harvard College commenced in 1902–03 under the leadership of Richard T. Fisher and J. G. Jack, instructors on the staff of Harvard's Lawrence Scientific School, Department of Forestry, at Cambridge. From 1908–12 the department became a division and in 1912 the division became the School of Forestry. Initially, a bachelor of science degree in forestry was granted for the program; it took one to four years to fulfill requirements, depending on the student's back-

Figure 1. Albert C. Cline, the third director of the Harvard Forest, surveying downed old-growth white pine in Petersham, Massachusetts, after the 1938 hurricane. In the space of 48 hours, some 70 percent of the volume of the Harvard Forest blew down, abruptly terminating 30 years of research on white pine silviculture and setting the stage for a new program of teaching and research on long-term changes in northeastern forest ecosystems. Courtesy of Harvard Forest Archives.

ground. Instruction was primarily in the classroom, although some fieldwork was done on private properties. By 1907, Fisher had concluded that the undergraduate degree should not be offered but that there should be a limited number of students studying for the master of forestry degree with a focus on research and limited classroom teaching. Years later Professor H. S. Graves, director of the Yale School of Forestry, wrote:

> I regard Fisher's work in education as one of his largest contributions to forestry. He properly resisted the idea, still held by many, that a practical man with a moderate knowledge of forestry can meet the requirements of the profession. The great influence which the Harvard Forest has exerted and will continue to exert is derived from the high standards in education which Fisher set, from the character of his teaching, and from the vision of the broad significance of forestry in our national life which has been emphasized at the institution.[6]

The standards and philosophy set by Fisher have continued at the Harvard Forest to this day.

Fisher's career spanned 32 years, until his untimely death in 1934. Early faculty members of the Harvard forestry program and many of his students and those who came later became renowned professional foresters and forestry educators and researchers. One of these, Austin Cary, joined the Harvard College faculty in 1905 as an assistant professor, and was greatly admired for his contributions to New England forest practices and for writing one of the earliest published manuals on forestry. He left in 1911 to assume a position at the Maine Agricultural College at Orono. Another early instructor, Ralph C. Hawley, a student from 1904 to 1906, became a highly regarded professor at the Yale School of Forestry and wrote *The Practice of Silviculture,* first published in 1921.[7] Harold O. Cook, M.F. (master of forestry) 1907, started with the state that year, becoming the chief state forester of Massachusetts in 1919 and served in this role until 1962. Many other early graduates became leaders in the forestry profession, as forestry was still a new field and Harvard was among the pioneering institutions teaching the subject.

The acquisition of the Harvard Forest in 1907 greatly affected the teaching of forestry. There was no endowment, and needed operating funds came from the sale of 10 million board feet of harvestable old-field white pine. Students gained practical field experience by doing course work on the forest in fall and spring terms and taking classes in Cambridge during winter term. In 1907, when graduate study was instituted, the school came to be administered by the Graduate School of Applied Science and was renamed the Division of Forestry. In 1914 the forestry faculty was combined with the Bussey Institute as the

Faculty of Applied Biology. At this time, undergraduate instruction was discontinued and Harvard Forest became a graduate program. Director Richard Fisher's memorandum to the corporation stated: "The staff of the School is unanimous in believing that the time has come to . . . organize squarely and exclusively as an institution for research and the training of advanced specialists. . . . The School of Forestry, therefore, proposes to give up entirely its general course, to devote itself strongly to the research which the elementary teaching has hitherto precluded."[8] There was a relationship not only with the Bussey Institute but also with the Harvard Business School, where Fisher had a joint appointment. This formal tie ended when Fisher gave up his professorship in the Business School in 1924. However, Harvard's interest in the economic or business aspects of forests has continued up to the last decade of the twentieth century, alongside a primary focus on the biological and ecological foundations of forestry.

This policy change in 1914–15 established the future operation of the Harvard Forest education program. It has had small numbers of students, generally 5 to 12 in residence; teaching is informal and students actively participate in forest operations. Silvicultural research was emphasized during the early period. There was collaboration in research as well as in providing advice to businessmen, landowners, and government agencies. The 1938 hurricane devastated the forest's growing stock. Although much of it was salvaged, this event greatly lowered the forest's economic value, and its management has not since greatly contributed financially to the program's operation.

In 1932 Harvard Forest became a department within the Faculty of Arts and Sciences and a program in its Graduate School, where it has remained. W. Shepard became director in 1935, following Professor Fisher's death. He was followed by A. C. Cline, M.F. 1923 (1939–42), when Shepard took a leave to do war work. Cline put a new teaching policy into effect. Two general methods of instruction were initiated on a trial basis — "the research project method and the so-called case method." This was a shift "out of the mainstream of teaching silvicultural research which the forest had followed since 1914."[9]

No students were accepted during the war, but Dr. Stephen Spurr joined the staff as an instructor in forestry in 1941 and was made assistant director in 1942. Along with two research assistants, he worked on a wartime camouflage research project. Out of this research came

Dr. Spurr's development of forestry uses for aerial photogrammetry and a textbook on the subject published in 1948. Principally a forest ecologist, Dr. Spurr wrote three publications while at the Forest, two coauthored by A. C. Cline. Spurr left the Harvard Forest in 1950 to go to the University of Minnesota and then the University of Michigan, where he later became dean of the School of Natural Resources. He had an outstanding professional career in forestry education and as a textbook author. He served as president of the Society of American Foresters and capped a distinguished academic career as president of the University of Texas.

In 1946, Dr. Hugh Raup, a botanist, was appointed director of the Harvard Forest, and the first postwar student was admitted. Dr. Raup had been a staff researcher at the Forest and on the faculty of the Arnold Arboretum. He had been encouraged by Professor Fisher "to study the flora of the Forest to see whether his biological interest could explain the results of many silvicultural experiments."[10] Dr. Raup remained director until his retirement in 1967, having been on the Harvard faculty for 35 years. He continued earlier philosophies of graduate education, and he commenced building a staff to carry out both research and teaching.

Graduate students from liberal arts colleges who had majored in biology began to be accepted in 1951–52 for the M.F.S. (master of forest science) degree. The program remained small, with little change in the basic philosophy of educating students for the master's degree. Doctoral students did their research at the forest but enrolled in one of the other departments in Cambridge. Because Dr. Raup came from the biology faculty, the ties with the campus and programs at Cambridge increased. The appointment of Ernest M. Gould, Jr., a forest economist, to the Forest faculty in 1947 further strengthened ties with the Cambridge economists, especially Prof. John D. Black, with whom Dr. Gould had studied for his M.F.S and Ph.D. Professor Black, a resource economist, had a major influence on the subject of forestry economics as adviser to students who became leaders in this field.

Over the years, Harvard Forest has supported a great diversity of research interests, as illustrated by a statement in the 1992–93 annual report: "Through the years researchers at the Forest have focused on silviculture and forest management, soils and the development of forest site concepts, the biology of temperate and tropical trees, forest ecology and economics and ecosystem dynamics."[11] Harvard Forest has always had an interest in historic human and natural disturbances in the forests of central New England, as "epitomized by the Harvard Forest Long Term Ecological Research (LTER) program established in 1988 through funding by the National Science Foundation."[12]

The most impressive educational programs at Harvard Forest have not necessarily been those that granted degrees but those that brought professional foresters to the Forest from all over the United States and the world. Some individuals visited for as long as a year, others for a few days. A series of two-week "Conferences on Forest Production" began in 1953 and were largely the responsibility of Dr. Gould, Dr. Raup, and the soil scientist John Goodlett (later replaced by Walter Lyford). From 1953 to 1956 the theme of these two-week conferences was "Forestry in Transition." The generally 15 to 20 professional foresters in attendance came from state, federal, private, and university employment. The diversity of these groups made for lively discussion both in the classroom and in the field, which was a major component of work during the day. Because participants were housed at the Forest, much informal discussion went on during mealtimes and in the evenings. The theme of the conferences from 1956 to 1959 was changed to "Investment Analysis as Applied to the Forest Resource." No conference was held in 1960, but they resumed in 1961 and went through 1965 with the theme "Balancing Forest Resource Use." The themes of these conferences reflect concerns of the times in forest-resource management, with the last series considering multiple-use issues. If held today, they would undoubtedly be focusing on biodiversity and ecosystem management.

Another important program, instituted in 1962, continues up to the present day: the Bullard Fellowships. This competitive program brings to the Forest midcareer scientists from all over the world for six months to a year of study and research. The interaction of these individuals — who generally have diverse interests — with one another, with the faculty and staff of the forest, and with visitors adds greatly to the intellectual milieu of the institution. Those who have had the honor to be granted a Bullard Fellowship or to interact with fellows, faculty, and staff would attest to this value of the Harvard Forest.

Harvard Forest hosts numerous groups interested in forest-resource use. It has excellent facilities and encourages their use at no or nominal cost in order to stimulate interest in forest-resource study and use. Forestry degree programs throughout the country often include a stop at Harvard Forest while students tour the Northeast on field trips, not only to see the Forest and learn about ongoing research, but to see the dioramas in the Fisher Museum (for more on the Fisher Museum, see page 231).

In this limited space it is difficult to accord recognition to all the many faculty members over the years who have made major contributions to Harvard Forest and its worldwide recognition as a distinguished forestry research and educational institution. Details may be found in the published annual reports on file at the Forest. All of the leaders of the Forest have had outstanding abilities in their fields. More than that, they have had avocations that were equally rewarding, and their interests and interactions with people outside of the realm of their specializations made them distinguished human beings. Of these outstanding people, three of the most recent directors and the current one certainly deserve particular acknowledgement for their leadership.

Between 1968 and 1970, Dr. Ernest M. Gould, Jr., served as acting director and became assistant director in 1970 until his death in 1988. Ernie, as he was known to everyone, gave continuity to the institution through three directors and was probably better known throughout professional forestry circles than any of the other faculty members. After his death in 1988 the annual report for 1987–88 summed up his impact on the Forest: "His passing marks the end of the Harvard Forest as a research center in forestry in the sense that was originally conceived by Professor Fisher . . . and as it was modified and extended by Professor Raup and Professor Zimmerman. . . . All of us will miss Ernie's direct friendliness, his cheerful willingness to consult on all manner of issues, from personal to professional, to regional or national. His wisdom and good sense undergirded many facets of the Harvard Forest community in ways that have made Petersham and the Forest an important and memorable place for many people."[13]

Following the directorship of Dr. Raup (1946–67), Dr. Martin Zimmerman became the Charles Bullard Professor of Forestry on July 1, 1970. He served as an interim director, as did Dr. Gould, during the three years after Dr. Raup's retirement. Dr. Zimmerman assumed this position after a distinguished career with the Cabot Foundation as a researcher in tree physiology. "The forest inspired Martin not only to do many of his physiological experiments on trees growing in the woods, but also to have an unusually broad interest in the technical and social problems of forest resource use and development.... Consequently, he came to take a special interest in the design and conduct of the long-term silvicultural experiments at the Forest." Dr. Gould described Zimmerman as a renaissance man with great abilities as an artist, a craftsman in stained glass, a builder of harpsichords, and a fine musician. He was an outstanding teacher who had "compassionate concern for each of his students." His tenure as director ended when death took him on March 7, 1984, at too young an age.[14]

Dr. John G. Torrey had moved to the Forest faculty in 1970, and became director following Dr. Zimmerman's death. Here was another individual who had been on the Harvard faculty for a long time and was familiar with his predecessors at the Forest, so he could readily carry on the traditions that had been established. Torrey had a "brilliant scientific career in the field of plant development and microbial symbioses. More importantly, he was a great mentor who guided the personal development of students, colleagues and friends through his wise understanding of science and people and his balanced approach to life."[15]

Dr. Torrey retired in June 1990 to pursue his interest in art collecting, particularly nineteenth-century British and American etchings. During his administration he oversaw the development of a program that will have a long-lasting impact on research at the forest. Along with Assistant Director Dr. David R. Foster, who succeeded him as director, Dr. Torrey was the principal architect of the "Long Term Ecological Research" (LTER) proposal to the National Science Foundation. This proposal involved multiple universities as well as disciplines: "The Harvard Forest is one of eighteen sites forming the Long Term Ecological Research (LTER) program of the National Science Foundation. Each site addresses ecological questions of a long-term nature; collectively the sites undertake comparative studies across ecosystems. The central theme of the Harvard Forest LTER is a comparison of the historically important physical disturbances and modern chemical disturbances in terms of their effect on forest ecosystem structure and function."[16] The long-term records of the forest will be valuable in explaining the historically important physical disturbance impacts. Dr. David Foster, an ecologist, joined the staff in 1983 and became assistant director of the Harvard Forest in 1988 when the position was vacated because of Dr.

Gould's death. As director since 1990, he oversees the Harvard Forest LTER program. Dr. Foster shares many traits with his predecessors, and so the Forest can look forward to very able leadership as it approaches its centennial year.

Since the mid-1970s the forest has increased its involvement with the rest of Harvard University, which reflects a return to some of the earlier philosophy of teaching undergraduates. Staff with faculty appointments teach classes in Cambridge and also teach students who travel out to the forest for field-oriented courses. Also, a number of those who hold faculty positions in Cambridge with the Graduate School of Design, the Kennedy School of Government, and the Earth and Planetary Science program are associates of the Harvard Forest. One popular course is the Harvard Forest Freshman Seminar, in which students come to the Forest for four weekends during the spring and focus on forest biology.

During the early to late 1970s summer undergraduate courses were offered at the Forest through the Harvard University Summer School. This has evolved into the Harvard Forest Summer Research Program, funded by the National Science Foundation, the Andrew M. Mellon Foundation, and the Harvard Forest endowment. Undergraduate students from a number of universities receive training, do independent research and study, and work on the Forest. In the summer of 1992 there was "a total of 34 undergraduate students and recent graduates in our summer program designed to provide first-hand experience in ecological investigations. Many students conducted independent research and all participated in a weekly seminar program and excursions to other research areas."[17]

A number of other teaching programs have been conducted over the years in conjunction with other departments at Harvard. Director Foster currently teaches "Forest Ecology" in the Biology Department and "Topics in Environmental Policy" with Dr. Charles H. W. Foster in the Kennedy School of Government. Landscape architecture students of the Harvard Graduate School of Design visit four weekends in the fall to consider the forest resource as a component of the rural environment, a subject that has become important in land-use planning and on national, state, and large industrial forests. The Forest is also used by the Department of Organismic and Evolutionary Biology and the School of Public Administration.

The Harvard Forest in Petersham, Massachusetts, has been an integral part of Harvard University throughout the Forest's history. Though it has at various times been closely associated with the Cambridge campus and at others has been more independent, it has always drawn from within the university for leadership. The importance of the Harvard Forest program has lain not in educating foresters for entry positions but in furthering the education of professionals, contributing to basic and applied forest-resources research, and exposing foresters to other disciplines associated with their work.

The Fisher Museum at the Harvard Forest

One of the outstanding public educational forestry exhibits in Massachusetts is the Fisher Museum at the Harvard Forest. The main theme of the museum is changing land use in central New England from the time of settlement, when forests covered the landscape, through a period when the forest was cleared for agricultural use, to the abandonment for agriculture and the land's reversion back to forest. This process is dramatically and artistically illustrated in a series of seven dioramas depicting the change over 230 years, from 1,700 to 1930. (Four of these dioramas are depicted on pages 44–48 of this volume.)

There are 16 other dioramas: a group of 10 that illustrate "silvicultural practices developed at the Harvard Forest for application to local forest conditions," and 6 that show "certain allied functions of modern forestry." The latter include a model on wildlife management, another on the control of soil erosion, and two models on forest fires; these models emphasize the wastefulness of developing forests only to have them destroyed through human carelessness. The large central model in the Fisher Museum is a reproduction of a stand of an old-growth forest on the Harvard Forest and a portion of Harvard Pond — a scene that suggests the great aesthetic and recreational value of the forest.[18]

The historical and silvicultural series were designed by Richard T. Fisher, the first director of the Forest. The models, constructed in the studios of Guernsey and Pitman at Cambridge between 1931 and 1941, are so lifelike that individual tree species can be identified.

Other exhibits in the museum illustrate land-use change in the town of Petersham. One map shows stone walls that once surrounded fields but now meander through forests. Other pictures and graphics show the devastation wrought by the hurricane of 1938, insect and disease damage to trees and wood, and research on tree-root development. Posters illustrate current research at the forest, and historical features of the forest resource.

Since 1988, Dr. John O'Keefe has been coordinator of the Fisher Museum and has developed additional exhibits and slide presentations illustrating the history and theme of Harvard Forest and its educational and research activities. He has also made it more user-friendly, opening the museum to visitors during working hours from Monday to Friday and staffing it with volunteers on Saturday and Sunday from noon to four P.M. May through October.

UNIVERSITY OF MASSACHUSETTS, AMHERST

Over the ridge not too distant to the west and south of Petersham is the town of Amherst and the primary unit of the multicampus University of Massachusetts. As mentioned previously, this large state university started as the Massachusetts Agricultural College (MAC), one of two Massachusetts land-grant colleges founded under provisions of the Morrill Act of 1862. During the 1930s it was designated the Massachusetts State College and in 1948 the University of Massachusetts. Forestry has had some recognition almost from the beginning. Although very limited in early years, the program has grown along with the rest of the university system. In contrast to its private neighbor, Harvard Forest, the public institution focused on undergraduate forestry training in its early years. Not until the 1950s did it develop graduate programs and become heavily involved in research.

The need for a forestry program was recognized by MAC president Kenyon L. Butterfield following his appointment in 1906. He reorganized several departments into a Division of Horticulture in concert with Frank A. Waugh, who became the division's first head. In the president's report to the state legislature he stated: "In the matter of instruction, for instance, I think we should have a professor of Forestry. I suppose that I have had more letters from prospective students asking about forestry instruction here than on any other subject."[19] Without waiting for a response from the legislature, he created a Department of Forestry as part of the Division of Horticulture in 1909. He hired as the first faculty member Franklin A. Moon, a graduate in 1901 of Amherst

College and in 1909 of the Yale School of Forestry. The 1911 course catalogue listed two courses, dendrology and silviculture. A year later two additional courses were listed: "Advanced Forestry," which included forest economics, policy and law, forest mensuration, forest management, and lumbering; and "Silvics and Silviculture," which was a field component of the silviculture course.

Before he could begin teaching these newly listed courses, Professor Moon resigned to accept a position at the New York State College of Forestry at Syracuse University, where he subsequently had a distinguished career. A Yale classmate of Moon's, William Darrow Clark, replaced him. Clark expanded the forestry curriculum by adding a course, "Introduction to Forestry," for students not concentrating in forestry. Of the four major courses, three emphasized practical fieldwork. There were few students in the program — in 1913, one senior and five juniors — although the program was favorably noted in an October 1916 issue of the student newspaper: "The course in forestry offered to the students of MAC is, in every sense of the word practical."[20]

The Mount Toby Experimental Forest, located five miles away in Sunderland, was acquired in 1916 from the heirs of John L. Graves. He had been willing to sell it to the college for $30,000, but the state legislature was not willing or able to appropriate that amount of money for the acquisition. At Graves's death in March 1915 the property was inherited by two maiden ladies who were willing to sell the property for $15,000; they did so when the legislature appropriated funds for its purchase in May 1916. Professor Clark was very pleased with the acquisition and noted that the diversity of forest types represented those found in the entire state "from the Berkshire Hills to Cape Cod" and, "even more rare . . . are found in every stage of development."[21]

World War I disrupted the progress of the forestry program at the Massachusetts Agricultural College. William Clark resigned in 1920 and was replaced by Laurence R. Grose, also with an M.F. degree from Yale. The 1921 course catalogue stated: "The forestry major is designed to give a grounding in the branches of natural science upon which forest development is based."[22] However, within a year the focus of forestry instruction had shifted to providing a service-type course to agriculture students who were "prospective owners or managers of farm woodlots."[23] This change apparently occurred because the state legislature, which had in 1916 taken away MAC's fiscal autonomy and even the autonomy of its curricular offerings, opposed any expansion of courses that did not deal with vocational instruction in agriculture. In part, too, this change may have resulted from national developments in forest policy. The passage of the Clarke-McNary Act in 1924 had as one of its four main objectives cooperation with states in reforestation and management, particularly "in providing nursery stock for the establishment of windbreaks, shelterbelts and farm woodlots on denuded or non-forested lands."[24] These legislative constraints led to the resignation of President Butterfield in 1924 and that of Professor Grose in 1930. Professional forestry education was at a new low, but this was to soon change when Robert P. Holdsworth replaced Professor Grose.

Professional Forestry Education at the University of Massachusetts

Professor Holdsworth led the forestry program for over 26 years, until he stepped down as department head in 1956 and retired in 1958. He was a 1911 graduate of Michigan State College and another product of the Yale School of Forestry, and also had a fellowship to the Royal Forest School in Stockholm, Sweden. He was a veteran of World War I and spent four years as a horseback ranger for the U.S. Forest Service in the West following his undergraduate education. Prior to entering into his graduate forestry training, Holdsworth had 11 years of experience in an import brokerage firm in Boston. His broad business experience and leadership qualities quickly benefited the fledgling forestry program. In addition, a change in the presidency of the college also created favorable circumstances to developing forestry at MAC. The new president, Hugh Potter Baker, a forester, came to the job in 1932 from a previous position as dean of the New York State College of Forestry at Syracuse University. Here was an ally for Holdsworth at the highest level in the college.

Even before President Baker's arrival, Holdsworth had initiated changes to move away from service courses aimed at agricultural students, reversing the philosophy that had been foisted onto Professor Grose by the administration and the legislature. The 1931–32 catalogue gave evidence that the program was once again directed at training students who intended to make a career of professional forestry. Four basic forest science courses were listed, and all entailed fieldwork on the Mount Toby Experimental Forest.

Professor Holdsworth developed a cooperative agreement with Dean Henry S. Graves of the Yale School of Forestry, which permitted the best students at MAC after their third year to work toward a Yale M.F. (master of forestry) degree. Following the first year at Yale, the student would receive a B.S. from Massachusetts State College (as it was now called) and then after another year at Yale would be awarded the M.F. This program was a forerunner of a close association between Yale and the post-World War II University of Massachusetts, when many graduates of the latter went on to Yale for the M.F.

Through President Baker's efforts and those of Professor Holdsworth, the forestry program continued to grow, despite the fiscal constraints caused by the Depression. The prospect for employment brightened during the 1930s with the New Deal administration of President Franklin D. Roosevelt. The Civilian Conservation Corps recruited foresters to plan and oversee projects and assured virtually all forestry graduates a job. These jobs provided good training for leadership and gave many forestry graduates of this period their first foothold in the profession.

During the 1930s three faculty members were added to the program. First, J. Harry Rich was hired to teach in the area of forest products and wood technology. Then, in 1936, Reuben H. Trippensee was engaged to teach wildlife management. Professor Trippensee was the first faculty member of the department to hold a Ph.D. He taught two courses, "Principles of Wildlife Conservation" and "Introduction to Wildlife Management." Trippensee was a pioneer in the field of wildlife management, having written two standard textbooks widely used in forestry and wildlife education. The third person to join the faculty was Arnold D. Rhodes, who came in 1937, after earning an M.F. at Yale, to teach dendrology, silvics, and silviculture. He and Holdsworth had more positive influence on the growth of the department than anyone else.

Although World War II brought some slowdown in the development of what had become the Department of Forestry and Wildlife Management, the program continued throughout the war, even though some faculty members were called into the service. Upon their return in 1946 and 1947, the department had a growth spurt, adding courses and faculty. By 1945–46, the dean noted in his annual report, three more forestry courses had been added, one in silvics, another in forest protection, and the third in harvesting of forest products. By 1949–50 there were 13 courses in forestry, four courses in wood technology, and five in wildlife management. Forestry could at last offer a full program to anyone who wished to major in the subject.[25] The extensive course offerings were possible because three faculty had been added. One, Paul Stickel, had experience with the U.S. Forest Service and was author of a textbook on seeding and planting of forests. He taught that subject, as well as forest protection (principally from fire). Two recent graduates of the Yale School of Forestry were added, Alton B. Cole and W. P. MacConnell, both of whom were MSC graduates who had returned to Yale after wartime service to earn M.F. degrees. Given the flood of veterans that entered the University of Massachusetts in 1948, Cole and MacConnell found themselves teaching students their own age or older. Cole was called back to the air force in 1951, because of the Korean Conflict, and was to make a career of the military except for a brief return to the faculty in the 1970s. Professor MacConnell has been a mainstay of the department since that time and holds the record for longevity on the department faculty — nearly 50 years as of this writing.

Two developments occurred as the decade of the 1940s ended. At that time the federal civil service required foresters employed in the U.S. Forest Service to come from programs accredited by the Society of American Foresters. The SAF carried out a thorough on-site review after Professor Holdsworth submitted an application for accreditation and filed a detailed report of the forestry B.S. degree program. Thus, the University of Massachusetts became one of the 21 accredited forestry programs nationwide; two others in New England had been accredited prior to World War II. Accreditation was a major step in aiding graduates to obtain other professional jobs and to be accepted in graduate school.

Two-Year Forestry Program in the Stockbridge School of Agriculture

A two-year program, called the Stockbridge School of Agriculture, was started in the Massachusetts Agricultural College following World War I to provide technical agricultural training. The school was named for Levi Stockbridge, who had been the MAC's farm superintendent and instructor in agriculture in 1867 and who later served as president of MAC from 1880 to 1882. When Holdsworth took over the forestry department in 1930 he felt that a two-year forest technology program leading to an associate's degree would be valuable in forestry, particularly to educate farmers in the management of farm woodlots. It was also a way to fulfill the desire of the legislature to provide vocational agricultural courses. What evolved were two programs, one in wildlife (this program was relatively short-lived and was abandoned in the early 1940s) and one in forestry. The one in forestry is the more significant. After World War II there were 15 to 20 students per class in the Stockbridge forestry program, and faculty were teaching both two-year courses and four-year (baccalaureate) forestry courses, often with much the same subject matter. The large number of two-year students may have partly justified expansion of the faculty in the Departments of Forestry and Wildlife Management. But, as graduate degree programs were initiated in the late 1950s, faculty had to deal with the complexities of ranging from the technician level to the master's, and ultimately the doctoral level. An increased teaching burden caused the combining of some associate (two-year) degree courses with those for the B.S degree.

When the Society of American Foresters did its 1962 accreditation of the University of Massachusetts B.S. program, the forestry department was told that it would lose SAF accreditation unless a separate two-year degree program with an independent faculty was initiated. Therefore the decision was made in 1963 to drop Stockbridge's two-year forestry program. However, a two-year wood utilization program was initiated to train individuals for wood industry and retail lumber-sales jobs. This program ended in 1972. It should be noted that these programs were very valuable for students who could not qualify for entrance to the B.S. degree program or were uncertain about their academic goals. However, many of them (probably over half) continued their education either at the University of Massachusetts or at other institutions — a few even to the Ph. D. level.

Expanding Definitions of Forestry and Forest Resources: The Holdsworth Natural Resources Center

For about 10 years, from 1953 to 1963, the Department of Forestry and Wildlife Management was housed in the so-called Conservation Building, which had once been the offices of President Clark. In 1963 work was completed on the new Holdsworth Natural Resources Center, finally bringing all the department's faculty together under one roof. Professor Arnold Rhodes, the department head since 1956, was the driving force behind the new building; he worked closely with the architects in its planning and design. Holdsworth Natural Resources Center, was designed not only for teaching but for research, with large classrooms, a library, laboratories and smaller research labs for faculty and graduate student use.

The increased growth and diversity of the Department of Forestry and Wildlife Management was overseen by Professor Rhodes. His philosophy was reflected in his remarks at the dedication of the Holdsworth Natural Resources Center in 1963: "Over the years departmental programs have broadened to embrace most of the major wildland resources with increasing emphasis upon the integration of the several uses of land, water, vegetation and people. The problem of the future of this nation of erupting population is to devise the means whereby man may live in harmony with his environment while yet benefiting from the economic, esthetic and spiritual values which the environment can provide."[26] Within the department, he built a staff to at least address the resources aspect of this philosophy. It was natural for the four major components — fisheries, forestry, wildlife, and wood technology — to form "sections," or minidepartments, and to elect their own leadership.

By the time the Department of Forestry and Wildlife Management moved into the new building, there had been additional diversification in its offerings. Fisheries biology was added to the wildlife biology program. The Cooperative Wildlife Research Unit added "Fisheries" to its name and thereby added fisheries biologists to the adjunct faculty. The growing emphasis on research, greater program diversity, a physical plant designed for graduate research, and numerous inquiries from potential students gave the impetus to the faculty to petition the Graduate Council in April 1966 for a Ph.D. program for all majors within the department. At this time there were 14 Ph.D.s on the faculty, with another to receive the degree shortly. The trustees approved the petition in June 1966.

Numerous faculty changes during the 1960s created an increasing diversity of research interests and course offerings. Dr. Charles F. Cole, a fisheries biologist, joined the faculty in 1964. Dr. Trippensee retired at this time and was replaced by Dr. Fred Greeley, who changed the wildlife program's emphasis from forest management to the zoological aspects of wildlife. In 1966 Dr. Carl Carlozzi joined the faculty to head up a new major, Natural Resource Studies. This program attracted students who wanted more freedom of course choices than that offered by a major in either forestry or wildlife management. Other additions in the department duing the late 1960s and early 1970s were Dr. Brayton

F. Wilson, in tree physiology; Dr. William W. Rice, a specialist in wood drying, in wood technology; Dr. Joseph S. Larson, in wildlife, with emphasis on wetlands ecology; and Dr. Michael Ross, in fisheries biology. There were also major changes in the Wildlife and Fisheries Cooperative Research Unit. Upon Dr. Sheldon's retirement, Dr. Wendell Dodge became unit leader; the assistant leader was a fisheries biologist, Dr. Roger Reed. Two additional staff members were added to the unit, one in wildlife and the other in fisheries.

When he stepped down as head of the Department of Forestry and Wildlife Management in 1972, Professor Rhodes was replaced by an alumnus of the class of '50, Donald R. Progulske. As an undergraduate Dr. Progulske had majored in wildlife management and minored in forestry; he earned his doctorate in wildlife biology at the University of Missouri in 1956. From there he went directly to the faculty at South Dakota State University, where he had served during the previous nine years as head of the Department of Wildlife and Fisheries Science.

During Dr. Progulske's tenure, undergraduate forestry classes burgeoned from an average size of 25 to 30 students to 70 to 80. These enrollments continued into the late 1970s and early 1980s. At just about the time the faculty considered implementing some limits on class size, enrollments started to drop. By the mid-1980s there was some question as to whether the forestry major could continue to survive because of low student enrollment.

Progulske remained department head until 1980. Because of fiscal constraints then in force, a national search for a new head was not permitted and the faculty elected Dr. Joseph Larson as chairman. When Dr. Larson went on to form and head the university's Environmental Institute in 1983, the faculty turned to another longtime member of the forestry faculty to serve as chairman of the Department of Forestry and Wildlife Management, Donald L. Mader. In poor health by 1985, Dr. Mader indicated his desire to step down as chairman and the university was finally convinced to support a national search for a new department head. Donald G. Arganbright, with a background in wood products from the University of California, Berkeley, became department head in 1986. Arganbright inherited a difficult situation, given the six years of transitory departmental leadership and declining student enrollments. Many faculty changes and another period of fiscal constraint meant that when a faculty member voluntarily left or retired, a replacement of that position's discipline was not assured. The forestry section suffered the most because its faculty had been in place the longest and were closest to retirement. As faculty numbers shrank, some key disciplines were no longer covered, and it was difficult for the forestry program to retain its accreditation by the Society of American Foresters. However, as of 1997 the program is still accredited and recent faculty additions bode well for continuation of accreditation.

In summary, forestry education within the University of Massachusetts and its predecessor colleges developed as a professional education program for a total of 42 years under the guidance of two men — Robert P. Holdsworth (26 years) and Arnold D. Rhodes (16 years). They were energetic, dedicated individuals who were able to take advantage of the times in which they served to develop a program that was highly ranked among those of all institutions nationally. Both Holdsworth and Rhodes served on the state Board of Natural Resources, which provided a close link between this state agency and the university. Succeeding department heads have not served in this capacity. In the 24 years since Professor Rhodes stepped down, there have been two department heads and two chairmen, whose average terms of service have been six years, compared with an average of 21 years for Holdsworth and Rhodes. Not only has the position of department head become much more complex because of additional academic programs, but the faculty is much larger and the university administration's demands on department heads is greater.

Forestry Research at the University of Massachusetts

In contrast to the situation at the Harvard Forest, research has been of secondary importance at the University of Massachusetts. In 1882 the Massachusetts Agricultural Experiment Station was established by the state legislature at the urging of MAC president William Clark. In 1887 the federal government passed the Hatch Act, which provided funds to assist states in establishing agricultural experiment stations, including forestry research. But because most stations were under the direction of agricultural professionals, forestry received minimal funding.

Federal funding of forestry research has been important to the University of Massachusetts. In 1923 an appropriation by Congress, initiated by Senator Henry Cabot Lodge, established a Forest Experiment Station of the U.S. Department of Agriculture (USDA), Forest

Figure 2. A managed pine stand in the Mount Tobey Experimental Forest, Sunderland. This forest, acquired by the University of Massachusetts in 1916, is still used for teaching and research. Holdsworth Natural Resources Center Library, University of Massachusetts, Amherst.

Service on the campus. The station's research focused on measuring growth on the Mount Toby Forest and the effects of the chestnut blight on the changing composition of the forest. The station remained for only nine years, at which point it was moved to New Haven, to be associated with the Yale School of Forestry. During those nine years it had three directors, all of whom achieved distinction in the field of forestry education and research: S. T. Dana, J. S. Boyce, and C. E. Behre.

The master's program in wildlife management created in 1942 under Dr. Trippensee's guidance was enhanced in 1948 with the establishment of the Massachusetts Cooperative Wildlife Research Unit under the direction of Dr. William Sheldon. This unit enabled the program to attract graduate students by offering research assistantships and also provided for advanced course offerings by Dr. Sheldon as an adjunct faculty member. This federally funded project was supported by the Wildlife Restoration Act of 1937, commonly known as the Pittman-Robertson Act, which provided funds to the states from the federal tax on firearms, shells, and cartridges. These funds were apportioned on the basis of the number of licensed hunters and a state's total area. Forestry did not at that time enjoy such dedicated research funds.

In 1954 Holdsworth gained support for forestry research from the College of Agriculture Experiment Station. This enabled the hiring in 1956 of the first forestry faculty member with a Ph.D., Donald L. Mader, a forest soils scientist from the University of Wisconsin. Although Dr. Mader was to focus on research, he also taught courses in forest soils. Professor Rhodes, who had just succeeded Holdsworth, now had some ammunition to proceed with a proposal to the university trustees for a master's program in forestry, which was approved in June of 1957. Another Ph.D., Harold B. Gatslick, joined the faculty to replace J. Harry Rich, who retired in 1958, and by 1963 a second position in wood technology was added with the appointment of Dr. R. Bruce Hoadley.

Forestry research received a major boost with passage in 1962 of the Cooperative Forestry Research Act (McIntire-Stennis Act). There was now a dedicated source of federal forestry research funds allocated to the agricultural experiment station to augment the Hatch Act monies, which had been doled out only sparingly to forestry research projects in the past.

Since inception of the doctoral degree program in the mid-1960s, research has been a mandatory portion of a faculty member's performance evaluation. Research publications in refereed journals are required if faculty are to earn tenure and then to progress in rank. The diversity of the faculty in disciplines other than forestry has meant that a wide range of research has been undertaken.

Some forestry research, mostly in applied silviculture, has been done by faculty over the years, much of it on Mount Toby Experimental Forest and the so-called farm woodlots adjacent to campus. The allocation of Hatch funds to forestry in the mid-1950s marked the beginning of more formal forestry research. A certain percentage of Hatch appropriations was required to be used in marketing research, and there was also a provision for "regional research," research undertaken cooperatively by faculty from various universities, both requirements taken advantage of by forestry faculty in the areas of forest soils and wood products.

One of the first regional projects was carried out by Professor Harry Rich, with other faculty from northeastern universities, to describe the marketing of wood products. This research comprised several different projects, with the final ones undertaken by Dr. Robert S. Bond, a forest economist, who joined the faculty in the fall of 1956. Most of these regional researchers were either forest or natural-resource economists. Following completion of the cooperative effort on timber-product marketing, several projects examined forest recreation, which was becoming a major use of the forest as a result of improvements in automobile transportation, the improved post–World War II economy, and greater leisure time for the working public.

Field research and teaching were enhanced by the gift to the university in 1951–52 of a 1,200-acre tract of forestland in Pelham by Mrs. Esther Hyde Cadwell, which became the Cadwell Memorial Forest. She offered it to the university because she could no longer afford the taxes and had not been able to find an acceptable buyer. The parcel was abandoned agricultural land that had been heavily cut over after naturally becoming reforested, and it thus provided research and teaching opportunities quite different from Mount Toby. Professor Herschel G. Abbott, who had joined the faculty in the mid-1950s to teach forest protection, dendrology, and subjects related to forest regeneration, used Cadwell for studies of planting, direct seeding, and the consumption by rodent populations of natural seed sources.

Dr. Donald Mader did extensive research on forest soils, some of which was carried out with other university faculty as regional research. He and Professor MacConnell initiated research on the Quabbin Reservoir watershed of the Metropolitan District Commission just to the east of Amherst. This large reservoir, created in the early 1930s to supply Boston and surrounding communities with drinking water, has a watershed of more than 50,000 acres. Though the watershed area is managed for forest products, its primary purpose is to protect the watershed to assure high-quality water. Professors MacConnell, Mawson, and Mader played a major role in initiating management of this vast resource because of a graduate student, Fred M. Hunt, who became the Quabbin watershed's first forester. Hunt set up a continuous forest inventory system and gathered the first data, from which an intensive management program has evolved. The watershed property has also provided a wilderness-type habitat for wildlife research.

One of the longest ongoing pieces of research in the department has derived from Professor MacConnell's interests in aerial photo interpretation of the forest. The project started as a land-use map of the entire state done from aerial photographs; more recently it has utilized the latest technology of satellite imagery. The work has found many users and attracted numerous grants from federal, state, river basin, and other regional agencies. The project has provided large amounts of funding for temporary and full-time positions as well as stipends for numerous graduate students over approximately a 30-year period. Massachusetts is uniquely fortunate to have such a store of land-use information at its disposal.

As new forestry faculty joined the Department of Forestry and Wildlife Management in the mid- to late-1970s, new research interests came to the fore. Dr. Brayton F. (Bill) Wilson did research on tree physiology; Dr. William Patterson worked on prescribed fire as a forest management tool, not only in Massachusetts but on a national scale; and Dr. Matthew J. Kelty undertook silvicultural research.

Another accomplishment of Professor Rhodes was the 1971 agreement with the Northeastern Forest Experiment Station to establish a unit in conjunction with the department to do research related to wildlife and urban forestry. This agreement brought a U.S. Forest Service research unit back to the campus after a hiatus of nearly 40 years. The first unit leader, Jack Ward Thomas, earned his Ph.D. in wildlife at the university while in this position, later transferring to Bend, Oregon, to take a position in wildlife research. From there he was appointed chief of the U.S. Forest Service in the Clinton administration. The unit continues, but has since been downsized and has gone through changes in emphasis; now its focus is primarily wildlife research.

As the Department of Forestry and Wildlife Management grew, the wood science and technology program, later called building materials and technology, became a separate section but remained involved in forest-product research. This research was greatly enhanced by the laboratory and woodworking machine room, which included experimental dry kilns, heretofore lacking, that came with the new building in 1963. One focus of research has been to improve the utilization of low-quality timber, of which there is a large supply in Massachusetts. Various species were tested for making particle board, oriented strandboard, and taking clear cuttings and regluing them into panels (dubbed the System Six method) for furniture and cabinets.

Drs. William Rice and Alan Marra have been the primary researchers in these areas. Dr. Rice focused much of his effort on wood drying; through his efforts and those of others, the Wood Processing Center was created at the Tillson Farm area on the eastern edge of campus. The center consists of a sawmill; wood-fiber laboratory complete with log crusher, hammermills, and a flaker; a 10 thousand board foot commercial-size dry kiln; an improved air drying yard; and a trailer that is used as a classroom, laboratory, and small conference area. Dr. R. Bruce Hoadley has worked on the design of wooden propeller blades for windmill electrical generation and is working on the "swelling pressure properties of wood and related areas of elastomer assembly of wood products and furniture joint analysis."[27] In addition, he is often called upon for legal testimony because of his expertise in wood anatomy and wood identification .

Before his retirement in 1977, Dr. Harold Gatslick worked diligently to promote wood-industry plant development in the state, especially for industries that would exploit underutilized species. With graduate students, Dr. Robert S. Bond studied locally important wood industries and their structure and marketing techniques, especially the pallet industry. Under later funding from the U.S. Forest Service and just prior to retiring in 1977 to become director of the Pennsylvannia State University's School of Forest Resources, Dr. Bond did extensive studies of labor in the primary wood-processing industries of the Northeast.

Over the past 30 years, as the department has changed its emphasis from primarily undergraduate education to include graduate education, research, and public outreach, research has been a major activity of the faculty in the Department of Forestry and Wildlife

Management — a contrast to the forestry program's first half century. This broadening of activities in forestry derives in part from the university's being a public institution and thus sensitive to changes in public policy.

Extension Forestry

Extension forestry has been an important component of the forestry program at the University of Massachusetts since its early establishment as the Massachusetts Agricultural College. When the rural sociologist Kenyon L. Butterfield became president of the Massachusetts Agricultural College in 1906, he asked the academic faculty to take on extension education, i.e., education of the general public. The then forestry professor, William Darrow Clark, responded to this request with a plan for a full-time person doing forestry extension and setting up demonstration plots throughout the Commonwealth on private lands of willing participants. Limited financial resources kept this plan on paper until the 1930s, when it was implemented under Professor Holdsworth's leadership.

Agricultural extension work became a cooperative activity between the U.S. Department of Agriculture and the land-grant colleges in 1914 with passage of the Smith-Lever Act. Again, as with agricultural research under the Hatch Act, the federal government provided matching funding to stimulate programs by states. It can be speculated that Professor Holdsworth convinced the college that Smith-Lever funds should be used to hire a person in this area. Robert B. Parmenter, Massachusetts' first extension forester, joined the faculty in about 1937 and held this position until his retirement in 1956. His role as extension forester was quite different from today. The norm at that time was for public foresters to perform services for private forest landowners. More like the early state service foresters, the extension forester dealt primarily with individuals, meeting with them on their lands, giving them advice, and even marking timber and assisting them with timber sales. Parmenter did, however, work closely with state district foresters to organize field meetings and did some radio broadcasts.

In 1958, John H. Noyes took over as extension forester. He was a native of Connecticut, with an undergraduate degree from that state's university and an M.F. from the Yale School of Forestry. Having come into the profession in 1939 following the hurricane of 1938, Noyes went to work with the U.S. Forest Service helping with the Timber Salvage Administration, a program implemented by the Roosevelt administration to recover the millions of board feet of timber the storm had blown down. Following World War II, Noyes rejoined the U.S. Forest Service and held a number of positions that broadened his experience. It was fortuitous that in his work with the U.S. Forest Service he was involved in both state and private forestry when the Massachusetts extension forester position became available. Professor Rhodes had known Noyes before the war when they were both at Yale. Rhodes respected his abilities, so he was hired.

Professor Noyes changed the way extension forestry was conducted in Massachusetts and made an impact on it throughout the nation. He worked with groups of people, developing many publications so that forest landowners could order these pamphlets and read up on topics before they actually met with a professional forester. He was the driving force in the founding of many organizations, such as the Massachusetts Christmas Tree Growers and the Massachusetts Land League (which became the Massachusetts Forestry Association). He worked not only with forest landowner groups but also with professional foresters to keep practicing foresters up-to-date on new developments. From the late 1950s to the early 1970s, when he moved into college administration to become assistant director of extension, Professor Noyes oversaw forestry extension's most productive period. His replacement stayed only three years, and fiscal constraints meant that no one was permanently put into the position. As they had been under President Butterfield, faculty were asked to take on extension in addition to their teaching and research duties. In practice, the teaching responsibilities took precedence over forestry extension services and the latter received little attention.

Again, as in the case with forestry research, there was national pressure on the Congress to provide for dedicated funds for forestry extension activities so as not to have to rely on agricultural Smith-Lever funds. Although conventionally considered a part of agriculture, forestry was often the "poor cousin" when it came to funding for research and extension activities, even in regions where forestry was more prominent than agriculture. In 1982, the Cooperative Forestry Extension Act was passed, which provided dedicated funds to be used exclusively for forestry extension. Although it has never been funded to the full authorization, as is also true for the Cooperative Forestry Research Act, the act has provided funding to strengthen the program.

In Massachusetts the act enabled the University of Massachusetts to hire Chistina Petersen as extension forestry assistant in 1985. Although it was only a part-time position, Petersen initiated a renewal of extension forestry activities with the state's forest landowners and the resumption of cooperative work with foresters in the state Division of Forests and Parks. Petersen resigned in 1994, but her efforts and those of an extension evaluation committee formed in the Department of Forestry and Wildlife led to the hiring of Dr. David B. Kittredge, Jr., as extension forester with a university faculty appointment. Kittredge, a Yale School of Forestry and Environmental Studies graduate, has responsibilities beyond extension for formal teaching and research in order to assure tenure consideration and permit future promotions.

Extension remains an important aspect of the University of Massachusetts program, but it has been greatly affected in recent years by cuts in the state budget. At one time there was a strong county-based extension program in addition to that found at the university campus, but cutbacks have greatly reduced these programs and eliminated forest-resource specialists at the county level. Recently, there has been a growing recognition of the importance of outreach by the university in agriculture and many other areas. This "outreach" not only provides technical knowledge to many businesses, but also gives the university greater visibility and recognition for its contribution to the state's economic and environmental well-being. Since three-fifths of Massachusetts is currently forested, there is good reason for extension forestry to help educate the landowning public and the cadre of professional foresters who work with them.

Forestry at University of Massachsetts Mirrors National Trends

Dr. Donald Arganbright, since 1988 the head of the Department of Forestry and Wildlife Management, resigned in July 1995 to accept a comparable position at Northern Arizona University. His tenure saw many developments in the university and in the College of Agriculture (now the College of Food and Natural Resources), of which the Department of Forestry and Wildlife Management is a part. Declining enrollments in forestry, a national phenomenon, required persuasive arguments at the college and university levels to permit the replacement of faculty who resigned or retired, especially in the face of reduced fiscal support at the federal and state levels. In August 1996, a new department head, Dr. William McComb, took up the reins. Dr. McComb, whose graduate studies were in wildlife, has had a wide-ranging teaching and research career at the University of Kentucky and, most recently, Oregon State University. His challenge is to keep a diverse faculty together as the various programs within the department seek funds to maintain or expand their programs.

Other important changes at the university have been more societal than institutional. For example, forestry was a male-dominated profession until the late 1960s. Susan Koons, '67 was the first female to earn a forestry B.S. degree at the University of Massachusetts. Since that time, many women have entered the profession of forestry and have distinguished themselves in teaching, research, and leadership. A University of Massachusetts forestry graduate student, Jane Difley, was the first woman to become president of the Society of American Foresters, a national professional organization with around 20,000 members, and the first woman to head the Society for the Protection of New Hampshire Forests.

Until women began earning doctoral degrees in forestry their faculty roles were not on the teaching staff but in extension. For a brief period in the mid-1970s, Nancy Arny Pywell was an extension forestry assistant; as discussed above, Christina Petersen was appointed to this position in 1985. Her appointment became possible as a result of funds made available under the 1982 Forest Resources Extension Act. At about the same time, Linda Deegan, a marine biologist, joined the department faculty.

Currently three women hold positions on the faculty: Ann Lewis, assistant professor of forestry, earned her Ph.D. degree from Harvard in the Department of Organismic and Evolutionary Biology in 1987, having initiated her studies with the late director of the Harvard Forest, Dr. Martin Zimmerman. Lucie K. Ozzanne became an assistant professor of building materials and technology in August 1995, after she completed her doctorate at Penn State University. Martha E. Mather, an adjunct assistant professor, is a fisheries biologist and assistant unit leader of the Massachusetts Cooperative Wildlife and

Fisheries Research Unit. Recruitment of additional minorities and women, in spite of strong efforts by the university and department, has been hampered by a shortage of candidates.

As of 1995, there is a new program in the department, arboriculture and park management. This marks the return of a two-year degree program to the department after a hiatus of 23 years (since the Stockbridge School of Agriculture wood utilization program was terminated). It is taught by Dr. H. Dennis Ryan, associate professor of arboriculture and urban forestry, and Thomas Houston, lecturer in arboriculture. This program had been housed in the Department of Landscape Architecture and Regional Planning for many years, but it is appropriate for it to be in the forestry department now, for urban forestry has become a nationally recognized submajor in other forestry education programs. The question may be posed as to whether it will become a full-fledged baccalaureate program in the future.

OTHER FORESTRY EDUCATION PROGRAMS

Three other programs in the Commonwealth in addition to the professional forestry education programs at Harvard and the University of Massachusetts have taught some forestry. Following World War II, Nichols Junior College in Dudley had a modest program to provide students with a forestry-conservation background. This was developed primarily because of the business-related opportunities and the college administration's recognition that such a program would be popular with students. During the early to mid-1950s, weekend field exercises were conducted at a camp in Rutland owned by the college to give students training in dendrology, silviculture, and mensuration. All of these courses were rudimentary because of time constraints and the college's hiring of a variety of individuals, mostly professionally trained foresters, to teach on a temporary basis. There was no organized curriculum at a professional level.[28]

Two nondegree programs at a vocational level were offered at the Essex Agricultural School in Danvers and at the Smith Vocational School in Northampton. The first was developed largely because two teachers at the school had received forestry degrees and had an interest in Christmas-tree and tree-nursery production. The Smith Vocational School program was more broad-based and actually was directed at training individuals to work in the woods and do logging. The school engaged faculty to teach these subjects, usually someone with a forestry degree, and had its own woodlot on which the students did fieldwork. The Smith School program continues today.

A number of programs at the local, state, and national level have made the general public more aware of the profession of forestry and have stimulated the expansion of forestry services. Professional forestry is not yet a century old in the United States and is not very well known or understood by the public. In Germany and the Scandinavian countries, forestry is a highly regarded profession. Here in the United States, too often foresters are thought to be despoilers of the forest resource, as opposed to stewards. The public views the cutting of trees negatively, rather than as a cultural activity to encourage or regenerate forest growth, improve wildlife habitat, protect watersheds, and provide a safe sylvan recreational experience.

PROFESSIONAL FORESTRY IN MASSACHUSETTS

Professional forestry in the state was largely related to state employment until the post-World War II years, when it became possible to earn a living as a private forestry consultant. As William Rivers documents elsewhere in this book, there has been a state forester since just before the turn of the century. In 1906, Alfred Akerman was replaced in that role by F. William Rane, who came to the post from the New Hampshire College of Agriculture and Mechanic Arts, where he had taught forestry. He became a lecturer in forestry at the Massachusetts Agricultural College coincident with his appointment as state forester.[29] In 1907, Rane hired Harold O. Cook, a recent M.F. graduate of Harvard College in Petersham, as the first forester for the state who had a professional forestry degree.

Cook had a long career with the state and became Chief Forester when Rane retired in 1919. In subsequent years the commissioner of conservation, often a political appointee with no forestry training, served as the titular state forester. In reality, whoever is chief forester acts in the capacity of state forester.

Harold Cook's career spanned over 50 years. His autobiography, *Fifty Years a Forester,* published by the Massachusetts Forest and Park Association in 1961, is a fascinating description of a forester's career.

Cook was heavily involved with the acquisition of state forest property, in reforestation, and in organizing the Civilian Conservation Corps program for Massachusetts in addition to his educational work in speaking to groups and giving advice on the ground to forest land-owners. As is still the case with today's chief forester, Cook had multiple responsibilities and was often called upon to undertake activities for which he had no formal training.

John H. Lambert, Jr., a graduate of the University of Maine (1929) and Yale School of Forestry (1930), came to work for the Massachusetts Department of Conservation in 1932 as a state forest supervisor in the Berkshires. He, too, had a long, distinguished career with the department and provided much of its professional leadership following World War II. Lambert officially replaced H. O. Cook as chief forester in 1962, although he had, for all intents and purposes, been unofficially carrying out the duties for 10 years or more.

The Cooperative Farm Forestry Act (known as the Norris-Doxey Act), passed by Congress in 1937, gave states matching funding to provide asssistance and educational programs to farm woodland owners, who at the time were the predominant owners of private forestland in Massachusetts. All of these activities gave further impetus to professional forestry in the state. But until the late 1940s, private forestry services were little in demand.

Federal legislation again made an impact on professional forestry with passage of the Cooperative Forest Management Act of 1950. This was an expansion of the Norris-Doxey Act in that it provided matching funding to states to employ foresters and to provide services to private woodland owners. Whereas the earlier act referred to "farm foresters," under the new act the term was "service foresters" — meaning assistance was not restricted to woodland owners engaged in some form of agriculture. Farms continued to be abandoned and were often inherited or purchased by individuals who had no interest in farming, but did wish to own forestland. Over the past half century, the number of these landowners, referred to as nonindustrial private forest landowners (NIPFLOs), has grown, but the average area of each ownership has declined.

As money was appropriated to increase the number of foresters employed by the state, professional foresters became increasingly evident. In Worcester County, for example, in the mid-1950s one district forester (state-funded) covered the entire county. By the mid-1980s the county had a forest supervisor, two assistants, three service foresters (north, central, and south), and two management foresters for the state forests in the county. Today, there is at least one service forester and at least one management forester in every county, with the exception of Suffolk, Dukes, and Nantucket counties.

The service forester's role has changed greatly. Much of the work is more regulatory: monitoring forest cutting under the Forest Cutting Practices Act (Chapter 132, Massachuesetts General Laws) and approving Forest Management Plans as required by the Forest Tax Classification Law (Chapter 61, M.G.L.), which is optional to forest landowners who wish to reduce their ad valorem tax. In the beginning of the public forestry assistance program, government foresters would spend much more time with individual landowners on the ground and even mark their timber for cutting and advise them on how to go about selling it. This activity is now the purview of the consulting forester — an individual or group who are private entrepreneurs providing professional forestry services for a fee.

By the 1970s, there were many federal programs to educate woodland owners about the importance of managing their forest land and, particularly, the advantages of hiring a professional forester to assist them in the sale of timber. There are increasing numbers of woodland owners who have no knowledge about the forest and how to manage it. Although too few have sought professional foresters' advice, the large numbers of Massachusetts owners, an estimated 235,000 owning 10 acres or more, has enabled consulting foresters to make a living doing this work. A September 1993 publication of the University of Massachusetts Extension System lists 87 private forestry consultants who will assist landowners with forest management for a fee. Not all of these are full-time consultants, as some have other jobs and some are semiretired.

SUMMARY

The development of forestry in Massachusetts has paralleled that of the United States as a whole, but genuine leadership has also been provided by Massachusetts organizations over the years. For example, some of the earliest lectures in the country about forestry were presented at the Massachusetts Agricultural College by B. E. Fernow, one of the first professional foresters to advocate and implement management of forests in the United States. The Commonwealth provided leadership to the profession through its two outstanding academic and research institutions at Harvard University and the University of Massachusetts. Although the former has emphasized graduate-level education and the latter, undergraduate studies, they have both made major contributions, even beyond their formal degree programs. The Harvard Forest with its Bullard Fellowships has made an international contribution in promoting contact among professional foresters, and between professionals and researchers. The Conferences on Forest Production brought public, private, and academic foresters together from this country, Canada, and even some other nations. The University of Massachusetts also conducted national and international conferences that were precedent-setting. One of the outstanding ones, "Trees and Forests in an Urbanizing Environment," held in August of 1970, brought together some of the leaders in this subject area and was instrumental in establishing the Northeastern Forest Experiment Station's new research unit on the campus at Amherst. In addition, the university's Department of Forestry and Wildlife Management has hosted numerous regional conferences for members of the forestry and wildlife professions.

Throughout the twentieth century, forestry itself has become increasingly complex. Both public and private forests are scrutinized ever more closely today by an increasingly environmentally aware public. The challenge is to educate landowners and students to manage forests as ecosystems and for biodiversity as well as for, or even instead of, timber or recreation. Up until 25 years ago, there was little doubt about what foresters did. They managed woodlands primarily for timber products, and recreation, wildlife habitat, and watershed protection were considered secondary uses. As different paradigms of the forestry profession emerge, Massachusetts can and will continue to adjust its forestry education programs to fit the changing times.

🍃 NOTES

1. Joseph S. Illick, "State Forestry," in *Fifty Years of Forestry in the U.S.A.* (Society of American Foresters, 1950), p. 226.
2. Massachusetts Agricultural College, *Fifth Annual Report* (Boston, 1868), p. 4. Cited in Nancy M. Gordon, *Forestry at the University of Massachusetts: A Provisional History* (unpublished, 1988), p. 3.

3. Massachusetts Agricultural College, *Eighth Annual Report* (Boston, 1871), p. 27. Cited in Gordon, *Forestry*, p. 4.

4. Massachusetts Agricultural College, *Thirtieth Annual Report* (Boston, 1893), p. 27. Cited in Gordon, *Forestry*, p. 6.

5. Samuel T. Dana, *Forest and Range Policy* (New York: McGraw-Hill, 1956), p. 79.

6. Harvard Forest, *The Harvard Forest 1907–1934: A Memorial to Its First Director, Richard Thornton Fisher* (Petersham, Mass.: Harvard University, 1935), p. 40.

7. David M. Smith, Jesup Professor of Silviculture at the Yale School of Forestry, coauthored revisions of this text and ultimately became the sole author. The most recent revision was coauthored by two additional individuals, one of whom is Matthew J. Kelty, of the University of Massachusetts faculty.

8. H. Raup and E. Gould, "Harvard Forestry School, History of Instruction," discussion draft, ca. 1955 (Harvard Forest Archives), p. 2.

9. Ibid., p. 5.

10. Ibid., p. 4.

11. David R. Foster (director of the Harvard Forest), *Annual Report of the Harvard Forest*, 1992–93 (Petersham, Mass.: Harvard University, June 1993), p. 5.

12. Ibid., p. 5.

13. John G. Torrey (director of the Harvard Forest), *Annual Report of the Harvard Forest*, 1987–88 (Petersham, Mass.: Harvard University, August 1988), p. 4.

14. *Annual Report of the Harvard Forest*, 1983–84 (Petersham, Mass.: Harvard University), no. pp.

15. Foster, *Annual Report*, 1992–93, p. 6.

16. Ibid., p. 16.

17. Ibid., p. 19.

18. President and Fellows of Harvard College, *The Harvard Forest Models* (Petersham, Mass.: Harvard University, 1941).

19. Massachusetts Agricultural College, *Forty-sixth Annual Report* (Boston, 1909), p. 63. Cited in Gordon, *Forestry*, pp. 7–8.

20. *Massachusetts Collegian* 27, no. 4 (24 October 1916). Cited in Gordon, *Forestry*, p. 9.

21. W. D. Clar, "The Mount Toby Demonstration Forest," *Yale Forest School News*, October 1, 1916 (University of Massachusetts Archives, Group 15, Series 14, "Mount Toby Reservation, General"). Cited in Gorden, *Forestry*, p. 28.

22. *Massachusetts Agricultural College Bulletin* 14 (January 1922), p. 81. Cited in Gordon, *Forestry*, p. 10.

23. *Massachusetts Agricultural College Bulletin* 15 (January 1923): 79; Massachusetts Agricultural College, *Sixty-first Annual Report* (Boston, 1924), p. 62; Anonymous, "A Brief Chronological Summary Concerning the Program in Forestry at the University of Massachusetts" (University of Massachusetts Archives, Group 25, Series F6/2), p. 2. Cited in Gordon, *Forestry*, p. 21.

24. Dana, op. cit., p. 222.

25. *Massachusetts Agricultural College Bulletin* (Boston, 1942–43), p. 35. Cited in Gordon, *Forestry*, p. 13.

26. "Dedication of Holdsworth Hall" (pamphlet), remarks of A. D. Rhodes (University of Massachusetts Archives, Group 25, Series F6/2), p. 3. Cited in Gordon, *Forestry*, p. 14.

27. Department of Forestry and Wildlife Management, University of Massachusetts, *Focus* 1977, vol. 11, 1977.

28. In 1958, Nichols College became a four-year institution emphasizing business management.

29. Massachusetts Agricultural College, *Fortieth Annual Report* (Boston, 1903), p. 99. Cited in Gordon, *Forestry*, p. 7.

Massachusetts Contributions to National Forest Conservation

STEPHEN FOX

🍂

OWARD THE END of the nineteenth century, Massachusetts forests helped inspire and launch what later became known as the
environmental movement. When the implacable processes of modern-
ization and industrialization reached a certain point — replacing older
powers of wind, water, and muscle with coal, petroleum, steam, and
electricity, and pulling rural residents from their farms into burgeoning
urban centers to work in shops and factories — a few individuals in
Massachusetts and elsewhere began to rethink the assumptions under-
pinning modern progress. Balancing the gains and losses, these re-
thinkers increasingly focused on the heedless wastes and unintended,
baleful side effects of their era's general rush to industrialize. Some
aspects of the natural world, they accordingly urged, should be guarded
from the relentless whoosh of modernity. In particular, dedicated
friends of Massachusetts trees and woodlands helped create a national
movement for forest conservation: both to protect some trees absolutely from human use, and to advocate more prudent commercial
forestry and timber cutting. By slow degrees, and just in time, Massachusetts forests found their defenders — with rippling effects on forest
policies at the national level.

This chapter highlights four individuals and two organizations, all
bred and based in Massachusetts, that were active in forest conservation
from the mid-1800s to the mid-1900s. Many other significant people
and conservation groups could have been included here; the state has
produced a long, honorable line of conservationists. But for this chapter the roster has been winnowed by the dual criteria of originality and
national influence. Everyone discussed here was immersed in the creation of something unprecedented, and these pioneers' work eventually
had impact beyond Massachusetts in conservation affairs around the

country. By standing apart from the dominant currents of their times and looking beyond the immediate priorities of everyday life, they helped invent a new reform movement. Alongside the colonists who had come ashore at Plymouth Rock, the revolutionaries at Lexington and Concord, and the Garrisonian abolitionists who insisted on eradicating the evil of chattel slavery, these early forest conservationists took their positions on the distinguished roll of Massachusetts idealists and reformers of conscience.

HENRY DAVID THOREAU

In the spring of 1845, as the forests of Massachusetts were yielding ever more products to the swelling hum of nineteenth-century industrial progress, Henry David Thoreau (1817–1862) turned around and repaired to Walden Pond in Concord for his two-year experiment in simplified living. At age 28, Thoreau was just beginning one of the most distinguished, eccentric careers in nineteenth-century American literature. He was still very much in process, seeking his particular place and voice, unsure of where he was headed. Retreating from his own recent life of quiet desperation, he went to the Walden woods — a moderate walk from Concord center — for selfish purposes, to pare everyday living down to essentials and examine them without flinching. By degrees he folded himself into the natural landscape, finding there a "sweet and beneficent society in Nature . . . an infinite and unaccountable friendliness all at once like an atmosphere sustaining me, as made the fancied advantages of human neighborhood insignificant." From the railroad track at the western end of the pond, the piercing locomotive whistle sounded like the scream of a hawk: but it only intruded briefly. Safe for a time in these woods, and even though absorbing the sought "tonic of wildness" with all his senses, Thoreau still accepted the prevalent notion — familiar to any contemporary carpenter or lumberman — of trees for human uses. Even at Walden, nature was yet assumed to serve a man's intentions.[1]

In the few remaining years of Thoreau's life after he left Walden, he moved fitfully toward a more heretical notion of trees for trees themselves. As he shifted between these two propositions — nature for itself versus nature for humans — Thoreau unconsciously anticipated an essential tension that would stretch across future efforts in forest con-

Figure 7.1. Thoreau's cabin at Walden Pond, Concord. Illustration for Walden, *by Henry David Thoreau (New York: The Heritage Press, 1939). Boston Public Library, Print Department, by permission of the estate of Thomas Nason.*

servation and, ultimately, the entire environmental movement. In his Walden phase Thoreau most valued human freedom, independence, and the inward declarations of his own individual voice. The later Thoreau turned more toward an outward-looking systematic study of nature, especially trees, with emphases on fecundity, generation, and interconnectedness. Alongside his older themes of humans drawing sustenance from nature, he increasingly focused on the internal processes of nature's self-cultivations, and a corresponding need to protect some of nature from human intrusion.[2]

This proto-conservationist Thoreau surfaced in his essay "Chesuncook," published by the *Atlantic Monthly* in 1858 and posthumously in *The Maine Woods*. Though he traveled mainly within Concord, Thoreau had made three forays into the seemingly endless forests of northern Maine. These woods left him with a surprising sense of their vulnerability to human misuse — and a dawning recognition that pine trees had their own purposes beyond any human intentions. "The pine is no more lumber than man is," he wrote, "and to be made into boards is no more its true and highest use than the truest use of man is to be cut down and made into manure." Veering toward a pagan animism, Thoreau declared his love for "the living spirit of the tree," not its human-derived products after death: "It is as immortal as I am, and perchance will go to as high a heaven, there to tower above me still." In conclusion, Thoreau recalled the royal forests of England, protected for the king's hunting. "Why should not we," he asked, "who have renounced the king's authority, have our national preserves . . . for inspiration and our own true recreation? or shall we, like the villains, grub them all up, poaching on our own national domains?" The first national parks and forests in the United States were not established until decades later.[3]

In the late 1850s Thoreau became fascinated by the process of forest succession — and thus came to render his major contribution to what later became the science of ecology. Concord's farmers had long observed that a white pine lot, if cut down, was usually followed by a stand of hardwood, and vice versa. Popular explanations for this incongruous succession of one species by another ran to dubious theories of spontaneous generation. Through patient observation over many seasons, Thoreau learned how seeds were dispersed by nature's own planting devices of wind, water, squirrels, and the eating habits of birds and other creatures, and why different seedlings then prospered under knowable circumstances. Recording the details in his journal, comparing the systematic husbandry of nature with the heedless practices of local farmers, Thoreau interpolated exasperated remarks on the urgent need for better forestry. Fieldwork led him on to conservation. Thus, on finding that one Concord farmer had burned over young pine-succeeding oaks to plant a rye crop: "What a fool! Here nature had got everything ready for this emergency, and kept them ready for many years . . . and he thought he knew better. . . . So he trifles with nature. . . . He needs to have a guardian placed over him. A forest-warden should be appointed by the town. Overseers of poor husbandmen." Here Thoreau again suggested that humans should yield on occasion to nature's own intentions. Trees, in short, by and for themselves.[4]

A strange irony: the tree studies that had sustained Thoreau and preoccupied his last years helped kill him. Late in 1860, while counting tree rings and measuring growth at Fair Haven Hill in Concord, he caught the cold that — along with tuberculosis — led finally to his death 17 months later. He left behind the draft of an undelivered lecture, "Huckleberries," which urged the preservation of the Concord River's banks for public walks and the conversion of some town property into a protected forest of 500 or 1,000 acres, "where a stick should never be cut for fuel, a common possession forever, for instruction and recreation." This early call to forest conservation stayed among Thoreau's papers, unread and unheeded. When finally exhumed and published years later, "Huckleberries" seemed ahead of its time — but also very much of its time, given that nobody thought it worthy of notice for a long while.[5]

CHARLES SPRAGUE SARGENT

Charles Sprague Sargent (1841–1927), a central figure in American forestry affairs of the 1880s and 1890s, was not much influenced by Thoreau. Born on Beacon Hill in Boston and raised at the family estate in suburban Brookline, Sargent came of intellectual age at a time when Thoreau had disappeared from the literary landscape, not to be revived for decades. Instead Sargent owed his tree career to reading George Perkins Marsh. A desultory student at Harvard and then a rich, aimless young man, Sargent remained unfocused until he picked up Marsh's

Man and Nature in the early 1870s. "If I have done nothing else but make you acquainted with George P. Marsh," Sargent later told a forestry colleague, "I shall feel that I have not lived in vain."[6]

For Sargent, a man not given to overstatement, the book became a conversion experience of nearly religious intensity. *Man and Nature,* published in 1864, was the first important call for forest conservation in America. Marsh — an authentic nineteenth-century polymath, a native of Vermont who lived abroad for much of his life — ranged across the entire ecological history of the Northern Hemisphere to show the dangers of wasteful lumbering and forest destruction. Droughts, erosion, floods, climatic disasters, even the declines of empires and civilizations of the old world had followed, and soon would threaten the new world as well. "Let us be wise in time," said Marsh, "and profit by the errors of our older brethren."[7] Absorbing the lesson, Sargent started tree work on a modest local level and steadily broadened his activities outward in concentric circles — rather like a cross-section of one of his especially beloved white pines. (Large and robust in stature, he conveyed a white pine's ramrod presence, endurance, and persistence, and some of its stubborn imperviousness as well.)

Having learned techniques of English landscape gardening in travels abroad, Sargent began by managing the opulent family spread in Brookline. From there he helped found the Arnold Arboretum in conjunction with Harvard University. In this lush public park, designed for both scientific purposes and "artistic effects," Sargent first planned to include every variety of tree and shrub that could be grown in Massachusetts. Later this design was cut back to include mostly North American species, with some outsiders, mainly from Asia. The plan remained ambitious. True to his white-pine nature, Sargent thought in the long term: His tax-free lease with the city of Boston ran for a thousand years — and was then renewable for another millennium.[8] He remained very much in charge of the arboretum for the next half century.

In 1876 Sargent prepared a report for the state Board of Agriculture on the Commonwealth's trees. As a botanist and horticulturist, he approached forest conservation as a matter of planting and cultivation rather than of sustained-yield forestry as long practiced in Europe. Drawn to young and growing trees, he preferred not to think about harvesting or reducing them to board feet. In that spirit, he urged the

Massachusetts Society for Promoting Agriculture, a private group, to encourage tree planting. In 1878 Sargent served on — and no doubt dominated — an award committee for the society that offered cash prizes totaling $1,400 for the best plantings of white pine, white ash, Scotch pine, and European larch. Intended "to increase the knowledge of arboriculture," the competition drew in only 12 tree planters across the state. When the results were assessed 10 years later, 8 of the 12 had withdrawn because of crop failures or inattention. Of the remaining 4, only one met the competition's stringent requirements. Thomas H. Lawrence of Falmouth received $100 for the best acre of European larch.[9] Forestry was as yet a very hard sell. The general supply of trees still seemed abundant; the American frontier yet beckoned, offering the promise of endless virgin land out west or up north; and the prevailing ethos, the late-nineteenth-century barbecue of laissez-faire economics and government, left little place for government regulation or even admonition.

On the federal level, Sargent nonetheless hoped to move from fact-finding surveys to informed policy recommendations to, eventually, some sort of government protection for forests on the public lands of the West. His preliminary survey in 1879 of forests in central Nevada led to his undertaking a major study a year later for the Interior Department. Sargent's *Report on the Forests of North America,* issued in 600 large pages as part of the 1880 census, was his first major publication and the first substantial study of the subject. It described 412 tree species, with details on their taxonomy, distribution, and characteristics in use, and concluded with dire warnings about the nation's shrinking forests. All across the West, Sargent declared, trees and humans dependent on them were threatened by wasteful cutting methods and simple, imprudent greed. Sargent stacked his argument by not counting trees under a foot in diameter, and so exaggerated the extent of forest depletion — as his critics in the lumber industry soon pointed out.[10]

The *Report* led to other federally appointed surveys by Sargent. After poking around the northern Rocky Mountains in 1883 and noting the unchecked depredations of miners, lumbermen, and stockmen, he published an article in *The Nation* magazine urging the creation of a federal reserve in the region of what later became Glacier National Park, in northwestern Montana. A political conservative, he disapproved of federal regulation of business affairs except on behalf of trees. "The fewer government officials we can have and the less machinery of that sort the better," he wrote an associate in 1883. "Still without government interference, Federal or State, I don't see how our mountain forests can be saved from entire extermination." Trees mattered more than any abstractions or political theories to Sargent.[11]

Though temperamentally unsuited to the task, Sargent saw the urgent need for patient public education about forest conservation. The only national organization in the field, the first American Forestry Association, had been founded in 1875 by John A. Warder, a physician and horticulturist from Cincinnati. After 1882 it was led by George B. Loring of Salem, Massachusetts, a farmer, a Republican politician, and a former United States commissioner of agriculture. The AFA held annual meetings, sponsored Arbor Day celebrations, and urged more prudent forestry practices by private owners, but made no significant appeals to government. The AFA's membership remained small, only a few hundred, and its real influence slight. Newspapers and public commentators often agreed that forestry sounded sensible, but the matter went no further. "There is a great deal of talk about forestry in this country, but I cannot find out that we have much of the thing itself," said J. B. Harrison of the AFA in 1889. "Forestry in the United States is a matter of talk, of Arbor Day oratory and essays at Forestry Congresses. We shall build nothing valuable on a basis of unreality."[12]

Sargent found common cause among the horticulturists and landscape gardeners of the AFA but deemed the group inadequate. In 1888 he launched his own weekly magazine, *Garden and Forest,* aiming to reach and expand the AFA's constituency on a national level. "Conducted" and apparently underwritten by Sargent, the magazine was published and edited in New York by a veteran journalist, William A. Stiles of the *New York Tribune. Garden and Forest* offered readers the carrot of soothing horticultural pieces along with the stick of stern calls to what was at first called "forest-conservancy," an uneasy combination, as it addressed different audiences in different tones. But it well mirrored Sargent's own twin priorities of both studying and saving trees. "In no other civilized nation of the world are forests so recklessly managed," the magazine declared in 1888. "As a consequence of this wanton and hideous waste of our national resources, millions of our people will be compelled to live on a lower plane of civilization."[13]

Sargent was a practical man. Within the Arnold Arboretum, his absolute domain, he could make and remake his environment, moving plants and people around as he wished. He took definite steps; he expected tangible results. Accordingly, in January 1889 he announced a three-part program in *Garden and Forest* for rescuing the beleaguered forests on the public lands of the West: withdrawal of all such lands from sale pending more study; protection of those lands by the United States Army from further unlawful pillaging by settlers and railroad and mining companies; and appointment of a federal commission of experts (like himself) to examine the public forests and recommend steps for their preservation and management, including a government-trained corps of professional foresters. Sargent's grand design was soon endorsed by the AFA and many newspapers around the country. Again, however, this was just talk. As a shrewd *Garden and Forest* editorial pointed out in October 1889, the best friends of forests and forestry lived far from the western lands, had no driving selfish stake in the matter, and operated only from tree-love and principle: "This interest may be a sentimental one, but it is none the less real." Against them were men who lived near and from the forests — lumbermen, stockmen, hunters, miners, all "despoiling what others would preserve" — pushed by the sharp, hardheaded goad of threatened livelihoods and profits. "These various interests are well organized; and the men who live on this accumulated wealth of the nation can afford to pay handsomely to preserve government indifference."[14]

Given such political and economic realities, parts of Sargent's program were carried out by subterfuge and presidential whim, not by the open democratic process so vulnerable to rich, self-interested lobbyists. The first national forests were authorized by an obscure amendment to a general land law that Congress passed unnoticed in March 1891; the amendment allowed the president to create "forest reserves" by withdrawing federal land from the public domain. Without needing congressional approval or the support of public opinion, President Benjamin Harrison — responding to discreet lobbying by Sargent and a few others — in two years established 15 reserves, a total of about 13 million acres. His successor, Grover Cleveland, added 7 million more acres by March 1896. As commanders-in-chief, presidents could simply order the army into guard duty on the new reserves; Congress had no power to object to the policy. As for the proposed forest commission, Sargent and his cohorts — notably Robert Underwood Johnson, an editor of the influential *Century* magazine — at first approached Congress, were rejected, and so instead persuaded the National Academy of Sciences to authorize the scheme at the request of a friendly secretary of the interior. With the Forest Commission, which also came to be known as the Sargent Commission, already under way they could then extract a congressional appropriation of $25,000 to fund it in 1896.[15]

For Sargent these developments played out between the poles of his new friendships with John Muir and Gifford Pinchot. These two men embodied the tension in Thoreau: nature for itself versus nature for humans. After working with Sargent for a few years, Muir and Pinchot split, bitterly, and came to define a philosophical schism within conservation that has persisted ever since. Muir, the Scotch-born, California-based naturalist and writer, helped found the Sierra Club in 1892 and served as its president for the rest of his life. His odd alliance with Sargent united quite different personalities: Muir, full of jest and whimsy, poetic and darting; Sargent, growling and irascible, always intent on his work to the exclusion of anything else. Hiking through a forest wilderness together, Sargent would barge ahead quickly, unswervingly, to collect ever more specimens, while Muir liked to saunter along, taking time to savor the rocks and flowers. They found common ground only in their love for trees. Sargent also knew that Muir, with his lyrical literary gifts, could reach and move audiences that were beyond his own more sober style. "Unlike you, I am not a poet," Sargent once told him, "and have to stick to dry and uninteresting facts displayed in uninteresting language which I cannot believe any one cares to read. You know how to do the trick and I don't, and that is the difference between us."[16]

Gifford Pinchot was the first American-born forester with a background of professional training in Europe. (His father, the owner of large forests in eastern Pennsylvania and a former vice president of the American Forestry Association, had suggested such work to his son.) Sargent, drawn to the young man's eagerness and personal qualities, provided crucial mentoring for his budding career. From 1890 to 1896, *Garden and Forest* ran 11 articles by Pinchot — among his first important publications — on forestry practices in Europe and the need for forestry training and forest protection in America. The magazine also praised Pinchot's forestry work on the Vanderbilt-owned Biltmore estate in North Carolina. Sargent gave Pinchot another major break in national forestry circles by adding him to the six-man Forest Commission, though Pinchot was much the youngest and least established of the group and the only nonmember of the National Academy of Sciences.[17]

The members of the commission all set forth in the summer of 1896 on a fact-gathering tour of the West, with Muir along in an ex-officio capacity. For months they examined forests along the northern Rockies to Washington, then down the coast, east to Arizona, and back up to Colorado, tolerating unpredictable transportation and lodgings. "I enjoyed Sargent ever and ever so much," Muir reported to Underwood Johnson, "— the only one of the Com. that knew and loved trees as I love them." Sargent wrote Muir, "It was the best trip I have ever made, and the pleasure and profit I got out of it was largely due to you." In drafting its report, however, the commission split into hard factions. The Sargent-Muir majority endorsed army patrols in the reserves and a total ban on outside commercial uses. Pinchot and another commissioner preferred regulated commercial use and the creation of a civilian, professional forest service. Sargent won on most points, though the final report did allow for some lumbering and mineral exploration. In February 1897, in the last days of his administration (thereby evading the lobby-driven political consequences), President Cleveland approved the Sargent Commission's request for 13 new reserves of 21.4 million acres. Sargent, it seemed, had carried the day.[18]

The ensuing political storm blew Sargent out of forestry work and started Pinchot on his ascent within the federal bureaucracy. Congress and the new administration of William McKinley suspended all but two of Cleveland's reserves and opened the existing reserves to mining and grazing — "so that the mining corporations can lay in a good supply of stolen timber," Sargent told Muir, "and squatters can acquire rights to what the mines do not want." Pinchot then enraged Sargent's faction by accepting appointment as a special agent of the Interior Department to make yet another study of the reserves, under the revised rules. "It was a great misfortune that he was a member of the commission," an ally wrote of Pinchot to Sargent. "The trouble is in his head and, it would appear from recent developments, in the lack of appreciation of proprieties usual among gentlemen." Sargent was humiliated. Having advanced Pinchot's career, he now felt betrayed by an ambitious, ungrateful former disciple who was helping dismantle his fondest hopes and plans. "One feeble part of the Forestry Commission," Muir wrote in exasperation to Sargent, "has thus been given the work that had already most ably been done by the whole, without even mentioning what had been done. For a parallel to this in downright darkness and idiotic stupidity the records of civilization may be searched in vain."[19]

Sargent and his friends could only commiserate among themselves. A year later Pinchot was named head of the Agriculture Department's forestry division. As Pinchot's career took off, Sargent withdrew in muttering defeat. At the end of 1897, following the death of his editor, William Stiles, Sargent stopped publishing *Garden and Forest* after 10 insolvent years. "It is useless," Sargent concluded, "to expend more time and money on a publication which cannot be made financially successful." The Pinchot version of forestry, with its emphasis on professional training and a more politically marketable, utilitarian, for-human-use approach, was taking over. Each new Pinchot success registered on Sargent like a kick in the face. "Clearly it is time to begin another crusade," Sargent wrote Muir early in 1899, trying to convince himself as well, "but who has the time and strength to do it and what good is coming out of it all? I confess I feel discouraged. . . . Of course Pinchot and his gang are largely responsible for this condition of things." The original forestry impulse, of dedicated amateurs working through voluntary organizations, was yielding to the Pinchot forestry of paid professionals in government bureaus.[20]

Despite the ethical slips of his early career, Pinchot turned out to be an effective conservation publicist, advocate, and administrator. With the advent of his friend Theodore Roosevelt as president in 1901, Pinchot became a favored member of the so-called "tennis cabinet" grouped around TR, an inner circle that engaged in vigorous manly exercise while discussing any topic on the boss's mind. As the most prominent conservationist in America, Pinchot made forestry seem practical, carefully limited, a matter of sensible efficiency and good political tactics. "We understand now that Forestry is a business," he told the annual meeting of the National Wholesale Lumber Dealers Association in 1903. "It is all based on the primary question, Will it pay? . . . If a forest is of no use, then it is useless." (That is, useless unless reduced to human purposes.) In 1905, Pinchot, with Roosevelt's support, was mainly responsible for creating the U.S. Forest Service within the Agriculture Department. As its founding chief forester, he ran his agency along standards of honesty and professionalism that lasted for years after his departure. Ever since then, his version of conservation and its origins has dominated most historical accounts, to the point that to most historians, "forestry" and "conservation" and "Pinchot" have become virtually interchangeable terms.[21]

For the remaining quarter century of his life, the vanquished Sargent played no significant part in national forestry matters. He finished compiling his sequoia-sized magnum opus, *The Silva of North America,* in 14 substantial volumes, and his enthusiasm for collecting botanical specimens remained undiminished. But his conservation work was over — and not only because of Pinchot's triumphs. Sargent's retreat was so sudden and total, such an abrupt break from the ferocious, effective activity of earlier years, that it demands comment. Safe within his arboretum, Sargent was an absolute monarch who permitted no argument and little discussion. But the more complicated outside world punished such rigidity. Even among his closest friends, Sargent remained imperiously difficult, selfishly fixed on his own purposes. In 1903, on a botanizing world tour with Muir, he grew impatient when Muir contracted ptomaine poisoning in Manchuria. "He never seemed to think of me sick or well or of my studies," Muir confided to his journal, "only of his own until he feared I might die on his hands and thus bother him. He was planning another botanical trip."[22] In the same spirit, Sargent could only participate in forestry as a dominant player. After the advent of Pinchot, wounded by his betrayal and refusing to share any power or responsibility, Sargent simply picked up his marbles and went home.

APPALACHIAN MOUNTAIN CLUB

Over the course of the twentieth century, the history of conservation has become more a record of organizations and bureaucracies than of individuals. Massachusetts contributed two bellwether groups, the Appalachian Mountain Club and the Massachusetts Audubon Society, which helped define the voluntary-organization sector of forest conservation on a national level. In counterpoint to the growing professionalization of forestry at the turn of the century, the older amateur roles still persisted in private groups outside government. The amateurs usually championed "preservationist" conservation to protect nature more absolutely from human damage and intrusion. Countering their utilitarian colleagues, they argued that nature had aesthetic and recreational as well as economic uses, indeed had uses beyond human purposes. The amateurs by definition did not make their livings as conservationists and thus were free to take controversial positions unrelated to salary or career matters; by the same token, however, they often lacked the technical knowledge and staying power of the professionals. Conservation as a livelihood generally extracted more sustained effort than it did as a hobby. All through this century, the amateurs and professionals have pursued common conservation goals, with some mutual suspicion, yet together achieving what neither camp could have accomplished alone.

The Appalachian Mountain Club, the first permanent organization of hikers and mountaineers in the United States, was founded in Boston in January 1876. Most of its organizers were college professors — a physicist, an astronomer, life scientists, geologists, civil engineers — whose indoor work pushed them outside to pursue recreation and natural beauty. "The study of natural science inevitably led man face to face with nature," said Charles E. Fay, an early AMC leader, in 1879. "Our Club stands as perhaps the sole representative on this continent of the interests of aesthetics as related to the realm of science." As time passed, the AMC became more aesthetic — in the broadest sense — and less scientific, more inclined to enjoy mountains and forests than study them. Enjoyment then implied protection: as early as 1879, a committee was appointed to help preserve "natural scenery" from encroaching progress. "The work of our Club is to a certain extent play-work, yet to a certain extent serious," an officer said in marking the AMC's tenth anniversary. "We are not bound down by the considerations of market values." Not a large organization, with average meeting attendance of about a hundred people, the AMC wielded influence beyond its numbers because its membership included prominent Bostonians of the day: John Greenleaf Whittier, Alice Stone Blackwell, Thomas Wentworth Higginson, Lucy Larcom, Lincoln Filene, Edwin Markham, Percival Lowell, and many others. Along with its blend of literally high purpose, scientific inquiry, and social contacts, the club tapped into the waning reform impulse that had so animated Boston for most of the nineteenth century. "It seems to me," said Higginson as president in 1885, "that if anywhere there is a universe in need of administration, it might well be turned over to the Appalachian Mountain Club." The idea was then dispersed beyond Massachusetts. In 1892 the AMC served as the organizational model for launching the Sierra Club in California, with John Muir as its focus and best recruiting device.[23]

Charles Eliot, a landscape architect and the son of Harvard's legendary president of the same name, joined the AMC in 1887. As head of the club's Topography Committee in 1890, he pushed the organization toward a novel idea: to own and protect patches of wild land and forest. "Opportunities for beholding the beauty of Nature are of great importance to the health and happiness of crowded populations," Eliot declared. "These opportunities are rapidly vanishing." With AMC help, Eliot first established a newly incorporated private group, the Trustees of Public Reservations. Then in 1894, in what the club's journal, *Appalachia*, called "the most important step since its organization in 1876," the AMC obtained from the state legislature the right to hold, tax-free, mountain and forest properties. Within a decade this concept had spread to private and public bodies in New Hampshire, New York, Maine, and Rhode Island, and onward from there. The first AMC acquisition, the Snyder Brook Reservation in New Hampshire, was bought in 1895 to save 36 acres of ancient White Mountain forest from logging. The Parsons Reservation (1897) protected 40 acres of Massachusetts mountain land, largely wooded, on Mount Grace in Warwick. The 10-acre Carlisle Pines Reservation in Massachusetts, acquired in 1902, included 100 great pines, up to 120 feet tall and 42 inches in diameter, believed to be the largest in southern New England. By 1913 the AMC held in trust 16 properties of 1 to 300 acres in three states.[24]

These reservations reflected and provoked a growing club interest in forestry, further extending the AMC's purposes from science to beauty to calls for political action. In 1892 the group gave $184 to assist lobbying efforts in New Hampshire toward preserving forests in the mountains and at the headwaters of principal rivers. A general AMC meeting in June 1893 heard a lecture on European forestry schools and techniques. Later that year, in discussing the New Hampshire forests, president Charles Fay called the club "an instrument of public good." This new emphasis continued through the decade. In 1899 a retiring club president addressed the question of "what we as Appalachians may do for our country." He blamed land abuse, flooding, and erosion on "indiscriminate" lumbering and "the influences of trusts for the cutting of timber and the manufacture of pulp and paper." By degrees the club was joining the nascent conservation movement of the reform-minded Progressive Era. To codify this drift, in 1900 the AMC's "Exploration" Committee was renamed "Exploration and Forestry," with an expanding emphasis on the latter aspect.[25]

Allen Chamberlain was the club's most persistent advocate of forestry. A reporter for several Boston newspapers, in 1895 he switched to freelance work, specializing in historical, outdoors, and conservation subjects. His writing often appeared in the *Boston Evening Transcript*, the favorite newspaper of the old-stock Yankee class that sustained the AMC. From his base in the club, Chamberlain became a tireless, articulate exemplar of the dedicated amateur in conservation, donating his time to many good causes around the country. "As a common or garden citizen," he wrote a Pennsylvania colleague in the fight to save Niagara Falls, "you will find me always ready to do what I can, and as a newspaper man I shall be glad to lend a hand." In 1898 Chamberlain and Joseph S. Nowell, another AMC leader, started the Massachusetts Forestry Association to lobby for forest legislation and better forestry practices on private land, especially by the state's farmers. This organization helped establish a state fire warden law, the office of state forester, and state forests and town forests; on a federal level, it worked hard for a decade to pass the Weeks Act of 1911. Described by Chamberlain in teasing irony as "the mildest and the sanest piece of socialistic legislation that has been drafted in a long time," the Weeks Act authorized designation of the White Mountain National Forest and other such forests in the East for the overt purpose of protecting the region's headwaters. (Later on the MFA's name was changed to the Massachusetts Forest and Park Association.)[26]

Within the AMC, which had larger and more diffuse purposes, Chamberlain kept urging the need for prudent forestry. As head of the Exploration and Forestry Committee in 1902, he assured members that he favored no limits on legitimate timber cutting. "A proper use of the forests is wholly desirable, and will tend to their perpetuation," he wrote in *Appalachia*. "It is to the ruthless waste of material, and to the stripping of the timber from those lands which are of little value for anything but forest growth, that we should stoutly object." Pointedly doing as well as talking, club members demonstrated good forestry practices on the AMC holdings. In 1905 a fire belt 20 feet wide was created around the border of the Carlisle Pines Reservation, and hardwoods and the smaller undergrowth were thinned in favor of young pines. On the Rhododendron Reservation in Fitzwilliam, New Hampshire — a stand of 300 acres donated in 1902 to save an enclosed 12-acre natural bed of rhododendrons, the largest in the area, from logging — club volunteers toiled to remove great heaps of slash, a fire hazard left behind by old logging operations. As Chamberlain reported in 1908, the worst five acres of slash were horse-hauled into 47 piles for burning, and further reductions were planned. All this for rhododendrons: the AMC, like other amateurs in forest conservation, still insisted on aesthetics. "Our friends the conservationists, that is the professionals, are exceeding loath to recognize this point of view," Chamberlain noted in 1909. "Nothing short of a wide public sentiment will ever bring them round, I fear."[27]

MASSACHUSETTS AUDUBON SOCIETY

The women of Massachusetts Audubon never lost sight of such aesthetic aspects. Their group, founded in 1896, was the first of the state Audubon societies and led within a decade to dozens of others and to an umbrella national organization based in New York. The Audubon movement became one of the most successful and durable players in national conservation affairs. Massachusetts Audubon, the key to the whole structure, always remained among the largest and most activist of the state groups, essentially free of commercial corruptions and true to the vision of its founders of protecting birds and their habitats. Bird protection thus eventually became part of the larger struggle for forest conservation.

The two key founders, Harriet Lawrence Hemenway and Minna B. Hall, came from long, eminent traditions of patrician New England reform. Hemenway's father, Amos A. Lawrence of the wealthy Boston textile family, had been a militant abolitionist who supplied guns and money to John Brown. He also founded two colleges and supported black education and political rights after the Civil War; his instincts for philanthropy and good works were passed on to his daughter. Harriet and her cousin Minna Hall grew up on the family's country estate in the

Figure 7.2. Turn-of-the-century editorial cartoon reflecting the growing public opposition to commercial clear-cutting. These attitudes helped persuade the National Academy of Sciences in 1895 to create the National Forest (Sargent) Commission, the precursor of the system of national forest reserves and the U.S. Forest Service. Massachusetts Department of Environmental Management.

then-rural Longwood area of Brookline, near the corner of Beacon and Essex streets. Harriet's first memories of birds — a childhood imprinting typical for most bird-lovers — were the sounds and sights of many orioles nesting high in the trees around the house each spring, and flocks of bluebirds among the apple blossoms in the orchard. The nearby land offered woods, meadows, and a pond, all teeming with plants and wild creatures. Children would gather collections of birds' eggs, although — Hemenway later insisted — they would take only two from a clutch, leaving the rest, and then exhibit the eggs in open little boxes covered with transparent muslin. Minna Hall, who lived across the street, never married; for her entire life she kept as her main residence the house in which she was born, eventually turning the grounds into a private bird sanctuary with houses and baths (and cats prohibited). In 1896 both women were in their late thirties, with time and money on their hands, and prodded by their Brahmin consciences to contribute to society.[28]

High fashion brought them to bird protection. The smartest women's hats of the day were lavishly adorned with bird feathers, sometimes with entire stuffed birds, uniting the trades of millinery and taxidermy. By one estimate in the mid-1890s, 5 million American birds of about 50 species were annually slaughtered to supply these needs of fashion. One day in January 1896 Hemenway read a gruesome article about the hunting of snowy egrets for their plumes in the Florida Everglades, with the untidy residue of gore and body parts and young birds left to starve in their nests. She told her cousin what she had read, and together they went through the rarefied *Boston Blue Book* to find sympathetic society women who might join them in foregoing feathers to save birds. "We then sent out circulars," Hall recalled, "asking the women to join a society for the protection of birds, especially the egret. Some women joined, and some who preferred to wear the feathers would not join." They enlisted William Brewster of Cambridge, a prominent ornithologist, to act as president, and held the first meeting of the Massachusetts Audubon Society at Hemenway's home on Clarendon Street in the Back Bay in February 1896. Charles Sprague Sargent agreed to be listed as one of the honorary vice-presidents on the letterhead.[29]

It was logical that women should spearhead a crusade for birds. Men had already taken up the larger aspects of conservation: trees, mountains, rivers, fish and wildlife, big-game hunting in the West. Many of these elements included troublesome, long-term commercial implications that had to be addressed. The comparative backyard scale of birding, its relative freedom from commercial aspects, even the aesthetics of birdsong and the flash of color on the wing: all attracted women in the late 1800s. Male birders at that time collected specimens with shotguns; women preferred to use binoculars. Even before the Audubon groups were launched, some of the most respected and widely read contemporary writers about birds were women such as Olive Thorne Miller, Florence Merriam Bailey, and Mabel Osgood Wright. In 1897 Bailey helped found the tenth Audubon group, in the District of Columbia, and for years she led its bird classes to instruct schoolteachers in basic ornithology. Wright helped start Connecticut Audubon in 1898 and served as its longtime president. As an editor of the national Audubon journal *Bird-Lore,* launched in 1899, she wrote up news of the multiplying state societies. "We are all in excellent fighting trim," she wrote an Audubon ally in New York in 1901. "Our Society is flourishing. . . . Connecticut may be slow about its laws but it's doing a deal of thinking." On the state level women dominated most of the early Audubon groups. In Massachusetts, William Brewster lent his name as the presidential figurehead while women such as Harriet E. Richards, secretary-treasurer for the first two decades, did most of the actual work.[30]

To save bird populations, the Audubon groups at first focused on specific measures to limit hunting for sport or business. The first federal legislation, the Lacey Act of 1900, outlawed the interstate shipment of any birds killed in violation of state laws. Audubon members worked toward the necessary state legislation and prowled their local retail outlets, looking for illegal merchandise. Another federal law, passed in 1913, protected migratory birds across state lines, by empowering a bureau of the Agriculture Department to regulate hunting seasons, and safeguarded some species entirely.[31] These steps limited the most immediate threats to birds. For the longer term, Audubon groups by degrees shifted to a more ecological, more complex, and more challenging emphasis on preserving bird habitats. Since that usually meant preserving trees as well, the Audubon movement came to include forest conservation among its purposes.

Massachusetts Audubon was incorporated in 1915, which gave it the right to receive and manage property. A year later a wealthy physician, George W. Field, offered the society his estate in Sharon as a bird sanctuary: 225 acres of meadows and forests, crosshatched with brooks and a pond. The society hired a warden to live on this first Moose Hill Bird Sanctuary to protect the land and distribute Audubon literature to the thousands of visitors it drew each year. A didactic "Nature Trail," with explanatory signs and tags, was added to the property in 1927, and conducted a walker along an encircling path for about a third of a mile.

The tags identified trees, flowers, and shrubs, explaining that birds especially liked wild or rum cherries, that chipmunks lived in an old stone wall, hibernating through the winter and bearing four to six young in the late spring. A walker's attention was directed to the six kinds of oaks, four of hickories, and three of birches along the trail, with more information about each species as it was encountered. An enormous dead chestnut, brought down after more than a century by bark disease, still provided shelter for squirrels, nuthatches, and woodpeckers, along with many insects and fungus growths. Under a pitch pine, the detritus of chewed cones and tips of branches was explained as the work of the red squirrel, "tyrant of the forest."[32]

Moose Hill and the other sanctuaries that followed it embodied the expanded purposes of Massachusetts Audubon, defined in 1931 as the protection of "useful or beautiful wild life." Those adjectives combined the ends of utilitarian and preservationist conservation. The stated definition of "wild life" was also revealing: "birds, beasts, forest, wild flowers."[33] Almost everything, that is, that lived in the woods. The original goal of bird protection and appreciation had broadened into more general conservation work. Harriet Hemenway and Minna Hall stayed active in Massachusetts Audubon to the ends of their long lives, justifiably pleased with what they had started.

BENTON MACKAYE

From their neighboring bases in small-town Massachusetts, Benton MacKaye and William P. Wharton (the subject of the next section) played crucial roles in national forest conservation during the three decades from 1920 to 1950. They differed in their respective forest values and priorities, they belonged to separate wings of the conservation movement (MacKaye was an impoverished Democrat, Wharton a wealthy Republican), and they never worked together to any substantial degree. Yet they shared and were informed by common histories. After difficult, unstable early childhoods, both boys were brought to live in villages in northwestern Middlesex County. To both, the nearby enveloping forests opened and beckoned, offering a friendly, known context that stayed reliable, year to year, even after schools and maturity took them away for long intervals. Woodlands gave them the surest, steadiest touchstones they had yet known. No matter how far MacKaye and

Wharton later went, the Massachusetts forests still endured when they came home, reminding them of why they spent their lives in conservation. They knew viscerally what they so often preached: the restorative powers of the woods. Both men looked and behaved like ancient swamp Yankees, barked and rooted in the Massachusetts woods for generations. But they were in fact relative nouveaux, acting with the zeal of recent converts to save forests that had once — in a long, slow, barely perceptible process — saved them.

MacKaye (1879–1975) came from an artistic family, gifted and dreamy, ambitious but impractical. His father, Steele MacKaye, was a noted playwright-director-producer of the 1880s; as a young man Steele MacKaye had known Emerson and Thoreau, and a hint of the more feckless aspects of transcendentalism, of Brook Farm and Bronson Alcott, stayed with him. The family moved around chasing thespian success, pursued by bills and creditors. By the age of 10 Benton had lived in at least seven homes, from New Hampshire to the District of Columbia. The MacKayes summered in Shirley Center, Massachusetts, a farming village of 71 people. This little time capsule, a stop on the railroad to Fitchburg but otherwise untouched by the nineteenth century, drew the boy into its steady simplicity: a few houses, a town hall, church, school, general store, and the surrounding forest. Benton and his young friends formed a secret Rambling Boys' Club "to give to the members," they explained, "an education of the lay of the land in which they live, also of other lands, taking in the Geography, Geology, Zoology, and Botany of them." After the death of his father in 1893, Benton, then 14, came to live year-round in Shirley Center with a sister and his Aunt Sadie. He became a Yankee by glad adoption, clicking into the unchanged folk rituals of small-town life, and gaining a surrogate father in a local farmer and political figure named Melvin Longley. MacKaye did chores on the Longley place and eventually was even allowed to drive the horse at haying time.[34]

In his teens MacKaye explored the land within walking distance of home, a radius of about four miles, taking special pains to map the forest ("my first stunt in forestry"). From Mulpus Brook, where he had learned to swim and noted a kingfisher in flight, he ventured on to the Squannacook River and saw a swimming muskrat, and then to Hunting Hill, the junction of the brook and river. He kept careful notes on these "expeditions," the start of a lifelong habit of self-recording. After his freshman year at Harvard he took his first real wilderness trip, into the southern edge of the White Mountains of New Hampshire. MacKaye and two companions waded the Swift River and struggled through a thicket of blowdown: "And it was hell. A scrambled mess of fallen broken trunks and boughs, a choking chaos impossible to describe." But he got through it and climbed Tremont Mountain, feeling at the summit his first mountaineer's weary satisfaction after a tough ascent.[35]

A career in forestry naturally followed. After graduation from the Harvard Forest School in 1905, he spent a dozen years in and out of Gifford Pinchot's Forest Service, sharing in that agency's early missionary zeal of proclaiming and practicing utilitarian conservation. MacKaye's postings around the country — down to Kentucky, out to Minnesota and then Puget Sound, back to the bureaucracy of wartime Washington — broadened his grasp of forestry on a national level, especially issues of acquisition and cutover land colonization. This professional life did not preclude volunteer efforts for aesthetic conservation. (Trees were MacKaye's vocation and avocation.) In 1908 he surveyed the Appalachian Mountain Club's Rhododendron Reservation; Allen Chamberlain noted the AMC's gratitude to MacKaye, "who, although not a member of the Club, has given his time, energy, and professional skill entirely without compensation to aid us." Later, in Washington, he conducted Sunday hikes along the abandoned Chesapeake and Ohio Canal towpath out to Great Falls, with running commentary on the dangers posed by automobiles and timber barons.[36]

In 1920 MacKaye quit government service and returned to Shirley Center for a long spell of freelance thinking and writing. In his early forties, he felt profoundly out of step with the main tendencies of his time. Though he called himself "an amphibian as between urban and rural life," most of modern industrial civilization offended him: its pace, noise, danger, clutter, waste, all in pursuit of trivial values of money and success, "an iron web of industry that threatens to strangle us." Spurning the popular culture of radio, movies, and screaming tabloids, he preferred folk music and dances he had first enjoyed as a boy in Shirley Center. "I would not 'go back' to the *old* school of color and melody," he made clear, "I would 'continue on' with the *eternal* school thereof — after its preposterous interruption by the machine-made forces of jazz and imbecility." Seeking a political alternative, he had joined the Socialist party in 1920 and — along with some 920,000 others of his progressive generation — voted for the socialist Gene Debs for president that fall. But he knew that Marxists shared the same modernist superstitions as capitalists, envisioning an identical, starkly mechanical urban future. As an antimodernist, MacKaye took his political cues mainly from the pre-Marxian utopian socialisms, spiritual and hopeful, of nineteenth-century New England; but here again he found few sympathizers among his contemporaries.[37]

MacKaye offered only fragments of these attitudes in his published writing. In print he dithered around — making his points with loose analogies, posing questions instead of answering them — and burying his arguments in thickets of soft verbiage that cried out for editing. By all accounts, he was more effective in person, impressing people with his vivid personality; widely if not deeply acquainted, he would bring diverse groups of his friends together and catalytically steer the conversation from gossip into serious matters. He carried himself like a stage Yankee: tall and lean, strong in the nose and mouth, smoking a pipe and spinning dry, pungent little homilies. Frugal and ascetic by taste or necessity, he kept his old house in Shirley Center free of electricity, indoor plumbing, and central heating. "He figures for me as Thoreau's latest continuator," his friend Lewis Mumford said later, "a Yankee of the Yankees, tart as a wild apple, sweet as a hickory nut." His vaulting idealism was usually grounded and tempered by a hard New England skepticism.[38]

MacKaye was always better at inspiration than execution. In the fall of 1921, in the unlikely venue of an architectural journal, he proposed a wild "Appalachian Trail" along the main divides and ridges of mountains from New England to Georgia. For a few years in the 1920s, MacKaye was intensely involved in a regional planning group with Mumford, Clarence Stein, and other American urban critics and architects inspired by the British visionaries Patrick Geddes and Ebenezer Howard. As an exercise in regional planning, the Appalachian Trail was only part of a larger MacKaye design for recreation camps, poised between rural and urban settings, which would replace "competition and mutual fleecing" with "cooperation and mutual helpfulness." Arguing that the East, where most of the population lived, especially needed more camping sites, MacKaye envisioned a chain of camps connected by a walking trail and sustained by volunteer labor. For the next few years MacKaye urged his idea on members of the Northeast's hiking community. As he explained in *Appalachia* in 1922, about one-third of the projected path already existed, mostly along AMC trails in New Hampshire and Forest Service trails through national forests of the South. The vast middle of the Appalachian Trail, through the most densely settled parts of the country, remained the knottiest problem.[39]

MacKaye began to lose interest, but the scheme was revived after 1926 mainly through the dogged efforts of two indefatigable hikers, Arthur Perkins of Connecticut and Myron Avery of the District of Columbia. They pushed it along to eventual completion, shorn of the founder's utopian regional vision, while MacKaye remained involved (and critical) at a distance. "It is a real *trail* — a path and not a road," he told Avery's Potomac Appalachian Trail Club in 1930. "The foot replaces the wheel, the cabin replaces the hotel, the song replaces the radio, the campfire replaces the movie. It is the trail of the *new pioneer,* not the old pioneer." (Avery just wanted to finish the damn trail, even at the expense of its pure wildness.) "To know humanity we must know forest history," MacKaye insisted in *Scientific Monthly* in 1932. The Appalachian Trail, then two-thirds complete at 1,400 miles, offered vital lessons in geological processes and the mutual interactions of plants, animals, insects, and fishes. "The primeval forest is a balanced and independent society," so unlike human modernity, he concluded. "In unravelling the forest civilization we reveal the contrasts of our own." Or so MacKaye still hoped; yet most of the trail's actual builders and hikers probably just wanted to take a bracing walk in the woods. Motives aside, though, the completed path — declared the nation's first national scenic trail in 1968 — did preserve a precious green ribbon 2,100 miles long, and MacKaye deserves first credit.[40]

The Appalachian Trail in turn helped spawn MacKaye's other major contribution to forest conservation, his cofounding of the Wilderness Society. Holding to his original vision of a truly wild trail, in the early 1930s MacKaye was appalled by suggestions for "skyline drives" and other motor-road intrusions into national parks and the Appalachian Trail. MacKaye found new allies in Robert Marshall, a young forester and mountaineer from New York who was endowed with great charm, energy, and personal wealth, and Harold Anderson of the Potomac Appalachian Trail Club. "You and Bob Marshall have been preaching that those who love the primitive should get together and give a united expression of their views," Anderson wrote MacKaye in August 1934. "That is what I would like to get started. . . . The present craze is to motorize everything."[41]

Marshall had met MacKaye in Washington during the Hundred Days of the New Deal; he was puzzled by him ("a grand fellow but very eccentric") yet liked his commitment to wilderness. Marshall brought his own expansive range of contacts across the country, enlisting such notable forest conservationists as Aldo Leopold, Robert Sterling Yard, and Ernest Oberholtzer, and thus enlarged the small founders' circle into a new national conservation group. After preliminary meetings they gathered in Washington in January 1935 and adopted a platform, drafted mainly by Marshall and MacKaye, which defined wilderness as "a human need rather than a luxury or plaything." The leaders chose their associates in the Wilderness Society very carefully. "I have in mind a long list of people who should NOT be admitted. We want those who *already* think as we do; not those who have to be shown," MacKaye emphasized. "There should be plenty of discussion and disagreement as to *how* and the *means* but none whatever as to ends."[42]

The society remained for years a small, tightly held oligarchy, sustained by Marshall's money and the carefully shared values of its founders. MacKaye served as the first vice president and, from 1945 to 1950, as president; well into old age he helped shape its policies. The protracted battles of the 1950s over national parks and monuments took an enlarged Wilderness Society onto the national conservation stage. Formerly isolated by his peculiar ideas, MacKaye took legitimate pleasure in the Wilderness Society's growing influence, which led finally to the landmark federal Wilderness Act of 1964.[43]

WILLIAM P. WHARTON

A few miles northeast of Shirley Center, the town of Groton was home to William P. Wharton, a ubiquitous leader — one with exceptional range and persistence — in many private conservation groups. His contributions have largely been lost to history, even to specialists in conservation, because Wharton was so modest and self-effacing. Of slightly less than average size, quiet and reserved, he dressed and spoke plainly. He sat through meetings without saying much and so was easily underestimated. He worked quietly behind the scenes, in correspondence and private discussions, never seeking credit — in fact, actively avoiding it. When the American Forestry Association gave him its Distinguished Service Award in 1955, Wharton sent somebody else to the ceremony to accept it. He seldom wrote for publication, even in the journals of the conservation groups he sustained so generously with his time and money. Twice married, he had no children, left behind no collection of personal papers, and, when he died, forgotten, at 96, after outliving his contemporaries, received few obituaries. During his life-time conservation was professionalized and bureaucratized; Wharton remained a dedicated amateur in every sense of the word, and that also has contributed to his current obscurity.

Wharton (1880–1976) came from a daunting background of wealth and high achievement. His paternal grandfather, of the prominent Virginia branch of the large Wharton family, had married a Bostonian and thus became a Yankee by marriage. His father, William French Wharton, was graduated from Harvard and Harvard Law and then embarked on a sober career of Boston lawyering and public service. In 1877 he married well, to Fanny Pickman of Beverly, and their first child, William Pickman Wharton, was born in August 1880. But Fanny died two months later, apparently from complications of childbirth, and the motherless boy was raised by relatives and servants. He probably lived in the Beacon Street home of his paternal grandmother, along with his spinster Aunt Nancy and Uncle Teddy (who soon became the hopeless, wastrel husband of the writer Edith Wharton).[44]

By the social conventions of his time and class, his father would have had little to do with his son's early childhood, and was quite busy anyway with his legal work and a rising political career that took him into the Boston Common Council, then to the state House of Represen-tatives. Early in 1889 the father reached high federal office with appoint-ment as an assistant secretary of state in the new presidency of Benjamin Harrison. His son, eight years old, went with him to Wash-ington. The father remarried in 1891, to Susan Lay, the daughter of the American ambassador to Canada, in a private ceremony attended by seven ambassadors and two Supreme Court justices, among others. The family then welcomed two more children, born in 1892 and 1894. By his teens William P. Wharton had lost the mother he never knew; had grown up in one household only to be taken to another in a strange city far from familiar surroundings; had acquired a stepmother at age 10;

had spent 12 years as an only child and then quickly gained two siblings. Money and social status had not provided him a stable childhood.[45]

In 1893 the family returned to Massachusetts and moved into a federalist mansion in Groton. The father commuted by train to his Boston law office while William was enrolled at the exclusive Groton prep school. After the upheavals and erratic schooling of his earlier life, he had to repeat his first year at Groton. Even the dullest Groton boys might still go on to Harvard, however. His college years passed with no great distinction. He then enrolled at Harvard Law School but left after one year. The young man still lacked a solid mooring. "I was one of those unfortunate fellows who didn't know what job they were cut out for," he wrote years later, "and just drifted along until something seemingly worthwhile turned up. A lover of the open spaces, I couldn't stand the idea of being shut up in city offices indefinitely, so took to the life in the open."[46]

He went back to Groton, bought abandoned farmland and wood-lots to grow trees, and became a gentleman farmer. Steadily adding to his land — which eventually exceeded 800 acres — walking his property each morning and soaking up the ongoing spectacle, he found in his fields and forests a permanent home. He planted white pine, then a small orchard. In 1912 he acquired Fiveoaks Farm, a spread of eighty acres, and ventured seriously into apples, dairy cattle, and hogs. Wharton's farming interests grew concurrently with his conservation work; again, Thoreau's tension between nature for humans and nature for itself. Travels along the Florida coast and to national parks of the West had sparked his concern for preserving wildlife and wild land. At home he banned hunting in his forest, protected birds, and deplored cats. He kept a shotgun to shoot red squirrels menacing bird nests. Once he found somebody hunting on his property, prosecuted the man, and then paid his fine. At Badacook Pond in Groton he planted wild rice for the ducks and built his beloved "shack," a small cedar-shingled cabin, where he would go to fish, think, and monitor his ongoing bird-banding project.[47]

The growing farm finally threatened to monopolize his time; "this farming job," he lamented in 1920, "has so tied me to a cow's tail as to turn me into a hopeless stick-in-the-mud." But agricultural reversals, ill health, and the family trust funds that relieved him of having to earn a real living then released him to full-bore conservation work. "As a farmer I haven't been much of a success," he reported with typical humility to his college classmates in 1928; but "my bird-banding hobby has proved a life-saver, and has given me many hours of pleasure and interest." He sold off his livestock and leased his orchard. Five years later, "Those wild life and forestry hobbies have practically become my occupation."[48]

Transmuting hobbies into his lifework, he toiled for a dozen conservation groups at every level, from town to nation. He sat on the board of the Massachusetts Forest and Park Association for 59 years. On the national scene, he served most notably in three influential organizations: National Audubon, the National Parks Association, and the American Forestry Association. Birding had first drawn him to conservation, and it remained his most durable passion. Wherever he went, in any environment, he would notice the birds. Starting in 1915, he served continuously as an officer and board member of National Audubon for 28 years, traveling faithfully down to New York for regular meetings. He was also the organization's most generous financial angel. Like other enlightened birders of his time, he moved on from protecting birds to preserving habitats. "God gave us a heritage," he told a group of Massachusetts birders in 1932, "of woods and waters and great open spaces and wild life such as few peoples have been blessed with. What we have done and are doing to it, often unnecessarily, makes the true lover of nature shudder to behold it. Fortunately it is not too late to save considerable areas from the hand of the despoiler."[49]

Wharton joined the National Parks Association upon its founding in 1919. For years he was one of its half dozen main supporters; after a crisis in 1935 Wharton stepped in, accepted the presidency, and became yet another group's principal source of income. He remained NPA president until 1953. The NPA guarded preservation practices in the national park system and urged the highest aesthetic standards in establishing new parks. At the same time — and with no sense of internal contradiction — Wharton was an influential director of the American Forestry Association, which had evolved into an adjunct of lumber industry trade groups; the AFA urged better private forestry practices with no government interference. To Wharton it simply depended on which trees were at issue, on which land. "Those things which on private lands and in national forests are essential material resources, to be used wisely and with caution," he explained in 1942, "in national parks acquire a sanctity comparable to great works of art. . . . People turn to the fundamental and immutable things to renew their courage and their hope. In the primeval parks and monuments these fundamental and immutable things can be found singularly unchanged."[50]

This catholicity was the most remarkable aspect of Wharton's sustained conservation efforts. In the balkanized conservation movement of his time, specific groups mostly kept to their own purposes of forestry, wilderness, wildlife, or national parks. Few individuals had Wharton's range because few as yet had fully heeded an ecological imperative: Aldo Leopold's challenge to think at right angles to Darwin, to slice across the biotic pyramid and thus see many species in their complex, mysterious interdependence. As Wharton walked around his Groton woods, watching and listening, and then meditated at his shack, he intuited this broader perspective. It made him one of his era's rare universal figures in conservation. "Whether man can adjust himself to [modern progress] in such a way as to keep his balance and his sense of values is a moot question," Wharton wrote in 1953. "Often I wish that man's brain could have directed his mental efforts into channels of deeper understanding of his proper place in a world where all life is worthy of consideration, and where the great gifts of the Creator should be used humbly for the good of all mankind."[51]

Ceremonial citations like the American Forestry Association award to Wharton in 1955 often sound too fulsome and overstated to take literally. But this one seems hard earned and richly justified: "It would be difficult, if not impossible, to find a citizen living today who voluntarily has devoted so much of his personal time, energy, and means to conservation . . . as an outstanding example of a private citizen whose approach to conservation has been based solely on the rock of unselfish public interest. . . . No man has done more for conservation in his native state of Massachusetts. No man has done more in throwing full support to all phases of the movement nationally."[52] In honoring and keeping alive the older tradition of the dedicated amateur in conservation, Wharton provided a personal bridge between the voluntary origins of the movement and the explosion of citizen environmentalism after the 1960s.

FOREST CONSERVATION AND MASSACHUSETTS

A unique set of historical circumstances has combined to give Massachusetts special prominence in the invention of forest conservation: a large presence of distinguished colleges and experts, a tradition of nurturing and tolerating Thoreauvian eccentrics, a history of spawning new reform movements, and a responsible patrician class that felt obliged to give back some of its good fortune. Behind all these factors, linking them, was the land itself. The lush primeval forest passed through long cycles, of woods to pastures to croplands and — in the twentieth century — back to woods again. European immigrants and their progeny cut down the trees, used the land, then moved away and let some of the trees return. The residents of Massachusetts, one of the oldest settled states in the country, witnessed this process before most Americans did; so the notion of forest conservation came up sooner and more forcefully here. "Massachusetts is the state in which efforts to preserve forests and trees and to use them economically have probably been made since earlier times and with more consistency than in any other," a national forestry journal noted in 1900. "Forest work can also be carried on more intensively there than in other states, and it is possible to give much more attention to aesthetic considerations."[53]

From the perspective of the 1990s, the state's creative role in such matters appears to have been most significant before the midpoint of the twentieth century. But this is to some degree a problem of historical perception. In the early years, individuals stood out more because, with little established context, they were making things up as they went along. Pioneers are more visible when they are working virgin land. Once conservation acquired the critical mass of environmentalism after 1960, individuals tended to fade into a vast, anonymous structure of private organizations and government bureaucracies. Experts today often speak only to each other in esoteric jargons impenetrable to citizen outsiders. Contemporary innovators still no doubt live and work among us, but they're harder to see now. The forest has come to obscure the trees.

Yet the "forest" remains the main point. The Massachusetts pioneers in forest conservation came in many forms: men and women, horticulturists, hikers, birders, hunters, professional foresters. Most were old-stock Yankees of middle- or upper-class backgrounds. (As it happens, Thoreau, Sargent, MacKaye, and Wharton all graduated from Harvard College.) Challenged in the twentieth century by new ethnic diversities and the relative decline of their own cohort, in preserving local forests the Yankee conservationists were also, in a way, preserving themselves. Trees and Yankees were both clinging to an endangered present, and yearning for an older, perhaps better time. But on balance the conservationists' motives should not be made more complicated — or more selfish — than the historical record suggests. Beyond backward-yearning ethnic and class patterns, and of greater importance, were these conservationists' shared affinities for trees and woodlands, and their generally selfless concern to protect them. This story starts and ends in the woods.

NOTES

1. Henry David Thoreau, *Walden* (Riverside edition, 1960), pp. 91, 80.
2. Robert D. Richardson, Jr., in Henry David Thoreau, *Faith in a Seed* (1993), pp. 4–14.
3. Henry David Thoreau, *The Maine Woods* (Perennial Library edition, 1987), pp. 163, 165, 212–13.
4. Kathryn Whitford, in *New England Quarterly*, September 1950.
5. Thoreau, *Faith in a Seed*, p. 252; Lawrence Buell, *The Environmental Imagination: Thoreau, Nature Writing, and the Formation of American Culture* (1995), p. 213.
6. Charles Sprague Sargent to Robert Underwood Johnson, November 25, 1908, Robert Underwood Johnson Papers, Bancroft Library, University of California, Berkeley.
7. Roderick Nash, *Wilderness and the American Mind* (3rd edition, 1982), p. 105.
8. S. B. Sutton, *Charles Sprague Sargent and the Arnold Arboretum* (1970), pp. 70–71; W. T. Councilman, in M. A. DeWolfe Howe, *Later Years of the Saturday Club, 1870–1920* (1927), p. 289.
9. *Garden and Forest*, January 2, 1889.
10. Charles Sprague Sargent, *Report on the Forests of North America* (1884); Sutton, *Sargent*, p. 92.
11. *The Nation*, September 6, 1883; Sutton, *Sargent*, p. 91.
12. Ovid M. Butler, in *American Forests*, October 1946; *Dictionary of American*

Biography, 10:444–45 and 6:417–18; *Garden and Forest,* October 23, 1889 and July 10, 1889.

13. *Garden and Forest,* October 13, 1897; March 14 and December 19, 1888.
14. *Garden and Forest,* January 30 and October 30, 1889.
15. Stephen Fox, *John Muir and His Legacy: The American Conservation Movement* (1981), pp. 110–12.
16. John Muir to Theodore P. Lukens, July 29, 1897, Theodore P. Lukens Papers, Huntington Library, San Marino, California; Charles Sprague Sargent to Muir, June 15, 1898, John Muir Papers, Holt-Atherton Pacific Center for Western Studies, University of the Pacific.
17. M. Nelson McGeary, *Gifford Pinchot: Forester-Politician* (1960), pp. 4, 24; *Garden and Forest,* July 30, August 6, 13, 1890; January 7, 14, 21, 1891; March 2, 1892; July 24, 1895; February 26, March 4, 18, 1896; February 21, 1894 and December 4, 1895; Sutton, *Sargent,* p. 159.
18. John Muir to Robert Underwood Johnson, July 30, 1896, Johnson Papers; Charles Sprague Sargent to Muir, November 5, 1896, Muir Papers; Fox, *Muir,* pp. 112–13.
19. Charles Sprague Sargent to John Muir, June 22, 1897, Muir Papers; Sutton, *Sargent,* p. 168; Muir to Sargent, October 28, 1897, Muir Papers.
20. *Garden and Forest,* December 29, 1897; Charles Sprague Sargent to John Muir, January 26, 1899, Muir Papers.
21. *Forestry and Irrigation,* April 1903.
22. Journal of John Muir, August 31, 1903, Muir Papers.
23. Allen H. Bent, in *Appalachia,* December 1916; Charles E. Fay, in *Appalachia,* June 1879; *Appalachia,* June 1880, December 1886, and July 1911; Fox, *Muir,* p.107
24. George C. Mann, in *Appalachia,* July 1897; *Appalachia,* March 1894 and June 1895; Allen Chamberlain, in *Appalachia,* October 1914; Harvey N. Shepard, *The Reservations of the Appalachian Mountain Club* (1913), p. 3.
25. *Appalachia,* February and December 1893, March 1894, and May 1899.
26. Marjorie Hurd, in *Appalachia,* December 1945; Allen Chamberlain to J. Horace McFarland, December 3, 1908, J. Horace McFarland Papers, Division of Archives and Manuscripts, Pennsylvania Historical and Museum Commission, Harrisburg, Pennsylvania; M. Richard Applegate, *Massachusetts Forest and Park Association: A History 1898–1973* (1974), pp. 3–8; *Forester,* October 1899 and January 1901; Harold O. Cook, *Fifty Years a Forester* (1961), p. 18; Chamberlain, in *Sierra Club Bulletin,* January 1910.
27. Allen Chamberlain, in *Appalachia,* May 1902 and June 1908; Chamberlain to J. Horace McFarland, March 13, 1909, McFarland Papers; and see Chamberlain, in *Outlook,* May 28, 1910.

28. *Dictionary of American Biography,* 6:47–48; C. Russell Mason, in *Bulletin of the Massachusetts Audubon Society,* February 1954; *Bulletin of the Massachusetts Audubon Society,* October and December 1951.

29. John H. Mitchell, in *Sanctuary,* January–February 1996; Mason, in *Bulletin of the Massachusetts Audubon Society,* February 1954; Massachusetts Audubon Society, *First Report* (1897).

30. *Notable American Women 1607–1950,* eds. Edward T. James et al. (1971), 1:83 and 3:683; Mabel Osgood Wright to William E. Dutcher, May 31, 1901, National Association of Audubon Societies Papers, New York Public Library Annex; Winthrop Packard, in *Bulletin of the Massachusetts Audubon Society,* October 1936.

31. Fox, *Muir,* pp. 153, 157-59.

32. Mitchell, in *Sanctuary,* January–February 1996; Harry George Higbee, in *Bulletin of the Massachusetts Audubon Society,* January 1928.

33. *Bulletin of the Massachusetts Audubon Society,* December 1931.

34. Paul T. Bryant, in *Living Wilderness,* January–March 1976; Laura and Guy Waterman, *Forest and Crag: A History of Hiking, Trail Blazing, and Adventure in the Northeast Mountains* (1989), p. 485; Harley P. Holden, in *Living Wilderness,* January–March 1976.

35. Paul H. Oehser, in *Living Wilderness,* January–March 1979.

36. Allen Chamberlain, in *Appalachia,* July 1909.

37. Benton MacKaye to Harvey Broome, September 5, 1932, Benton MacKaye Papers, Dartmouth College; MacKaye, in *Survey,* May 1, 1925; Mackaye to Harvey Broome, April 3, 1932, MacKaye Papers; MacKaye's Socialist Party card, box 79:15, MacKaye Papers; MacKaye to Lewis Mumford, March 9, 1927, MacKaye Papers.

38. Lewis Mumford, in *Living Wilderness,* January–March 1976.

39. Benton MacKaye, in *Journal of the American Institute of Architects,* October 1921; Lewis Mumford, in *Living Wilderness,* January–March 1976; Mumford to Mackaye, October 14 and December 22, 1926, MacKaye Papers; MacKaye, in *Appalachia,* December 1922.

40. Benton MacKaye to Clarence Stein, May 19, 1930, MacKaye Papers; Waterman and Waterman, *Forest and Crag,* pp. 488–93; MacKaye, in *Potomac Appalachian Trail Club Bulletin,* November 26, 1930, box 63:14, MacKaye Papers; MacKaye, in *Scientific Monthly,* April 1932.

41. Benton MacKaye, in *Appalachia,* June 1934; MacKaye to Clarence Stein, June 13, 1932, MacKaye Papers; Harold Anderson to MacKaye, August 12, 1934, Wilderness Society Papers, Wilderness Society, Washington, DC.

42. Robert Marshall to Robert Sterling Yard, October 26, 1935, Wilderness Society Papers; Fox, *Muir,* p. 211; Benton MacKaye to Yard, June 25, 1935,

Wilderness Society Papers; George Marshall, in *Living Wilderness*, January–March 1976.

43. Fox, *Muir*, pp. 211–12, 266–72, 287–89.

44. R. W. B. Lewis, *Edith Wharton: A Biography* (1975), p. 50; *Groton Historical Series*, ed. Samuel Abbott Green (1899), 4:397–98.

45. Marion Stoddart, in *The Life of William P. Wharton 1880–1976* (videotape, Groton Historical Society, 1990); *Boston Evening Transcript*, February 11, 1891.

46. Harvard College Class of 1903, *Fiftieth Anniversary Report* (1953), p. 862.

47. *American Forests*, March 1940; interview with Isabelle Beal of Groton, May 21, 1996.

48. Harvard College Class of 1903, *Fourth Report* (1920), p. 322; *Twenty-Fifth Anniversary Report* (1928), p. 1035; *Sixth Report* (1933), p. 183.

49. *Boston Globe*, December 15, 1976; William P. Wharton, in *Bird-Lore*, September–October 1914 and November–December 1916; Wharton, in *Bulletin of the Massachusetts Audubon Society*, January 1932, March and May 1952; *Audubon Magazine*, September–October 1943; Wharton, in *Bulletin of the Massachusetts Audubon Society*, October 1932.

50. Robert Sterling Yard to John C. Merriam, November 17, 1930 and Yard to George D. Pratt, February 26, 1929, John C. Merriam Papers, Manuscript Division, Library of Congress; Harold Ickes to Franklin D. Roosevelt, May 3, 1940, PPF 1811, Franklin D. Roosevelt Library; Fox, *Muir*, p. 187; *American Forests*, October 1925 and December 1938; William P. Wharton, in *National Parks Magazine*, July–September 1942.

51. Aldo Leopold, *A Sand County Almanac* (Ballantine edition, 1970), p. 189; Harvard College Class of 1903, *Fiftieth Anniversary Report*, pp. 863–64.

52. *Bulletin of the Massachusetts Audubon Society*, November 1955.

53. *Forester*, July 1900.

Town Forests:
The Massachusetts Plan

ROBERT L. MCCULLOUGH

*T*HE GROTON memorial town forest, 400 acres and more bounded by the Nashua and Squannacook rivers near Groton center, is approaching its seventy-fifth year. Established in 1922, the forest has fulfilled the promise of those who first championed the town forest movement a decade earlier: cultivation of a sustained yield of timber consistent with recreational, educational, aesthetic, and other beneficial uses. In truth, Groton's reserve is a model town forest firmly grounded in community welfare. Dedicated as a memorial to residents who served in World War I, the forest was created with land donated by a local benefactor and with pasture and woodlot from the town's poor farm. Members of Groton's 4-H Club transplanted seedlings, WPA labor conducted timber-stand improvement during the Depression years, and the local garden club long ago began nurturing a wildflower sanctuary. Active forestry management continues today with harvesting typically undertaken at five-year intervals. Most recently, 20 acres of white pine were cut during the spring of 1996. Proceeds are reinvested in timber-stand improvement, and the town forest committee, not funded under the municipal budget, keeps a well-balanced ledger. The forest also invites recreational use, and town members explore secluded paths on foot and with bicycles.[1]

From their origins, town forests such as Groton's have played an important role in the larger quest to reverse deforestation and reclaim idle farmland, goals that became rallying points for municipal forestry during the early decades of the twentieth century. Massachusetts' wooded townscapes, now abundant, are testimony to that endeavor. As with so many aspects of natural resource conservation, Massachusetts became a vanguard in the movement for town forests. As early as 1905, the Massachusetts Forestry Association (MFA) shaped the beginnings of a campaign that soon gathered momentum in several New England states and eventually became national in scope. Harris A. Reynolds, the association's tireless secretary from 1911 to 1953, guided that campaign steadfastly. The MFA's mission, as Reynolds so astutely put it, was to make forestry part of people's everyday lives, and town forests have always been a quiet place to do just that. Where once policy-makers could argue the need for more and better forests, they now can ponder strategies that accommodate uses as diverse as timber cropping and ecological demonstration. The debate has changed, but it remains enveloped by sylvan canopy.

Town forests did not suddenly sprout on barren soil — far from it. They are a vital link in an evolving woodland ethic cultivated by Massachusetts towns for nearly four centuries. This continuum of forest and community began with the vast common weald that once encircled the nucleated villages of Massachusetts Bay and other colonies. Woodsmanship, the practice of culling forest resources without killing trees, was part of Anglo-Saxon culture transplanted from rural England during the Great Migration. Where individual routine blossomed into collective voice, guiding the course of new communities, the beginnings of forest conservation can be observed. Today, that process continues to mature.

Although these common lands were soon given up to private ownership, public lands — typically ecclesiastical allotments known as glebe, parsonage or church lots, together with school lots, all set aside by town proprietors to subsidize the costs of community institutions — endured much longer. Some exist today in the guise of town forests. The largest part of Massachusetts' history of communal woodlands is one of timber-products utilization guided by a stewardship applied consistently to community benefit. For much of the twentieth century, the town forest movement nurtured and refined that stewardship, all the while encouraging recreational and educational forest uses. Only during the last 50 years have the latter pursuits grown dominant in local woodlands, threatening to erase part of a working landscape essential to a complete understanding of the region's forest and urban history.

A MASTER PLAN TO RECLAIM IDLE LAND

The movement for town forests in Massachusetts emerged amid changing attitudes about America's woodlands, a reordering that took shape
during the second half of the nineteenth century. Concern about wasteful cutting practices and depleted timberlands, the introduction of
professional forestry and forestry science, focus on the role of forests as
part of larger ecosystems, the influence of woodland cover on water
supplies, and the culling of forest reserves from the public domain in
western states, all propelled this transformation. Reform-era prog-
ressivism that helped to synthesize the conservation movement also
fostered progress in urban and regional planning. These events made it
easier for citizens to sift unrefined policy into workable, community-
sized initiatives. The ancient bond between town and forest in many
parts of Massachusetts offered fertile ground for these seeds of opinion.

Amid shifting outlooks, selection of one event to mark change is
seldom easy. However, the appointment of Bernhard Fernow in 1886 to
head the U. S. Department of Agriculture's newly created forestry
division stands out as a milestone for local forestry. Fernow, a Prussian-
born professional forester, was especially knowledgeable about Europe's carefully managed communal forests. He encouraged a similar
program in America and can be given a large share of the credit for
inaugurating the town forest movement. In an 1890 editorial letter for
Charles Sprague Sargent's journal, *Garden and Forest,* Fernow wrote:
"In Germany I know of communities where not only all taxes are paid
by the revenue from the communal forests, but every citizen receives a
dividend in addition." Suggestions that American towns could produce
comparable lucre were enticing, and Fernow's comments were bor-
rowed countless times by those who publicized town forests during the
years to come. Fernow frequently pointed to Zurich's ancient city
forest, the Sihlwald, as a model of efficient forest utilization. There,
management by city foresters had begun as early as the fifteenth century, and technical working plans were in place by 1697. Modern
forestry practice originated with a series of nineteenth-century management plans, the results of which were carefully scrutinized by American foresters who made frequent pilgrimages to the Sihlwald.[2]

Germany's communal forests were rooted in a village structure
quite similar to Massachusetts' first settlements. The nucleated village

of Anglo-Saxon culture and its counterpart, the Mark Society of Germanic civilizations, both developed as communal agrarian societies with dwellings clustered to form a village nucleus. Outlying arable, pasture, woodland, and waste land were held in common, and communities were defined by the margins of this varied landscape. In England, feudal tenure buttressed by a unified central monarchy steadily suppressed communal ownership of land, eventually limiting common rights to those acquired by grant or by prescription through timeless use. A great many were extinguished by a legal process known as enclosure. In Germanic states, however, these common lands ripened into well-defined community-owned resources. It is ironic that Massachusetts' Anglican towns, where vast common lands had been renounced by the beginning of the seventeenth century, turned to Germany two centuries later for the model that would help them reclaim public lands in the form of town forests. The value of these ancient common rights did not escape Fernow, who remarked, "Through all the changes of centuries, these so-called servitudes (certain rights in the substance of the forests) have lasted until our own times, much changed, to be sure, in character, and extending by new grants especially to churches, charitable institutions, cities, villages, and colonists."[3]

Fernow was practical in his endorsements for community forestry in America, often cautioning that towns should not expect immediate returns but should plan instead for the distant future. Nevertheless, he wisely understood the educational value of such a program during an era of policy reform:

> If every community will concern itself in the rational use of the land within its borders, if every town and every county will give profitable occupation to its waste lands by utilizing them for forest-growth, the movement would not only increase the financial prosperity of each community, the efforts of those who work for a rational forest-policy in the country at large would be subserved by every communal forest established. In fact, no better method of forest reform could be suggested than by beginning forestry in each town."[4]

Unfortunately, Fernow's successors at the U.S. Forest Service were not as farsighted about the prospects of municipal forestry in America, and the federal government did not participate in the town forest movement until Franklin Roosevelt's administration. Instead, the task was left to private forestry associations such as the Massachusetts Forestry Association and to state forestry programs. Many state laws enabling towns to acquire municipal forests subsequently required management assistance from state foresters whose programs were aided by federal funds. An informal and effective system of collaboration between states and towns quickly developed.[5]

Massachusetts policy-makers had already responded to concern about the state's depleted forests and polluted waters. A law enacted in 1882 allowed towns to purchase land for "the preservation, reproduction and culture of forest trees for the sake of the wood and timber thereon, or for the preservation of the water supply." Acquisition was sanctioned by either direct purchase or eminent domain, but title vested in the state as a trustee for towns. Ironically, although recreational uses were clearly a secondary goal, the bill received support from those who sought a metropolitan park system, and it became known as the Massachusetts Public Park Law. A number of important forest parks, or reservations, as they are sometimes called, were founded during the ensuing years. These include Lynn Woods, Prospect Hill Park in Waltham, Forest Park in Springfield, and Indian Ridge in Andover. Portions of Middlesex Fells, too, initially were acquired by a group of trustees who subsequently conveyed the Fells to the Metropolitan Park Commission in 1894. Forest parks qualify as a discrete category of community-owned woodlands devoted to recreational use, and they are distinct from town forests, although the latter often double as recreational lands. Often placed in scenic locales, forest parks are usually kept a cautious distance from timber cropping, sometimes in accordance with the express wishes of those who donated land or money. The distinction between forest parks and town forests remains an important one in Massachusetts and in several other New England states as well.[6]

Thus, when the Massachusetts Forestry Association organized in 1898, it did so in the midst of a prevailing mood of reform. Its charter identified the need to promote afforestation of unproductive lands, to encourage the planting and care of shade trees, and to educate the public about forestry management. Education was achieved in part via a steady flow of published materials, and town forests were promoted as early as 1905. Only after the appointment of Harris Reynolds, however, did a program for town forests fully develop. In 1912, the MFA reprinted a short bulletin by George H. Maxwell, a California lawyer who vigorously advocated government control of rivers and waters as a means of converting arid or waste lands to productive use. Titled "Forests for Towns and Villages," Maxwell's article had been published already by the Society for the Protection of New Hampshire Forests (SPNHF). He recommended municipal forestry for the entire country, remarking that German communal forests supplied an annual quota of fuelwood to the local citizenry and sold sufficient timber to meet all public expenses. Although Maxwell remained an obscure figure in the field of forestry, his article was publicized at a pivotal moment by both the MFA and the SPNHF, the region's two most influential private forestry organizations. Reynolds later credited Maxwell's contribution with being the genesis of the town forest movement in Massachusetts.[7]

The year 1913 proved to be one of consequence for both Harris Reynolds and town forests. Reynolds married a woman of German descent, Alice Hecker, and the couple spent their honeymoon in Europe observing Zurich's Sihlwald and communal forests in Heidelberg, Frankfurt, and Munich, accompanied during part of their excursion by William Wharton, a member of the MFA's executive committee and later its president. Reynolds also honed his ample literary skills, producing three of what would become a respectable corpus of articles and monographs about town forests. The first, "A Citizens' Movement to Reduce the Tax Rate," was published as a bulletin by the MFA to convince communities that turning waste lands into forests would improve local tax rates. In the second, which appeared in the journal *American City*, Reynolds discussed the MFA's ambitious plan to establish an extensive network of branch associations in towns throughout the state to be assisted by trained foresters. As he described it, the appointment of foresters in every city and town and the acquisition of municipal forests were the MFA's principal objectives. In the third article, written for *Landscape Architecture*, he suggested that landscape architects could fill the multifaceted position of city forester as capably as commercial foresters. Also in 1913, Massachusetts amended its town forest enabling law so as to permit towns to own and manage forests independently.[8]

With passage of this amendment, town forests in Massachusetts were given a statutory purpose: cultivation of trees for the production of wood and timber for common benefit. A year later, Fitchburg adopted an ordinance designating four unused parcels of city-owned land as a municipal forest, and the town forest movement was under way. Town forests became popular in New Hampshire and Vermont, and in other states, too, particularly New York and Pennsylvania, where enabling laws had been enacted a few years earlier. Several midwestern states developed active programs as well. Massachusetts towns, however, seized the idea with an enthusiasm that paid tribute to the state's history of community and forest, long intertwined, and their initiative eventually outlasted programs in many other states.[9]

PINE PLANTATIONS

The movement's first decade in Massachusetts was dominated by efforts to encourage towns to organize town forest committees, acquire suitable lands, and transplant seedlings, primarily coniferous types such as white, red, and scotch pine or spruce. At the MFA's annual meeting in 1914, William Colton, a member of Fitchburg's branch association, carefully outlined the procedure for starting a town forest, identifying types of available land, unredeemed tax lots for example, and describing appropriate forestry work. This included conducting inventories, drafting compartment maps, undertaking improvements such as fire lanes or roads, and creating working plans to govern planting, thinning, and harvesting. Contests exhorting committees to establish town forests were launched by the MFA in 1914 and 1915. Hoping to establish working forests of efficient size, the MFA required towns to obtain at least 100 acres, officially designate the area as a town forest, and plant a minimum of 50 acres with white pine seedlings. Judging focused on carefully identified criteria including size of land area, quality of planting, potential for commercial productivity, recreation, aesthetics, fire prevention, water and soil protection, and various improvements such as roads. Unfortunately, fewer than 10 entries were submitted each year, the minimum required by contest rules, and no winners were declared.[10]

Nevertheless, activity in two important forests did occur. In Fitchburg, the city forester, Page Bunker, prepared a working plan and supervised planting on lands that included a former woodlot for the

Figure 8.1. Dedication ceremonies held on May 6, 1916, for the Walpole Town Forest, Massachusetts' first comprehensively planned town forest. Left to right: George Plimpton, donor of the land; Calvin Coolidge, then lieutenant governor of Massachusetts and later, as president, convenor of the 1924 National Conference on Outdoor Recreation; and Charles S. Bird, Jr., a member of the Walpole town planning committee and, later, chairman of Governor Alvin Fuller's (1928) state-wide Committee on Needs and Uses of Open Spaces. Walpole Historical Society.

town's poor farm and several parcels devoted to watershed protection. Walpole developed a far more elaborate scheme as part of a comprehensive town plan produced by the landscape architect and planner John Nolen. Nolen had completed his work by 1914, but Charles S. Bird, Jr., head of the city's planning committee, inquired about the MFA's contests after a local benefactor, George Plimpton, agreed to donate land near the Neponset River for a high school park and town forest. Nolen set to work again, proposing winding roads, open meadows, and scenic vistas for a town forest that proved to be as much park as forest. However, he did retain a consulting forester, George Carlisle, to recommend tree species and supervise planting. A dedication ceremony was conducted on Arbor Day in 1916, and Lieutenant Governor Calvin Coolidge planted a symbolic first tree before relinquishing the task of planting remaining seedlings to the town's schoolchildren. The forest was developed according to Nolen's plan, and the pattern of trails that he devised still remains. Today, however, entry points are not well defined, and interpretive evidence of Walpole's important contribution to the town forest movement is absent.[11]

The onset of World War I caused the movement to stall, and momentum did not return until after 1920. All the while, however, progress had been occurring independently on local watershed lands. Industrialization during the last quarter of the nineteenth century had fostered rapid growth of urban centers, and a great number of Massachusetts cities and towns had been forced to develop new and larger sources of water. Many of these systems depended on surface drainage, and lands surrounding newly constructed reservoirs were purchased to protect water quality. The ability of forests to retard runoff, equalize the flow of streams, and thus prevent pollution and sediment from reaching water bodies steadily gained credence. Massachusetts' 1882 enabling act for local forests gave legislative sanction to these theories, and many an old cow pasture became a young pine plantation.

The New England Water Works Association was chartered in Boston that same year, giving shape to a professional body of municipal engineers and portending a merger between forestry and water-supply management. Beginning with the 1887 paper evaluating forest influences by the MIT engineering professor George F. Swain, the association's journal chronicled the patient growth of forestry on watershed lands. By 1911, presentations such as that by Boston forester Edward Bryant outlined very detailed silvicultural practices for watershed forestry, a realm that eventually would become quite specialized. Thereafter, forestry became a topic of frequent discussion at association meetings. Forestry work had actually begun in a number of communities by this time, well before the MFA's contests were publicized. For example, Fall River's reservoir commission began measuring water levels in Watuppa Pond before 1900 and solicited help from state foresters to increase the efficiency of water collection. A working plan and type map, prepared by Harold Cook (who later became state forester), were in place for the city's 5,000-acre watershed by 1909 — one of only a few formal plans in New England at the time. Other cities — Brookline, North Adams, Pittsfield, and Westfield, for instance — all began planting prior to or shortly after World War I.[12]

The MFA doggedly sought an alliance with water utilities, and the match often worked. Addressing a gathering of New England Water

Works Association members in March, 1911, Massachusetts State Forester Frank Rane placed special emphasis on the economic advantages of timbered watersheds. Observing that municipal forestry offered lucrative opportunities, Rane argued that utilities had everything to gain by converting idle lands to profitable use. He also pledged assistance from the state's forestry program, and his text was reprinted in bulletin form by the MFA. By far the most extensive planting on municipal lands prior to World War I occurred on watersheds, and many became model town forests.[13]

Successful watershed plantations also served as useful demonstration forests for the MFA after 1920. That year marked the start of the town forest movement's most prolific decade, a success impelled by several factors. In 1920, the state legislature passed a bill authorizing the state forester to provide free seedlings for town forests, and a year later the MFA offered to plant 5,000 trees on any newly established forest of 100 acres or more. These incentives prompted similar offers from a number of local organizations, including the Berkshire Forestry Association, the Springfield Chamber of Commerce, and the Hampden County Improvement League. The New England Box Company also offered to plant seedlings in any town forest in Franklin County. An array of published materials continued to emphasize the benefits of local forests in the broadest possible manner, from commercial to recreational, and all were aimed at public education. Harris Reynolds maintained a steady pace of writing, producing a 1925 monograph titled "Town Forests: Their Recreational and Economic Value and How to Establish and Maintain Them," published by the American Tree Association with a foreword by Charles Lathrop Pack. These enticements yielded prodigious return, and by 1930, 90 forests had been established on more than 25,500 acres with over 3 million trees planted.[14]

Forests in Petersham and Russell were among the state's most capably managed. Town officials in Petersham began harvesting timber on a portion of the poor farm in 1921, and established a fund to pay for reforestation of open land that same year. Silvicultural work commenced in 1926 with the help of students from Harvard Forest, and a type map was prepared. The following year, a town forest committee took shape under the aegis of Richard T. Fisher and Albert C. Cline, respectively director and assistant director of Harvard Forest, and a third member, Daniel Broderick. Pine and spruce plantations were established that year on six acres of abandoned fields near the old town farm buildings. Two other parcels, the Shaw Tract and the Monroe Tract, were added later, and Petersham's forest soon became a prototype for other communities. Russell, a small village in Hampden County, began purchasing lands in 1923 to protect water supplies and to reduce the cost of town services to a few struggling hill farms. Acreage steadily increased, spreading into neighboring Blandford, and forestry management progressed according to a working plan prepared by state forester C. A. Galarneau. A full-time forester, Elmer R. Foster, was eventually hired, and Russell's forest affirmed the union between municipal forestry and water-supply management that the MFA so actively pursued.[15]

WEEDING, THINNING, AND RELEASING

By 1930 the town forest movement had begun to grapple with an assortment of stubborn problems. Many communities had neglected young plantations, and coniferous seedlings were quickly overtopped by sprout hardwoods. In response, the MFA placed greater emphasis on stewardship, and the need for silviculture — weeding, thinning, and releasing — replaced earlier emphasis on land acquisition and planting. These events coincided with inauguration of the annual Conference for Town Forest Committees in 1928, sponsored by the MFA and held continuously until after 1960. At the conference's first meeting, held in Boston, Albert Cline stressed the need for weeding in order to improve composition and quality of tree stands. Subsequent conferences included field demonstrations in towns such as Westfield, Russell, Fitchburg, Groton, Ayer, and Petersham. Each conference elected an executive committee to plan the following year's conference, and this committee gradually acquired more autonomy as the MFA began channeling its energies in other directions. Both committee and conferences added much-needed structure to the movement, and the committee's reports were published regularly in the MFA's informative newsletter, *Forest and Park News*.[16]

Commercial productivity also received closer scrutiny after 1930, and a skepticism about the ability of communities to produce marketable timber began to afflict the movement. Inconsistent municipal administration, lax bookkeeping, competing local interests, and a fickle timber economy all presented barriers to successful management.

Competent oversight notwithstanding, Petersham's forest illustrated the formidable quandaries facing those who advocated sustained yield cultivation on small tracts of community woodland. After initial improvements in 1926, Petersham's forest was left with only mature or very young stands. Establishing a desirably short period between yields was not possible until an even distribution of age classes existed. Allowing mature trees to age beyond their greatest vigor lessened their value for the commercial market because of increased potential for disease. Cost-saving features, a portable sawmill, for example, were key to any ledger balancing but were not practical until yield periods became relatively short. Nominal returns during the interim did little to encourage local financial support for indispensable silviculture. Not surprisingly, many communities facing similar difficulties soon lost interest in their town forests.[17]

Partly in response to these factors, and partly as a result of alliances between a cadre of conservationists and planners, recreation began to assume a larger role in the town forest movement. As early as 1924, at the National Conference on Outdoor Recreation, Reynolds had hinted that recreation might prove to be the greatest benefit from town forests. Although the cultivation of marketable timber characterized this particular class of community woodlands (and today remains an important element if one is to understand the movement's origins), the MFA had to work hard to sustain the momentum of local forestry. The country's worsening economic condition aggravated circumstances, and in 1933 the MFA changed its name to the Massachusetts Forest and Park Association (MFPA) as a way of adjusting to these trends. In correspondence to Benton MacKaye, Reynolds sought advice about this change, and his remarks set a tone for the period: "Am short on office assistance, cash, spirit and ideas — Am think(ing) of moral bankruptcy — Where can I get a quart of pre-war?" For his part, MacKaye had been working with the Committee on Needs and Uses of Open Spaces, established by Governor Alvan T. Fuller in 1928. MacKaye's plans, regional in scope, employed forests as means of controlling metropolitan sprawl and attempted to connect these wildlands with recreational trail systems. The value of open spaces as a means of balancing irrepressible urban growth rapidly gained acceptance and ultimately influenced local planning as well.[18] Between 1930 and the onset of World War II, the number of town forests in Massachusetts did not increase significantly. At the annual Conference for Town Forest Committees in 1938, the year the U.S. Forest Service launched a community forest program, Reynolds reported 105 town forests. Possibly incredulous at the Forest Service's long period of absence from the field, Reynolds was nevertheless gratified that federal participation had finally arrived.[19]

Although Reynolds and the MFA had awakened national interest in town forests, impetus for the government's program came from Franklin Roosevelt, who asked Nelson C. Brown, friend and faculty member from the New York State College of Forestry at Syracuse, to assist. Brown traveled to Europe to study German and Swiss communal forests and, upon his return, authored a substantial collection of articles promoting community forestry. Although Brown served Roosevelt's goal of public education very well, much of his writing failed to adequately consider the movement's progress in Massachusetts and other New England states and, more important, to isolate some of the troublesome problems that had surfaced. One such article, "Community Forests — A New Idea in the American Forestry Program," appeared in *Southern Lumberman* in 1939. Undoubtedly Reynolds and others who had struggled to build the movement during the preceding decades felt the irony in Brown's choice of words. The title of a 1938 bulletin by the MFPA, "The First Quarter Century of the Town Forest in Massachusetts," was surely not coincidental.[20]

Nevertheless, the Forest Service's program did spark a period of renewed interest prior to World War II. Productivity remained at the center of debate, however, and comparisons between national and community forests were inevitable. Reynolds argued that the period of acquisition for national and state forests had passed its heyday and that the future of new public forests rested with communities. He also contended that local forests were ignored unfairly by professional foresters and lacked crucial financial support. At the core of Reynolds's arguments lay the conviction that town forests could produce higher yields per acre than national forests in western states. Soil quality on abandoned farms in Massachusetts was higher, the growing season longer, and water more plentiful. Transportation costs to large market centers were lower, making shipment of low-grade lumber worthwhile. By-products such as wood fuel could also be marketed more easily. All these factors offered opportunity for more intensive management and a higher rate of return. Acces-

sibility during all seasons also increased recreational benefits and provided added opportunities for employment.[21] Despite the apparent merits
of these arguments, skepticism about commercial productivity continued
to daunt the movement, and the Forest Service's program did little to
change that perception. Fairly stated, however, fear of government interference in local matters also contributed to the movement's weakness in
the field of timber production.

Capitalizing on the increased public awareness of community forests generated by the Forest Service, the MFPA and the Conference for
Town Forest Committees jointly sponsored a regional conference on
town forests in the fall of 1940. Delegates representing 14 states jour-
neyed to Springfield, Massachusetts, to attend the two-day symposium,
which included field trips to Westfield, Russell, Petersham, and Northampton. Although a variety of topics were addressed, including the
need for technical assistance from professional foresters, the relationships between local, state, and federal governments received especially
close scrutiny. The conference closed with a bluntly worded resolution:
"It is the sentiment of this meeting that a community forest should
grow out of local interest and meet local needs. We are opposed to any
form of federal or state control of such areas. We believe, however, that
close cooperation should be maintained with state agencies in drafting
and carrying out plans of management." This policy statement was
significant, at least for Massachusetts' town forests, because it set clearly
defined boundaries in the struggle to address the problem of consistent
management. All agreed that assistance (financial as well as technical)
from government foresters was essential, but few were willing to toler-
ate any form of bureaucratic oversight. Questions about the capacity of
towns to produce marketable timber were thus drawn more sharply
into focus.[22]

Not surprisingly, those who administered state forestry assistance
programs wanted assurances that their efforts and funding were not
wasted. Toward that end, the Massachusetts legislature passed a bill in
1941 requiring towns to obtain approval of plantation lands before trees
could be distributed for planting. A year earlier, Reynolds had conducted a survey of the state's town forests and had found widespread
neglect of young plantations. At about the same time, he had grown
increasingly concerned about management practices on small, privately
owned woodlots. Recognizing the need to span a gap between owners

of modest-sized tracts of timber, towns among them, and government forestry programs aimed at large-scale operations, he conceived the idea of establishing a nonprofit organization to provide technical assistance to the former. The New England Forestry Foundation was created in 1944 by the MFPA to provide complete forestry services at cost, from survey to harvest, and offered private owners an alternative to government foresters. Reynolds was appointed secretary of that organization as well. The foundation sought to demonstrate that owners of small tracts could produce a profit if their lands were managed properly. A network of consulting foresters soon developed in several New England states, and their services were offered to an assortment of woodland owners, including towns. Working plans for town forests in Greenfield, Groton, Needham, North Adams, Pembroke, Pittsfield, Russell, and Walpole were the result. The MFPA also developed a concise policy: sustain public support, improve local administration, and generate management plans.[23]

Greater public cognizance of community forestry during this period, in part the result of the Forest Service's campaign and in part the result of well-publicized state programs, led to other developments that ultimately affected town forests in Massachusetts. In 1941, the Society of American Foresters instituted a special committee on community forests and named Reynolds its chairman. Other members included Nelson Brown and U.S. Forester Joseph Fitzwater, who later was replaced by George Duthie. The committee quickly confronted the seesaw contest between recreational and commercial uses by cautioning against unrealistic economic goals. Rather, greatest emphasis was given to conservation education, best achieved through recreational use. Logging activities became a means to reduce the costs of multiple-use management, the forest policy the committee sought to advance through public education. The matter of local control was also confronted, and the committee initially stressed the authority of local town forest committees. Later reports issued during Reynolds's chairmanship, however, looked with envy at profitable communal forests in Germany and argued for greater control by state programs and the appointment of full-time community foresters. Committee members also encouraged the U.S. Forest Service to create a separate division for community forestry and to allocate sufficient funding.[24]

The onset of World War II caused an interlude in the promotion of town forest programs, but opportunity lingered. With supplies of coal and oil scarce, cordwood became an increasingly important resource, and Reynolds was appointed director of Massachusetts' wood-fuel production. Fortuitously, the thinning sorely needed in many town forests generated a timely crop of cordwood. Reynolds quickly turned the situation to advantage, inviting regional wood-fuel production managers to attend the annual Conference of Town Forest Committees in 1942. Many committees subsequently marked selected trees and allowed volunteers to do the culling, often charging only a half cord for welfare. Toward the close of the war, emphasis on employment opportunities also surfaced, and the MFPA publicized self-paying work projects, borrowing a page from Roosevelt's New Deal. The MFPA also hired a forester, David Miner, to inspect town forests across the state. His report, published in 1949, revealed that many forests lacked management plans and required silviculture. By this time, 35 years after the establishment of Fitchburg's town forest, 127 towns had cultivated forests on almost 40,000 acres and had planted more than 8,500,000 trees.[25]

Although post war enthusiasm helped to rekindle interest in town forests, the surge was a fleeting one. Between 1942 and 1944, a legislative initiative that would have provided federal subsidies for community forests had failed, and this defeat struck an ominous note. Although Roosevelt had sponsored the bill, he later abandoned his proposal when advised that community forest projects would not pay for their costs. This advice, tantamount to admission that town forests were unprofitable, was undoubtedly rooted in the U.S. Forest Service at a time when their community forest program was only a few years old. That program, never much more than a clearinghouse for information and census taking, all but ended with the retirement of George Duthie in 1949. Unquestionably, the inability of towns to produce consistently marketable timber influenced policy-makers in the Forest Service at a critical juncture. This in turn contributed to a weakening of their community forest program.

On the other national front, the SAF committee sputtered, barely managing to sustain momentum. Brown acknowledged that the movement had not met the expectations generated by profitable European communal forests, and Reynolds complained about the absence of forceful sponsorship by a national agency. His committee report for

1951, the year he requested appointment of a new chairperson, carried a tone of irritation. Three years later, the committee was dissolved for lack of a "concrete and specific assignment."[26]

The collapse of national initiatives in turn caused a weakening of state programs. Town forests in Massachusetts suffered an even greater misfortune in 1953 when Harris Reynolds perished following a heart attack. It is a testimony to Reynolds's Herculean effort during the preceding 40 years that the town forest program in Massachusetts managed to sustain momentum during the decade following his untimely death. Town forest committees continued to gather at annual conferences, and *Forest and Park News* faithfully reported these events. By the early 1960s, 147 Massachusetts towns had dedicated forests totaling more than 43,000 acres, a marvelous legacy to the memory of Reynolds. In 1957, however, passage of enabling legislation for local conservation commissions foretold a new movement that would hasten the decline of town forests. Conservation commissions, intent on preserving a variety of ecologically important lands, soon gained overwhelming popularity, obscuring any local interest in timber management that still lingered. Remarkably, more Massachusetts towns formed conservation commissions in the five-year period between 1957 and 1962 than had formed town forest committees during the preceding 50 years. These trends may have reflected a decreasing public interest in the state's forests as well. Many town forests survive today, and a few of these still produce timber; a significant number continue to protect water supplies. Many others, however, are more properly classified as ecological preserves and are overseen by conservation commissions, often without complete understanding of the origins and objectives of the town forest movement. Noticeably absent, too, are the commitments to forestry management that are part of that movement's heritage.[27]

THE FUTURE OF EVERYDAY FORESTS

The true history of Massachusetts' town forests can be found, not on these pages, but in the woodland places that contribute so serenely to our communities. There, in the landscape where it belongs, history is transformed into something more tactile than the written word, and greater insight is the reward. Any who seek out these timbered enclaves, and seek one must for many are well hidden, will quickly understand why conservation is so deeply rooted in our culture. Remarkably, too, the individual visions expressed in these local patches of forest are singularly creative, often quite different from one place to the next. Collectively, these very personal affirmations of a woodland ethic offer a fresh outlook on the broader history of forests and conservation in America. Their resiliency, too, is a tribute to the ability of forests to accommodate human use. Indeed, their value as everyday places is beyond measure.

Today, an array of examples entice exploration. Pembroke's J. J. Shepherd Town Forest honors a former state representative and district fire warden. Its 100 acres, planted with red pine in the 1950s, are managed according to a working plan prepared in the mid-1980s, and the town forest committee continues to meet several times each year. Stands of pine shelter picnic areas as well as nature walks, and a portion of the land has been kept open for Little League baseball fields. In Westford's town forest, plots were assigned to demonstrate the value of thinning and pruning white pine to promote rapid growth and to improve the commercial quality of timber. Those tracts are now mature, and the town forest committee continues to function. However, little harvesting has been conducted; ironically, an adjoining watershed forest currently demonstrates more intensive management.

In contrast to Westford, Natick's town forest committee once set aside plots as natural resource preserves during the 1950s and prepared an informative manual. However, the town forest committee is now defunct and the woodland is underutilized. In Duxbury the Frederick Knapp Town Forest is no longer under active forestry management, and the town forest committee, too, has ceased to exist. The forest's 32 acres of white pine are, however, part of a large central green belt owned in part by the Duxbury Rural and Historical Society, the Massachusetts Audubon Society, and the Duxbury Conservation Commission. This extensive weald also protects local water supplies. No better opportunity exists to merge and interpret demonstrations of timber cultivation, ecosystem protection, and history.

So often, the answers to questions that perplex and divide our society can be found in the history that fills our landscapes, if only we take the trouble to look. This is certainly true for the current debate about forest use. By most standards, the town forest movement was unsuccessful in the production of commercially saleable timber. Yet if one peers a little more carefully into these forests, important features begin to take shape. The continuum of working forest and community in Massachusetts is an ancient one, but one guided throughout by strong ties to stewardship. That tradition of stewardship deserves to be carried forward, if only to demonstrate the enormous cultural endowment represented by these timberlands. Town forests, a link between the utilitarian woodscapes of earlier periods and today's conservation areas, the latter managed with equal utility as natural ecosystems, are perfect places to sustain that continuum. With these backyard reminders, we achieve better understanding of past cultures, we sharpen perceptions of our own culture, and we make better decisions about our environments. In doing so, we help not only our own generation but those to come.

Town forest and community are bound in other important ways as well. Local woodlands have played a valuable role in the evolution of community form, and they are as much a part of urban and village history as they are of forest history. The shifting balance between public and private land has been a fundamental force in the evolving structure of Massachusetts towns and villages, and that tension continues. The instantaneous popularity of conservation commissions during the early 1960s can be explained in large part by concern for the overwhelming, unfathomable pace of change in our society. Acquisition of conservation lands offered communities an opportunity to confront that change in emphatic terms. Yet urbanization continues to swallow open environments whole, nullifying even the most carefully conceived efforts at large-scale planning. As a consequence, we are being forced to concentrate our energies in manageable, pocket-sized realms; to claim and reclaim habitable communities from within, all the while reliant on a human sense of place and scale. Public lands will remain indispensable to this campaign. If, in the future, we pause to consider the time when New England communities first embarked on a sustained effort to reclaim their public lands, we will begin with the town forest movement.

Finally, our success in constructing habitable communities will depend upon alliances among those allegiant to both natural and cultural resources. Unfortunately, such alliances have proved all too elusive in the past. It is the intricate layering of history in our landscapes that creates a sense of place. In town forests, cultural and natural history intertwine to the extent that distinctions between the two become unimportant. There, communities can continue demonstrating forest policy that successfully accommodates recreation, timber production, and ecosystem management. There, too, we can add to the understanding of those who seek interpretation of our built environment, a society whose very foundations were erected with wood. Surely, too, these town forests are sheltered places where such alliances can be steadily nurtured.

What is to become of town forests in Massachusetts, or, for that matter, in New England? Simply suggesting that towns have much to gain by sustaining a centuries-old tradition of forest ownership and utilization will not make it so. At the very least, there must be a concerted effort among policy-makers to reinforce forestry management at the local level. Achieving consistent silviculture, an essential component if cultivation of timber is to be anything more than symbolic, should be the product of a partnership between federal, state, and local governments. Such a partnership would supply the required funding, technical assistance, and public interest, all the while ensuring that the goal of multiple utilization within a diverse and carefully sustained ecoystem is rigorously pursued from one generation to the next. The federal government's Forest Legacy Program, part of the Forest Stewardship Act of 1990, encourages the U.S. Forest Service to build precisely that type of partnership. Town forest enabling legislation, still valid in all New England states, remains a viable tool as well.

More is needed, however, to link town forest programs with community efforts to preserve both cultural and natural resources. A nonprofit organization chartered to reclaim town forests could provide the foundation for such an alliance. In addition to encouraging local interest in forestry, such an organization could collect and hold the valuable but widely scattered records of New England's town forests. These records are in great danger of being lost or destroyed as offices are moved from one place to another. Developing systematic communication between towns and state or federal foresters, often a difficult undertaking, might also be possible. Time and time again, Massachusetts has been a place of innovation in matters of conservation, and rejuvenation of its town forests would be a shining and much-deserved tribute to Harris Reynolds.

NOTES

1. See Groton, Mass., *Annual Reports* (1922): 11–13, (1935): 73–74; H. S. Ripley, "Forest Management Plan for the Groton Memorial Town Forest" (July 1952), records of the New England Forestry Foundation. Harlan Fitch is a longtime member of the town forest committee.

2. Bernhard E. Fernow, "Communal Forests," *Garden and Forest* 3 (July 16, 1890): 349. For a very thoroughly written biography of Fernow, see Andrew D. Rodgers, *Bernhard Eduard Fernow: A Story of North American Forestry* (Princeton, N.J.: Princeton University Press, 1951).

   For the most comprehensive study of Zurich's Sihlwald, see Ulrich Meister, *Die Stadtwaldungen von Zürich*, 2d ed. (Zurich: Druckerei der Neuen Zürcher Zeitung, 1903). A number of visiting Americans published articles in various journals. For a good example, see Gifford Pinchot, "The Sihlwald," Parts 1, 2, and 3, *Garden and Forest* (July 30, August 6, August 13, 1890): 374, 386, 397–98. For a more recent work, see James P. Barrett, "Recreational and Timber Opportunities on Swiss and German Town Forests," *Forest Notes* 140 (Spring 1980): 2–5.

   German city forests were also influential, and those in Villengen, Baden-Baden, Freiburg, Darmstadt, and Frankfurt were often visited by Americans.

3. Bernhard E. Fernow, "Report upon the Forestry Investigations of the U.S. Department of Agriculture, 1877–98," House Documents, 55th Cong., 3rd sess., 1898–99, vol. 71, serial 3813 (Washington, D.C.: GPO, 1899).

   For a general discussion of open-field systems and the origins of community in England and Germany, see C. S. Orwin and C. S. Orwin, *The Open Fields* (Oxford: Clarendon Press, 1954). See also Howard L. Gray, *English Field Systems* (Cambridge, Mass.: Harvard University Press, 1915); W. E. Tate, *The English Village Community and the Enclosure Movements* (London: Victor Gollancz, 1967); and Franz Heske, *German Forestry* (New Haven: Yale University Press, 1938).

4. Bernhard E. Fernow, "Communal Forests," *Garden and Forest* 3 (July 16, 1890): 349.

5. Gifford Pinchot, "Forest-Policy Abroad," *Garden and Forest* (January 1, 1891): 8–9, (January 14, 1891): 21–22, (January 21, 1891): 34–35.

6. Massachusetts Laws of 1882, Chap. 255, Sec. 1–8, adopted May 25, 1882. See also "The New Forestry Law of Massachusetts," *The American Journal of Forestry* 1 (April 1883): 304–7.

   For a discussion of Middlesex Fells, see Medford Historical Society, *Round about Middlesex Fells* (Medford, Mass.: Medford Historical Society, 1935); and Metropolitan Park Commission, *Annual Report* (January 1905): 42–44.

See also Sylvester Baxter, "The Lynn Public Forest," *Garden and Forest* 2 (October 30, 1889): 526–27; M. C. Robbins, "Forest Park, Springfield, Massachusetts," *Garden and Forest* 4 (December 2, 1891): 566–67; and Susan Blake, "A Communal Forest for Andover," *The Forester* 3 (November 1, 1897): 132.

7. M. Richard Applegate, *Massachusetts Forest and Park Association: A History,* 1898–1973 (Boston, Mass.: MFPA, 1974). See also George H. Maxwell, "Forests for Towns and Villages," *Bulletin of the Society for Protection of New Hampshire Forests,* n.d.; reprint, Massachusetts Forestry Association, n.d. (c. 1912); and Harris Reynolds, "The First Quarter Century of the Town Forest in Massachusetts," *Bulletin of the Massachusetts Forest and Park Association,* no. 163 (December 1939).

8. Harris Reynolds, "Notes on European Town Forests (1913)," records of the Environmental League of Massachusetts; "A Citizens Movement to Reduce the Tax Rate," *Bulletin of the Massachusetts Forestry Association,* no. 104 (May 1913); "Establishment of Foresters in Towns and Cities through State Forestry Associations," *The American City* 9 (November 1913): 412–14; and "An Opportunity for the Young Landscape Architect," *Landscape Architecture* 4 (October 1913–July 1914): 47–51. See also Massachusetts Acts and Resolves, 1913, Chapter 564, "An Act Relative to Public Domain," pp. 483–85.

9. For Fitchburg, see Page Bunker, "A Town Forest in America," *Forest Quarterly* 13 (March 1915): 4–7; and Guy Hubbard, "The Municipal Forest in Fitchburg, Mass.," *The American City* 24 (February 1921): 121–24.

10. William Colton, "Organization and Management of Town Forests," *MFA Bulletin* no. 115 (1914). See also Harris Reynolds, "Town Forest Contest," *MFA Bulletin* no. 112 (June 1, 1914).

11. John Murphy, "The Town of Walpole Establishes a Communal Forest of 200 Acres," *American City* 15 (August 1916): 144–53. See also letter of George Carlisle to Charles S. Bird, 4/25/1916, records of the Walpole Historical Society.

12. George Swain, "The Influence of Forests upon the Rainfall and upon the Flow of Streams," *Journal of the New England Water Works Association* 1 (March 1887): 11–26. See also Edward Bryant, "Practical Forestry for Water Works," *Journal of the New England Water Works Association* 25 (June 1911): 243–46; reprinted by the MFA as an undated, unnumbered bulletin.

See also Massachusetts Forest Service, F. W. Rane, State Forester, Harold Cook, assistant in charge, *Forest Working Plan for Land Belonging to the City of Fall River on the North Watuppa Watershed* (Boston: Wright & Potter Printing Co., 1909).

13. Frank Rane, "The Reforestation of Watersheds for Domestic Supplies," *Journal of the New England Water Works Association* 25 (June 1911): 234–42. Reprinted in *Eighth Annual Report by the State Forester of Massachusetts,* 1911, 58–59; also reprinted by the MFA as an undated, unnumbered bulletin.

14. *Massachusetts Acts and Resolves,* 1920, Chapter 604, titled: "An Act to Provide for the Purchase and Development of State Forests," pp. 668–69; see specifically Section 5. See also MFA, "Why Massachusetts Needs Town Forests," *MFA Bulletin* no. 132 (1921); and MFA, "Summarized Report of the Third Annual Conference of Town Forest Committees," *MFA Bulletin* no. 150 (1930).

15. For information about Petersham's town forest, see annual town forest committee reports, 1930–38, records of Harvard Forest, Petersham. For information about Russell's town forest, see "Second Conference of Town Forest Committees," *MFA Bulletin* no. 147 (November 8, 9, 1929): 4; and Harris Reynolds, "The Russell Town Forest," *MFA Bulletin* no. 170 (1946);

16. Harris Reynolds, *Report on the First Conference of Massachusetts Town Forest Committees, January* 10, 1929 (Boston: MFA, 1929). See also "Second Conference of Town Forest Committees," *MFA Bulletin* no. 147 (November 8, 9, 1929): 4; and "Summarized Report of the Third Annual Conference of Town Forest Committees," *MFA Bulletin* no. 150 (1930).

17. Letter to Spencer H. Palmer, N.H. State College of Forestry, 2/24/33, probably from Albert C. Cline. See also "The Management of a Small Forest for Sustained Yield: The Petersham Town Forest," undated but probably 1926. Both documents are in the records of Harvard Forest, Petersham, Mass.

18. Harris Reynolds, "Town Forests," *Playground* 18 (July 1924): 224–36. See also letter of Benton Mackaye to Harris Reynolds, 9/26/32, and reply of 10/4/32, both in the Mackaye Collection, Dartmouth College Archives. For information about the Governor's Committee on Needs and Uses of Open Spaces, see Benton Mackaye, "Progress Report," typewritten manuscript, 4/4/28, and "Suggested Classification of Open Spaces," undated typewritten manuscript, both in the Mackaye Collection, Dartmouth College Archives.

19. "Town Forests Endorsed by U.S. Forest Service," *Forest and Park News* 3 (January 1939): 1, 4.

20. Harris Reynolds, "The Town Forest in Massachusetts," *A Planning Forum* 3 (October–November 1939): 34–36; and Harris Reynolds, "The First Quarter Century of the Town Forest in Massachusetts," *Bulletin of the Massa-*

chusetts Forest and Park Association no. 163 (December, 1939). See also: Nelson Brown, "Community Forests — A New Idea in the American Forestry Program," *Southern Lumberman* 161 (December 14, 1940): 154–58.

21. Harris Reynolds, "Town Forests — A Neglected Opportunity," *Journal of Forestry* 37 (May 1939): 364–67. See also "Report of Committee on Community Forests," Journal of Forestry 49 (February 1951): 132–34.

22. "Town Forests in the Northeast," *Forest and Park News* 4 (November 1940): 3.

23. *Acts and Resolves of Massachusetts,* 1941, Chapter 455, titled "An Act to Provide Demonstrations in Forestry Practices and to Encourage the Rehabilitation of Forest Lands," p. 529. See also Richard Applegate, *Massachusetts Forest and Park Association: A History: 1898–1973* (Boston: MFPA, 1974); and Harris Reynolds, "Bringing Forests to the People," *MFPA Bulletin* no. 165 (November 1941).

    The New England Forestry Foundation was brought into being with the hope of improving the quality of management practices on private woodlands. The services of its foresters were offered to a variety of woodlot owners, from wealthy property holders to farmers seeking to improve marginal returns. However, Reynolds may have been most interested in reaching a class of landowners who were engaged in speculation and who typically employed clear-cutting. By studying markets for forest products in well-defined regions, he hoped to demonstrate that owners could realize greater profit after employing a professional forester. Although town forests were not the primary focus of foundation efforts, Reynolds nevertheless touted the availability of foundation foresters in a number of the MFA's publications aimed at promoting municipal forestry. For example, see Harris Reynolds, *The Russell Town Forest MFPA Bulletin* no. 170 (Jan. 1946), and "Work of the New England Forestry Foundation on Watersheds," *Journal of the New England Water Works Association* 62 (June 1948): 133–40.

24. "Report of the Committee on Community Forests," *Journal of Forestry* 40 (February 1942): 112–17. See also reports in *Journal of Forestry* 41 (May 1943): 332–34; *Journal of Forestry* 42 (May 1944): 348–51; and *Journal of Forestry* 44 (November 1946): 1005–7.

25. "Town Forests Aiding in Wood Fuel Campaign," *Forest and Park News* 6 (December 1942): 1, 4; "War Demonstrates Value of Town Forests," *Forest and Park News* 7 (November 1943): 1, 4; and Harris Reynolds, "A Survey of the Town Forests in Massachusetts," *MFPA Bulletin* no. 171 (November, 1949).

26. "Summary of Recommendations Presented by the Forest Service on February 16, 1940, to the Joint Congressional Committee on Forestry with Respect to a Forest Program for the United States," records of the National Forest Products Association, Forest History Society, Durham, N.C. The document is attributed to Ferdinand Silcox.

Various correspondence between Roosevelt and members of his administration discusses the fate of this legislative initiative. See specifically letter from Claude Wickard to Franklin D. Roosevelt, 5/12/41, and letter from Earl Clapp to John Bankhead, 10/10/41, both in the U.S. Forest Service Collection, National Archives, Records of the Office of the Chief. See also Memorandum from Wayne Coy to Franklin D. Roosevelt, 5/16/42, in Edgar B. Nixon, *Franklin D. Roosevelt and Conservation, 1911–1945* (Washington, D.C.: GPO, 1957).

For information regarding the SAF committee , see: "Report of the Committee on Community Forests," *Journal of Forestry* 49 (February 1951): 132–34.

27. *Acts and Resolves of Massachusetts,* 1957, Chapter 223, titled "An Act Authorizing Cities and Towns to Establish Conservation Commissions to Promote the Development of Natural Resources, and to Appropriate Money Therefor," pp. 141–42. See also MFPA and Massachusetts Association of Conservation Commissions, "A Guide for Town Forest Committees and Conservation Commissions," *MFPA Bulletin* no. 179 (1962). For a discussion of the history of conservation commissions in Massachusetts, see Andrew Scheffey, *Conservation Commissions in Massachusetts* (Washington, D.C.: Conservation Foundation, 1969).

*T*he sounds of the Hall Tavern household coming to life, and the first milking underway in the barns of the nearby Hall Tavern Farm, caused 12-year-old Bob Healy to stir in bed and open his eyes. Although it was barely sunrise, he sighed contentedly thinking of the long summer ahead far removed from his home in the Chicago suburb of Evanston, Illinois. Bob and his siblings were free to roam the 500 acres of Deerfield River bottomland and forest assembled by his father, starting in 1905, to fulfill his mother's desire to spend family summers near her home town of Shelburne Falls, Massachusetts.

The Hall Tavern, once a coach stop on western Massachusetts' historic Mohawk Trail and a hostelry for eighteenth-century travelers and the nineteenth-century work crews building the Hoosac railroad tunnel, had become the Healy family's summer home, a welcome respite from Mr. Healy's regular duties as the Illinois state's attorney. Yet the summer would not be unmitigated pleasure, Bob knew, because his job in the farm operation was to take the cows daily up to the Pocumtuck Mountain woodland pastures. The pail of grain he carried, and the border collie who kept him company, were usually inducements enough for the livestock to follow him, but Bob would still have to travel up the main woods road, manage the heavy rail pasture gates, and then return to the mountain in the early afternoon to round up the cows for the evening milking, a daily roundtrip of about four miles in the heat of the summer that caused him to do quite a bit of grumbling.

In recent years, Bob had begun to notice how the livestock would browse selectively on the hardwood sprouts, leaving more and more of the little pines to take over the pastures. In fact, the boy had overheard his father discussing with neighbors how the forest and farm supported each other naturally—the forest providing a dependable source of fuel, building materials, and forage and the farm, through selective grazing, hastening the growth of what would become the third great pine forest since colonial days. In the eighteenth century, these forests yielded the stately "broad arrow" mast white pines so favored by British surveyors-general. In 1949,under the guidance of Bob and his son, Jonathan (Jay) Healy, the Massachusetts commissioner of food and agriculture, the Hall Tavern would be moved to serve as the visitor center for Historic Deerfield, and the Hall Tavern Farm, still in Healy ownership, would become the oldest continuously managed private forest in the entire Massachusetts Tree Farm system.

The Massachusetts Forest Today

CHARLES H. W. FOSTER

W HAT ABOUT the Massachusetts forest today? First, we know
that it is very extensive, occupying 3.2 million (64 percent) of
the state's approximately 5 million acres of land. In the past 150 years,
the proportion of nonforestland to forestland has virtually been re-
versed. Not since Colonial times have we become so markedly a commonwealth of forest dwellers.

Second, despite Massachusetts' position as the third most densely
populated state in the nation, almost 3 million of these 3.2 million acres
are classified as timberland — that is, capable of growing 20 cubic feet
or more of industrial wood per acre per year. The amount currently
available is simply staggering. As of 1985, the U.S. Forest Service reported some 20 million board feet on the stump throughout southern
New England (up 50 percent since the last measurement, in 1972). From
growth alone, the Massachusetts forest could provide materials for
housing a quarter of a million people each year.

Third, the Commonwealth's forestlands are predominantly privately owned. More than 1,400 ownerships (in excess of 250,000 acres)
are designated as Tree Farms. There are no national forests in the
Commonwealth, and less than 500,000 acres of state, municipal, and
nonprofit conservation ownerships. With the average private holding
now at barely 10 acres, there are probably a quarter of a million
individual forest owners in Massachusetts. Significantly, the average
owner today is over 50 years of age, a circumstance that portends a
massive turnover in ownership early in the twenty-first century.

Fourth, the average forest in Massachusetts is largely unmanaged,
despite the fact that the value of the timber alone may represent the
cash equivalent of as much as $1,000 per acre. State foresters estimate
that perhaps one acre in four displays any evidence of actual management activity. Massachusetts forestry experts consider these observa-

tions to be quite reliable. They are based upon periodic state inventories conducted by the U.S. Forest Service in cooperation with the Massachusetts Bureau of Forestry.

The first formal, quantitative look at the forests of Massachusetts was a cooperative effort by the office of the state forester and the Bureau of Statistics of Labor. The work was begun in 1905 under the direction of State Forester Alfred Akerman and finished under State Forester Frank Rane in 1907. The methodology used was for the census employees to interview local assessors and to have them sketch the forested areas in their towns as best they could on maps supplied by the State Forester's Office. From this survey it was determined that the state was 37 percent forested.

The next survey of the Commonwealth's forest resources was carried out by the foresters of the Department of Conservation during the period 1915–28. It was determined that survey lines running across the town from one boundary to another at a spacing of one mile would yield statistically reasonable data. The project was staffed by a seasonal crew, usually consisting of three forestry students and a team leader. The leader was responsible for transporting the students to the starting point and from the end point of their lines each day. In addition to this, the leader was responsible for gathering information on the forest's status and use, such as wood-using industries in the town, gypsy moth infestation, and any other relevant information. This survey showed that 54 percent of the state was forested and that another 8 percent was in "transition land," consisting mostly of abandoned pastureland. From this, the department's Chief Forester H. O. Cook deduced that the present and prospective total potential forestland in the state amounted to 62 percent of its area. In addition to providing information about the extent of the forest, this survey also provided information about its size. During that period Massachusetts forests were quite young with 80 percent of the forest area in stands less than 35 years of age (trees less than 6 inches in diameter), and only 4.5 percent of the area in trees greater than 10 inches in diameter, what might be considered "saw timber" size. The reasons for this, Cook said, were "not far to seek, because under current conditions in this state as soon as a growth has attained some commercial value, even for fuelwood, the owners commence to cut it off."

Subsequent inventories were conducted in 1952, 1972, and 1985 by

Figure 8.2. Forest scene at the Metropolitan District Commission's Quabbin Reservation in central Massachusetts, the Commonwealth's largest (50,000 acres) and best managed public forest. Photo by David W. Haas. Courtesy of the Boston Public Library.

the Forest Survey Unit, a branch of the U.S. Forest Service's Northeastern Forest Experiment Station, in cooperation with the state. These surveys were increasingly quantitative, revealing a steady increase in individual tree size and timber volume but a relatively stable proportion of the state's area in forest. Meanwhile, however, three other Massachusetts data sources had begun to fine-tune these national inventory findings.

In the mid-1950s, the Commonwealth adopted the Continuous Forest Inventory (CFI) system for its 285,000 acres of state forestland. Nearly 1,500 one-fifth-acre plots were installed and 63,000 individual tree measurements taken in the course of three separate visits. A fourth remeasurement is planned for 1997–98 to determine the amount of forest growth that has occurred since 1977–1978.

In 1951, University of Massachusetts experts prepared a statewide set of land-use and vegetation maps from aerial photographs, on which they classified the landscape into 104 relatively homogeneous units of forest and wildlife habitat. Remeasurements occurred in 1971 and 1984 and refined these classifications into 21 broad land-use types. These maps reveal not only the extent and nature of the forest, but its relationship to other land uses. By 1985, for example, the acreage of the forest statewide was found to have declined less than 3 percent in the intervening decade and a half. More important than sheer acreage was the emerging juxtaposition of forest and other cover types, a complexity that shows promise for a state management strategy predicated increasingly upon broad environmental forestry objectives, not just wood.

More particular information on individual forest ownerships is available from statistics on lands classified under Chapters 61 and 61A of the Massachusetts General Laws, measures that reduce and defer taxation on tracts of privately held forestland voluntarily committed to professional forest management. An owner of at least 10 contiguous acres whose land is subject to a state-approved forest plan, may petition local assessors for a reduction in the annual tax assessment. As of 1992, some 275,000 acres of Massachusetts forestland had qualified for such classification.

In 1995, a special legislative commission was established and charged with the study and investigation of the extent and adequacy of the management of state and privately owned forestland in the Commonwealth. Chaired by Senator Robert D. Wetmore (D-Barre), himself a forest landowner, the Wetmore Commission sought ways to better utilize the forest resource while simultaneously encouraging the development of healthier and more valuable forests.

Given these encouraging developments, it is ironic that most of the Massachusetts forest, far from being the storehouse of values and products that the Pilgrims encountered, has become an underrated, unappreciated, and underutilized resource. Why that is can be seen through the lens of history.

In the early period of Massachusetts' history, the forest played a dominant and integral role in the growth of the Commonwealth. First it had to be rolled back to make room for settlements. Its products then proved indispensable as fuel and building materials and consequently formed the basis for later trade and the growth of personal wealth. From what we now know of the modern forest owner, the situation today is markedly different. The land and the forest on it are no longer the owner's principal economic assets. Nowadays, the importance of attributes of the forest such as site and setting have in many instances outstripped the importance of any expectation of direct economic return. This has led many modern forest owners to regard the forest-land's values as watershed, wildlife habitat, recreation, and aesthetics more highly than its value as a source of wood products. The reluctance to manage forests stems in part from a fear of diminishing such indirect returns, but also from a perceived inability to obtain dependable, professional management and utilization services. Rightly or wrongly, the image of the forest operator remains that of a person insensitive to long-term natural values.

At the Seventh American Forest Congress, convened in Washington, D.C., February 20–24, 1996, and attended by a large contingent of forestry leaders and landowners from Massachusetts, the prevalence of these practical and attitudinal constraints became obvious. Nevertheless, among the tabulated responses receiving the highest general approval was the vision of the forest sustainably providing a range of goods, services, experiences, and values that contribute to community well-being, economic opportunity, social and personal satisfaction, spiritual and cultural fulfillment, and recreational enjoyment — in short, the broadest possible view of the value of forest in its largest sense. Given Massachusetts' long concern with its forest, the Commonwealth could and should be in the vanguard of states working toward these broad social objectives. How can history illuminate the path toward such ends?

First, we now know that the forest does not exist in isolation from external events. Some of these events are natural, such as the six major hurricanes since 1635 that have been verified by historical records and radiocarbon dating. Other disturbance effects are of human origin: the use of fire by native populations, land clearing by the early colonists and successor farmers, and the massive agricultural land abandonment that triggered the forest's most recent return and subsequent harvest at the turn of this century.

Second, the Massachusetts forest has turned out to be remarkably resilient to these types of disturbances. The new forests may not always be the same as those they replace — a pure stand of birch repopulates an old burn, white pine invades abandoned farmland or pasture, hard-

Young Dicken Crane, a sixth-generation descendent of Zenas Crane, the founder of the paper industry in Berkshire County, waited anxiously for his father, Frederick Goodrich Crane, to return home from Crane & Co., the historic manufacturer of paper for the nation's currency, located in nearby Dalton. Upon his arrival, the daily "peer and poke" routine would begin. Trailed by his four children, Fred Crane, a Yale-trained chemist, would wander through portions of the 1,300-acre Holiday Farm inspecting operations and seeing generally what was going on. On one such occasion, Fred Crane had pulled down an old wasp nest and explained to his attentive offspring that nature was really the first paper maker.

Thirty years later, in 1997, University of Massachusetts graduate Dicken Crane, the president of Dicken Crane Logging, was in the woods in "south county" just before daybreak firing up his articulated skidder (woods vehicle) and preparing to cut logs from a 50-acre woodlot in Sheffield. As he glanced through the pasture-origin pine-hardwood forest, now ripe for a harvest cut to release an understory of sugar maple, he could see the rock face and crest of Mount Everett towering above him.

As the skidder warmed up, Dicken reflected on how forestry had changed over the years, and what would be needed as the twenty-first century approached. For the most part, logging was no longer the cut-and-run operation it used to be. The professionalism evident in Scandinavia and other European countries was beginning to take hold in the United States. Mechanization was gradually replacing hand labor, generally to the benefit of an always hazardous profession and with less damage to the forest itself. But as these operational improvements occurred, the public perception of what should be done with the forest had fragmented.

Some citizens felt that forests and everything that occurred within them should be left to nature alone; others argued that forest management could actually hasten the development of the desired natural qualities and still yield important material and economic benefits to society. Berkshire County, Crane thought, could be a crucible for this search for a pragmatic accommodation of values.

woods succeed the pine after harvesting. But expressed in human terms, we have been blessed with a remarkably forgiving forest, one that provides us with a continuous and unusually varied set of options. Now, however, there is a new factor to consider when we speak of the forest's resilience: a growing realization that the appearance of a forest does not necessarily indicate its ecological health. The future Massachusetts forest may not recover from modern chemical and climatic stresses as well as the past forest did from physical and biological disturbances.

Third, the bulk of forest usage to date has been opportunistic rather than purposeful. Forest resources were largely taken for granted by aboriginal people. For the original European settlers, forest removal commanded priority attention. At the turn of the twentieth century, a completely unplanned new forest spurred by agricultural land abandonment led to a massive period of harvest and utilization, until that resource surplus had again been used up.

Currently, one can only conclude that unlike previous periods in its history, Massachusetts is substantially out of touch with its forests — ironically, just as the resource itself has recovered to a new state of abundance. Thus, if any single policy is needed to shape the future, it would be to awaken and reinvigorate the historic connection between Massachusetts citizens and their forests. Several steps would contribute measurably to attaining this objective.

Expanding our knowledge about the forest and forest processes and disseminating this knowledge to the public would help appreciably. At present there is no comprehensive research plan for the Massachusetts forest, nor any established system for making the necessary research investments. The result has been isolated and disconnected pockets of knowledge fitted to individual areas, investigators, and interests, but little understanding of the resource as a whole. Such an ineffectual research and development program would be regarded as a scandal in any other billion-dollar industry.

If the state of expert knowledge about the forest is deficient, public awareness of forests can only be described as appalling. Massachusetts citizens, though confronted daily with the forest, can barely distinguish among prominent tree species. The ecological functions of the forest are but dimly understood and are rarely reflected in public policy. At this rate, our twenty-first-century citizens, though they may turn out to be computer-proficient, are likely to be environmentally illiterate. Yet the current fragmentation of forest ownership and the fabric of town forests, conservation lands, and open space already in place where people reside seem almost ideally suited to reintroducing present and future Massachusetts citizens to their forests.

Doing more with the forest on a proactive rather than reactive basis must be a major component of any future forest strategy. Expanding outlets for fiber, such as the new energy and products markets envisioned by the Wetmore Commission, would help stimulate responsible management activity. Accelerated forest-improvement practices such as weeding, pruning, thinning, partial harvesting, organized through publicly supported youth and community projects, could enhance the value of the resource while educating participants to its future potential.

Steps to bridge individual ownerships would encourage the management of forests as whole systems, thereby ensuring broad ecosystem and societal benefits. To do this, planning and management need to occur within the framework of entire landscape units, not simply individual ownerships or tracts. Preference should be given to units where there is a preexisting human sense of forest place or where one can be created through the establishment of "neighborwoods." Linkages between ownerships should be advanced that are both natural (such as corridors connecting lands in their natural state), and human (such as provisions for cooperative action to protect, manage, and utilize forest resources). Consistent with historic tradition, any such arrangements should to the extent possible be based upon incentives, not regulation.

That such an approach can be both practical and locally well received is illustrated by several recent developments. For example, the small forested western Massachusetts town of Plainfield, in conjunction with the state-run Massachusetts Forest Stewardship Program and the University of Massachusetts–based Coverts Program, has established two "neighborwood" stewardship projects involving eight landowner families and nearly 500 contiguous forest acres where management occurs cooperatively. Farther to the east, in the vicinity of the Quabbin Reservoir, Boston's main water supply, a more ambitious program is underway with the interest and support of affected landowners. The state-designated 400,000–acre North Quabbin Forest Legacy corridor includes portions of the 19 towns and three central Massachusetts counties between Quabbin Reservoir and the New Hampshire border. A private local organization, the Mount Grace Land Conservation Trust, is actively encouraging the joint conservation and management of North Quabbin's mix of public and private forestlands on a voluntary basis. The prospects for an expanded, ecosystem-based approach in Massachusetts are likely to be enhanced by recent legislation permitting jurisdictions to enter into agreements with one another for environmental purposes.

Finally, the greatest challenge ahead for the Massachusetts forest will be to ensure that the next cycle of harvest and utilization, at least the third since the arrival of the colonists, occurs by design rather than default, so that the resource can be employed sustainably for years to come. To do so, Massachusetts' public and private officials must build support for a forest strategy that mixes market and regulatory forces and ensures an orderly conversion from the present to the future forest. Blocks of potentially permanent forestland must be identified and designated, then secured through agreements with private owners and, if necessary, state, local, and nonprofit land purchases. The state's successful farmland preservation program could serve as a model here. So too could Forest Legacy, which provides federal grants to the state for the acquisition of conservation easements to protect key regional forests against ownership fragmentation and conversion to nonforest uses. Whatever the course of action, the conservation of the future Massachusetts forest will require a different kind of initiative by the state's forestry leaders in regular and open consultation with the private sector. Once the strategy has been developed, it should be ratified at a statewide Massachusetts Forest Congress.

Just how might such an agenda be accomplished? Massachusetts has a wonderful reservoir of human resources devoted to forestry, but the present system of support and services is badly fragmented. For example, as many as a dozen types of intermediaries are now required in order to extract wood products from the forest and deliver them to the ultimate consumer. Each participant consumes a share of the value added. These inefficiencies raise costs for consumers, and offer only modest economic incentives for the forest landowner to manage his or her forests. Forestry services are equally fragmented. The most recent Massachusetts directory lists 89 professionals offering fee-based consulting assistance. Massachusetts' lone forester working for the state Cooperative Extension Service is forced to divide his time between outreach and teaching responsibilities at the state university. At present, there is no concerted, coordinated forest-planning capacity anywhere in state government. The state has 16 service foresters but all are federally funded. Given the uncertainties of the federal fiscal picture, it would be prudent for Massachusetts to provide directly for its own resource service needs.

One good prospect is the Forest Products Trust Fund, placed on the state's statute books in 1991 as a means of sharing state forest revenues with cities and towns where they are situated. This modest revenue stream of $300,000 in average annual timber sales should be augmented by a portion of the state sales tax revenues derived generally from wood, paper, and forest-related products and services. The authorization should be framed to provide incentives for the use of Massachusetts-grown and processed forest products. The availability of a dependable financial base would permit many of the initiatives described above. It would also provide meaningful financial resources to cities and towns, encouraging them to engage actively in forest planning and development. Consistent with historic tradition, the private and nonprofit sectors should take the lead in bringing about these needed changes in public policy.

Can these ambitious goals be achieved? We think so. The late Hugh M. Raup, director of the Harvard Forest for more than twenty years and a student of what he called the "forests of the here and now," expressed great faith in "the contriving brain and the skillful hand of man." He believed firmly that humankind could not and should not be separated from nature. A botanist rather than a forester, Raup particularly favored the observations of the great historian of the American grasslands, James Malin. "The potentiality of man to solve problems," Malin once wrote, "has not yet been exhausted, and the potentiality of the resources latent in the earth to be brought into the horizon of usefulness is still beyond the power of man to conceive. The key to the situation is not the earth, but the minds of men determined to realize their own potential." This optimistic view of the future forest can and should be Massachusetts' own as it enters the twenty-first century.

🍂 SOURCES

For the vignettes on the Hobbamock and Winslow families in Plymouth, I am deeply indebted to James W. Baker of Plimoth Plantation, Inc., for the program training manuals, books, and special research reports and access to interpretive specialists he placed at my disposal. Other sources consulted on Native Americans were Harold E. Driver (1961), *Indians of North America;* George E. Hyde (1962), *Indians of the Woodlands;* Peter Farb (1978), *Man's Rise to Civilization: The Cultural Ascent of the Indians of North America;* Elizabeth Tooker (1979), *Native North American Spirituality;* and John Demos (1995), *The Tried and True.* Additional Colonial period references included Alexander Young (1841), *Chronicles of the Pilgrim Fathers;* John Demos (1970), *A Little Commonwealth;* and John Demos (1972), *Remarkable Providences.*

Annotated bibliographies prepared by the Massachusetts State Library and the Massachusetts State Archives at the request of the Special Commission on Forest Management Practices confirmed the dates of forest-related Colonial statutes. For an overview of early Massachusetts forest and environmental history, five references proved exceptionally helpful: John Bakeless (1961), *The Eyes of Discovery;* Charles F. Carroll (1970), *The Forest Civilization of New England;* William Cronon (1983), *Changes in the Land;* Sheila Connor (1994), *New England Natives;* and Edward T. Price (1995), *Dividing the Land.*

The vignette on the Sheldon family and the description of the Connecticut Valley in the 1700s draw heavily on source materials provided by Historic Deerfield, Inc., through the courtesy of Joseph Peter Spang. In addition, the classic two-volume work by George Sheldon (1895, 1896), *A History of Deerfield;* the later work of John Demos (1994), *The Unredeemed Captive;* and two publications available through Historic Deerfield, *Historic Deerfield: An Introduction,* and the school magazine *Cobblestone* (September 1995) all contributed to this section of the chapter. I am also indebted to C. John Burk of the Department of Biological Sciences, Smith College, for his account (*Rhodora,* January 1994) of the *Evolution of a Flora by Early Connecticut Valley Botanists.* Edmund Delaney's 1983 book, *The Connecticut River,* provided a concise background history of the valley.

The vignette of the Pliny Freeman farm in Sturbridge and much of the description of the forest environment of early nineteenth-century

Massachusetts were greatly facilitated by Jack Larkin of Old Sturbridge Village, Inc., and the use of its archives. Larkin's own work (1988), *The Reshaping of Everyday Life: 1790–1840,* proved most helpful. In addition, the Village's training notebooks and various issues of its magazine, *Rural Visitor,* synthesized much useful material. Special reports such as John Englund (1982), *Sawmills in Worcester County;* Myron O. Stachiw (1988), *Economy of a Countryside;* and Martha Lance's 1993 doctoral dissertation (University of Pennsylvania) focusing on Sturbridge and Southbridge, "The Fathers Lived in the Forest," were consulted extensively. Gordon C. Whitney and William C. Davis (*Journal of Forestry,* April 1986), "From Primitive Woods to Cultivated Woodlots," provided a parallel glimpse of the forest resource in nineteenth-century Concord.

The vignette on Bob Healy is derived largely from a personal interview with his son, Massachusetts commissioner of food and agriculture Jonathan L. Healy. Additional references used include the profile of outstanding Massachusetts tree farms (June 1991), *Massachusetts Tree Farms,* and Phil Lussier (1993), *Hall Tavern Farm Forest Stewardship Trail Curriculum Guide,* published by the Mary Lyons Education Fund, Inc., Shelburne Falls, Mass.

To place the Deerfield River in the context of western Massachusetts, two publications were consulted: Walter E. Bickford and Ute Janik Dymon (1990), *An Atlas of Massachusetts River Systems,* and Deborah E. Burns and Lauren R. Stevens (1988), *Most Excellent Majesty: A History of Mount Greylock.* The three-volume set of memorabilia from the Mohawk Trail and Savoy State Forest Civilian Conservation Corps camps assembled by Bernice O'Brien of the Massachusetts Department of Environmental Management, provided a unique picture of forest conservation activities in western Massachusetts during that period.

For the later part of the nineteenth century and the early twentieth century, several sources were consulted: William H. Clark (1948), *The First Fifty Years of the Massachusetts Forest and Park Association;* state forester Harold O. Cook's personal reminiscences (1961), *Fifty Years a Forester;* and Perry H. Merrill (1981), *Roosevelt's Forest Army: A History of the Civilian Conservation Corps.* Douglas MacCleery (1992), *American Forests: A History of Resilience and Recovery,* provided a useful overview of modern forest history.

The vignette on Dicken Crane was based almost exclusively on a personal interview. However, background information on the Crane family was acquired from *The Berkshire Hills* (1939), a volume in the American Guide Series compiled and written by members of the Federal Writers' Project of the Works Progress Administration for Massachusetts.

Current Massachusetts forest statistics are drawn from David R. Dickson and Carol L. McAfee (November 1988), "Forest Statistics for Massachusetts"; William P. MacConnell et al. (October 1991), *Land Use Update for Massachusetts;* Robert T. Brooks et al. (February 1993), *Forest Resources of Southern New England;* statistical reports on Chapters 61 and 61A of the Massachusetts General Laws compiled by the Massachusetts Bureau of Forest Development and from material included in the interim report (June 1996) of the Special Commission on Forest Management Practices. The April 1996 special supplement of *The Forestry Source* (Society of American Foresters) summarized the results of the Seventh American Forest Congress.

For the recommendations on regional and ecosystem approaches, three sources were especially helpful: Massachusetts Bureau of Forest Development (1993), *Forest Legacy Needs Assessment;* Susan M. Campbell and David B. Kittredge, Jr. (*Journal of Forestry,* February 1996), "Ecosystem Management of Multiple NIPF Ownerships"; and Alisa D. Godoletz and David R. Foster (*Conservation Biology,* in press), "History and Importance of Land Use and Protection in the North Quabbin Region of Massachusetts."

Recommendations for action at the local level were inspired by Robert L. McCullough (1995), *The Landscape of Community.*

For the concluding observation, I am indebted to Benjamin B. Stout's 1981 collection of the writings of Hugh M. Raup, *Forests in the Here and Now.*

Finally, a source of help and guidance has been the Massachusetts Historical Society (especially Virginia Smith and Peter Drummey), which hosted an early meeting of the forest history authors, encouraged this project, and helped track down some of the more obscure references.

Authors' Profiles

Robert S. Bond, a specialist in forest economics and forest management, was for 20 years a faculty member in the University of Massachusetts' Department of Forestry and Wildlife Management, before going on to direct Pennsylvania State University's School of Forest Resources. He is a past president of the Massachusetts Forestry Association.

Charles H. W. Foster, a specialist in natural resources and environmental policy, is an adjunct research associate and lecturer at Harvard University's John F. Kennedy School of Government. He is a former Massachusetts commissioner of natural resources, secretary of environmental affairs, and dean of the Yale University School of Forestry and Environmental Studies.

David R. Foster, a botanist and forest ecologist, is director of the Harvard Graduate Program in Biology, director of the Harvard Forest, principal investigator for the Harvard Long-Term Ecological Research Project, and a member of the editorial boards of *Ecology* and *Ecological Monographs*.

Stephen Fox, a social historian and writer with a special interest in the environmental history of private conservation groups, is the author of five books in the general area of American history, including *The American Conservation Movement: John Muir and His Legacy* (University of Wisconsin Press, 1986).

Nancy M. Gordon, a former lecturer in history at the University of Massachusetts, Amherst, and Mount Holyoke College, is an independent consulting historian. She holds a license to practice forestry in Maine.

William A. King has practiced law for the past 40 years. He served for 10 years as a council member and officer of the Appalachian Mountain Club, and is currently president of the New England Forestry Foundation.

Robert L. McCullough, with a background in city and regional planning, historic preservation, and the law, is the author of *The Landscape of Community: A History of Communal Forests in New England* (University Press of New England, 1995), the definitive work on the subject.

John F. O'Keefe, educated in both social relations and forest ecology, is the coordinator of the Harvard Forest's Fisher Museum in Petersham and a member of the steering committee for the state's primary forest education program, Massachusetts Project Learning Tree.

William H. Rivers, a career professional with the Massachusetts Department of Environmental Management, is currently the statewide management forester for the department's Bureau of Forestry.

General Bibliography

Albion, Robert G. *Forests and Sea Power: The Timber Problem and the Royal Navy.* Cambridge: Harvard University Press, 1926.

Applegate, M. Richard. *Massachusetts Forest and Park Association: A History, 1898–1973.* Boston: Massachusetts Forest and Park Association, 1974.

Bailyn, Bernard. *The New England Merchants in the Seventeenth Century.* Cambridge: Harvard University Press, 1955.

Baker, George, P. *The Formation of the New England Railroad System.* New York: Greenwood Press, 1968.

Baxter, Sylvester. "The Lynn Public Forest." *Garden and Forest* 2 (October 30, 1989).

Blake, Susan. "A Communal Forest for Andover." *The Forester* 3 (November 1, 1897).

Bradford, William. *Of Plymouth Plantation.* Samuel E. Morison, ed. New York: Alfred A. Knopf, 1952.

Brooks, Robert T., et al. *Forest Resources of Southern New England.* Resource Bulletin NE-127, USDA Forest Service. Broomall, Pa.: Northeastern Forest Experiment Station, 1993.

Brown, Nelson C. *Community Forests.* Foreword by Franklin D. Roosevelt. Washington, D.C.: USDA Forest Service, 1939.

Buell, Lawrence, *The Environmental Imagination: Thoreau, Nature Writing and the Formation of American Culture.* Cambridge: Harvard University Press, 1995.

Burns, Deborah E., and Lauren R. Stevens. *Most Excellent Majesty: A History of Mount Greylock.* Pittsfield, Mass.: Berkshire Natural Resources Council, 1988.

Campbell, Susan M., and David B. Kittredge, Jr. "Ecosystem Management of Multiple NIPF Ownerships." *Journal of Forestry* (February 1996): 24–29.

Carroll, Charles. "The Forest Civilization of New England: Timber, Trade and Society in the Age of Wood, 1600–1688." Doctoral dissertation, Brown University, 1973.

Clark, Christopher. *The Roots of Rural Capitalism.* Ithaca, N.Y.: Cornell University Press, 1990.

Colton, William W. "Organization and Management of Town Forests." *Massachusetts Forestry Association Bulletin,* no. 15 (December 10, 1914).

Commonwealth of Massachusetts. *Census of Massachusetts,* 1837, 1845, 1855, 1865, 1875, 1885, 1895, 1905.

Commonwealth of Massachusetts, Department of Natural Resources, Division of

Forests and Parks. *Annual Reports* for 1964, 1966, 1967, 1968, 1969, 1974, 1977, 1978, 1979, 1980, 1981, 1983, 1984, 1985, 1986, 1987, 1989, 1990, 1991, 1992–93.

Commonwealth of Massachusetts, Water Resources Authority. *Report on Wholesale Water Charges.* Boston: Massachusetts Water Resources Authority, 1996.

Condit, Carl. *American Building.* Chicago: University of Chicago Press, 1982.

Connor, Sheila. *New England Natives: A Celebration of People and Trees.* Cambridge: Harvard University Press, 1994.

Cook, Harold O., with Lewis A. Carter. *Fifty Years a Forester.* Boston: Massachusetts Forest and Park Association, 1961.

Cronon, William. *Changes in the Land: Indians, Colonists and the Ecology of New England.* New York: Hill and Wang, 1983.

Dana, Samuel T. *Forest and Range Policy.* New York: McGraw Hill, 1956.

Delaney, Edmund. *The Connecticut River.* Chester, Conn.: Globe Pequot Press, 1983.

Defebaugh, James. *History of the Lumber Industry in America.* 2 vols. Chicago: American Lumberman, 1907.

Dickson, David R., and Carol L. McAfee. *Forest Statistics for Massachusetts: 1972 and 1985.* Resource Bulletin NE-106, USDA Forest Service. Broomall, Pa.: Northeastern Forest Experiment Station, 1988.

Duddleson, William J. Supplementary Report to Andrew J. W. Scheffey, *Conservation Commissions in Massachusetts* (q.v.). Washington, D.C.: Conservation Foundation, 1969.

Federal Writers' Project, Works Progress Administration. *The Berkshire Hills.* New York, N.Y.: Duell, Sloan and Pearce, 1939.

Fishlow, Albert. *American Railroads and the Transformation of the Ante-Bellum Economy.* Cambridge: Harvard University Press, 1965.

Fox, Stephen. *John Muir and His Legacy: The American Conservation Movement.* Boston: Little, Brown, 1981.

Godoletz, Alisa D., and David R. Foster. "History and Importance of Land Use and Protection in the North Quabbin Region of Massachusetts." *Conservation Biology* 11 (1997): 227–35.

Hawley, Ralph C., and Austin F. Hawes. *Forestry in New England.* New York: John Wiley & Sons, 1912.

Harvard College, President and Fellows. *The Harvard Forest Models.* Petersham, Mass.: Harvard University, 1975.

Harvard Forest. *The Harvard Forest 1907–1934: A Memorial to Its First Director, Richard Thornton Fisher.* Petersham, Mass.: Harvard University, 1935.

Hindle, Brook, ed. *America's Wooden Age: Aspects of Its Early Technology.* Tarrytown, N.Y.: Sleepy Hollow Press, 1975.

————. *Material Culture of the Wooden Age.* Tarrytown, N.Y.: Sleepy Hollow Press, 1981.

Heske, Franz. *German Forestry.* New Haven: Yale University Press, 1938.

Hyde, George E. *Indians of the Woodlands: From Prehistoric Times to 1775.* Norman, Okla.: University of Oklahoma Press, 1962.

Illick, Joseph S. "State Forestry." In Robert K. Winters, *Fifty Years of Forestry in the U.S.A.* Washington: Society of American Foresters, 1950.

Innes, Stephen. *Creating the Commonwealth.* New York: Norton, 1995.

Irland, Lloyd C. *Wildlands and Woodlots: The Story of New England's Forests.* Hanover, N.H.: University Press of New England, 1982.

Lance, Martha B. *The Fathers Lived in the Forest, Their Children Lived off Them: Rural New England Sawmilling and the Timber Trade, 1730–1870.* Doctoral dissertation, University of Pennsylvania, 1993.

Larkin, Jack. *The Reshaping of Everyday Life: 1679–1840.* New York: Harper & Row, 1988.

MacConnell, William P. *Land Use Update for Massachusetts with Area Statistics for 1971 and 1984/85.* Research Bulletin 740, Massachusetts Agricultural Experiment Station. Amherst, Mass.: Massachusetts Agricultural Experiment Station, 1991.

MacKaye, Benton. *The New Exploration: A Philosophy of Regional Planning.* New York: Harcourt, Brace, 1928.

Malone, Joseph. *Pine Trees and Politics.* Seattle: University of Washington Press, 1964.

Massachusetts Forest and Park Association. *A Conservation Land Use Plan for the Town of Groton, Massachusetts.* Boston, Mass.: Bulletin 175, 1952.

Massachusetts Forest Service. *Forest Working Plan for Land Belonging to the City of Fall River on the North Watuppa Watershed.* Boston: Wright & Potter Printing Company, 1909.

McCullough, Robert. *The Landscape of Community: A History of Communal Forests in New England.* Hanover, N.H.: University Press of New England, 1995.

McGaw, Judith. *Most Wonderful Machine: Mechanization and Social Change in Berkshire Paper-Making, 1801–1885.* Princeton: Princeton University Press, 1987.

Medford Historical Society. *Round About Middlesex Fells.* Medford, Mass.: Medford Historical Society, 1935.

Meister, Ulrich. *Die Stadtwaldungen von Zurich.* 2nd ed. Zurich, Switzerland: Druckerei der Neuen Zuercher Zeitung, 1903.

Merrill, Perry H. *Roosevelt's Forest Army: A History of the Civilian Conservation Corps.* Montpelier, Vt.: Privately published, 1981.

More, Muriel. *Massachusetts Forest Resources: A Working Guide to Action.* Amherst, Mass.: Massachusetts Department of Environmental Management, 1985.

More, Thomas A. "Municipal Forest Management: A Massachusetts Survey." *Journal of Forestry* 82 (July 1984): 417–19.

Morison, Samuel E. *Maritime History of Massachusetts, 1783–1860.* Boston: Houghton-Mifflin, 1961.

Murphy, John A. "The Town of Walpole Establishes a Communal Forest of 200 Acres." *The American City* 15 (August 1916): 149–53.

Nash, Roderick. *Wilderness and the American Mind.* 3rd ed. New Haven: Yale University Press, 1982.

Olmsted, Frederick L., Jr. "Landscape Problems in the Improvement of Spot Pond Reservoir, Metropolitan Water Works." *Journal of New England Water Works Association* 15 (March 1901): 272–87.

Olson, Sherry, H. *The Depletion Myth: A History of Railroad Use of Timber.* Cambridge: Harvard University Press, 1971.

Orwin, C. S. *The Open Fields.* Oxford: Clarendon Press, 1954.

Pinchot, Gifford. "The Sihlwald." Parts 1–3. *Garden and Forest* (July 30, August 6, August 13, 1890): 374, 386, 397–98.

Price, Edward T. *Dividing the Land: Early American Beginnings of Our Private Property Mosaic.* Chicago: University of Chicago Press, 1995.

Powell, Sumner C. *Puritan Village: The Formation of a New England Town.* Middletown, Conn.: Wesleyan University Press, 1963.

Rackham, Oliver. *Ancient Woodlands: Its History, Vegetation and Uses in England.* London: Edward Arnold, 1980.

Reynolds, Harris A. "A Citizens Movement to Reduce the Tax Rate." *Bulletin of the Massachusetts Forestry Association,* no. 104 (May 1913).

———. *Town Forests: Their Recreational and Economic Value and How to Establish and Maintain Them.* Foreword by Charles Lathrop Pack. Washington, D.C.: American Tree Association, 1925.

———. "The First Quarter Century of the Town Forest in Massachusetts." *Bulletin of the Massachusetts Forest and Parks Association,* no. 163 (December 1939).

Reynolds, Harris A., and Philip T. Coolidge. "The Russell Town Forest: A Forest Management Plan." *Bulletin of the Massachusetts Forest and Parks Association,* no. 170 (January 1946).

Ripley, Harrison S. "Forestry Management Plan for the Groton Memorial Town Forest." Unpublished report, New England Forestry Foundation, Groton, Mass., undated.

Robbins, M. C. "Forest Park, Springfield, Massachusetts." *Garden and Forest* 4 (December 2, 1891): 556–67.

Rodgers, Andrew D. *Bernhard Eduard Fernow: A Study of North American Forestry.* Princeton: Princeton University Press, 1951.

Scheffey, Andrew. *Conservation Commissions in Massachusetts.* Washington, D.C.: Conservation Foundation, 1969.

Sheldon, George. *A History of Deerfield, Massachusetts. 1895–96.* Reprint, Somersworth, N.H.: Somersworth Publishing Company, 1972.

Stout, Benjamin B., ed. *Forests in the Here and Now: A Collection of the Writings of Hugh Miller Raup, Bullard Professor of Forestry (Emeritus), Harvard University.* Missoula, Mont.: Montana Forest and Conservation Experiment Station, 1981.

Sutton, S. B. *Charles Sprague Sargent and the Arnold Arboretum.* Cambridge: Harvard University Press 1970.

Thoreau, Henry David. *Walden.* New York: Riverside, 1960.

U.S. Department of Commerce, Bureau of Census. Census of Manufacturers, 1910, 1920, 1929, 1939, 1947, 1958, 1967, 1977, 1987, 1992.

Wallace, Floyd and Associates. *Report on Metropolitan District Commission.* Boston: Metropolitan District Commission, 1984.

Waterman, Laura, and Guy Waterman. *Forest and Crag: A History of Hiking, Trail Blazing and Adventure in the Northeast Mountains.* Boston: Appalachian Mountain Club, 1989.

Whitney, Gordon C., and William C. Davis. "From Primitive Woods to Cultivated Woodlots: Thoreau and the Forest History of Concord, Massachusetts." *Journal of Forest History* (April 1986): 70–81.

Williams, Michael. *Americans and Their Forests.* Cambridge, England: Cambridge University Press, 1989.

Winthrop, John. *Life and Letters of John Winthrop.* Robert C. Winthrop, ed., New York: Da Capo Press, 1971.

Wood, William. *New England's Prospect.* Originally published in 1634. Alden T. Vaughan, ed. Amherst, Mass.: University of Massachusetts Press, 1977.

Woods, John B. "Municipal Forestry in Pittsfield, Massachusetts." *The American City* 21 (September 1919): 225–28.